DISCOVERING BYFIELD

BY

JOHN S. H. RUSSELL B.E.M.

A pencil sketch by F. C. Gill drawn in 1849, looking towards the village of Byfield from the roadway to Farndon Hill Farm; it shows a typical rural scene of the day, with a post mill and, further over, a horse and man ploughing. The view is the same area of foreground and vista of the village in the background as does the photograph on the previous page, taken by Andrew Spackman in July 2005; a time factor of over one hundred and fifty years between the sketch and the photograph.

The capture of each scene from the same vantage point, one using the skill of the artist with his pencil, the other the skill of the photographer with his camera, make comparisons of the overall scene over a period of time possible.

Dedicated to Jill for her tolerance of me for nearly fifty years

Published by John Russell
The Grove, 42 Banbury Lane, Byfield, Daventry, Northants, NN11 6UX, England

First published 2005

ISBN 0-9551505-0-7

Front cover photograph: Byfield Church and surroundings from the south west, Spring 1973
Back cover photograph: Byfield from the south, Spring 1973
Cover photographs by Cameron Fraser

Typeset at The Corner House, Byfield

Printed by Thornton Printers, The Old Chapel, Nottingham Road, Alfreton, DE55 7GL

THE AUTHOR

There is perhaps nothing more English than the traditional English village, with its own identity and spirit, its own traditions and history, and of course its characters. The village of Byfield is no exception and one of its true stalwarts is the author of this book, John Russell.

For those readers that live or have lived in Byfield over the last 60 years, you will need very little introduction to John Russell. John has been at the heart of the village since he was just a small lad clowning around at school during those dark days of World War II. But few will really know of the lifelong devotion John has shown to this small English village in the heart of rural Northamptonshire.

John was born on the 19th of August 1936 in the same house in Bell Lane, Byfield as his own father Les, had been born in 34 years earlier. Strangely enough though his father had not lived there all of his life, he had moved for a short while around the corner to Westhorpe Lane and then moved back into the house when he bought it in the early 1930's.

At just four and half, a very skinny little boy was marched off to the village school where he was determined to entertain the other children with his pranks and tomfoolery. Sadly just a few months later John's mother was struck down by TB, or consumption as it was called in those days and passed away. Despite the very sad loss of his mother, John remained positive about life and preferred to fool around at school rather than take life seriously. But despite his lack of attention to his studies, he managed to pass his eleven plus exam, much to the surprise of some and especially to John himself. And so in 1947 he began his secondary education at the very well respected, Towcester Grammar School. Like many village children, John came from a family that was more familiar with manual work than academic studies and he was never really encouraged to continue with his education on a full time basis. Once he reached sixteen, his father, who was the local shopkeeper, did want the very best for John and he paid for him to undertake an indentured apprenticeship as a motor mechanic with Grimsbury Motors in the nearby town of Banbury. This was the start of a career that John would follow all of his working days, albeit at levels much more senior than those early days of oily overalls and endless cups of tea in the pit.

During this time, National Service was still in operation. John's call up was delayed until he completed his apprenticeship, but at 20 he joined the Royal Air Force as a direct entry tradesman and underwent his basic training at Cardington and Padgate, he was then moved to RAF Cottesmore. John recalls that this was a time when the world was going through one of its most dangerous periods, the height of the Cold War. RAF Cottesmore was home to the V bombers of 10 and 15 Squadrons and the Victor bombers were on a continuous 4 minute alert to scramble. With his motor mechanic skills, John was tasked with others in maintaining "Tugmasters" that towed the bombers to and from the airfield under the watchful eye of the Commanding Officer Group Captain Johnny Johnson, a Battle of Britain veteran and ace pilot. Although for 21 months John was away from Byfield, he never really lost his involvement with the village, returning home in his Ford 10 Tourer every Friday to keep goal for the local football club, Byfield Athletic, on the following Saturday.

Like most of the other village lads of the time, he was a regular at the local village dances. One such evening in 1955 he remembers with great fondness, as this was when he first met Jill, who was to become his wife just five years later. It was another one of the great coincidences in his life because they met at Eydon Village Hall, the same village that his father had met his mother many years before.

After leaving the RAF in November 1958 John returned to Grimsbury Motors for one year when he was offered a job with C&W Knight of Fenny Compton, as the Fleet Engineer. Here he was responsible for taking care of the company's plant and machinery and its 25 lorries, which were used to haul aggregates to customers. John is quick to point out that it was also twice as much pay as he had been used to!

On the 23rd of July 1960 John and Jill were married at Fenny Compton Methodist Chapel and I am very proud to say that my own father, Les Henning, was John's best man – John had been my father's best man five years earlier. The happy couple moved into the house that they built in Banbury Lane, Byfield where they have lived to this day.

John's career in the Motor Trade continued to develop and in 1968 he joined the Ministry of Transport in Northampton as its Professional and Technological Engineer covering the Northampton district. He then became the Station Manager for the Ministry's Depot at Weedon, where he and his staff of 10 would test around 800 buses per year along with 13,000 heavy goods vehicles. During his years with the Ministry John was involved in a number of important national projects including reorganising the car testing scheme (the MoT). John retired from the Ministry on the 2nd of February 1995 having completed 27 years of loyal service.

Loyalty is perhaps one of John's strongest characteristics, dedication is another. Both are shown in abundance when one looks at what John has achieved in Byfield and the surrounding district. He became involved in village affairs initially through the football club when he was asked by the then Secretary of the club, Arthur Shenton, to represent it on the Village Hall Committee. During November 1960, Byfield proudly opened its new Village Hall, but found itself £300 in debt and in need of funds urgently. Jill came up with the suggestion of running a weekly bingo session and on the 14th of February 1961 the first number was called and the first winning house was completed – with John at the helm of course. The Friday night bingo became incredibly successful with coaches picking up people from a number of the surrounding villages so that folk could attend. It continued right up until 1992, with John having been directly involved for exactly 25 years. John also served on the Village Hall Committee for twenty two years, ten of which as its Chairman, and during this time John not only took on one project to extend the hall in 1968, but a further extension in 1975.

John was becoming ever more intertwined with the village and in 1967, at just 31, he was elected onto the Parish Council and six years later became its Chairman, a position he was to retain for a staggering 24 years. In 1983 he was elected to the Daventry District Council as an Independent candidate where he was involved with the East Midlands area of the Sports Council and the National Committee of Personnel and Human Resources. His work with the District continued for 19 years and he served two terms as its Chairman from 1992 to 93 and from 1995 to 96 – something no other Councillor has ever achieved. During his time on the Council he was twice invited to Buckingham Palace, and as Council Chairman he very proudly recalls shaking hands with both the Queen Mother and Princess Diana.

Perhaps John's most notable achievement for the village to date has been the Brightwell Recreational Ground Project. In 1985 both the Cricket Club and the Football Club were given notice to quit their grounds. Something needed to be done to secure their future and John was the man to do it. Having played for the village football club for 20 years, during what was its most successful period ever, and having been the President of the Cricket Club since 1968 – despite never having played cricket – John needed no more motivation. John rallied the people of Byfield and with his band of helpers managed to raise £16,000, which was matched by a further £48,000 from a Government grant. Enough to level a new playing field in the heart of the village, and mainly as a result of John's drive and enthusiasm, the whole project was completed in just 2 years and 4 months.

John's list of personal achievements goes on, but perhaps the culmination of his life of long dedication and loyalty to the village and the wider community was when, in 1990,

he was awarded the British Empire Medal. Choosing not to go to Buckingham Palace to receive it in order that his father-in-law could be present at the ceremony, he was presented with the medal by John Lowther, the Lord Lieutenant of Northamptonshire – a truly remarkable achievement for the son of the local shopkeeper!

Today, John still retains that devilish sense of humour and always has a funny tale to tell whenever you meet him. Although he tells me that if he has one regret in life it was that he wasted his early days at school clowning around, he is testimony to what can be achieved through working so well with others - and having fun must be part of that. John is an infectiously positive and cheerful person and thrives on getting things done. When I asked him what irritates him, he was quick to point out negative people and negative thinking.

You will seldom find John sitting in front of the television, unless there is sport on. He prefers to be working on one of his many projects such as the historical village photograph project. He has boundless energy and continues to swim every week – something he has done for the last 29 years! Occasionally he will find time to sit and read – usually factual history books. Holidays are fine, but they tend to take up valuable project time, although he does find time to go for walks with Jill in various parts of the country. His home and his garden are also very important to him, one only has to walk up the driveway to his house to realise that it belongs to a very caring couple – even the squirrels feel at home there!

Village life has dramatically changed over the last 50 years and society has become much more self-centred with people more concerned about the value of their house than about the value of the community in which they live. There are however still some people that dedicate their lives to making the environment better for all that live in it, John is without doubt one such person. His love for the village of Byfield is clear for all to see. The only thing that has greater importance to John is of course Jill, who has tirelessly stood by him and supported him all the way through his work ever since they met all those years ago in Eydon Village Hall.

When I asked him how he would like to be remembered in 50 years time, he thought a while and replied – "well at least he achieved something". John is without doubt an achiever, a role model for any youngster and a true gentleman, and I am very proud to be his godson and to have had the opportunity of writing this very brief introduction to him.

Andrew Henning

Andrew Henning
23 May 2005.

CONTENTS

FOREWORD

A proof-reader's responsibility is to correct errors where necessary, but not to dominate. All art is a collaboration however, and I have given modest help to an acceptable degree, but I have not been a "ghost writer".

John Russell has had recourse to antiquity and, through the present, hopes to reach out to posterity. The declared objective of the author is to mention his native village as it was recorded in the Saxon chronicles; to refer to formalized recording of property in the Doomsday Book, to bring it up to the present and to hope that in fifty years' time it will be used as a source of information for those who are interested in how we live today.

He traces ownership largely by reference to the Byfield Enclosure Act of 1779.

He has impressed me with his assiduity in pursuing verifiable facts and at the same time acknowledging where records are vague.

The accumulation of the relevant body of detail must rank in the process of enlightenment; when, as in this book, it is unclouded by dogma or prejudice, it could become the stuff of history.

He walks towards the village in turn from all points of the compass and describes a system of land and property tenure which has shaped it in stages of tenancy, purchase, grant or inheritance.

Certain family names recur and may be found to-day on the Electoral Roll and other official documents. A thrill of pride may be evoked as names are mentioned and their owners recognise kinship.

Some long lists of names of inhabitants could be boring were it not for the reflection that they represent the sequential, inexorable flow of life. The thread of life runs through the narrative as one is reminded of the phrase: "Life is a comedy to those who think; a tragedy to those who feel."

The natural, salty dry humour of the author provides its own sense of comedy, but we could cite one or two examples to be found in anecdotes.

First there is the account of a schoolboy who entertains his fellow scholars by producing a psychedelic arc of brilliant green urine; the result of taking some patent kidney pills. His commercial instincts may have been realised in profitable sale of the pills. We are not sure of his motives; were they scientific demonstration or rampant boasting?

Secondly, a group of mischievous youths were playing around a railway truck from a nearby mine. When one released the brake the wagon rolled, gathering speed, and en route, thundered through a junction before crashing some distance away. The crossing controller complained "He never whistled" (the usual warning of an approaching train).

Comedy that could have ended in tragedy. The name of the youth remains a secret.

He also writes of the courage and tenacity of a widowed mother of eleven children, overtaken by the tragic loss of her husband, who struggled gamely, worked hard and brought up a decent family. Pathos also plays its part. War is a tragedy and a waste. The second son of the same woman, joined up during World War One! He was killed in action. His mother travelled to the military cemetery overseas; found his grave and brought back the cross, eventually to be installed in Byfield Church. Two acts of courage both admirable, both illuminating the path of human life.

Other flashes of comedy, notably a railway joke, lighten the mood, but I shall not steal a march on the writer; who would like you to read his book.

John refers to the part played by Byfield and the surrounding villages in two World Wars. Troops were billeted, prisoners of war assisted in the growing of crops and performed other tasks; military exercises in which villagers vanquished soldiers took place, and the use of Chipping Warden fields as an aerodrome for training and operational flights; all bear testimony to this area's contribution.

The gift of the Brightwell Recreation Ground; and the growth and usage of the village hall. John's comments bear testimony to the important part he played.

This book is not an ego trip for the writer, however. A more intimately domestic account of the family store gives a valuable description of an age that has passed. It is a slice of life; a facet of local history, and I urge you to read it.

George Spencer
23 May, 2005

Acknowledgments

Without the help and support I have received, the writing of this book would have been impossible.

May Haynes for her encouragement, which prompted me to start.

Andrew Spackman with his help in guiding me in the purchase of my laptop, and getting me up and running. Plus his expertise in the systems and procedures needed, including the page layout and typesetting of the book, before it was forwarded to the Printers.

All the lenders of photographs to the Byfield Photo Museum, who have given me permission to use their photographs, together with the other lenders whose photographs give so much useful information. The museum is a collection of over 2,500 photographs relating to Byfield, from 1860 onwards. Digital copies are stored on CD, together with detailed information about each item. There are also albums of all the pictures for loan, and the collection is constantly expanding.

John Roddis and Oliver Tynan for their guidance at the outset.

The late Valerie Tarling for the legacy she has left to the village of Byfield. A mass of historical data, running to some four hundred pages compiled in date order. This was accrued over a long period, and was collected from a considerable number of sources.

This work is a memorial in itself to Valerie Tarling.

Byfield Parish Church for loan of the Memorial Books.

Bryan Martin for his work on recording the history of the buildings, the occupancy and then completing a matrix of his own property. This matrix, then when used as a standard, guided others into investigating the history of other village properties using a common method.

John and Margaret Roddis, who together photographed, copied, collated and enhanced the detail of the 1779 Byfield Enclosure Map. This work has made it possible to use the Map, which is now in a readable and usable format, and can be used for further historical research.

Philip Johnson for his work in copying details from the Byfield census and burial records, spending much time at the Northamptonshire County Council Records Office. Also for the use of the details of the history and past occupancy from the various village properties he and his teams have investigated.

George Spencer for his expertise and guidance.

Russ Mallace for his contribution on the progression of the development of Brightwell, also Jean West for the detail of the more recent improvements to the Village Hall.

Some most valuable information was gleaned with chats with: Frank Holmes: Denis Judd: Dick Haynes: Fred Hutt: Cyril Nichols: Winnie Eyles and Barbara Smith, all sadly no longer with us.

Amazing wartime vivid recollections of the time of their childhood in Byfield, after arriving from the bomb damaged areas of London, from Dolly Buckle, Sylvia Lowe and Norman McKenzie.

Other details from:

May Haynes: Joyce French: Polly Harris-Watson: Pat Deacon: Mary James: Ken Lamb: Jessie Jones: Fred Steel: Cecil Laurie: Les Jones: Rex Partridge; Doris Perehinec: Maurice and Rita Smith: Bryan Martin: Ann Codling: Josephine Milnes: Norman Thurman: Margaret Roddis and valuable snippets from many others.

The field names were taken from various documents, but specifically from the Field Map of Byfield, compiled by Percy Shepherd and added to by Peter Codling, again both no longer with us.

Lastly, but not least, I thank my old friend Colin Thornton and family for printing this book.

INDEX OF MAPS

MAP ONE

THE LOCATION OF BYFIELD IN "MIDDLE ENGLAND

TAKEN FROM A MODERN MAP

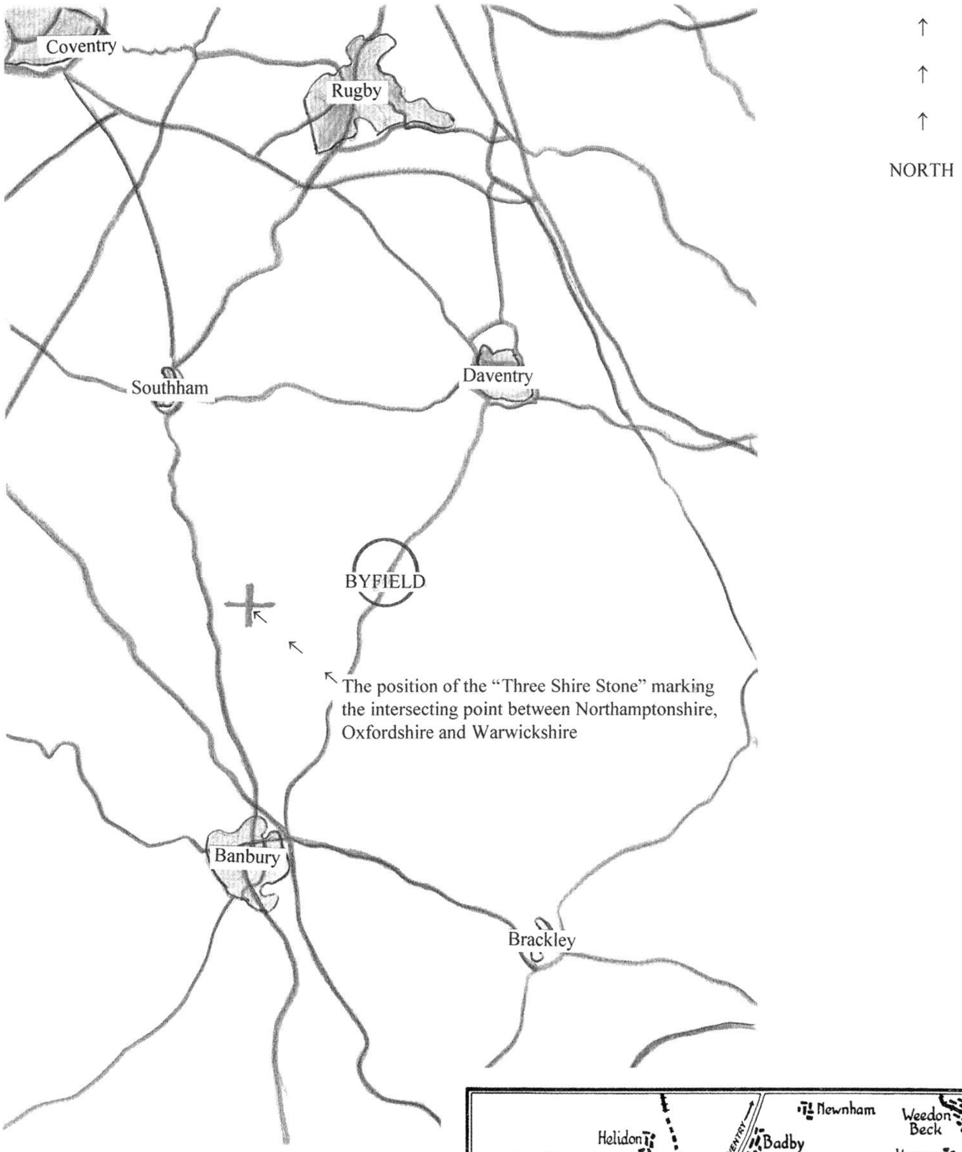

Coventry

Rugby

↑
↑
↑

NORTH

Southham

Daventry

BYFIELD

The position of the "Three Shire Stone" marking the intersecting point between Northamptonshire, Oxfordshire and Warwickshire

Banbury

Brackley

MAP TWO

THE LOCAL DISTRICT AROUND BYFIELD

TAKEN FROM A 1930s MAP

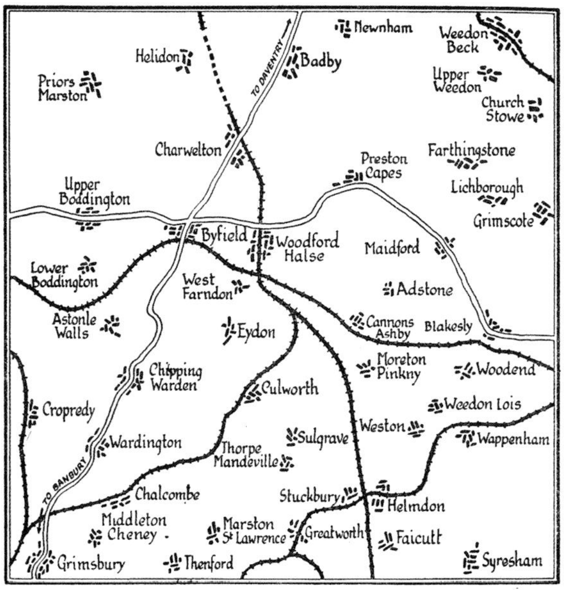

Newnham

Helidon

TO DAVENTRY

Badby

Weedon Beck

Priors Marston

Upper Weedon

Church Stowe

Charwelton

Preston Capes

Farthingstone

Upper Boddington

Lichborough

Grimscote

Byfield

Woodford Halse

Maidford

Lower Boddington

West Farndon

Adstone

Astonle Walls

Eydon

Cannons Ashby

Blakesly

Chipping Warden

Moreton Pinkny

Woodend

Cropredy

Culworth

Weston

Weedon Lois

Wardington

Sulgrave

TO BANBURY

Thorpe Mandeville

Wappenham

Chalcombe

Stuckbury

Helmdon

Middleton Cheney

Marston St Lawrence

Greatworth

Faicutt

Grimsbury

Thenford

Syresham

Map Three

Byfield from the
1779 Enclosure Map

The centre section of the map outlined in <u>black</u> is the area containing the 142 Old Inclosures and Homesteads in the centre of the village which are referred to on detailed maps numbered four to nineteen and in the script.

The outer section of the map outlined in <u>blue</u> is the area containing the 112 allotments of Tracts of land in the rest of Byfield parish which are referred to on detailed maps numbered four to nineteen and in the script.

Outline details taken from the 1779 Enclosure Map.

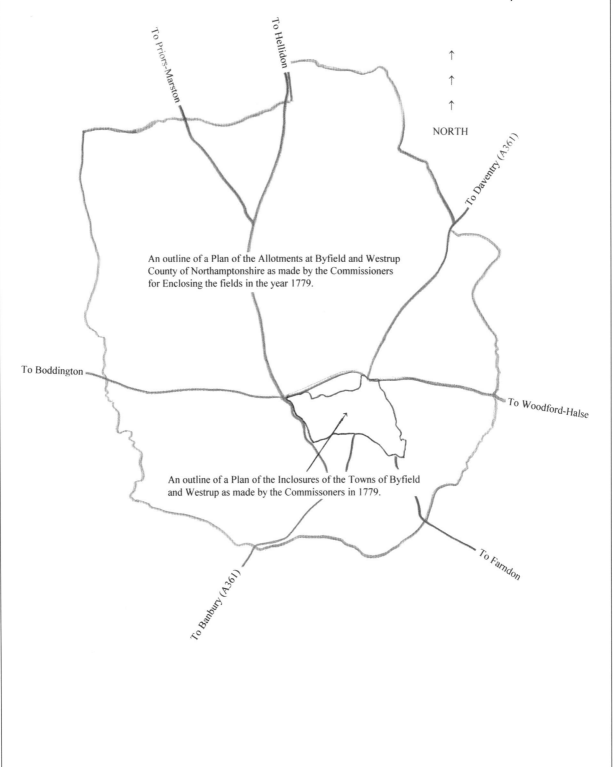

To Priors-Marston

To Hellidon

↑
↑
↑
NORTH

To Daventry (A361)

An outline of a Plan of the Allotments at Byfield and Westrup County of Northamptonshire as made by the Commissioners for Enclosing the fields in the year 1779.

To Boddington

To Woodford-Halse

An outline of a Plan of the Inclosures of the Towns of Byfield and Westrup as made by the Commissioners in 1779.

To Banbury (A361)

To Farndon

DISCOVERING BYFIELD

(See Maps One, Two and Three)

Byfield is a large village situated in the south west of Northamptonshire; it is a halfway house on the main road from Banbury to Daventry. The geographical location can also be readily found as the village is four miles east of the intersection of the "Three Shires" of Northamptonshire, Oxfordshire and Warwickshire **(see Map One for the location of Byfield)**.

The population is now, in 2004, around 1300, and as the 1841 census shows a population of 1079, the population has altered very little in some 160 years! There was a variation over those years, the numbers "dipping" through the middle period, with a low being the year of 1891, when the census shows a population of 737. Details from the surrounding district show this as a general trend, and it was not until around 1960 that the Byfield population reached the 1000 mark again.

Byfield census records as reported in the Northamptonshire Directories

Census	Population
1801	842
1841	1079
1851	1060
1871	840
1881	787
1891	737
1901	792
1911	809
1921	879
1931	863

A glance at a physical map of England and Wales reveals a belt of upland running from the south-west in a north-easterly direction, of which the Cotswolds are the most prominent ranges. Although the altitude decreases as we enter Northamptonshire, some hills around Byfield are over 700 feet in height; some of the highest land in the county.

Byfield lies in a fertile part of middle England on the iron- and fossil-rich Jurassic limestone. Although relatively high it does not have any natural trading through routes, even though some pass quite near by. The Portway passes through Kirtlington in Oxfordshire and on via Chipping Warden and Preston Capes to Daventry. It preserved the Roman name in the eighteenth century but was probably of British origin.

The Roman Watling Street was one trading route, as was the Welsh Lane with its wide verges used by drovers taking animals from the Welsh pastures to the eastern seaports. It was inevitable that some of the users of these routes would deviate onto the Banbury to Daventry road into Byfield **(see Map Two for the local Byfield district)**.

It is fascinating and rewarding to look to see what can still be found in an old English village; it is interesting to look at the trades, crafts and livelihoods that were engendered and see what remaining evidence there is of these past ways of life.

Looking at the known facts of the history of Byfield, the first real milestone detailing modern history of the Parish is the 1779 Enclosure Act passed by Parliament in the eighteenth year of the reign of King George III.

The practical detail is recorded on an Enclosure Map and in associated papers. The map of the Parish is divided into two parts, the first being the Village itself with a survey of Old Inclosures and Homesteads; the second is a detail of Proprietors/Owners of the rest of the land in the Parish **(see Map Three)**.

Two separate lists of numbers, one for the Old Inclosures and Homesteads, and one for Proprietors/ Owners, coincide with the numbers on the Map.

Obviously there are many sources of information and many pertinent dates relating to the village of Byfield, but this date of 1779 is an ideal point at which to start.

INTRODUCTION

Recorded history outlines the events, and happenings, together with the various legislation imposed by Kings, or passed by Parliament. This recorded history also shows the effect and implications on the Nation's people over which, in most cases, they themselves had little or no control, and to recognise the effect and implications on villages such as Byfield.

Doomsday (day of judgement) gave the name of the Doomsday Book drawn up by William the Conqueror in 1086. He sent his officials to each part of the Country, to ascertain the facts and the way of living of the people, in each of the towns and villages in the land. William intended it to be a record of his fiscal rights, and the information collated was to be used to calculate how much each place could afford to pay in taxes.

An elaborate system of dues and customs was the inevitable accompaniment of feudalism, which had started in the eighth century, with the great landowners each a little monarch under the King, within the limits of their lands; they were known as nobles or lords.

The tyranny of King John of England was against all classes in his Kingdom. While he was waging a losing war on the Continent, the leading Barons of the day secretly met together and were sworn to compel the King to respect the rights of his notable subjects, so on June 15th 1215 the King was forced to affix his seal to the Great Charter; the Magna Carta.

The epidemic of the Black Death, that swept through Europe in the 14th century, had an effect on rural areas, with the influx of people fleeing the towns and cities in an attempt to escape the intensity of the spread of the disease. Local history reveals that people were fleeing the city of Oxford in droves to distance them from the infection. The Black Death was at its worst in Northamptonshire from May to October 1349.

The effect of war was felt by the nation's civilian population. All conflicts had some effect, especially those where local men were conscripted to take up arms, or when the conflict was close at hand. In local areas in this part of the rural countryside around Byfield the impact of battles such as the battle of Edgecote "Loosecoate Field" in 1469, during the Wars of the Roses (1455–1485), stood out; the battlefield being only three miles south of the centre of Byfield village.

The Battle of Edgecote "Loosecoate Field"
The conflict between the Partisans of Edward IV and a body of insurgents, in which the former was defeated and the Earl of Pembroke with two of his brothers and eight other gentle-

men were taken to Banbury and beheaded. The Insurgent force was estimated at 20,000 strong and the King's troops between 17,000 and 18,000. At the end of the conflict 5,000 men were left dead on the field.

The Civil War battles – of Edgehill in 1642 continuing on to the final battle at Naseby in 1645 – would have had a considerable impact.

The First World War because of the high loss of life had a considerable effect as families became much depleted.

During the Second World War, a wartime within living memory, battle-damaged aircraft crash-landed on and around local airfields, such as Chipping Warden, when returning from mass bombing raids over German cities. Later, over the local area, ground troops were preparing all their weapons and equipment for the D-Day landings on occupied Europe; all part of a huge invasion force which turned southern England into a massive military camp.

There was sadness within the local population when loved ones failed to return from the conflict. The direct effect of air-raids, blast netting over the school windows, the blackout, air raid wardens, dads in the Home Guard, rationing, were the other little things that only happen in wartime.

All of these events and others in history had a considerable effect on the lives of the people, but none more so than the long-term effects of the Enclosure Acts (see the following section).

The Enclosure Acts: (copied verbatim)
These were a series of Acts of Parliament which provided for dividing and enclosing common fields and pastures, and other common lands and grounds within the Manor, Parish and liberties of any given parish, and relocating and consolidating disparate strips under diverse ownership. The practice of enclosure of common land began as early as the reign of King Henry VII , and its prevalence in the Tudor period, contributed to the pauper class in the 16th century.

Enclosures continued to be made at every opportunity, and the riots of the fifteenth century were the most active demonstration of hostility. Late confiscations of what was regarded as common property caused much heartburning and sullen discontent. By the beginning of the eighteenth century, up to three million fields had been enclosed in the Midlands alone.

The General Enclosure Act of 1801 was the last enclosure act to be passed by parliament. This 1801 act meant that the process became even simpler. Woods and waste land disappeared, making way for a new pattern of hedges, walls and fences.

These Acts brought order into land ownership by the reallocation and consolidation of lands in private and common ownership. Prior to the Enclosure, as far as can be assessed, one third was common land, the rest being held freehold by farmers, the Lord of the Manor and the Rector.

The Control of Moles

Prior to the Enclosure there was an agreement between the inhabitants of Byfield and John Walton of Byfield to kill moles in the common fields for a period of 20 years. This agreement was signed on the 1st day of January 1645 by thirty six inhabitants of Byfield headed by Thomas Knightley.

From the details recorded within the allotments in the Enclosure, it is possible from the date of the specific enclosure in a given area, to follow lines of progression of ownership. Land and Property was sometimes freehold, sometimes leasehold, or copyhold. Even the tenants and users of the land or property are recorded, and one is able to ascertain what effect the Enclosure Acts had on future generations.

Definitions of Land Tenure

Freehold: *Property and land that could be held freehold without encumbrance charge or mortgage.*

Leasehold: *Property and land were leased from the Lord of the Manor for a defined number of years at ground rent, with the land reverting back at the end of the period.*

Copyhold: *Where property and land were leased for 300 years at a ground rent. Copyholders had clearly defined rights: they could build a house on the rented plot, which could be sub-let and passed though the family for a small fee, or the copyhold itself could be sold to a third party, who would have to pay a fee to the Lord of the Manor, but would then start a fresh 300 year term.*

At the beginning of the 19th century only a few properties were freehold, but many were leasehold. The vast majority were copyhold. As the 19th century wore on, more and more copyholders purchased their freeholds from the Lord of the Manor.

The demise of the copyhold system came finally with the 1922 Law of Property Act, which gave copyholders the undisputed right to purchase their freeholds.

The Enclosure as it affected Byfield began in 1778, in the reign of King George III.

In the past, parcelling of land into small strips, unhedged and often un-drained, made economical cultivation extremely difficult, and in the preamble to the text of the Act, its necessity is urged from the fact that private enclosures and common land had become inconveniently mingled, with the result that these old enclosures were declared "incapable of any considerable improvement". These strips can be readily seen around the Byfield area by the ridge and furrow patterns. One owner had multi strips usually 220 yards long and 8 yards wide in various places to share ground quality, cultivated on a three year rotation with the third year fallow. Livestock was grazed on the

uncultivated land in the fallow year, and on the commons and wastes which surrounded the open fields. This is readily emphasised by a terrier of glebe land in Byfield dated June 11th 1702 which clearly indicates in its 113 entries the diverse and intricate land holding of the tenants on the glebe land.

The enclosures ensured that the majority of land was transformed more or less into the landscape we see today, with larger tracts of land separated by hedges or fencing. The legislation within the act specified that all allotments were to be fenced within one calendar month. These procedures made the land considerably more productive, and were conducive to a structure which progressively increased the efficiency and productivity for the future.

The act sets out the steps to be taken in defining the new enclosures of the Parish. It appointed Commissioners with powers given to them to act within the specific Enclosure Act, and embodied an oath of impartiality. The acts also determined the duties of the holders of the new allotments.

In Byfield Parish the Commissioners were:
Reverent Henry Homer of Birdingbury
Thomas Bazely of Priors Marston
John Chamberlain of Cropredy
James King of Daventry
John Watts of Sulgrave.

The Rose and Crown was chosen as the meeting place of the Commissioners; non-attendance was considered a refusal to sit.

Preliminary steps were:
1. The valuation of the Parish by Quality men, who were:
   Richard Shortland of Helmdon.
   John Brothers of Wyken
   William Collingridge of Fulwell
2. A survey of all common and enclosed lands:
   The Surveyors appointed were:
   Edward Linnell of Thorpe- Manderville
   George King of Daventry

The work was to be completed by September 1st 1778.

This Act had a big influence on the lives of the people, who were initially hostile, the future being uncertain, especially for the lower working classes.

A satirical comment regarding the Enclosure of common land in the eighteenth century, taken from a Penguin Book of Quotations:
The Law doth punish man or woman
That steals the goose from off the common
But let's the greater felon loose
That steals the common from the goose.
Anon

However, history has shown that the organisation brought by the Allotments in the Enclosure Act did progressively produce results with the methods and systems used within agriculture, also in commerce and industry, thus increasing production and efficiency.

The progress, specifically in the development of mechanisation, reduced the need for manpower especially on the land. An encyclopaedia records: "Until 1750 the World carried on its daily work in much the same way as it had done for more than two thousand years, which we may sum up very broadly by saying, that there were no machines before 1750, such as now perform most of man's work for him". This was the start of what became known as "The Industrial Revolution" and this advancement placed at the disposal of the majority goods which previously only the wealthy could afford to buy.

Locally, as elsewhere, there was a diversification of labour into industry; also, with the expansion of national and international business and commerce, the employment options extended to the working-class labourer, expanded to a degree never before dreamed of. The detail in the census returns from the village of Byfield shown in 1841, and up to and including the 1901 census, clearly indicate this trend. The inventive processes were advanced even further, especially in the First and Second World Wars. Invention and production, especially of machines, were speeded up by acute demand and necessity, as also more recently by an explosion in the developments in the field of electronics, especially in the field of computer technology.

Some of the allotments within the Enclosures in 1779 were considerable tracts of land, especially to the Lord of the Manor William Henry Chauncy esq., and the incumbent Rector of the time, the Reverend John Knightley allotted for Glebe and Tithes.

Glebe and Tithes:

Glebe is land belonging to the Church or Ecclesiastical Benefice, for the use of the incumbent Minister.

Tithe is a tenth part, and was originally a tenth part of the produce of the soil within the parish the produce of handicrafts, or merchandise or the products of animals kept.

From the 8th century the church has had the right to the tithe from which a Rector received an income. (If incumbents received an income from large tithes they were rectors; if they received income from other means they were vicars.)

In 1836 the tithe was altered into an annual rent charge, with a value based on the price of corn, (in Byfield in 1885 this was a net income to the Rector of £625 p.a. from 516 acres). In 1925 an arrangement was made to gradually wipe out the tithe altogether, in the course of the following 85 years by annual payments. The fund is managed by an ancient institution called Queen Anne's Bounty, which pays out money to incumbents (clergy holding a benefice such as rectors or vicars).

There was also land allotted in smaller measure to others specifically to offset the loss of previously owned land, mostly to gentry or yeoman farmers; these allotments were still of a considerable size.

The allotments to individuals were divided by hedging and fencing, reflecting the use to which specific fields were to be put to suit the owner's needs. Immediately after 1779 arable and livestock units tended to be small. Initially the progressive increase in size was linked to the availability of more modern methods, using more modern machines.

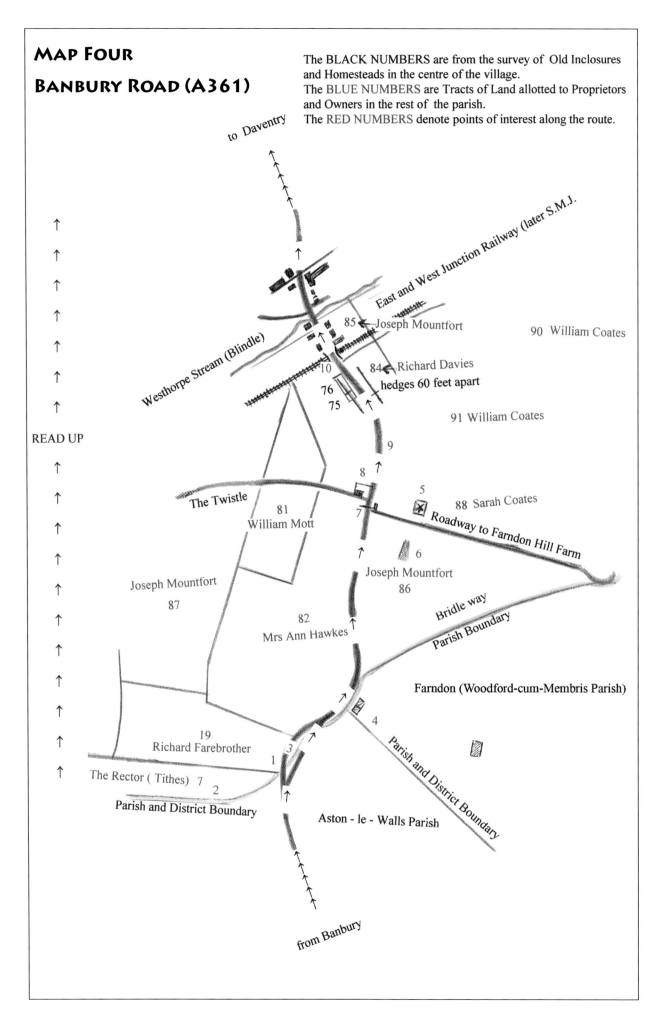

Map Four
Banbury Road (A361)

The BLACK NUMBERS are from the survey of Old Inclosures and Homesteads in the centre of the village.
The BLUE NUMBERS are Tracts of Land allotted to Proprietors and Owners in the rest of the parish.
The RED NUMBERS denote points of interest along the route.

to Daventry

East and West Junction Railway (later S.M.J.

85 Joseph Mountfort

90 William Coates

Westhorpe Stream (Blindle)

10

84 Richard Davies

hedges 60 feet apart

76
75

91 William Coates

9

READ UP

8

5

88 Sarah Coates

The Twistle

7

Roadway to Farndon Hill Farm

81
William Mott

6

Joseph Mountfort
86

Joseph Mountfort
87

82
Mrs Ann Hawkes

Bridle way

Parish Boundary

Farndon (Woodford-cum-Membris Parish)

4

19
Richard Farebrother

1   3

The Rector (Tithes) 7
2

Parish and District Boundary

Parish and District Boundary

Aston - le - Walls Parish

from Banbury

12

CHAPTER ONE

THE START OF OUR JOURNEY ALONG THE HIGHWAYS AND BYWAYS OF BYFIELD

(See Map Four)

Byfield can be discovered, through the mind's eye, at a leisurely pace from our own favourite armchair. On this route as we are entering Byfield at the Parish boundary, it is fitting perhaps to start on the road from Banbury, the North Oxfordshire town the services from which generations of Byfield people have obtained their various requirements.

Before starting the journey northwards and the descent into the village we pause to look back towards the south. From this high point at 628 feet (192 metres) above sea level and at a spot known by the locals as "Half Crown Corner" **(see Map Four, point of interest number 1)**. This title and its origin are unknown to me! The Parish Boundary is one mile from the village centre, the road which became the B4036 and later was upgraded to the A361. Before this it was "The Turn pike"; it was officially named the Banbury Road in the 1950s, its name as long as it had been "the way to Banbury".

We start by looking back into history to the time of the Enclosures and occasionally before. From this high point as we look away from the village to the south through a gap in the greenery, the hedge in front of us is the boundary between Byfield Parish and the Parish of Aston-le-Walls. (The Enclosure map of 1779 shows the "parishes" as "Lordships"). Also today it is the division between the Districts of Daventry and the District of South Northamptonshire **(see Map Four, point of interest number 2)**.

If we take the panorama from left to right starting by looking south over into Oxfordshire, the town of Banbury is clearly visible in the middle distance, the stream of vapour from Kraft Ltd, a food and drinks producing factory being a clearly dominant feature. The site was originally developed by Birds, of Birds Custard fame, after its move from Birmingham. Since Birds, it has had several names including General Foods, Maxwell House, Jacob Kraft Suchard, and now Kraft Ltd.

The Peddling Representative

Before the motor car became commonly available, in a period between the First and Second World Wars, the representatives of Birds the Birmingham based company, known then for their brand of custard, periodically visited all of the company's retail outlets, using other various modes of transport.

One such outlet visited was Russell's of Byfield. One quality that the Representatives required as well as the obvious one of

promoting the company's wares was that of physical stamina. The representative suitably dressed in a dark suit, bowler hat and bicycle clips on his trouser legs, started his journey from his home in Birmingham on his "upright two crossbar bicycle", and rode to Birmingham Railway Station where he and his bicycle caught the Banbury train. On alighting at Banbury Station he then cycled the ten miles to Byfield and Russell's. How many other customers he visited on this round is unknown. It is obvious that Birds Representatives in those days did not require the services of a Fitness Centre or the like, for their cycling excursions would keep them fighting fit.

As we pan to the right, we see the village of Claydon and beyond it Farnborough. In the middle distance is the Edge Hill range of hills, the site of the first battle in the Civil War in 1642. Our eyes are now travelling over the point where the three Counties of Oxfordshire, Warwickshire and Northamptonshire converge. Slightly again to the right is the Wireless Mast on the edge of the escarpment above Radway; to the right again is the Beacon of Dassett and we are looking into Warwickshire.

In line with the dam of Boddington Reservoir we look over the village of Boddington in the middle distance and see the shining white clad building of the motor museum at Gaydon. Motors now on a site where in the "Cold War" those mighty "V" Bombers flew! We look further towards the Malvern Hills, and shift again to the right, the high rise flats of Leamington Spa and the chimney of Stockton Cement Works. In the middle distance are the white sails of Napton Windmill and behind it the high rise flats this time in Coventry. These were built after the Coventry blitz of the Second World War, and the fires from the raids could be clearly seen from here.

Turning on to the right we see the Post Office Tower just out of Byfield Parish in the Parish of Charwelton. It rises from its base at 727 feet (222 metres) with the top of the tower well over 1100 feet. Just in front of the tower and the Ordnance Survey Triangulation pillar, is the boundary between the parish of Charwelton and the parish of Byfield. The contour line indicates a height of 704 feet (215 metres). Only a fraction of the line is in Byfield Parish and this point is the highest ground in the parish. Right of the Tower we are looking in the direction of Arbury Hill; the highest point in Northamptonshire at 737 feet (225 metres). As we pan further right we see the one remaining mast on Borough Hill at Daventry of pioneering BBC fame! This mast is now used for the mounting of an ever increasing number of satellite dishes which relay masses of data over vast distances.

On the same site 350 years ago King Charles I made camp for his 10,000 men before being defeated at the Battle of Naseby, while his "Billet" was the more comfortable Wheatsheaf Inn in the Town.

We are now looking towards Leicestershire. Across this entire panoramic vista in the past there were emergencies such as impending invasion, or more joyous occasions, including Royal celebrations when bonfire beacons were lit all over the Country. From here we would have seen the glow of these fires, through the Thames Valley in Oxfordshire, at Long Compton in Warwickshire, and one near Market Harborough in Leicestershire.

* * * * *

All this from Byfield's "Half Crown Corner"!

CHAPTER TWO

BANBURY ROAD

(See Maps Four and Four "A")

Having taken an overview across Byfield and its surroundings we now walk into the village from this point at "Half Crown Corner" (**See Map Four point of interest number 3**). At an imaginary walking pace, through our mind's eye we face Byfield! This ancient route was trodden perhaps by Stone Age Man and certainly by the Saxons from whose language the name Byfield is derived, "bye" meaning a habitation, and "felde" a field.

We can imagine this route has known a great variety of "the trodden foot", of both Man and Beast. Animals have been ridden and driven, both by drovers on foot and drivers in carts. This road surface has been passed over by all shapes and sizes of powered vehicles from the early steam vehicles to motors driven by the internal combustion engine. Wooden wheels, iron wheels, solid rubber tyres, pneumatic inflated tyres and tracks all used this old Turnpike road.

Moving forward, using the map to see which land the proprietors had been allotted, the land immediately to our left is the apex which comes to the very edge of the Parish. This land was allotted to the Rector John Knightley with an area of 139 acres 2 roods and 17 perches, for Tithes. It was a large tract of land sweeping down and round to the Boddington Road, (**see Map Four Proprietor/Owner number 7**).

Land measure
1 acre = 4 roods.
1 rood = 40 sq. rods, poles or perches.
1 sq rood, pole or perch = 30.25 sq. yards.
1 acre = 4840 sq. yards.

The next land on the left was allotted to Richard Farebrother in lieu of settlement — an area of 33 acres and 11 perches, (**see Map Four proprietor/owner number 19**)

On the right side of the road the hedge is the boundary between Byfield Parish and the Parish of Aston-le-Walls. When we reach the two stone-built semi-detached cottages, the hedge at right angles to the road, and going down the right side of the first cottage, is the boundary between Aston-le-Walls Parish and the Parish of Farndon (Woodford-cum-Membris), (**see Map Four point of interest number 4**).

The cottages were built by Thomas Kench of Eydon, a well-known and respected local builder in the 1950s, to accommodate staff of Solden Hill House.

Solden Hill House, an impressive stone building, is just visible from the road. It is not in Byfield Parish but it is interesting to state that it was built for Captain James Gerald Murland M.C., J.P. in the 1920s. It was purchased by a Mr Nicolle, a gentleman from the island of Jersey in the 1940s, and in the 1950s was acquired by the present owners as a school for young adults with learning difficulties under the guidance of Mr Fred Apps for the sum of £10,000.

If you look slightly over to the right, you can see Red Hill Wood and Farm. This is the area where the "Elephant Man" (Joseph Merrick) who was befriended by Lady Knightley of Fawsley Hall came to find peace and solitude in the wood where he was able to roam undisturbed. (Joseph Merrick died in London in May 1890).

Joseph Merrick
Joseph Merrick was a physical abortion who could not be contemplated without the feelings of horror; repulsive in his deformity; became known as the "Elephant Man", an unscrupulous showman made capital out of him until stopped by the authorities.

After years of unhappy experience best left to the imagination, he was befriended by Sir Frederick Treves, who rescued him and secured him two rooms at a London Hospital.

It was Merrick's great desire to visit the country. The kindness of Lady Knightley made this possible; she offered the use of a cottage on her estate as a "holiday home". Elaborate arrangements were made for the journey, but when Merrick was presented at the cottage where he was to stay, the good lady ran away shrieking. Friendly aid was at hand however.

"Merrick was conveyed to a gamekeepers cottage which was hidden from view and was close to the margins of a wood" (Redhill Wood).

"The man and his wife treated him with great kindness, and he spent the most supreme holiday of his life. He could roam where he pleased. He met no-one in his wanderings, for the wood was preserved and denied to all but the gamekeeper and forester."

Footnote by J.R. *The maternal grandfather of the author rented the farm/gamekeeper's cottage in 1917; but due to the 1920s and 1930s recession went into voluntary liquidation.*

Back to the Road! The hedge across the front of the cottages, and across the entrance to both Solden Hill House and Golden Hill Farm, is the boundary between Byfield Parish and the Parish of Farndon (Woodford-cum-Membris); the parish boundary then follows the line of the hedge and bridleway, heading directly towards the hamlet of Farndon.

A DISAPPEARED LANDMARK, BYFIELD WINDMILL, TAKEN DOWN IN 1913.

This is a photograph taken in the early 1900s of Byfield Windmill in Banbury Road, which was situated 200 yards along and to the left of the roadway to Farndon Hill farm. It was dismantled in December 1912.

This photograph is annotated BH18 in the Byfield Photo Museum. Lender Mrs Janet Blake.

As we descend the hill, the tower of Holy Cross Church comes into view; it is interesting to note that the gilded weathercock on the top of the spire is within a very few feet of the same height above sea level as our starting point in the parish near Half Crown Corner.

The land to the right, an area of 19 Acres, 1 rood and 10 perches, was allotted to Joseph Mumford **(see Map Four proprietor/owner number 86)**. The lower boundary of this allotment is the driveway to Farndon Hill farm. The farm itself is in the bounds of the hamlet of Farndon. The Wotherspoon family lived here in the late 1800s and some of them are buried in the southwest corner of Byfield Churchyard in the area which at the time was referred to as "The New Ground" having been consecrated in 1894.

If you looked up this driveway 200 yards on the left and prior to December 20th 1912, you would have seen a windmill — a post mill. A mill on this site is shown on the 1779 Enclosure Map, on a site indicating a small mill yard. The land around the yard was allotted to Sarah Coates being an area of 42 acres 2 rods and 13 perches **(see Map Four proprietor/owner number 88)**. The owner of the windmill from 1894 was John Henry Bromley, an eminent member of the local community, a yeoman farmer and landowner (Sarah Coates was J H Bromley's great-great-aunt). We have millers shown in the Northampton Directories: Thomas Boot was recorded as

a miller in 1866 and John Elliman (1828-1923) in 1874; John Elliman later retired to live in Westhorpe. There were sites where older mills had ground the local farmers' corn in the area; one on the road to Charwelton, (in fact just in Charwelton parish), was deemed much older, as 13 century coins were found in its foundations when it was dismantled in 1914 by the Checkley family. The oldest-recorded mark on this of Byfield Mill was 1820. It was probably then not the mill shown on the enclosure map, but a later one on the same site, **(see Map Four point of interest number 5)**.

In 1911 a large bonfire was built on the village side of the windmill, obviously far enough away as not to endanger the mill. The bonfire was lit by Miss Audrey Potter, aged 10, daughter of W. H. Potter, as part of the village celebrations to mark the coronation of King George V.

By a very interesting coincidence, to the right of the driveway to Farndon Hill farm and about the same 200 yards in, you would have seen in the 1970s a yellow drilling rig, **(see Map Four point of interest number 6)** which, strange as it may seem, was actually drilling for coal half a mile underground. We still have the final core section of the drilling process. Drilling at this site was not an isolated incident, as it was taking place over a fairly large area around Byfield.

This photograph was taken in February or March 1980 and is of a Drilling Rig drilling in a process of excavating for coal near the Banbury Road, ironically almost on the same site as was the Byfield Windmill.

This photograph is annotated RP62 in the Byfield Photo Museum. Lender Rex Partridge.

The field shown around the Windmill is an area considerably less than the land allotted to Sarah Coates, when fields were named. This was then called Tollgate Ground!

Shown on an early Ordnance Survey map, the original of which is deemed to be 1834, is a small section of ground with a building, on the left hand side of the drive-way adjacent to the road, marked Toll Gate! Obviously the gate had to be located before the intersection with the Priors Marston road (The Twistle) to prevent intentional deviation to avoid payment. This was the southern site of the Turnpike Tollgate **(see Map Four point of interest number 7)**.

The 1841 census shows a Thomas Gardner aged 23 as a Toll House keeper and Emma Gardner aged 20 living in "Old Toll House". The 1861 census shows one John Blabey.

Tolls and Toll gates

An interesting note from a contemporary encyclopaedia states:

"Although tolls for the upkeep of British roads were levied as early as the 13th century, many years passed before it became general. The first Turnpike Act was passed in 1663, and this allowed the operators to charge tolls to pay for and repair roads. As much as 11,500 miles of turnpike road were built between 1750 and 1780, (at the time of the Byfield enclosure!). With these, new toll roads had become well established. A gate was installed across the highway to prevent travellers from passing until the toll was paid. Often the enterprise was in private hands, and the toll went as a return to the "trust" of the persons who financed the cost of building or keeping the road in order. Under George III (reign 1760 to 1820) turnpike roads were the rule."

In the first ten years of his reign 1450 Acts were passed. With the toll system providing the funding, and with self-taught engineers improving road construction, the speed of traffic doubled.

On the left hand side of the road at this point is the Priors Marston road known as "The Twistle," a name probably taken from an ancient field name of Twist Hill.

Continuing down the hill until we come to the Westhorpe stream, this adjacent land was allotted in 1779 to a Mrs Ann Hawkes, the total acreage being 45 Acres 17 Perches (**see Map Four proprietors/owners number 82**).

This land from the Twistle to the stream was later farmed by the Checkley family.

One interesting point, the farmer Benjamin Checkley erected a fence adjacent to the stream using willow wood as posts; inevitably these grew into mature trees which still stand in 2004. A barn on the corner, now demolished, was built on the side of the Twistle and in more modern times was always known as Checkley's Barn (**see Map Four point of interest number 8**). The last of the Checkley family to own this farm was Benjamin's daughter Elsie Checkley, who had been an attractive girl in her youth! Latterly the elderly Elsie, still a spinster, could be seen dressed in her old gabardine Mac and Wellington boots, bending over the handles of her wheelbarrow as she went up the hill to "Checkley's Barn" with feed for her one or two cows, kept as pets more than for any commercial undertaking,

This land is now owned by Mrs Janet Blake.

The Westhorpe Stream was originally called "Blindwell Brooke" (or Blyndwell)

As we continue down towards the left hand bend entering the village, the land to the right was allotted in two parts to William Coates; one with acreage of 37 acres 2 roods and 33 perches, the other of 22 acres 1 rood and 22 perches (**see Map Four Proprietors/Owners numbers 90 and 91**).

Byfield from Turnpike.

This is a photograph of the Banbury Road clearly showing the width between the hedges, also it shows that "Bridge Villa" has not as yet been built (1898) but the railway bridge and new fencing are in the picture. This dates the photograph at between 1866 and 1898.

This photograph is annotated JR45 in the Byfield Photo Museum. Lender Jean Eyles.

Just before the bend on this turnpike, on the right hand side of the road, was a mile post indicating a distance to Banbury of 9 miles and to Daventry of 8 miles **(see Map Four point of interest number 9)**.

As we turn the left hand bend into the village, we have descended about one hundred feet.

As we proceed the roadway appears abnormally wide; the reason for this is that within the legislation of the Enclosure Act it stated that all new turnpike roads should be sixty feet between the hedges, and other new roads forty feet between the ditches, which should be four and a half feet wide. When physically measured in 2004 the hedges are sixty feet apart.

Byfield's hedgerows

A survey of the hedgerows in the parish of Byfield by John Roddis was carried out in 1988/89. Detailed recording of all the hedgerows included the species and the ages of specific hedges, using a formula devised by Doctor Max Hooper of The Institute of Terrestrial Ecology. (The formula is: taking 30 metres stretch of hedge, count the independent species of trees and shrubs, the age of the hedge equals 99 times the number of species minus 16; this theoretically then gives the age of the hedge.) Using this formula the left hand hedge at this point is deemed to be an estimated two hundred and fifty years old. So we can state fairly confidently that this hedge was originally planted at the time of the enclosure in 1779!

The right hand hedge is on the line of the original but is of much more recent planting.

As we descend towards the railway bridge **(see Map Four point of interest number 10)** on the left there was the first of two small allotments of land. A survey of the Old Inclosures and Homesteads in 1779 shows that this site was allotted in two parts; one to Thomas Price of 4 perches **(see Map Four Old Inclosures/Homesteads 75)**, and the other to Edward Brown of 8 perches **(see Map Four Old Inclosures/Homesteads 76)**.

On the right, 2 acres 2 roods and 6 perches were allotted at the time of the enclosure to Richard Davies **(see Map Four proprietors/owners number 84)**, this was later named Doctors Close. One would presume that perhaps the Doctor kept his pony here, which he would have used in the shafts of his "Gig" to visit his patients! This site is now home to the Clayton family.

The second plot, which went down to the Westhorpe stream, was allotted to J Mountford being some 3 acres 23 perches **(see Map Four proprietors/owners number 85)**. These two allotments **84** and **85** were later separated by the East and West Junction Railway in 1866.

If we had been here around 1866 we would have seen the surveyors planning the route of this section of this new east to west railway. (This single line, when completed, would run from Blisworth to Broom Junction, via Towcester – Blakesley – Moreton Pinkney – Byfield – Aston-le-Walls sidings – Fenny-Compton, – Kineton – Ettington – Stratford-upon-Avon). Not many railways ran across the Country; most of the big Companies ran lines in competition with each other on the more lucrative north to south routes.

The Act of Parliament authorising the construction of the East and West Junction Railway was passed on June 23rd 1864. The construction of the Railway was started with Lady Palmerston cutting the first sod later in the same year on August 3rd. The contractor was T. R. Crampton M.Inst.C.E. If you had been on the road bridge in the autumn of 1873 you would have seen the first passenger train on the line.

Later the line was to become the Stratford Midland Junction Railway; it then became a part of several divisions of the London Midland and Scottish Railway. When nationalised it became part of British Railways and finally being British Rail. The last scheduled passenger train ran over the line in 1952, and the line was closed in 1965.

The large modern brick-built house on the right, constructed in the 1990s, is built entirely on ex-railway property, on a site which in the 1940s and 1950s was used as garden allotments.

The brick-built house, on the left with its "date stone" of 1898, was built by Henry Buckley in the garden of the forge and named "Bridge Villa". The 1901 Census shows that Henry, a retired blacksmith, lived in this house, with his son having taken over as Blacksmith living in the original house called "The Forge". Later Bridge Villa was lived in by the Over and Fletcher families. Mr Fletcher was a teacher at Byfield School in the Second World War, and went on to teach at Brackley Magdalen School. After the war the occupiers were Arthur and Miriam Cook, which was history to some extent repeating itself, as Miriam was the daughter of Arnold Humphris, the blacksmith at "The Forge". In 1955 Bridge Villa and adjacent land was purchased by Stuart Douglas.

On to the Forge on the left, the property had one small building on it in 1779 and was extended in the 1800s to the building that we see today. It has been a private house since the late 1950s. Before that, as the name implies, it was a Blacksmiths Forge. Records show the Blacksmiths were: 1877 – Henry Buckley (1852–1931); 1900 – his son William Buckley; 1906 – J Humphris and son; 1914 – Arnold Humphris; the Humphris family were originally from Eydon, where in his youth Arnold had been a Sunday School teacher and occasional organist. Arnold the Blacksmith will be remembered for always wearing a white shirt, unusual attire for a blacksmith!

In 1950 the property was purchased by Charles Henry George (Harry) Bland (1910–1971) and his wife Esmie Bland as a private house and named "The Old Forge". One couple who for a time lived with Mrs Bland were David Porter and his wife Liz. Liz was a descendant of the old Byfield family of Coates.

A definitive footpath runs along from the Twistle between The Forge and the Old White Lion, and continues to the right across the road and continues alongside the Westhorpe stream through to the Farndon road.

The pair of semi-detached houses on the right was built by the Brown and Preston families, (Mrs Preston was a member of the Brown family), in the 1950s. The Brown family operated a market garden to the rear of these houses on the site of what is now Thomas Close **(see Map Four A point of interest number 11)**.

Map Four A
Banbury Road (A361)

The BLACK NUMBERS are from the survey of Old Inclosures and Homesteads in the centre of the village.
The BLUE NUMBERS are Tracts of Land allotted to Proprietors and Owners in the rest of the parish.
The RED NUMBERS denote points of interest along the route. Detail taken from a modern map some detail from the 1779 Enclosure Map with other detail added.

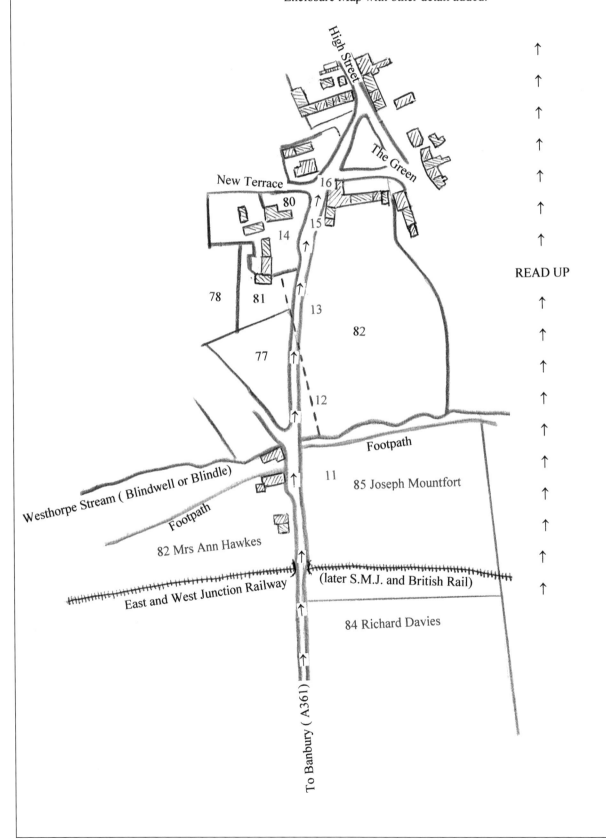

This photograph of the White Lion in Banbury Road was taken between 1911 and 1924, when Joseph Maycock was the Landlord. The older lady is Mary Ann Maycock the Landlady.

This photograph is annotated JR679 in the Byfield Photo Museum. Lender Mrs Mary James.

The Old White Lion was built around the middle of the 1800s as a Public House; the site was virtually the footprint as the actual building.

Records show the Landlords were: 1866 – Thomas Mason: 1874 – Thomas Sewell, Castrator, Beer seller and Veterinary Surgeon: 1884 – Samuel Batchelor: 1885 – Mrs Priscilla Batchelor: 1894 – William Gascoigne (who was also the Honorary Secretary of Byfield Liberal Club): 1901 – Edward Gardner: 1907 – Joseph Maycock (at the time the brewers were Hopcraft and Co): 1928 – Harold Cave: 1940 – Horace Walters (1882–1963): 1950s – Thomas Pollard (1910–1970): and in the 1960s Jeff Pollard until closure.

Mr and Mrs Robert Nixon purchased the property from the brewery to convert to a private dwelling for £2,000. The dwelling is now lived in by a member of the Lamb family.

A day in the life of a signalman!

In the 1950s the brother-in-law of the then landlord of the White Lion, Tom Pollard, was Billy Grubb who worked on Byfield Station as one of the signalmen. Billy was partial to a pint and he used to take his refreshment in the bay window of the bar of "The Lion". Having set the home signal on the Stratford side of the station at stop, Billy waited for the two toots on the stationary engine's whistle, carefully put down his pint if it was unfinished, quickly mounted his bike and rapidly rode along "The Station Fields" (now part of the Brightwell complex) to the signal box, pulled the lever and let the train into the station.

The land between the Old Forge and the Old White Lion has since been purchased. This was previously the gateway into the field behind.

The detached house on the right side of the road was built in the late 1970s

We have now reached the Westhorpe stream. This stream rises in the parish and flows via the rivers Cherwell, Isis and Thames to an outfall to the sea at the Thames estuary.

We have walked into Byfield on the Turnpike Road; now on the left we reach the junction with Banbury Lane, which prior to 1824 was the turnpike route. A meeting of the Turnpike Trustees on March 18th 1824 was convened to consider the propriety of diverting and improving that part of the road which passes through the village (see the transcript in the paragraph below). The reason for this was that the narrow lane was becoming of inadequate width for the traffic, and it was said that a convoy of circus wagons were attempting to negotiate this lane when one became wedged in the lane. It is doubtful if this was the sole factor for the re-routing, but it probably "triggered" the action.

A transcript of the notice to convene a meeting, which was reported in the Northampton Mercury, recorded verbatim hence the old style and spelling. Additional notes by J.R.

Edgecott 26 February 1824.

Sir

We the undersigned, being two of the trustees of the Turn pike Road leading from Banbury, in the county of Oxford, to the south End of Mill Field, in the Parish of Lutterworth in the County of Leicester, do hereby direct you to convene a meeting of the said Trustees, to be holden at the Griffin Inn, in Chipping Warden, in the County of Northampton, on Friday the 18th day of March next, at Twelve o'clock Noon, for the Purpose of considering the Propriety of diverting and improving that Part of the said road which passes through the village of Byfield.

T CARTER

M H BARTHOLOMEW

Notes by J.R.: Thomas Carter was the Lord of the Manor. The Carter family were preceded by the Chauncy family and were succeeded by the Cartwright family as Lords of the Manor in Byfield. There was direct lineage between the three families.

The Bartholomew family lived in Blakesley Hall, and 89 years after this letter were responsible for building the first workers' cottages in New Terrace and Banbury Lane in Byfield .A link with the generations of the Bartholomew family has not as yet been positively made!

Looking at a more modern map that shows this "new route" we continue on the roadway, the route of which went over land that was originally allotted in 1779 to Joseph Mumford, an area of 3 roods 16 perches **(see Map Four "A" Old Inclosures/Homesteads 77)** on the south side joining with his other allotment numbered **85**.

All of the properties subsequently built on the right of the road, including the housing estate Edwards Close **(see Map Four "A" point of interest number 12)** up to the

junction with the Green, were all built on land originally allotted in 1779 to George Hitchcock, an area of 2 acres 2 roods 38 perches **(see Map Four "A" Old Inclosures/ Homesteads 82)**, and was named Thomas Edwards Close after a Byfield Charity, as was and still is the policy of Byfield Parish Council.

This specific Charity was bequeathed by Thomas Edwards of Hampton in the Parish of Bugbrooke in the County of Warwickshire; a Yeoman who, by his last will and testament proved in the prerogative Court February 29th 1725, bequeathed as follows.

The Thomas Edwards charity (copied verbatim)

"Item, I do give to the poor in Byfield in the County of Northamptonshire, the sum of ten pounds to be sett out in interest, and that the said interest to be laid out in Bread and given at the discretion of the Minister and Church Wardens and the Chiefest Inhabitants of the Parish yearly, on the 13th of February or the nearest Sunday to it."

The houses in the close were built in the 1970s by Dennis Price Ltd, who was hoping to name it "Holy Cross View". The one larger house in Thomas Close was built to maximise the value of that specific part of the site, Dennis Price Ltd having been refused planning permission to extend the site into what was then British Rail land and is now part of the Brightwell Recreation Ground. The site benefits the housing balance within the Parish with its large numbers of bungalows, and offsets the other sites in the village which are biased to larger houses.

Continuing on the right is Judd's garage, originally used by Bertie Waterhouse **(see Map Four point of interest number 13)**. The original premises were built of corrugated iron. That building was moved by Dennis Eyles and is now used as an agricultural store on the Farndon road. Records show that Bertie was operating in 1928, (the premises had a telephone number Byfield 14).

The new building was erected by Denis Judd, an entrepreneur, in two phases, initially still utilising the old corrugated iron building. Denis not only repaired cars and light vehicles but ran buses and a coal merchant's from this site, (by this time the telephone number was 43). Today the premises are still a retail garage and M.O.T. Testing Station operated by Brian Haynes and Ken Quinney (with the same telephone line but with the increase in the number of digits to become 260243).

The site opposite the garage was allotted in 1779 to William Thornton, an area of 1 rood 16 perches **(see Map Four "A" Old Inclosures/Homesteads 81)**, (the 1777 Militia list shows William Thornton as a farmer), together with adjoining land to the north, part of which was sited on the roadside in "New Terrace", allotted to John Gibbons, an area of 16 perches **(see Map Four "A" Old Inclosures/Homesteads 80)**, together with allotments 77, with part of **78** and **81**, became the premises and land that went with the New Inn public house **(see Map Four "A" point of interest 14)**.

One would assume that the William Thornton who was allotted the land in 1779 was the father of the William Thornton who was the first landlord of the New Inn. The

This photograph is of Judd's Garage in Banbury Road taken in the 1950s. It shows Denis in his smock together with all the items fitments and tools that you would expect in a rural country garage.

This photograph is annotated BH161 in the Byfield Photo Museum. Lender David Adkins.

This photograph is of Banbury Road showing the "Old" New Inn when it was still thatched. The date of the photograph is around 1900, and the pub sign shows the brewery supplying the premises was Phipps of Northampton.

This photograph is annotated BH4 in the Byfield Photo Museum. Lender Mr Dick Haynes.

1841 census shows that William Thornton was born in Byfield. He was 45 in 1841 and was a farmer, so he was born in 1796.

The landlords were: 1841 – William Thornton, Farmer and Tax collector: 1869 – Thomas Thornton, Higgler: 1877 – Charles Gibbard: 1884 – Samuel Howes junior: 1901 – William Hickman: 1910 – Thomas Cary (whose daughter Daisy married Jim Smith later to be manager of Byfield Ironstone): 1931 – Reginald Knight: 1936 – Jim Berrill, (who had been a master mariner): 1952 – Eric Williams, followed by George Plumb, Eric Dobson, Graham Taylor and Steve Newby.

Higgler!

Is taken from the word higgle (form of haggle), one who makes a fuss over buying or selling; a Pedlar, a Dealer, one who drives a "hard bargain" especially when dealing in animal livestock.

The public house was drastically altered in the 1920s from a thatched, stone building, to what we see today. Over the years the Bicester and Warden Hill fox hunt regularly met here.

Latterly the land was owned by Grand Metropolitan Brewery together with the Cross Tree Public House,

previously The New Inn. The land was sold to a developer and the public house sold to Wolverhampton and Dudley Brewery.

Of the houses on the right the first one next to the garage is named "The Doll's House", obviously due to its size. Occupiers included Tom and Sissie Pollard and the McKenzie family. This house was built, as was the pair of semi-detached houses above it, by a Banbury dentist Herbert Peake, just before the Second World War. The manhole covers on the property have the name R.W.M. Peake cast into them.

The next brick building on the right has a lean to extension which has been used by a number of businesses **(see Map Four "A" point of interest number 15)**.

In the late 1920s the house only was used by Percy T Jarvis trading as a saddler, tennis racquet maker (restrings and repairs) and radio dealer. Later he used the lean-to extension. This extension was used in the Second World War as the Headquarters of the Byfield Home Guard. Interestingly, Percy Jarvis was the sergeant and the previously mentioned Denis Judd the officer in our "Dad's Army". Later the premises were used by F. W. Boddington as a shop selling bicycles, models, toys and knitting wool. It has since been a second-hand bookshop and a wood worker's workshop.

This photograph is of Percy Jarvis outside his shop in Banbury Road in the 1930s. As you can see from the detail, Percy was an entrepreneur. He was a harness and collar maker, he repaired and restrung tennis rackets, sold and repaired bicycles, repaired radios, and, before mains electricity was available, supplied and recharged accumulators for the radios. In whatever leisure time he had, he was a keen cyclist, a good club standard tennis player and also an amateur artist. Both of his two daughters were born in the house.

This photograph is annotated JR279 in the Byfield Photo Museum. Lender Mrs Mary Thomas

Byfield Home Guard:

Byfield had its Home Guard and all able-bodied men were recruited, unless they were needed for any special duties. The men were drilled and trained in the use of hand weapons. On Sundays when the ironstone workings were idle, a firing range was set up there between large banks of earth. With regular troops in the locality who needed to be kept occupied, mock battles were arranged between different contingents including the Home Guard. Officer Judd told many stories. One was that sometimes the Home Guard managed to defeat the regular troops by local knowledge of the area. While the regular troops were poring over maps and map references, officer Judd told his men to go to Checkley's barn and turn left!

We now get to the site of the butcher's shop, presently a private house but we are told it was previously a boys' school. As yet we have no documentary evidence that this was the case.

When it was a butcher's shop there was a "lean-to" extension on the front of the building which served as the actual shop. Phil Montgomery was the butcher in the late 1940s. Phil had a cousin who also had a butcher's shop in the High Street. Phil Montgomery was followed by George Freeman (**see Map Four "A" point of interest number 16**).

This photograph was taken in Banbury Road as it joins High Street in the snow of 1947. The now dismantled butcher's shop can be seen on the right, which was a lean-to built onto the main building. Phil Montgomery is looking out of the doorway. The "Snow Diggers" are, left to right: Peter Hince, Bert Wingrove and Les Jones.

This photograph is annotated JR322 in the Byfield Photo Museum. Lender Betty Potter

Map Five

High Street (A361)

The BLACK NUMBERS are from the survey of Old Inclosures and Homesteads in the centre of the village.
The BLUE NUMBERS are Tracts of Land allotted to Proprietors and Owners in the rest of the parish.
The RED NUMBERS denote points of interest along the route.
Detail taken from a modern map some detail from the 1779 Enclosure Map with other detail added.

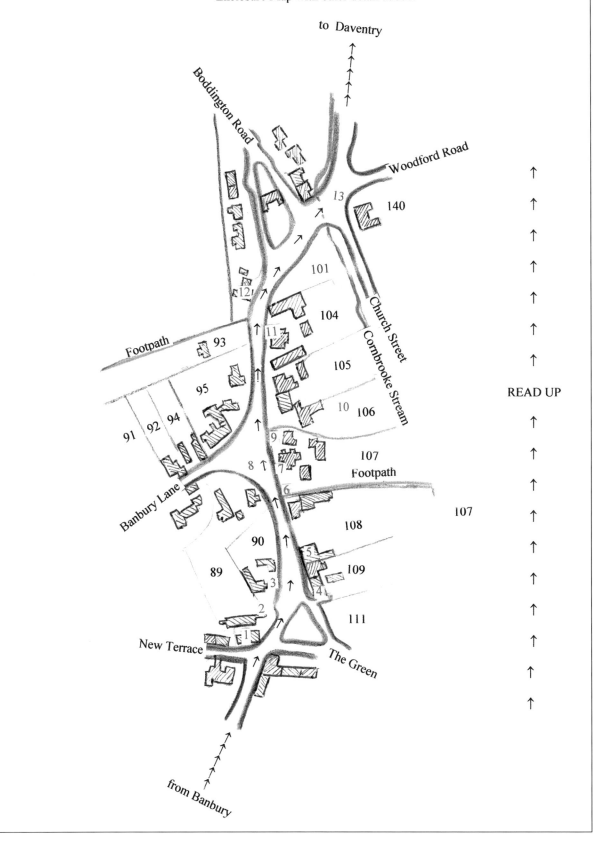

to Daventry

Boddington Road

Woodford Road

13   140

101

Church Street

Cornbrooke Stream

104

Footpath   93

11

95   105

10   106

91 92 94

9   107

8   7   Footpath

6

107

108

90

5

89   109

3   4

2   111

New Terrace   1

The Green

from Banbury

READ UP

CHAPTER THREE

HIGH STREET

(See Map Five)

Moving from Banbury Road into the High Street, on the left is a large house on the corner of New Terrace and High Street, now known as Flora Inns House **(see Map Five point of interest 1)**. These premises were up to 1966 the village doctor's house and surgery. The doctors were: 1901 – Doctor Albert Adam Hope (1875-1939); 1939 – Doctor Theodore Edward Waine; 1946 – Doctor Wilfred Hampton Parkinson. On his death his ashes were interred in the churchyard in June 1967. As the Doctor's family, wished to remain in the house, the link with the house and the general medical practice in Byfield was severed. When Mrs Parkinson moved out the premises were sold. The traditional doctor's house and surgery then became an annex for the school for adults with learning difficulties at Solden Hill House, and was later named "Flora Innes House".

The progression in the mode of a Doctor's Transport
Doctor Albert Adam Hope was the doctor of Byfield from the start of the 1900s up to the Second World War. Within that period his daily rounds to visit his patients progressed from a Horse and Gig, with a certain Joseph A Smith aged 16 as his "live in" carriage driver, on to one of the first "clutch-less" motor cycles with its handsome wicker side-car. The combination had to be push started. If the push was un-assisted then he, the rider, had to leap onto the moving vehicle. This meant the Doctor had to be lissom and fit. To stop the machine, before using the brakes the engine had to be "de-compressed". This stops the engine firing, allowing the combination to be brought to a standstill. Finally the Doctor purchased a motor-car. At first early models were fitted with a "wet clutch" which, to the uninitiated, is a clutch running in a bath of oil; the friction plates being of steel and the clutch plates being fitted with a series of cork inserts. When failure of the unit occurred prior to the Doctor wishing to go on holiday, Dennis Judd vividly describes in his book "Living in the Country" how he, as a motor engineer, being unable to obtain genuine replacement parts, replaced the corks with some supplied by the Doctor himself, taken from his store of empty medicine bottles.

Moving on there was a small brick building within the curtilage of Flora Innes House, adjacent to the rear access to the back of "The Lawns" in Banbury Lane **(see Map Five point of interest 2)**. This building was used initially by Doctor Hope as a consulting room before moving it into the main house. A number of business people rented the premises. In the 1930s a son of Doctor Hope, J Hope, ran a radio and electrical shop there, with a telephone number of Byfield 13! The building was later used by F W Boddington (Jack) for demonstrating his model railway layouts.

Dispensing medicines
The Doctor's surgery was not manned by medical staff, but the elderly lady called for a repeat prescription! The only "Staff" on the premises were the sons of Doctor Hope, Raymond and Oliver, who dealt with the matter, mixing the medicine in the bottle returned by the patient. On returning at a later date for a further repeat prescription, she told the doctor that the yellow medicine she had been given last time was much better for her ailment than the red medicine he had given her before!

The next building on the left, a stone house converted and extended by Mr and Mrs Cobden (parents of Mrs Dot Montgomery, wife of Tom Montgomery formerly the Byfield high street butcher) and now named "Windwhistle", was originally built on an Inclosure allotted in 1779 to William Chambers, an area of 1 rood and 26 perches **(see Map Five Old Inclosures/Homesteads 90)**. Before 1957 this house was attached to a row of cottages known as Post Office Yard. Previously, before the post office moved opposite, it was known as Tomalin's Yard **(see Map Five point of interest 3)**. This row of cottages clearly shown on the 1779 Enclosure map was pulled down in 1957 for road widening. Prior to this these houses were occupied by a large number of Byfield people, mostly as their first marital home. The families who lived there included the Spriggins, Eyles, Smith, Jones, Tomalin, Partridge, Huntley, Fenimore, Russell and Vine families, and many more.

Opposite here on the right side of the road at this point prior to the 1880s was a row of cottages. These were built on an Inclosure allotted to Henry Thornton **(see Map Five Old Inclosures/Homesteads 109)**.

The first, bottom, cottage became the village post office in 1890 to 1929 and returned in the 1990s and is the present post office **(see Map Five point of interest 4)**. The first Postmaster in these premises in 1890 was John Jones (1851–1933).

Sale of the Post Office Premises
Block of Freehold property, known as the Post Office Property, was sold at auction at The New Inn Byfield; on Wednesday February 2nd 1898, at Three for Four o'clock in the afternoon. By the direction of the Trustees of the Will of the late Samuel Amos Bush Esq. (Verbatim)

The Post Office is shown in this photograph in the High Street occupying the bottom cottage of a row, adjacent to the Village Green. The row of cottages opposite became known as "Post Office Yard" because of its location opposite the Post Office. The date of the photograph is around 1912. This photograph also shows the merchandise on display outside the shop of W. T. Potter.

This photograph is annotated BH9 in the Byfield Photo Museum. Lender Mr Dick Haynes.

Known as the Post Office Property, Situate in the Village of Byfield, Comprising of a Stone-built and Thatched Dwelling House, containing 3 bedrooms 2 living rooms and a pantry, with garden at the rear, in the occupation of William Russell, at a rental of £10 per annum; a well-built Dwelling House, now used as a Post Office, containing 4 Bedrooms, Sitting Room, Post Office, Kitchen, and Scullery, with Garden at the rear, in the occupation of Mr John Jones, at a rental of £19 15s. per annum.

Two Dwelling Houses now converted into one, containing 4 Bedrooms, 2 Living Rooms, 2 Pantries, and a Back Kitchen, with Garden at the rear, in the occupation of Miss Bull at a rental of £10 per annum.

An entry in the Byfield Parish Council minute books recorded the meeting of 29th January 1908, in which Mr John Jones was asked by the Council "to trim and light the lamp to enable people to see to post letters".

Street (footway) lighting
Street lighting was not installed until 1934, after there had been a debate by the parish council as to whether the lighting should be powered by gas or electricity. Fortunately electricity was decided on.

John Jones was followed as Postmaster by Henry Hatwell, in 1911. (Records in the Northamptonshire Directories of 1914 show that Henry Hatwell was also a civil servant

running a Ministry of Labour Employment Office. Other records also show that Henry Hatwell became Byfield's very first Scoutmaster in 1911.) From 1922 William Arthur Russell became Postmaster, then in 1929 William Russell built a new Post Office further down the High Street on the opposite side of the road to the Rose and Crown Public House **(see map five point of interest 12)**, and the post office function moved there.

John Jones – Notes by J.R.
The Local Government act of 1894, (which had a very difficult passage through Parliament) legislated for the formation of Parish Councils. In Byfield Parish the procedure was started by the Overseers calling an open parish meeting in the boys' school room (known by all as the "Tithe Barn" but was never used as such; now the site of the new Rectory). On Tuesday 4th December at 7.30 p.m. John Jones was elected unanimously by the meeting to supervise the methods and procedures that would enable a Parish Council to be formed. At the first council meeting on Tuesday 1st January 1895 at 7.15 p.m. John Jones chaired the meeting which elected from the assembled candidates members who would form the first parish council for Byfield. Those newly-elected councillors then elected the first Chairman of Byfield Parish Council, who was the Rev. Francis Henry Curgenven, the Incumbent Rector of the parish. Evidently John Jones possessed ability but not social standing. He then stood down and the newly-elected Chairman took the chair.

The Council then invited John Jones to accept the office of Clerk to the Council, which he accepted at a salary of £2.0.0. p.a. John Jones, a true servant of Byfield, died in 1933 at the age of 82.

Overseers

These were officers appointed in each parish under the Poor Relief Act of 1601 to provide for the poor. These roles were succeeded by the National Assistance Act of 1948.

The vacated post office premises then became a retail shop and were extended to include some of the adjacent cottages. Records show that Albert Joshua Walker J.P. was a clothier here in 1929, (with a telephone number of Byfield 29). Prior to this Mr Walker also traded in Woodford Halse; in 1920 he advertised a three piece suit for 30/-.

The shop became the Cooperative store in 1935 as part of the Banbury Cooperative Society. It was then purchased by a Mr Hughes and became Acorn Stores. The premises were extensively altered, with an extension to the shop and a store room to the rear; the first storey over all of the shop being let as flats. Later the Post Office function was added; this brought it back from whence it came in 1929. In the 1990s, the business was sold, returning once again to a Cooperative Store but this time under the auspices of the Gloucester, Oxford and Swindon Cooperative Society.

The next building in the terrace was a stone cottage occupied by various postmen including, in 1898, William Russell, at the age of 64, with his wife Fanny.

The house at the end of the terrace was built of brick **(see Map Five point of interest 5),** now a private dwelling, within an allotment to Mary Shaw **(see Map Five Old Inclosure/Homesteads 108)**. This property had formerly been used as commercial premises firstly by Edward Cornelius Dodd Cramp, a Clock and Watch maker, from 1884 until 1928. (ECD Cramp died in 1934 aged 85 as detailed in Byfield burial records). He was always known as Crampy-Dodd, due to the fact that the Cramp family married into the Dodds or the other way round. Crampy-Dodd fancied himself as a bit of an amateur hypnotist, and tales of his exploits in the local ale houses are long remembered and are still repeated. These exploits are vividly described in Dennis Judd's book "Living in the Country".

Prior to Crampy Dodd being the village clock and watch maker, the Northamptonshire Directories record that, from 1847 to 1877, the Byfield clock and watch maker was Benoni Pearson Durran. With a Christian name like Benoni one would suspect he was of Italian extraction. The Byfield Census records show Benoni was born in Middleton Cheney, Northamptonshire. The Durran family were later to have a clock and watch makers shop in Banbury.

Clocked by a Clock!

Most villages had a clock and watch maker and repairer. They would repair almost anything which had a clockwork mechanism. It was not an unusual sight to see a parishioner carrying a time piece for repair to the clock-mender.

An incident occurred in one village where a man was scurrying along, late for a doctor's appointment. On reaching the corner of the street, he collided with another man who was carrying a grandfather clock on his shoulder. Both men fell heavily, with the clock skipping along the highway! The man, who was then even later for his doctor's appointment, spluttered and said "Why don't you wear a Bl—y wristwatch like every one else?"

After Crampy Dodd had vacated the premises, for a short time it was a hardware store which was run by W. T. Potter.

By 1903 the premises had on specific days became a sub branch of a Bank; Gillett & Co. (sub-branch Manager Thomas Rose) open Tuesdays 2–4 pm.; drawing on Glyn, Mills, Currie & Co. London E C. Later it became a Barclays Bank Ltd – sub-branch open 10.30 a.m. till 12 noon on market days, and also on Tuesdays 2 to 4 p.m. drawing on its head office at 54 Lombard Street, London E.C.3. Two of the tenants living in the accommodation, which was part of the bank premises, were Bill Smith and his wife Ethel.

Walter William (Bill) Smith (1882–1975) was awarded the Military Medal in the First World War.

The last occupants of the "Bank House" were the Henning family, who purchased the property as sitting tenants. It then became a private house in the 1950s.

The next two cottages on the right are two of the oldest cottages in the village; they are situated at right angles to the road and are clearly shown on the 1779 enclosure map, within the area of 2 roods and 30 perches allotted to a Mary Shaw. It has been suggested by some architectural historians that parts of these two cottages are in fact medieval. The Rand family lived here in the cottage nearest the road. James Rand, a farmer, lived in the Manor House from 1894 to 1898. His daughter Lillian lived in the cottage until her death, having become Mrs Lillian Pettit. The other cottage until recently was lived in by a member of the Checkley family. Stanley, son of the previously referred to Benjamin, and brother to Elsie of Banbury Lane, was a well known character. (Stanley Checkley died on October 1st 1976 aged 81.) He had the distinction of joining the Northants Yeomanry in 1910 at the age of 16, and was the first villager to join the British Forces in France.

Moving on, still on the right, immediately behind the two old cottages a footpath runs through to Church Street. Today it is metalled and runs through a modern housing estate at the Church Street end. The Inclosure on the right of High Street next to the footpath was a tract of land of 3 acres 18 perches. Running from the High Street down and along Church Street towards the Church, this was allotted in 1779 to Thomas Orton **(see Map Five Old Inclosures/Homesteads 107)**. This field at some stage was named "Alley Close" obviously named after the "alley" from the High Street through which the field was accessed. "Alley Close" was the traditional village sledging field, and in the deep snow of 1947 much sledging was enjoyed. The villagers witnessed an unusual event with a certain Gratton Darbishire, a local farmer and professional photographer, skiing down the steep slope and over the road, easily clearing the six foot wall on the opposite side into the field. Seeing a person skiing was not a common sight, especially as it was during a long period of austerity, when the minds of people were far from a pastime that was the forte of Kings and Gentry.

On the corner in High Street next to the footpath was a small brick building built in the 1800s **(see Map Five point of interest 6)**. This became another bank sub-branch in 1914, open on a part-time basis. It was Capital & Counties Bank Ltd. opening 10.30 a.m. to 12 noon, and on market days also opened from 1.30 to 3.30 p.m; drawing on head office, in 39 Threadneedle Street, London EC. By 1920 it had become Lloyds Bank Limited (sub-branch, Manager Herbert John Vick,), open Tuesdays 2 to 4 p.m. and drawing on head office, 71 Lombard street, London E C 3. It continued as a bank until the 1950s. It became a model shop, a wool shop and a barber's. The building has since been demolished to make way for parking space for a new bungalow built on the site.

Further on within the same site of 3 acres and 18 perches, which was in 1779 allotted to Thomas Orton, once there was a Thatched "L-shaped" building with a single storey shop fronting on to the road. The second part of the "L" was two storey living accommodation. This was one of the most picturesque buildings in the parish **(see Map Five point of interest 7)**. The premises are shown on the 1882–83 Ordnance Survey Map as a Post Office.

It was in 1840 that the famous "Penny Black" stamp was introduced.

In 1847 the Northamptonshire Directories record Thomas Seear (1813–1889), as grocer, ironmonger and Postmaster. In 1869 the post office was also a money order office and Post Office Savings Bank, and letters arrived by "Foot messenger" from Daventry. In 1874 the directories indicate that Mr Seear had retired. Alfred William Budd then became Sub-Postmaster, and he was also a grocer and agent for W. & A. Gilbey, wine and spirit merchants. In 1890 the Post Office moved to the premises previously referred to in the High Street **(see Map Five point of interest 4)**, adjacent to The Green.

After the Post Office moved, first the premises were used by Oliver and Son Contractors.

Sale of Several Freehold Properties

To be sold at auction by Castle, Son, and Booth At the New Inn Byfield. On Wednesday February 2nd 1898, at Three for Four in the afternoon. By the direction of the Trustees under the Will of the late S. A. Bush Esq.

Lot 2: All that Valuable Freehold Property (Verbatim)

Situate in the Village of Byfield, comprising a Range of Buildings , now used as Offices, and containing on the upper floors, Five Rooms; on the ground, Four Shops and Rooms, now used as Offices and Stores, Kitchen Pantry, and Coalhouse, together with an Enclosure of Land adjoining, in which are a Barn, Brick-built Stable with Loft over, and wood-erected lean-to Shed with galvanised roof; the whole being in the occupation of Messers Oliver and Son, Contractors,

at a rental of £35 per annum. A good Grocers Business has been carried out on these premises.

There is a capital Well of Water upon this property.

Land Tax last payment, 9s 2d.

Note by J.R.

T. Oliver and Son of Horsham, Sussex, were the contractors building part of the Great Central Railway, contract number 4; this was the section between Rugby and Charwelton, a distance of 15 miles 77 chains, with a contract cost of £513,308. This section included the construction of: 5 viaducts; 46 bridges; 32 Culverts; 12 cuttings; 13 embankments; 6 sets of sidings; a junction and a tunnel (Catesby) which was nearly 1¾ miles long; the tunnel was faced with Staffordshire Blue Bricks, and some 30 million were used in its construction.

All of the construction of contract number 4 was administered from these premises in Byfield. Further detail of the construction of "The Great Central", including details of the building of this section, can be found in "Echoes of the Great Central" by John M. C. Healy.

On the death of Samuel Amos Bush, the then owner, it was purchased at auction on February 2nd 1898 by James Richard Hutt (1864–1941) for four hundred and twenty pounds, and converted into a drapers shop.

Indentured apprenticeship for young James Hutt (copied verbatim)

Memorandum of an Indenture made this fourteenth day of October one thousand eight hundred and seventy eight, between William Sedgwick of Byfield in the County of Northampton Draper and Clothier of the one part and James Hutt of Byfield of the other part, whereas James Hutt of the Parish of Byfield has agreed to place himself as an apprentice with the consent of his Father for the term of three years from the day of the date hereof to learn the trade of Draper and Clothier. In consideration of the same the said James Hutt and his Father agree to pay the same William Sedgwick the sum of fifteen pounds.

Notes by J.R.

The detail continues and includes the payment being at five pounds a year for three years. This means that James Hutt was an apprentice from 1878 to 1880. The document of Indenture was signed by James Richard Hutt, James Hutt his father and William Sedgwick, and was witnessed by William George Sedgwick.

Within the Byfield Photo Museum we have a pristine photograph of James Richard Hutt outside his shop with all the varied merchandise that was on sale on display outside the front of the shop. The year of 1899 has been authenticated by a date beside the shop doorway advertising a sales promotion. This was determined by computer scanning and picture enhancement.

James Richard Hutt also had a shop in Parsons Street Woodford Halse, at the time of the construction and initial operation of The Great Central Railway; a very prudent move with a demand for various garments, footwear and other merchandise, from both construction workers and railwaymen.

This photograph taken in 1899 is of J. R. Hutt's shop, showing Mr Hutt and his dog and the vast and diverse array of merchandise which he sold from these premises.

This photograph is annotated AS149 in the Byfield Photo Museum. Lender Mrs J Milns.

In 1911 the thatch was taken off the roof of the Byfield shop and a brick-built first storey added. The work was carried out by the building firm of G Johnson of Hinton. This alteration totally destroyed the character of the building. The advantage of the extra floor was that it enabled more stock to be held, giving a greater choice to the customers.

After J R Hutt died his wife Kate continued to run the shop for a time. It was then divided into two smaller shops; one was a greengrocer's run by the Brown family, the other became a card shop and newsagent at first operated by Colin Thornton then by Herbert Eichler.

The premises were purchased by the Gabriel family; Mrs Gabriel continued selling clothing in one of the small shops for a time.

Byfield's own Fred Dibnah

In the 1960s it was realised on the Quinquennial Inspection of the Church fabric, that the top of the spire was unsafe due to the fact that the ferrous ties holding the top were corroded and had expanded, lifting the adjacent and constituent stone structure.

A restoration fund was set up with several money raising schemes, one being the purchasing of some small cardboard replica steeples in which parishioners' coins could be saved.

The Incumbent Rector, the Rev. Andrew Freer, made the statement that, if the necessary funding was raised, he would personally re-mount the Cockerel back on its pinnacle perch.

By 1969 the funding had been raised. The repaired and re-gilded cockerel had been displayed to promote the fund in the window of Hutt's old shop, which at the time was being rented by Colin and Greta Thornton as a greeting card and newsagents. The cockerel was taken from the shop to the base of the church tower. True to his word made in haste or not, Andrew climbed up the 120 winding steps to the top of the tower, and the proud re-gilded Cockerel was hoisted from the ground by the Byfield children to join him. With the bird secured to his back, Andrew mounted the external ladder secured to the spire and climbed up to position the most prominent land mark in the local area back to its rightful perch. The Golden Weather-Cock would now continue to indicate the wind direction as it had for many years before. Andrew's very worthy efforts were filmed by the local professional photographer Gratton Darbishire, who also scaled the spire as a true professional would! The Rector's noble efforts were shown on National Television.

A few days later, before the scaffolding was removed, Churchwarden Fred Hutt having expressed a wish also to scale the spire, he was initially having second thoughts, but the Rector would have none of it. Finally, whether he volunteered or was ordered, he made it, but remarked that he was glad it was a "one off."

The "Old Hutt's Shop" became so dilapidated that a demolition order was put on it by the local District Council. When the building was being demolished a cruck beam was found to be the main structure for the roof. This rang alarm bells regarding the historical significance of the building!

The demolition order was lifted, but by then the cruck beam had fallen down, as had most of the rest of the structure. The living accommodation was saved, but the shop area was completely demolished and Mr and Mrs Gabriel built a modern bungalow on the site.

To the left of the road opposite the shop is the memorial green. Mounted on this green is the stump of an Ancient Bartering Cross, the square base of which is medieval. Records show that the broken stump of the shaft of the cross together with its base was restored to its vertical position in 1947 by the Ministry of Works. It is now deemed by English Heritage as being of such historical importance that it is registered as listed building number UID 560514 **(see Map Five point of interest 8)**.

Very close to the Bartering Cross was an elm tree that had stood as a landmark on this site for over 200 years, but sadly it succumbed to Dutch Elm Disease and was felled in the autumn of 1979. This elm was planted by John Maud in 1753 assisted by eight yeoman farmers namely: Bromley; Brightwell; Hitchcock; Dodd; Potter; Harris and two others.

Yeoman
A man of common rank next below a gentleman.

Gentleman
A man of gentle or noble birth; one without a title could wear a coat of arms and, more generally, every rank above the rank of yeoman; one above the trading classes; a man of refined manners.

In 1809 there was a celebration in commemoration of the Sovereign, King George III, entering upon the 50th year of his reign, on the 25th of October 1809. This was celebrated at Byfield by the ringing of bells early in the morning of the day. After divine worship, 110 children of both sexes assembled in the School House and were feasted with roast beef and plum pudding, ale etc. provided by the benevolence of the Rev. Henry Knightley. A sheep, cost raised by subscription, was roasted upon the Cross Hill, cut up, and distributed to the poor with bread, etc. and a band of music paraded the streets.

Also on this green is the war memorial unveiled on Friday September 20th 1920, by Sir W Ryland Adkins K.C. M.P., Chairman of Northamptonshire County Council. It now has inscribed on it the names of those who gave their lives in two World Wars. The memorial stood adjacent to the ancient elm and became unsafe, due partly to the tree roots, and was moved to its present position in the 1970s funded by public Subscription.

In recent years the Byfield Branch of the Royal British Legion have won the best kept war memorial in the County a considerable number of times. In 1972 this area was one that was registered as a Village Green, and as such the maintenance of the main area is funded through Byfield Parish Council.

On the right of the road opposite the end of Banbury Lane, still within the allotment to Thomas Orton **(see Map Five point of interest 9)**, is a former butchers shop and off licence; known as the Cross Tree Public House.

Owners/occupiers were: 1851 – William Gardner (1819–1888); 1884 – James Smith, carrier and beer house; 1894 – Mrs Smith; 1901 – John Eyles (General Ag. Lab. in the 1901 census); 1903 – Arthur James

This photograph is of the unveiling of the War Memorial on September 20th 1920, by Sir W Ryland Adkins, Chairman of Northamptonshire County Council.

This photograph is annotated JR1039 in the Byfield Photo Museum. Lenders Mr and Mrs Harris-Watson.

Montgomery, butcher; 1910 – W H Stevens, horse breaker beer retailer, Phipps and Co; 1924 – William Montgomery (1894–1948), beer retailer (with Arthur James); 1928 – Mrs Louisa Montgomery (with William); 1940 – Arthur Philip Montgomery, butcher (with William); William Thomas Montgomery into the 1980s.

The confusion of the Three Cross Trees!

In Banbury Road and High Street there have over the years been three Cross Trees:

The first was the "Cross Tree Elm" planted in 1753, the name "Cross" having been taken from the ancient bartering cross on the site.

The second was the butchers shop and off licence known as "The Cross Tree Public House" named originally in the 1880s after the ancient elm.

The third, named after the other two were no longer there, was the public house in Banbury Road, previously called the "New Inn"; a title that was difficult to illustrate on a pictorial pub sign. A competition was launched to get a name that could be easily illustrated on a sign. Mr Arthur Shenton, a well known user of the establishment, suggested "The Cross Tree". This was taken up, so the "New Inn" became the third "Cross Tree".

Behind the butchers shop and off licence was the slaughter house and a cottage. The cottage was occupied in the 1940s and 1950s by the Carvel family.

The next dwelling on the right is a stone house. The buildings and the land running through to Church Street

are clearly shown on the 1779 enclosure map, an area of 3 roods and 3 perches, allotted to James Harris **(see Map Five Old Inclosures/Homesteads 106)** who was also allotted land off the Priors Marston road **(see Map Twelve Occupiers/Owners 75)**.

James Harris and his allotment 75 off the Priors Marston Road – Notes by J.R.

This relatively small allotment to James Harris, recorded on pages 55 and 56 of the written particulars within the Byfield Enclosure of 1779, gives a very good example of the kind of detail within the procedures relating to individual allotments, made by the Commissioners.

Detail (Copied Verbatim)

To and for the said James Harris – Owner of some old lands, one cottage, common, two lots of bushes and two plots of thorn and in lieu thereof and of all his other estates, rights and interests in and over the said open and common fields.

One plot or parcel of land or ground containing three acres two roods and twenty three perches as now staked and set out. And the annual value of four pounds and two pence upon the quality. Bounded on part of the North and on the East by an allotment to the said John Bromley. On the South by an allotment to the said Cressent Boote. On the West by an allotment to the said John Edwards and on the remaining part of the North by the said Thomas Bromley.

The hedges, ditches, mounds and fences for inclosing which said allotment on the East against the allotment to the said John Bromley against the allotment to the said Cressent Boote, and against the allotment to the said John Edwards. The said

This photograph is of Byfield High Street taken just before the First World War, showing the butchers and off licence and the grocery store. One interesting aspect, further down the road on the right, is the thatched malt house of the Rose and Crown Public House.

This photograph is annotated BH6 in the Byfield Photo Museum. Lender Mr Dick Haynes.

Commissioners do hereby award and order and direct and appoint, shall be made and at all ties thereafter maintained and repaired by and at the expense of James Harris and the owners and occupiers by the time being.

Back to the Inclosure number 106 allotted to James Harris on High Street. As well as the stone house there was a brick built building later used as a bakehouse; this was built in the middle of the 1800s and shown, on the 1882–83 Ordnance Survey Map, as being sited on the right hand side looking into the site from the road.

Owners and occupiers, of the house and bake house: the Smith family were bakers here from 1910 until the 1960s, Alfred Smith senior (1879–1965) and Alfred Smith junior (1911–1985). Mrs Alice Smith (1880–1960) was well known for her splendid tasty ice-cream! The male members of the family loved singing and would burst into song at any opportunity; they were also very socially minded, being part of many village organisations, such as the Pig Club, Cricket Club and the Village Hall.

Up to 1914 the village castrator William Sewell slept in the loft over the bake-house.

In the yard of the Bakehouse, from 1928 until 1948, Ernest Victor Vine ran a cobblers shop; the building was a wooden shed. This was later moved and used as the first tennis pavilion on the Brightwell Recreation Ground (**see Map Five point of interest 10**).

Zip Zine and the chase

Ernest Victor Vine lived in Post Office Yard in the end house with the gable window facing the road. He was a man small in stature; so much so that when he was in the Byfield Home Guard and they were marching, Victor was always bringing up the rear; his Lee-Enfield Rifle 303 appeared bigger than him! His W.W.II gaiters looked more like W.W.I Puttees almost reaching up his little short legs to his knees. Victor Vine had a nickname given to him by the children which was "Zip Zine". His wooden cobblers shop was in Alf Smith's yard. This yard had a brick and cinder pathway running down from High Street to Church Street.

The children teased Zip Zine, and one trick they used was to wait until they could hear the rapid hammering of the nailing on of a new sole. Knowing that Zip had a mouthful of tacks they then, putting their heads round the door, would call Zip names. The chase was on! the children madly making for the High Street or down the cinder path through the scrub bushes to Church Street, followed by a red-faced Zip Zine spitting tacks high into the air.

The land on the left side of the road on the corner of Banbury Lane was allotted in 1779 to a Samuel Batchelor, who is recorded in the 1777 Militia list as being a servant, an area of 2 roods and 1 perch (**see Map Five Old Inclosures/ Homesteads 95**). Later a number of cottages were built. Tom Alcock, painter of signs, lived there in the 1930s. Other families lived there including the Needams, Holtons, Lovells, Boddingtons, Goddards and others. It was known as "The Hollies"; the cottages later became one dwelling.

Moving on, at the right side of the road at this point was a large stone house which is on the roadside frontage of a plot of land that went though to Church Street and was allotted in 1779 to Mary Coates, the area being 2 roods 11 perches (**see Map Five Old Inclosures/ Homesteads 105**). In the late 1880s Henry Golding built a single-storey extension on the north end of the house to use as a retail grocer's shop. He took over the agency of W. A. Gilbey, wine and spirit merchants, formerly held by Alfred William Budd. An entry in the Parish Council records shows that the council expressed concern when a fence appeared in front of his property between the house and the road.

The grocers on his property were: 1890 – Henry Golding; 1903 – Golding & Adams; 1914 – John Adams (1867–1936) telephone number Byfield 8. In 1949 the business was taken over by Roy Plant, followed by Minnie, Pratley, Davies and others until it closed as a grocer's shop and became a furniture reupholstering business. It is today a kitchen design and tile shop.

Roy Plant built the bungalow on the bank opposite the shop to live in, due to the fact that the traditional accommodation, which went with the shop, was not available as it was still owned and lived in by the descendants of John Adams.

The next building on the right, formerly The Rose and Crown Public House, was then, and has been probably over the years, the busiest area in the village of Byfield! The area of land on which this building stands was allotted in 1779 to Thomas Cox with an area from High Street to Church Street of 2 roods 21 perches (**see Map Five Old Inclosures/Homesteads 104**).

The unusual situation with regard to this specific allocation was the fact that the Commissioners sat to make their decisions in this very building, the "Rose and Crown".

The building was of considerable age at the time of The Enclosure, as a very busy Coaching Inn and a Hostelry. It was also being used as a stopping stage for the mail coaches. It was the forerunner of the post office of Thomas Seear in the 1840s, although the only method of transporting mail over journeys of any distance still relied on the horse in his day. Certainly the transport of mail by rail to and from Byfield Railway Station had come by the 1870s.

The present building is only part of what was there in 1779, as there was a large malt-house on the edge of the road, (**see Map Five point of interest 11**), and a brewhouse on the east of the main building. Records show that Alfred Brightwell said that his family brewed beer here, and it was sold at a penny a quart. This malt house building adjoined the boundary of the previously described property, leaving only a gap between the present building and the malt house through which the stagecoaches and other traffic would pass to enter the busy court yard. The stabling for the horses, and the ostlers' accommodation, was on the opposite side of the courtyard from the hostelry and was also of considerable size! These buildings are clearly shown on the 1882/83 Ordnance Survey Map.

The conditions of the Inn Keepers victuallers licence (records from 1630) copied verbatim.

That the above bounden (name) shall observe and keep all the Articles contained in his licence for victualling which are as followeth:-

1. *That he suffer not unlawful games to be used in his house or ground.*

2. *That he entertain no town dwellers to tipple in his house, but wayfaring men only in their passage or journey.*

3. *That he permit no tippling in his house on the Sabbath day or holiday time of service or sermon or any time after 9 o'clock at night.*

4. *That he suffer none to lodge in his house above one day and night together, but such as he will answer for.*

5. *That he buy no goods off any wayfaring man or suspected person unless he know them to be of honest conversation.*

6. *That he sell no less than a quart of his best ale or beer for a penny and five quarts of the smaller.*

7. *That he observe all other orders mentioned in the King's proclamations concerning ale houses.*

8. *That he shall not entertaine any notorious rogues or vagabonds.*

9. *That he shall not willingly suffer any tobacco taken in his house.*

10. *That he shall not make any deputy to sell his ale or beer.*

11. *That he allow no flesh in his house in Lent or other tymes prohibited by lawes and statutes of this realme.*

Within the Byfield Photo Museum is a photograph of a painting, which was painted in 1858, and is of a view of the Rose and Crown from the north (cattle market side) of "Club Night". The painting shows a crowd of people in front of the building having received their once a year payment from "The Club", a sick and dividend savings club, in essence a philanthropic society! This painting has within the crowd a lady in a red shawl and a young girl in a white dress. The painting, cape and dress are still held in the possession of the Harris-Watson family handed down to them from earlier generations!

The G.P.O. and the Mail Coaches.
In 1710 a General Post Office was set up, under the control of a Postmaster General.

The first Mail Coach Service began in 1784 operated by a John Palmer, and lasted half a century, but died out entirely, with the advent of the Railways.

The owner at the time of the Inclosure was Thomas Cox. It is not known whether he was the publican. Publicans from 1847 were: Thomas Lake maltster and farmer (Robert Lake Lord 1823–1875, was the maltster for the inn), followed by: 1866 – Thomas Brightwell, licensed victualler and farmer of 88 acres, he grew his own hops and barley, manufactured his own malt; 1890 – Thomas Henry Brightwell (1827–1893) who also is shown as a thrashing machine owner; 1894 – George Elkington; 1903 – George Ford, the brewer is shown at this time as Hopcraft and Co; 1914 – Thomas George Whiston, who advertised accommodation for cyclists; luncheons, dinners and teas; parties catered for; good stabling. Mrs Whiston

was known throughout the district as "The Painted Lady" due to her liberally applied make up; also the family had two very good looking daughters who obviously attracted customers especially the young men of the day; 1931 – Mr Vance; 1935 – Harold Hince, publican and petrol sales (telephone number Byfield 65) until closure.

History uncovered in the Rose and Crown
In 1954, when the lounge was being renovated, a 16th century Tudor fire place was discovered.

Denis Judd operated his taxi service and garage from here before moving into the premises in Banbury Road; after this Dave Roberts ran a garage business from the site.

Notes by J.R.
Mr Vance, Landlord of The Rose and Crown, 1931–1935.
One of the vehicles operated by Denis Judd was a Minerva which was garaged on the site which in 2004 is the garage forecourt shop.

When entering the garage on one occasion it was noticed that something was dripping onto the Minerva from the loft space. On closer inspection this was found to be blood. Investigation then found that Mr Vance had attempted to take his own life by cutting his throat. Medical assistance was rendered and on this occasion Mr Vance survived, only sadly to succeed on a later occasion.

Minerva a car maker in Belgium producing cars from 1899 to 1939
(Detail from an encyclopaedia of cars)
Sylvain de Jong, founder of one of Belgium's most famous marques, began making Minerva and Romania cycles in his Antwerp workshops in 1897. Minerva produced large prestige models up to 1928. (Minervas were driven by the Kings of Belgium, Norway and Sweden, and in fact by Henry Ford). Smaller models continued to be produced up to the company's demise in 1938.

In the Second World War the building, which was accessed by the external stone steps, was a billet, and on the ground floor of the main building; the room adjacent to the road was a cookhouse.

When the public house closed, it was purchased in 1963 by Ken and Margaret Lamb, and used as private accommodation, whilst it was attached to a retail garage and petrol forecourt. Ken also incorporated the running of his taxis from here as well as continuing to use "Chimneys" in Banbury Lane.

On the left side of the road was a small paddock. This was part of a larger Inclosure in 1779 allotted to Joseph Cox, a total area of 1 rood 37 perches **(see Map Five Old Inclosures/Homesteads 93)** which at the time when Byfield Cattle Market was at its height housed a very strong spring. The water from it ran across the turnpike and was used to wash the animals' feet, together with the carts and premises of the market. Prior to the Second World War the site was purchased by Denis Judd. It was sold in the late 1950s to Alec and Barbara Smith, who built a bungalow on it at the top of the paddock. The stone was obtained from a condemned cottage which had been at the rear of the present post office, on the left of the driveway going down to "Brookwell".

The next building, a brick-built detached building on the left opposite the Public House, was purposely built as a Post Office, built by William Arthur Russell in 1929 **(see Map Five point of interest 12)**. The post office function thus moved from further down the High Street. Two rather unique aspects: one was that a well had to be sunk to provide water to the dwelling, as mains water was not as yet available, and the other was that the telephone number was Byfield 1 (one), the first number to be connected to the Byfield new manual exchange that was actually housed in this very building.

In the Second World War this had to be manned night and day, which meant sleeping on a bed next to the manually-operated switchboard.

Postmasters were: 1929 – Russell; 1946 – Montgomery; then Payne, Thornton, Morley, Frisby and Daniels, until closure in the late 1990s. The post office function then went back from whence it came **(see Map Five point of interest 4)**, in the premises adjacent to The Green.

The land to the right of the road down to the Cornbrook Stream was also allotted in 1779 to Thomas Cox, an area of 1 Rood, which is 1210 square yards **(see Map Five proprietors/owners 101)**. This piece of land is the same-sized area today.

This land had for a considerable time been a cattle and livestock market, which was probably initiated in the 1860s. When the first passenger train ran into Byfield station in 1873 it is recorded many butchers came to the stock sale. Mutton sold for 8½d – 10½d (3p – 4p) per lb, Lamb 1s (5p) per lb, Beef 9d – 10d (3p – 4p) per lb, and Pork 12s – 13s (60p – 65p) for a score (20lb).

An interesting detail appeared in the Northampton Herald in an article: "Great Christmas Sale and Show of fat cattle and sheep, Tuesday December 7th 1875, comprising animals of rare excellence. Auctioneer Septimus P Graves".

An article more recently in the Daventry Weekly Express, July 2001, recalled past history of Byfield Market, in this case 126 years previously and again in the year 1875; it indicated that there was a fat stock sale held every month.

Details from the Northamptonshire Directories indicate that the auctioneers were: 1877 – Graves Miller and Eales; 1884 – Graves and Miller, (Septimus P Graves, home Southam, Samuel Miller, home Banbury); 1894 – Miller and Abbotts. The final closure of the market was in 1928, when most of the goods and chattels, plus the goodwill, went to the newly established market of Midland Marts, which had been built in Grimsbury on the north east side of Banbury in 1924.

The Miller family of auctioneers, originating from Balscote, near Banbury, were related to the Reading family who farmed Pitwell in the 1890s and the North family who also farmed Pitwell in the early 1900s.

This site of the old cattle market was used as a billeting area, with army officers being housed in Nissen huts in the Second World War.

After the war, with the huts removed, the concrete bases became a favourite place for "ice skating" by the village children, especially on winter's nights, and more especially the one under the street lamp.

We have reached the junction of the five roads coming in to this busy part of Byfield, now known as "Fiveways", previously known as "The Sale Ground" or "The Market", previously to that "The Bridge" and prior to that "Town Green" **(see Map Five point of interest 13)**.

This is a photograph of Byfield Market in 1919, and indicates a fair throughput of animals.

This photograph is annotated JR110 in the Byfield photo Museum. Lender Mr Alan Holton

CHAPTER FOUR

DAVENTRY ROAD

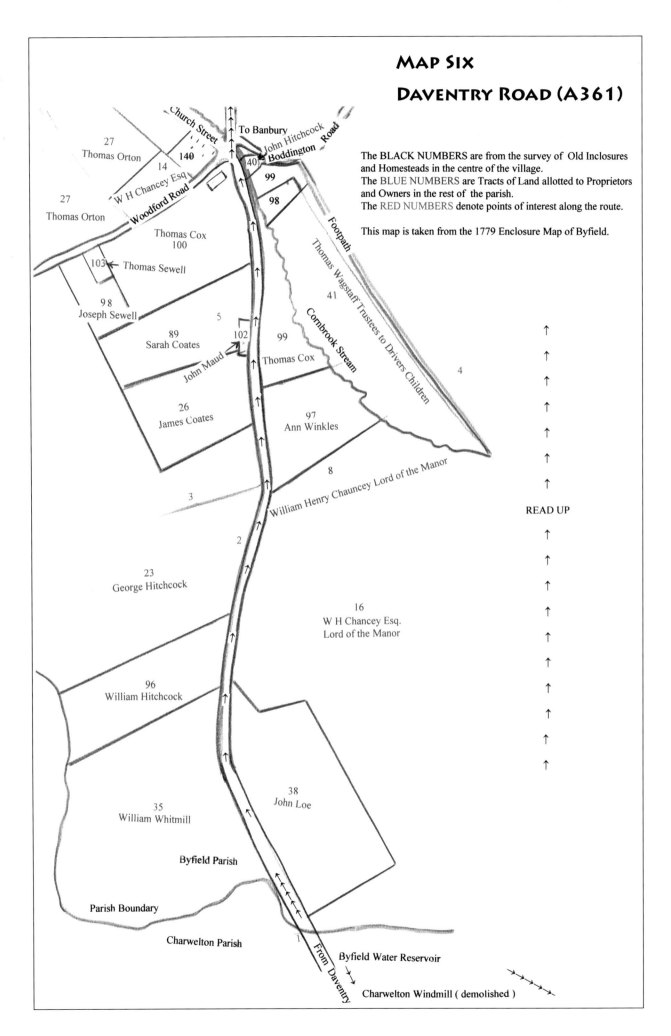

MAP SIX

DAVENTRY ROAD (A361)

The BLACK NUMBERS are from the survey of Old Inclosures and Homesteads in the centre of the village.
The BLUE NUMBERS are Tracts of Land allotted to Proprietors and Owners in the rest of the parish.
The RED NUMBERS denote points of interest along the route.

This map is taken from the 1779 Enclosure Map of Byfield.

Church Street

To Banbury

John Hitchcock

Boddington Road

27
Thomas Orton

140

14

W H Chancey Esq

40

99

98

27
Thomas Orton

Woodford Road

Thomas Cox
100

103 ← Thomas Sewell

98
Joseph Sewell

5

89
Sarah Coates

102

John Maud

99
Thomas Cox

Footpath

Thomas Wagstaff Trustees to Drivers Children

41

Cornbrook Stream

4

26
James Coates

97
Ann Winkles

8

William Henry Chauncey Lord of the Manor

3

2

READ UP

23
George Hitchcock

16
W H Chancey Esq.
Lord of the Manor

96
William Hitchcock

38
John Loe

35
William Whitmill

Byfield Parish

Parish Boundary

Charwelton Parish

1

From Daventry

Byfield Water Reservoir

Charwelton Windmill (demolished)

38

CHAPTER FOUR

DAVENTRY ROAD A361

(See Map Six)

This route is entering the village from the north east, using the main road, the old turnpike, now the A361.

But before we start our journey from the boundary of Byfield parish, it is worth travelling back to the village of Badby and starting our walk towards the Byfield parish boundary. Coming up the hill out of Badby looking over to our right we see Arbury Hill, the highest point in Northamptonshire (737 feet or 225 metres). Moving on to the next highest point we see Sharmans Hill (734 feet or 224 metres) which is almost equidistance between Badby Village and the village of Charwelton, but the actual summit is just in the parish of Hellidon.

One important historical event took place on this Sharmans Hill. In 1913 King George V and Queen Mary, together with the German Kaiser, and other members of the Royal Family, visited the site at the end of the biggest military manoeuvres ever staged in this country. Over 50,000 men had taken part. Obviously there were a large number of people who had come to see the spectacle, among whom were members of the Byfield Hutt family, Mrs Connie Hutt and her son Richard (Dick). Dick's son Tim tells us of them relating about seeing the Kaiser departing in an airship back to Germany.

As we continue to walk towards Byfield, the next hill on our right is Charwelton Hill (675 feet or 206 metres). Old maps show a windmill on this hill. The mill was pulled down in the First World War by the Checkley family, then farmers of Charwelton Hill farm on whose land the windmill stood. Coins were found in the foundations dating back to 1340–1399, the time of John of Gaunt.

John of Gaunt, Duke of Lancaster (1340 - 1399) 4th son of Edward III married to a Castilian princess. Detail Sir Keith Feilings, "A History of England" first edition 1950.

Byfield records show a Richard Thornton as a millwright in 1690.

On the right, adjacent to the roadside, is the underground reservoir that supplies Byfield with its head of water, the supply having been pumped all the way from Pitsford reservoir, on the north side of Northampton. Prior to this the first "mains" water supply was provided by the Woodford water company from a spring at Hinton. Before that, water was supplied from the many wells, springs and pumps in the village.

As we approach the bottom of the hill we reach the boundary between Charwelton and Byfield Parishes (see **Map Six point of interest 1**).

The first land on the right as we enter Byfield parish is

land allotted in 1779 to the Lord of the Manor William Henry Chauncy Esq. It was a large tract of land, 256 acres 2 roods 18 perches (see **Map Six Proprietor/Owner 16**). When named, the land adjacent to the road was called "Second Blinkers" and the land behind "Dodds Barn Ground" with Dodds barn on it. The next land again on the right was named "First Blinkers". Dodds Farm was well-known in the 1860s, the time when Mr Aubrey Cartwright Lord of the Manor, owned the land. Dodds farm was farmed by Joe Spencer in the 1940s and 1950s.

Also on the right, encroaching into this large tract of land, there was adjacent to the roadside an allotment in 1779 to a John Loe, of 46 acres 2 roods 11 perches (see **Map Six Proprietor/Owner 38**).

Over a large proportion of this area, on the right of the road, iron ore was mined from 1915 until 1965. Owners were: 1915 – J W Payne; 1931 – Geoffrey Treadwell; 1940 – Byfield Ironstone, and then Stewarts and Lloyds until closure in 1965.

The first land on the left on entering the Parish was allotted to William Whitmill, 33 acres 2 roods 33 perches (see **Map Six Proprietors/Owners 35**), later known as "Post Ground". Records show that the Bromley family sold two fields in 1925 on the death of Mrs Mary Elizabeth Bromley. Further to our left land was allotted to William Hitchcock, 11 acres 1 rood 27 perches (see **Map Six Proprietors/Owners 96**).

A short distance on, still on the left side of the road, a mile post indicated Daventry 7 miles, Banbury 10 (see **Map Six point of interest 2**).

The next land adjacent to the mile post was a bigger tract of land allotted to George Hitchcock, 106 acres 2 rood 26 perches (see **Map Six Proprietors /Owners 23**). All of these three allotments were bordering on their eastern boundary with the Hinton (Woodford-cum-Membris) parish. Part of this land was named "Turnpike Field". Whether this reflects that adjacent to this land a toll gate was sited across the Turnpike may be pure conjecture!

This allotment was later to become part of Hinton House Farm. Hinton House was built around 1900 and was sited just outside the Byfield Parish boundary in Hinton (Woodford-cum-Membris) parish, but adjacent to this land. Hinton House was built by a Mr Charles Cunningham Church, who built the farmhouse from which his farm bailiffs ran his farm, with some of the cottages on this land making the holding a small estate. Bailiffs in this farm house were: 1898 – John Franklin; 1903 – Thomas Wyatt (1852–1908); 1910 – William Quarterly; 1924 – Tom Forrester, Bailiff for Mr M. H.

This photograph shows the Ruston Bucyrus 5W "Walking Dragline" with its 135 feet boom, which was used for taking off the top soil and overburden to enable the Ruston Bucyrus Face Shovels to extract the iron-bearing ore. This machine was operated principally by two Byfield men, Denis Gregory and Maurice Tomalin.

This photograph is annotated AS262 in the Byfield Photo Museum. Lender Tim Hutt.

Pelham. It is interesting to note that several Byfield men were gardeners at Hinton House, among them in the 1930s Arthur Carvel a member of an old Byfield family. Today the gardener at Hinton House is another Byfield man, Peter Paybody.

A pond adjacent to some of the cottages on this land is still named Hitchcocks pond **(see Map Six point of interest 3)**, named after the proprietors who were allotted the land in 1779. Mr Bolton, a ship owner, purchased Hinton House. In 1953 it was sold at auction, and the Byfield holding was subsequently purchased by Mr Dennis Gulliver, a farmer. He was a keen cricketer and cricket continued to be played on this land as it had been previously on the left of the farm driveway, fairly close to the Daventry Road. Byfield cricket team played there between the First and Second World Wars.

As we come into the village towards the cross roads, the first of the last two enclosures on the right was allotted to Ann Winkles, an area of 7 acres 1 rood 28 perches **(see Map Six Proprietors/Owners 97)**, the field to be later named "Plough Pikeard". The last enclosure was allotted to Thomas Cox, an area of 4 acres 1 rood 12 perches **(see Map Six Proprietors/ Owners 99)** later named "Grass Pikeard". The land to the west behind "Grass Pikeard", named "First Faulkners", was one of the sites of the last ironstone mining to take place in Byfield before closure in 1965 **(see Map Six point of interest 4)**.

It is interesting to note that all the land on the right from the Parish Boundary, with the exception of a thirty yard gap at what today is the driveway entrance to Manor Farm house and buildings down to the Five Ways junc-

tion, is all part of Dodds Farm; a total area of 120.596 acres. The land directly to the west of Dodds Farm, some 239.607 acres, makes up the majority of the land holding of Manor Farm. The total land holding of both Dodds and Manor farms makes up the majority of the area farmed today by E. W. and R. W. Watts, and is now all called Manor Farm

On the left were two allotments of similar size, allotted in 1779 to a brother and sister of the Coates family. The first, of 9 acres 3 roods and 17 perches, was allotted to James Coates **(see Map Six Proprietors/Owners 26)**, and the second, of 9 acres 36 perches, to Sarah Coates **(see Map Six Proprietors/Owners 89)**.

The Enclosure Map shows a site marked "stone pit" in the centre of this allotment **(See map six point of interest 5)**.

The Coates family married into the Bromley family, who married into the Hornsby family. Tracing the family line back through the Bromley and Coates families indicates that James and Sarah Coates were the great-great-great-uncle and aunt to the present owners. There is a small allotment to John Maud of 2 roods 4 perches on the roadside encroaching into the Sarah Coates allotment **(see Map Six Proprietors/Owners 102)**.

The last allotment on the left, before we get to the five ways road junction, was allotted to Thomas Cox, an area of 12 acres 1 rood 30 perches **(see Map Six Proprietors/ Owners 100)**. On a large part of this land, which was known as "Dolls Hill", the Daventry Rural District Council, the local Housing Authority, built Council Houses. The first houses were completed in the late 1920s.

CHAPTER FIVE

FARNDON ROAD AND CHURCH STREET

MAP SEVEN

FARNDON ROAD AND CHURCH STREET

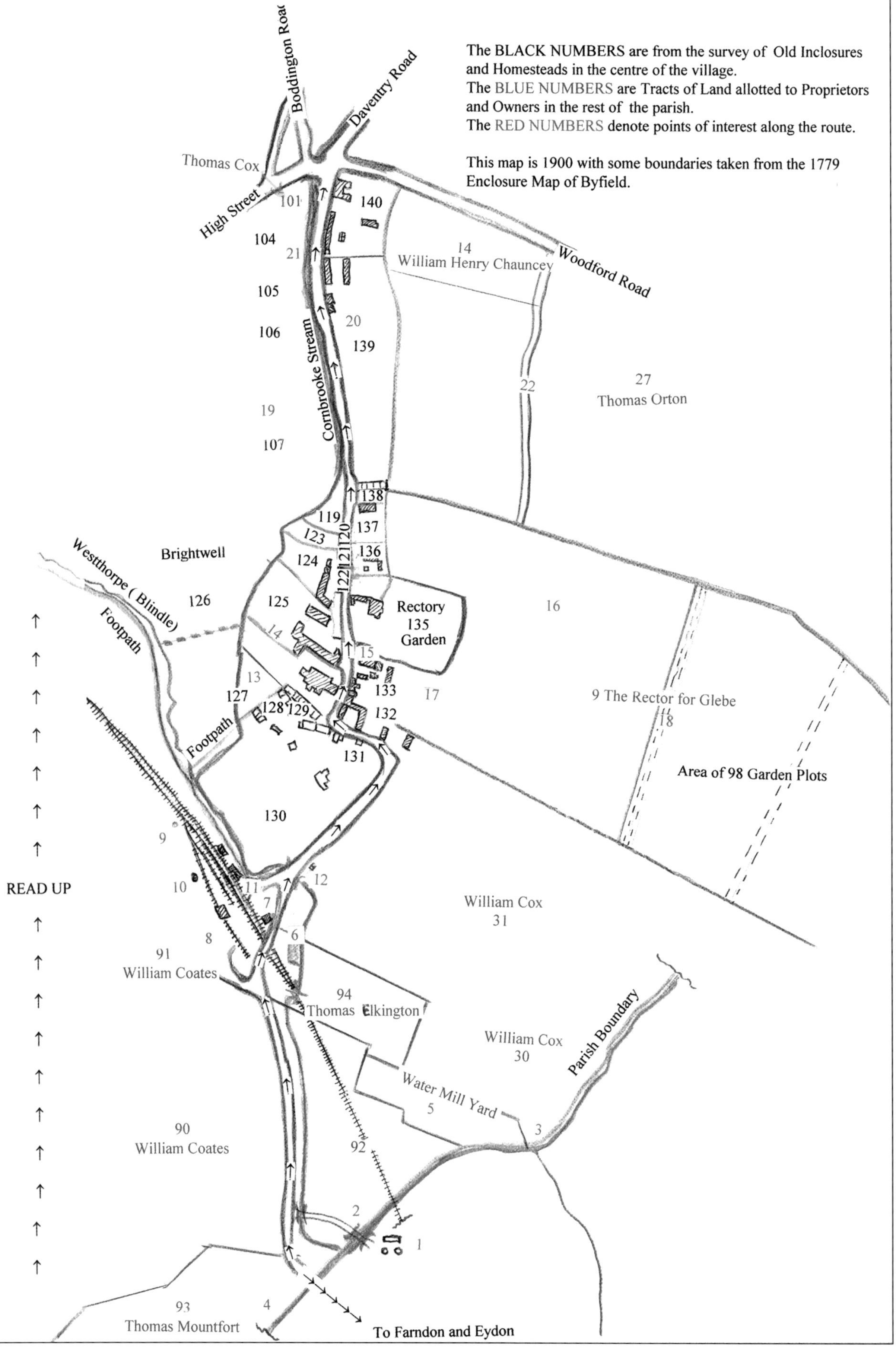

Boddington Road

Daventry Road

Thomas Cox

High Street

The BLACK NUMBERS are from the survey of Old Inclosures and Homesteads in the centre of the village.
The BLUE NUMBERS are Tracts of Land allotted to Proprietors and Owners in the rest of the parish.
The RED NUMBERS denote points of interest along the route.

This map is 1900 with some boundaries taken from the 1779 Enclosure Map of Byfield.

101
140
104
21
14
William Henry Chauncey
Woodford Road
105
106
Cornbrooke Stream
20
139
27
Thomas Orton
19
22
107
138
119
137
123
122 121 120
136
Westthorpe (Blindle)
Brightwell
Footpath
124
126
125
Rectory
135
Garden
16
14
15
13
133
17
9 The Rector for Glebe
127
128 129
132
18
131
Area of 98 Garden Plots
130

READ UP

9
10
11
7
12
William Cox
31

8
6
91
William Coates
94
Thomas Elkington
William Cox
30
Parish Boundary

90
William Coates
92
Water Mill Yard
5
3

2
1

93
Thomas Mountfort
4
To Farndon and Eydon

FARNDON ROAD AND CHURCH STREET

(See Map Seven)

This route into Byfield is from the south east. It has the name Farndon road, but it is also the road to Eydon. Walking towards the Parish boundary into Byfield, sited on the left in a field adjacent to the roadway hedgerow, is the old garage building, built by Bertie Waterhouse in the Banbury Road. This was later moved by Dennis Eyles to its present site to become an agricultural store. This land was allotted to Thomas Mountford in 1779; an area of 15 acres 1 rood and 27 perches (**see Map Seven Proprietor/Owner 93**).

To the right at this point are the modern Sewage Treatment Works which (**see Map Seven point of interest 1**) are actually in the parish of Hinton (Woodford-cum- Membris) but the road to them is in Byfield parish, as the boundary at this point adjacent to the works is the stream! (**See Map Seven point of interest 2.**) The works are accessed by a bridge over that stream, which flows in the direction of Windmill Hill in Charwelton parish, until it joins the stream coming from that direction (**see Map Seven point of interest 3**) when the then larger stream turns southeast towards its link with the river Cherwell south of Hinton.

Records show that a sewage scheme was put forward as early as 1922, but the present treatment works were built in 1928. A statement was made at Byfield Parish Council that wherever possible every landlord should be compelled to link up with the sewage. The works were extended in 1937 and have again been extended and updated quite recently to include the processing of Woodford sewage. Bosworth and Wakeford of Daventry were the contractors who installed the Byfield sewage system in the village; as you would expect, their name is on numerous manhole covers in the parish. At the point where the sewage outfall joins the stream, the flow would be almost all of the water that flows from Byfield parish, from both foul and surface water sources, including the two streams that rise in the parish; namely the Westhorpe stream and the Cornbrook stream.

Byfield is therefore one of the summits of the system. The water meanders from here for well over a hundred miles to the point where it joins the sea at the Thames Estuary. On its way it will be retained in lakes, tanks, lagoons and cisterns to be used again and again for hundreds of different purposes. Obviously these facts indicate the geographical position and height above sea level of the village.

Geography of Northamptonshire
It is also interesting to note that the county is unique in the fact that, even though some of the watercourses mark its boundaries, no water runs into Northamptonshire from any other county.

Leaving the stream, the boundary crosses the Farndon road and continues to the left in a southerly direction up towards Half Crown Corner (**see Map Seven point of interest 4**).

The land to the right was an allotment to William Coates of 9 acres 3 rod 20 perches. This land was sold out of the Coates/Bromley family on the death of Mrs Mary Elizabeth Bromley in 1925. Part of the land was named later as "Farndon Gap" (**see Map Seven Proprietor/Owner 92**).

The land on the right, on the Byfield side of the stream, was called Watermill Yard. Allotted to Sarah Coates, the Mill would be more likely used for grinding corn rather than cutting wood (**see Map Seven Point of interest 5**).

Records show that when Watermill Yard was also sold out of the Bromley/Coates family, in 1925 on the death of Mrs Mary Elizabeth Bromley, the description of the site at the time stated that there was "a stone-built and slated hovel with yard and dipping bath".

The next land on the right was allotted in 1779 to Thomas Elkington; an area of 6 acres 3 roods and 4 perches (**see Map Seven Proprietor/Owner 94**). This Allotment was later owned by the Church and named "Clock Meadow"; the reason for this was that the rent from the field was used to pay for the winding of the Church clock.

This same land in the 1860s was sold to the East and West Railway. Sections of the railway were used for goods traffic in the late 1860s, including being used in the construction of various sections of the line. The financial credibility of the company was sometimes in doubt.

The building of the Great Central Railway in the 1890s was a great financial boost to the line as the route crossed the E. & W. J. R. It was able to transport much of the material and equipment for the construction of "The Great Central" with all its subsequent parts and subsidiaries, including those linked to the extensive Woodford marshalling yards, plus the railway workers' purpose-built housing being constructed in Woodford village.

The 1901 census of Byfield gives an indication of the number of professions, trades and skills of people residing in the parish of Byfield, who were living or just "billeted" here. Being involved with this revolutionary new form of transport meant a change to a "totally new way of life" for some people.

The building of the Woodford West Junction connection two miles to the east of Byfield in 1899 also boosted the diversity of destinations available to users of the East and West route. This connection was to a lesser degree also beneficial to users of the Great Central route, which was of course a much bigger concern.

The next land on the left was allotted to the Coates family **(see Map Seven Proprietor/Owner 90 and 91)**. Part of this land was covered by two spinneys; one named Half Moon Spinney and the other Pole Spinney. Later in the 1920s they became one, and were named Humphreys Spinney after the owner of the land at the time.

The fields around the spinney were later named Comb Stile and Top Hill, Twist Hill, Middle Hill, Granary Ground (aptly close to Byfield windmill), Russet Hill, Cow House Ground, The Plain and Rough Hill. All of this land was sold out of the Bromley family in 1925. The details recorded of the auction details state that on the Cow House Ground was a large corrugated iron implement and cattle shed, with two enclosed yards, and also two thatched open hovels. Cow House Ground is the field to the south of what is now the Byfield Civic Burial Ground, and traces of the barns can still be found; they were used up to the 1950s.

Walking up the slope, that prior to the closing of the Railway in 1965 had been the "Station approach", on the left side of the road was the Station goods yard entrance. This had been part of the William Coates allotment; closest to the road which is now village plots of garden ground. These were previously owned by British Rail but have since been purchased by the Byfield Parish Council, in the early 1980s, together with the rest of the station area for a total sum of £4,000.

As we reach the top of the slope, we are standing on what was the station railway bridge, which was deemed to be unsafe and dismantled in the late 1980s; the detailed inspection of the bridge having been triggered by the collapse of the bridge in Pit Lane.

There is an interesting incident regarding the dismantling of the bridge. The operator of the navvy, with its heavy dismantling ball swinging from the end of the jib, was pounding the British Rail blue brickwork, when a rather smartly dressed man attracted the attention of the operator and duly stated "I would not do that if I were you. I am from the Gas Board and there is a high pressure gas main across that bridge." This resulted in a rapid cessation of the brickwork pounding. A temporary loop of 4 inch yellow gas main was then routed through the old station area. Later, on completion of the new roadway, the gas main was reinstated along its original route. What future generations will make of a 4 inch yellow gas pipe running though this old station area with no gas in is anybody's guess!

Looking over to the right, adjacent to the road retaining bank, we are looking at the site of the old station pond, which was constructed by diverting the stream **(see Map Seven point of interest 6)**. Water was pumped from here, first by using donkey power, later steam and then electrical power, to raise the water into a large brick water tower on the Station side of the bridge **(see Map Seven point**

of interest 7). Some Ordnance Survey Maps also show a force pump further downstream from the pond.

The 1901 Census shows that the driver of the pumping engine was William Bull. An interesting additional use of steam power was the inclusion of a "Direct Current Generator" coupled to the steam pump shaft, which provided lighting to the station buildings and platforms. This electric lighting provision was the first in the parish, (it was to be 1928 before mains electricity was generally available in the parish).

Byfield station was the only intermediate water pick-up point for the steam engines between Towcester Station and Stratford-upon-Avon Station. Obviously stream water untreated was suitable for all station purposes; watering engines, cattle, and sheep and horses, gardens, flushing lavatories, cleaning; in fact everything except for human consumption. Drinking water had to be fetched by hand from Byfield House. Curiously, the station was never connected to mains water up to the date it closed in 1965, but later, in the early 1990s, water was installed from a water main in Farndon road to service the garden allotments, the new burial ground, cricket and football pavilion, the cricket wicket and the scout headquarters.

As we look to the left of what was the station area, to our immediate left was the "Timber yard" started by John (Jack) Hutt (1867 – 1902) in the late 1890s **(see Map Seven point of interest 8)**. Sadly he died of an accident in the High Street in 1902. Jim was taking a number of scythes in an open cart to the Woodyard to be sharpened by probably the only powered wet-stone in the parish (steam), when the horse was frightened by a dog, the horse shied, and the scythes moved round and cut Jim Hutt's leg to such an extent that the loss of blood caused his death.

The 1901 census gives us the names of John Hutt, English Timber Merchant, and his employees; listed those were: Fred Faulkner – Steam Roller Driver; William Carvel – Timber Sawyer; John J Steel – Engine Driver at Saw Mill; John Luddington – Labourer Timber Carter; Walter Luddington – Timber Carter; John Bradbury, Nelson Chapman and Jabez Chapman – all Sawyers at the saw mill. (The names of Luddington, Bradbury and Chapman are common with the Silverstone area of wood and timber workers.) The Byfield Church Memorial book records Henry Wingrove (1875 – 1954) as a Sawyer.

The Woodyard after the death of John Hutt was run by John Bradbury, who later took on a partner, Jim Over. In 1906 it was "Over and Bradbury"; in 1920 "Over and Co", whose telephone number was shown as Byfield 23. Over's employees included Billy Lane, a man of small stature who was in charge of the horses, up to five of which were used to haul big loads of round timber from the felling site to the saw mill. To see Billy controlling those huge horses was a pleasure to behold.

Other employees were : Alf Holt, George Shaw, George Plummer, Maurice Smith, Peter Hince, David Caswell, Gordon Tomalin, Jack Boddington, George Horne (who sadly lost a leg in an accident when loading round timber), Jack Burditt (who was killed after being struck by a chain connected to a steel hawser which snapped), David Widdows, Jack Eyles, Frank Walters, Cyril Pickersgill,

This photograph is of Byfield Woodyard as it was in the 1890s. It shows a steam engine powering a saw. The proprietor of the Woodyard at this time was Jack Hutt. The 1901 Byfield census gives John J Steel, aged 40, as Engine Driver at the Saw Mill; Nelson Chapman, aged 48, and Jabez Chapman, aged 14, are both shown as Wood Sawyers, as were William Carvel, aged 23, and John Bradbury, aged 25. John Bradbury was later to take over the running of the business.

This photograph is annotated JR703 in the Byfield Photo Museum. Lender Mr Vic Perry.

Lionel Booden, Frank Binderman, Arthur Wheeler, George Stevens, Harry (Pagel) Burt, Paddy O'Rourke, Bill Gardner, Tom Bilson, Bill Tomalin and others.

The operation moved to Fawsley House main "Banqueting Hall" in the early 1960s. Imagine those large powered saws in the classical building, quite a change from when the Knightley family were in residence, and a change from today, with the Banqueting Hall's pristine décor returned as it now is part of a high-class hotel.

The road into the Timber yard was also the goods entrance to Byfield Railway Station, now the entrance to the Byfield Civic Burial Ground **(also see Map Seven point of interest 8)**.

In the days when the Station was at its operational height, to the right of the goods entrance driveway just into the site was a weighbridge, together with the normal sidings with coal yard, cattle pens and a covered shed used to unload perishable merchandise. Also there was the station's wooden jibbed crane, and a "down line" mushroom-design slave water tower fed from the main brick tower on the "upline". The square feed pipe to the down line water tank can still be seen at ground level today **(see Map Seven point of interest 9)**, as can the concrete base block of the wooden jibbed crane **(see Map Seven point of interest 10)**.

Railway terminology.
"Up line" was the direction towards London! "Down line" was the direction away from London (even if the line did not actually go to London)!
Note by J.R.
Even though geographically Byfield is higher than London, as proven by the flow of the village streams if you were travelling on the railway you would be travelling up to go down, or the other way round!

The first Station Master is recorded in the 1874 Northamptonshire Directory as George Marshall followed by: 1894 – Frederick Lawyer; 1906 – William Days; 1914 – Frederick Trenfield; 1949 – George Holton until closure in 1965. George Marshall, Frederick Trenfield and George Holton are all buried in Byfield Churchyard.

George Marshall (1824 – 1898) the first Station Master at Byfield Station.
To reach the position of Station Master George Marshall would almost certainly have been a career railwayman, probably starting as a trainee clerk or some such minor post.

The 1881 Byfield census shows that George Marshall was born in 1824 at Newnham, Gloucestershire, and his wife Alice was born in 1821 at Monmouth (Newnham to Monmouth is a distance of 12 miles). Their daughters, of which there were three, were born as follows: the eldest, Julia, in 1851 at Oxford, Alice in 1856 at Kingswood, Gloucestershire, and the youngest, Charlotte, in 1866 at Fenny Compton. One interesting point is that all of these places had "main line" stations located on the Great Western Railway, and would indicate the progression within the Great Western Railway Company of George Marshall's career. The pinnacle of that career was a change of railway company to the newly-constructed East and West Junction Railway, with the post of Station Master at Byfield Station. Another interesting point was that the Great Western Railway, with the London to Bristol line completed in 1841, was a "Broad Track Gauge" of 7 feet; this gauge was used at the instigation of the great engineer Isambard Kingdom Brunel. In 1850 a Royal Commission ruled that the British National Track Gauge should be 4 feet 8½ inches. The Great Western Railway had modified most of its track by the 1870s, but only finally completed the task in 1892.

So it transpires that the East and West Junction Railway was probably the first standard gauge railway that George Marshall worked on, previously only being familiar with the broad gauge system.

As we move forward down the other side of Station approach towards the village, immediately to our left is what was the passenger entrance in the operational days of the railway, and is now the entrance to "Brightwell". The layout was the "standard East and West Railway design" signal-box, which was later extended at both ends when an innovation of an electrical safety system was devised for "single line" working. There was a ticket and Station Master's office, a waiting room, ladies' and gentlemen's lavatories (note, not toilets!), a lamp room, a cycle shed and a converted Lancashire and Yorkshire coach, serving as a staff mess room and store and the "Up line" waiting room (see Map Seven point of interest 11).

As well as passengers being accommodated by the railway, there was of course a wide variety of outgoing freight, including milk from the farms transported in churns, supplying urban areas with their daily "Pinta", timber from the wood-yard, hay and straw, and iron ore from the local mines. There was also livestock from the Byfield cattle market, and horses and ponies from the Byfield horse and pony sales held on what today is Jubilee Close. At times the station was very busy transporting livestock, an example of which is indicated by a large livestock sale held at Byfield market in 1916, when more than a thousand sheep and three hundred head of cattle were sold. All of these were shipped by rail in 50 cattle wagons split into three special trains. The animals being driven along Church Street to the Station, would have ensured fine roses and a profuse crop of vegetables in the adjacent cottage gardens.

The local fox hunts also sometimes transported horses and hounds to a day's hunting by rail. It is interesting to note on the inventory of rolling stock on the S. & M. J. R., taken in January 1916, that the list of "Coaches" included a hound van and 10 horse boxes. A separate list of " Goods Vehicles" includes cattle wagons; this indicates

This is a photograph of Byfield Station taken from the Farndon Road bridge in the early 1960s by Mike Ward. It shows that Byfield Station was a typical East and West Railway station lay-out.

This photograph is annotated RP178 in the Byfield Photo Museum. Lender Mike Ward.

that grooms travelled with the horses, but drovers did not travel with the cattle.

Interesting details of the S.M.J. and some snippets from "Warwickshire" by Vivian Bird and added notes by the Author.

This Railway between Stratford Old Town Station and Broom Junction closed around 1960 after the passenger services had ceased on June 16th 1947.

The line had come to Broom Junction at Stratford Old Town Station on June 2nd 1879, to join the Evesham and Redditch line. It was 46 miles long, originating at Blisworth, Northamptonshire, on the London North Eastern line. During its passenger days this S.M.J. line made two interesting innovations. On April 20th 1911 it introduced the "Rail phone" giving telephone conversation between the train and a fixed point, with the Mayor of Stratford in the train and Marie Corelli, the novelist in Stratford. The novelty was short-lived, but was developed as a train control device.

Then in 1932, in the L.M.S. days, came the "Ro-railer, a single-deck half-cab bus, with separate steel flanged wheels to be used on the track and pneumatic-tyred wheels on the road; the change of operation was by a system of eccentric cams. This enabled it to travel the metals from Blisworth and change to the road at the Stratford Old Town Station, from where it continued on the road to the railway's Welcome Hotel.

This vehicle was built to L.M.S. specifications by Karrier Motors of Huddersfield; the body was constructed by Cravens of Sheffield. It was said to be capable of 75 m.p.h. on rails and 60 m.p.h. on the road; the second figure may have been overstated due to the operating weight of the vehicle with all of its dual-purpose equipment.

Byfield Station was, in its heyday, tended by the very keen station staff. Such was the standard of the garden that it regularly won the competition for the best-kept station garden on the line.

In August 1911 Byfield was again awarded first prize for the best kept station. The Stationmaster at the time was William Days who received £1 for this; his staff signalman Maycock got 10 shillings and signalman Cornell also got 10 shillings.

Adjacent to this garden was signalman Billy Grubb's "chicken run". How official this was we can only hazard a guess. The run contained fruit trees; a plum and an apple still survive today, but are in very poor condition. When the Brightwell field was being extended in the 1980s the site which included Billy's chicken run was being tidied up. Buried deeply, teeth down, under the perimeter wire was a huge Band Saw blade, about thirty feet long with large one and a half inch teeth, which had been used to stop the scratching hens from escaping from under the perimeter wire. Obviously the blade had itself at some time escaped from the Timber yard.

Byfields Civic Burial Ground

It was realised in the early 1980s that the Churchyard was finally running out of space for burials and that an alternative site for interment, based on a historical number of nine burials a year, was required within five years.

Funding

The Parish Council realised it was possible that, having located a suitable piece of land, it might be that an application to the Daventry District Council would need to be made for compulsory purchase of the land if the owner was not willing to sell at a reasonable price. To save embarrassment in not having the funding for the purchase when the sale was agreed, the Parish Council decided to levy a rate on the Parish, to go into a special fund solely for land purchase, of £1,000 per year. With around 500 houses this equated to £2 per house per year.

On a casual remark by Denis Judd to the Chairman of the Parish Council, suggesting that perhaps the old station area was a suitable site, this remark resulted in the Byfield Parish Council purchasing the whole area from British Rail, having already purchased land adjacent to the Brightwell Recreation Ground from the same source.

The purchase price for the old station area was £4,000 plus legal fees, and for the additional Brightwell land £1,700 plus legal fees. The funding having already been accrued, these purchases were made without the need to borrow.

A sub-committee of Parish Councillors was set up and given powers to co-opt others, one important inclusion being that of the Rector of Byfield, Rev. W. P. Kentigern-Fox. This sub-committee was led by Councillor Brighid Buchanan-Wollaston. The brief of the committee was to forward a plan to the Parish Council to develop the site, and also to table draft rules and regulations, within national legislation, for the use and management of the site, including when nominated the consecrated burial area.

The site was developed and the burial area fenced. The new burial area was consecrated by the Bishop of Brixworth, Suffragan Bishop of Peterborough, the Right Reverend Paul Barber, on Saturday May 4th 1991.

The Buchanan-Wollaston family expressed a wish to erect a set of oak memorial gates in the memory of the father of the family, Brighid's husband Nigel, at the entrance to the new Civic Burial Ground. This offer was gratefully accepted by the Parish Council. The gates were made locally and erected, and a memorial plaque suitably mounted and inscribed as such (verbatim)

IN LOVING MEMORY OF
NIGEL RICHARD BUCHANAN- WOLLASTON
10.12.21 – 24.2.83

Actor, Navigator, Farmer, Lecturer, Potter in Byfield from 1975

How happy is he born and taught

That serveth not another's will

Whose armour is his honest thought

And honest truth his utmost skill

Sentimental Recollections

A number of people interred in the civic burial ground had specific links with the Station and or the Woodyard. The first to be interred, on the 16th of January 1992, was Fred Horton, who had approached the Parish Council Chairman three years before he died, requesting to be buried in this ground. Fortunately Fred's request was possible as all the necessary practical procedures were in place when Fred died.

Fred came to Byfield at the age of sixteen to live with the Selwood family. His first job was on the Stratford Midland and Junction Railway at Aston-le-Walls sidings, putting the destination labels under the retaining clips on each of the railway wagons. This start, plus the love of "his village" and the family he lived with, is reflected on the epitaph on his grave. "It was Fred's wish when he departed to rest here where life really started".

Dick Haynes worked for a time at the Wood yard. Dick planted a sapling, a Black Poplar which has grown into a mature tree, and this species of the Aspen tree family can grow to a height of 100 feet. One characteristic of these trees is, that the leaves flutter even in the slightest breeze. This tree reminds us all as we see the shimmering fluttering leaves, of the man who planted it, who is at rest just fifty yards away.

Fred Waddoups, buried here, worked as a lad in Byfield signal box and later on the "Foot plate" of engines based on the Great Central at Woodford. In the Byfield Photo Museum we have photographs of Fred working this line, through Byfield.

Tom Lane was interred here under the place where his father Billy Lane (1877-1954) worked with those huge horses bringing the round timber to be processed. Tom also was an engine driver on Byfield Ironstone bringing iron ore down to "the main line" sidings ready to be taken to the ironworks for smelting.

Bob Hutt of the well known Hutt family is buried in the spot where his uncle John Hutt started the wood business here over a hundred years ago.

Arthur Wheeler lies at rest now at the spot where he worked in the Wood yard, and when the site was to become a burial ground Arthur's brothers Bill and Albert erected the perimeter fence to enclose the consecrated ground. Sadly today both Bill and Albert have departed this life.

Close by Billy's chicken run and to the back of what were the buildings before demolition of the station, is a definitive footpath running from the Farndon road though to the Banbury road, over a route once "The Station Fields" now part of the Brightwell recreation complex.

Back to the road, and walking in towards the village and the church, we pass over the Westhorpe (Blindle) stream; on the right is a small green building; a mains gas pressure reducing unit, **(see Map Seven point of interest 12)**.

Mains gas was available in Byfield in 1911, the supply being coal gas from Woodford gas works.

The land on the right allotted to William Cox was an area of 36 acres 1 rood and 32 perches **(see Map Seven Proprietor/ Owner 30 and 31)**; apart from one small paddock this land is now owned by the Church and farmed today by Mr John Rogers.

An aerial photograph of Church Street in 1959, shows the cows in the milking yard of Darbishire's farm. The old National School (Tithe Barn) can be clearly seen, together with other interesting features.

This photograph is annotated JR152 in the Byfield Photo Museum. Lender John Russell.

The Inclosure on the left allotted to Richard Hickcock was an area of 2 acres 3 roods and 30 perches **(see Map Seven Old Inclosures/Homesteads130)**; this land is now owned by the owners of Byfield House, Mr and Mrs Davidson-Houston.

On the left, this new house on the corner behind the high wall was built by The Rev. and Mrs Moira Fryer in the 1990s in what was a part of the garden of Byfield House. The land on which Byfield House now stands was an Inclosure allotted to William Cox, an area of 3 acres 22 perches **(see Map Seven Old Inclosures/Homesteads 131)**, as was the land on the right, on the other side of the road, an area of 1 rood 27 perches. A barn on this side of the road has a "date stone" showing a date of 1779 **(see Map Seven Old Inclosures/Homesteads 132)**, which almost inevitably means that the barn was built by William Cox when he was allotted the land.

Byfield House was built by John Newbury in the very late 1890s, as was the front wall of the stable block which since has been converted into a very desirable dwelling. The rear wall and both the gables of the stable block are part of the original building, possibly built by William Cox at the same time as he built the barn over the other side of the road.

The conversion of the original barn to a stable block was done at the time by John Newbury, who built Byfield House, as the roof structures and form are the same on both buildings.

The site, on which today a double garage now stands, is shown on the 1779 Enclosure Map as a small cottage. The garage has built into the structure a "date stone" detailed I.M.1645. The date stone was perhaps the date the small cottage was built. But it is possible that a stray soldier (a roundhead or a royalist!) could have been a "stone mason" who decided to carve his name on this piece of stone in Byfield; and, if so, was it before June 14th or after? It is interesting to note that the form of the stonework at the eaves of the "small cottage", and that on the "stable block", are both similar and still remain today.

Civil War notes

On the 12th of June 1645 King Charles I hunted at Fawsley. On the 13th of June he spent the night at the Wheatsheaf Inn at Daventry whilst his 10,000 men camped on Borough Hill. The next day, the 14th of June, he fought the Battle of Naseby and lost!

When Byfield House was being built the front boundary wall was found to be partly made up of animal bones, indicating that the house was being built, as had been previously thought, on the site of a Tannery.

This in fact ties up with details in the 1777 list of all the men in the parish of Byfield "capacitated" to serve in the militia. This list includes the same William Cox who was allotted this land in 1779 as a Tanner; also a Humphrey Shotton, probably an employee of William Cox, is listed as a Tanner.

"Militia"

An army; a body of men enrolled and drilled as soldiers but only liable to home service.

Byfield records also show that a Joseph Cox is listed as a Tanner in 1690.

John Newbury had come from Honiton in Devon to the village of Byfield. The 1901 census indicates that Mr Newbury brought several of his previous employees to Byfield, as shown in the following table.

What links were there?

The 1901 census records John Newbury as a Yeoman; this would mean he was a man of substance!

1901 census (copied verbatim)

Street/House	Name	Relation to the Head	*	Age	Profession or Occupation	**	Where born
Byfield House	John Newbury	Head	M	44	Yeoman	Employer	Devon, Honiton
	Elizabeth J Newbury	Wife	M	45			London, Hackney
	Walter Mickleburgh	Visitor	M	44	Mechanical engineer	Employer	Devon, Ottery St. Mary
	Sarah A Colman	Servant	S	48	Cook (Domestic)	Worker	London, Islington
	Kath Furniss	Servant	S	14	Housemaid (Domestic)	Worker	Northants, Dodford
Church Street	William Bradbeer	Head	M	40	Groom	Worker	Devon, Honiton
	Hannah Bradbeer	Wife	S	38			India, Madras
	Edna Bradbeer	Dau't	S	12			India, Bangalore
	Gladys Bradbeer	Dau't	S	4			Hants, Christchurch
	Irene Bradbeer	Dau't	S	2			Devon, Kilmington

* Marital status   **Employer, Worker or Own Account

These entries throw up much interesting detail and enable the imagination to run riot! One would presume that William Bradbeer was in Bangalore, India at the time of the birth of his eldest daughter in 1889; if so he was there at the height of British influence!

Queen Victoria had just been made Empress of India in 1877; history shows that from then until after the First World War British rule, with its western influence, built factories, railways, hospitals, modernised cities, irrigation systems, schools and universities, and trade was brisk.

Was John Newbury also there then? Perhaps in the army or a civil servant! Was William Bradbeer his groom? Also, with William Bradbeer's wife being born in Madras India in 1863, was she of British or Indian descent? One would suspect with a name like Hannah it would be the former!

What was Walter Mickleburgh, the visitor who was also born in Devon, in the same year as his host, doing in Byfield? Was he working as a self-employed engineer, perhaps on the building of The Great Central Railway?

Looking at diverse and scattered birthplaces, of both the Newbury and Bradbeer entries, gives rise to all sorts of speculation! Certainly William Bradbeer appears to have been a much-travelled man.

Mr Newbury also brought with him the Clegg family. James Clegg was a cowman, while Mrs Sarah A. Clegg and daughter Ethel B. were both lace makers working at home. Son Fred was a grocer's errand boy, and Walter L. S. was at 6 years of age a schoolboy. (He was later to become the husband of Lottie and father of Beatrice who became the wife of Fred Tuckey). They lived in a tied cottage in Church Street. Mr Newbury attempted to negotiate with the Northamptonshire County Council to move the site of his house towards the east, to enable the road to be straightened, prior to the house being built, but to no avail.

To commemorate the coronation of King Edward VII on June 23rd 1902, Mr and Mrs Newbury presented to the children of the village, cups and saucers to the girls, and mugs to the boys.

Later occupants of the house were: 1920 – William Frederick Strick Humphreys (1870–1947), telephone 44; 1947 – Mrs Glwadys Humphreys (1876–1960). It is interesting to note that Glwadys was the daughter of Sir Richard Dancy Green-Price and Lady Green-Price. 1960 – Blakemores, followed by Mrs Rolls (related to the Blakemores) and Rev Anthony Fryer. Today the house is lived in by Mr and Mrs Davidson-Houlston.

The stables at Byfield House were used as billets in the Second World War.

This part of Church Street was at the time of the enclosures known as Tanners Town End, obviously named after the leather tanners who worked in this part of Byfield.

The land to the south of the Churchyard was in two plots, one Inclosure allotted to Simon Gibbs 1 rood 10 perches (see Map Seven Old Inclosures/Homesteads 128), and the other to Davis Fox Cox 36 perches (see Map Seven Old Inclosures/Homesteads 129). The name of the site

This photograph was taken in Farndon Road in the 1920s. It shows Byfield House with its adjacent farm buildings and ricks.

This photograph is annotated AS446 in the Byfield Photo Museum. Lender Mike Fennell.

Chapter Five: Farndon Road and Church Street

is shown in the 1891 census as "Tan yard" (obviously an abbreviation of Tanner); the number of cottages shown on this site on the 1900 Ordnance Survey Map was nine.

The occupants included the families of Brooks (who were a family of Thatchers), Jennings, Butler, Callow, Grubb and French. We also have a record of Walter Selfe, a single man who lived at the bottom of "Gooseberry Lane", which ran from the Church down the side of the Churchyard to the stream. He was employed by the Post Office, was church organist in the late 1890s and early 1900s, and was also a member of the Byfield Band.

A brief comment on the Churchyard and Church. The Churchyard has been extended five times; two major and three minor extensions.

The first major extension was on the south-west corner using part of the land that in 1779 was allotted to the then Church Curate The Reverend "Mr" Copeland (1750 – 1789) an area of 2 Acres 3 Roods 10 Perches **(see Map Seven Old Inclosures/Homesteads 127)**. The division between the existing Churchyard and the additional land was a diagonal wall, which is clearly shown on the 1882/83 Ordnance Survey Map The land to the south-west of the wall was used to enlarge the burial ground. This extra land was consecrated in 1894 by the Bishop of Leicester, who was then Suffragan Bishop within the Diocese of Peterborough. It became known as "The New Ground" **(see Map Seven point of interest 13)**.

Detail in the Byfield burial records show a Sarah Ann Gardner, aged 52, buried on November 3rd 1894 with an unofficial addendum note "last grave on the old ground" and it also shows a record of a William Gardner, aged 70, buried on November 29th 1894 with the unofficial

The diagonal wall which divided the original church yard (old ground) and the land originally allotted to the Rev "Mr" Copeland in 1779 (new ground) is clearly shown on this photograph. The wall is shown on the Byfield 1882-1883 Ordnance Survey Map but not on the 1900 Ordnance Survey Map, so it was obviously taken down between these dates.

This photograph is annotated J.R.14 in the Byfield Photo Museum. Lender Mr & Mrs Harris-Watson.

addendum note, "first grave on the new ground". Both burials were administered by the Rev. Francis Henry Curgenven. There is no indication, as yet found, as to whether the two Gardners were in fact related. Census records show that Sarah Gardner was the wife of Samuel Gardner of Westhorpe, who was an agricultural labourer; William Gardner was a Beer Seller and husband of Jane Gardner, living in Banbury Road.

This "New Ground" was part of one of two allotments that were made up of what was much later to become Brightwell land. These two plots were separated by the Cornbrook stream, before it was diverted as shown on later maps.

The three small additions were "ten poles from Robert French" of wasteland at the top of "Church Lane" consecrated by the Bishop of Peterborough D Herbert Marsh in the summer of 1821, and in 1849 two small plots of land were added to the Churchyard purchased from Mr William Coates and Mr Hands.

The eight evergreen trees down the central causeway of the Churchyard were planted by the Reverend F. H. Curgenven in his third year as Rector; this would then be in 1875 (detail parish records). The other major extension was in 1933 when the Church purchased a plot of land to extend the north-west side of the Churchyard. This land was purchased from Mrs Cricilla Bromley of Church House, an area 171 feet by 41 feet 3 inches for £80. This land was consecrated by the Bishop of Peterborough in 1936 (see Map Seven point of interest 14).

The Church is said to be the third on the site; the present building was completed in 1342. Records show that the Church was part of the Diocese of Lincoln in 1200, and that the first in the list of Rectors was John of Exton in 1242. There have been six members of the Knightley Family that have served as Rectors; some of these are interred in the Church or Churchyard. The body of John Mabletoft who died aged 76 (Rector over the period 1721 – 1763) is interred as well. There are only three Rectors interred in relatively modern times. Charles Wetherell, Rector from 1819 to 1867 (48 years), is actually interred in the Church, in a clearly marked grave in the Chancel, on the left hand side quite near the High Altar. Francis Henry Curgenven, Rector from 1872 to 1901 (29 years), is interred in the Churchyard adjacent to the south side of the Chancel. His grave is marked with a tall granite cross. Close to his grave, in the south wall of the Chancel, is a stained glass window also erected in his memory. David Henry Stanley Mould, Rector 1955 to 1961 (6 years) is interred on the south-west side of the Burial Ground in the 1933 extension (Rev. Mould was the first Byfield Rector to be inducted into an additional parish in 1955 to make the Benefice Byfield with Eydon.)

The body of The Reverend W. Copeland, Curate of Byfield from 1770 until his death on 26th February 1789 and burial on March 2nd 1789 aged 39, is in the church in the centre aisle, in a position of what is today under the site of the low altar. He was the son of Andrew Copeland of Hammersmith, and he studied at Magdalen Hall, Oxford: matric. 10th December 1766 aged 18 years, B.A. 1770, M.A.1775 (detail Northants and Rutland clergy).

Also buried in the centre aisle of the church, but nearer west between the front two blocks of pews, about halfway, is the body of the Reverend Gilbert Gilbert (Christian and Surname the same) the Church Clerk, whose body was interred on December 26th 1862, aged 64.

The Church itself, the earliest mention of the bells is in 1552, when there were three bells and a Sanctus Bell. Bells were added in 1703, 1791, 1905 and 1991; there is now an octave of eight bells in the tower.

New Year truly celebrated.

Thomas Allen, Sexton at Byfield Church for 50 years, rang out the old year and rang in the new, without a break on fifty consecutive occasions, dying in 1888. The 1881 census shows he was Sexton and Gardener aged 75 and a widower. This indicates that he was 82 when he died.

The external profile of the Church has altered little over the years; we know that the spire was added after the tower was built, and was repaired and a lightning conductor fitted in 1874.

The pitch, height and type of roof of both the Chancel and the Nave, have been altered at least three times. The east wall of the north aisle, the whole of the north wall of the chancel, and the old vestry, which stood right at the end of the east end of the north side of the chancel, were pulled down. The north aisle was lengthened and the two chancel windows re-used but in different positions. The extended east part of the north aisle was made into an organ chamber and vestry. An arch was constructed between it and the Chancel. (Today there is little evidence of this work on the outside of the building, with the exception of the different structure of the eaves of the roof on the east end of the north aisle.)

To commemorate the Diamond Jubilee of Queen Victoria in 1897, a new chiming clock was mounted with a face on both the east and west side of the tower. This was funded by public subscription, the cost being £130 - 6s - 2d. Due to the countrywide demand on the nation's clockmakers the new clock was not installed until 1898.

The six tower gargoyles, four of which are now in the south porch, were removed in 1952. Also removed were the four large octagonal turrets which had long stood on the four corners of the tower. (The turrets were deemed to be unsafe, but when demolition started they proved to have an unexpected resilience and strength, probably due to the fact that the stones were inter-linked for extra strength and stability.)

The inside of the church has been altered a number of times. The altars have been in at least three different formats; there have been at least three different pulpits; at least two fonts in three different positions; three organs in three different positions. The seats have been taken in and out in an amazing array of formats. There have been at least four methods of illuminating the building: candles, lamp-oil, gas and electricity. There have been at least four methods of heating: coal/sticks, coke, oil, and electricity.

On the right of the road directly opposite the east end of the Church was a row of cottages on an Inclosure allotted to Thomas Elkington, an area of 30 perches (see

The cottages on the right of this photograph show a complete row reaching nearly as far as the National School (Tithe Barn), the end of which can be clearly seen. The east end of the Chancel of the Church can be seen together with, on the south side, the white granite cross of the Reverend Francis Henry Curgenven's grave. The photograph was taken in 1904.

This photograph is annotated JR19 in the Byfield Photo Museum. Lender Mr & Mrs Harris-Watson

This photograph is of Church House, with members of the Bromley Family in the foreground. This photograph was taken around 1900, and the farmer living there then was John Henry Bromley.

This photograph is annotated BH69 in the Byfield Photo Museum. Lender Mrs J Blake.

Map Seven Old Inclosures/Homesteads 133). This site was later owned by the Bromley family up to 1925 when the cottages were sold to William F. S. Humphreys of Byfield House and were used to house members of his staff. Occupants of these cottages have been: Franklin, Boddington, Marlow, Clegg, Tomalin, Smith, Ellard, Mayes, Kehoe and Ted Lewis (1889–1957). Ted was a long-time servant of the Church, serving as clock-winder, boiler stoker and sidesman.

Back to the road on past the Church, the house on the left abutting the Churchyard was once known as Church Yard House, but later always as Church House. This house was built on an Inclosure allotted in 1779 to William Coates (1742–1797) an area of 1 acre 1 rood 24 perches **(see Map Seven Old Inclosures/Homesteads 125).**

Other occupants were: William Coates (1772–1837); William Coates (1806–1854); William Bromley (1800–1879) who married Elizabeth Coates (1803–1875). This was the coming together of two big farming families in Byfield. 1890 – John Henry Bromley; 1916 – Mrs Mary Elizabeth Bromley; 1928 – James Reginald Bromley; 1933 – Mrs Criscilla Bromley; 1936 – d'Aulnis de Bouvill, Baron William Yan; 1937 – Cecil Cockerill; 1960s – Maurice and Daphne Greaves. Today the property is owned and occupied by Mr and Mrs Reed and family.

Records in the 1851 Byfield census show that William Coates farmed 137 acres.

Auction details regarding the sale of Church Farm Byfield Thursday 18th June 1925 on the death of Mrs Mary Elizabeth Bromley. (Verbatim)

Freehold Farm extremely well-situated with residence in the village of Byfield and known as Church Farm. For many years in the occupation of the Bromley family, and contains an area of 110 acres 2 roods 1 perch.

The House which is substantially built of Stone with Thatched Roof contains :-

In the Basement :- 2 Excellent Cellars.

On the Ground Floor:- Entrance Hall and Vestibule, Drawing Room, Dining Room, Breakfast Room, large Kitchen, Scullery with Copper and Sink Pantry.

On the First Floor:- 5 Bedrooms with Box Room over.

There is a fine Old World Garden.

The Water Supply is good, there being a force pump for Hard Supply and also Soft Water.

The Farm Buildings Comprise of: -

Range of Thatched (except where otherwise stated) buildings, viz: Dairy with 2 Rooms over, Tiled Store Barn with Loft over, Loose Horse Box with Loft over, and Nag stabling for three, also with Loft.

There is a good Barn adjoining the Street and a Slated Cow house for 4 Cows, with 2 enclosed yards.

There is also a 7-Bay Wagon Hovel, Slated Loose Box and Dove Cot, Meal House Piggeries, Cow house for 5 Cows, and a Bull pen adjoining, a Slated Cow house for 4 Cows, Large Barn Slated Cow house for 6 Cows, Cart Horse Stable for 4 Horses, with Loft over.

Included in this Lot is the Freehold Dwelling House or Tradesmen's Residence:- Which is built of Stone with Thatched Roof, and is at present occupied by Mr Thomas Young!

This Residence known as "The Cottage" contains:-

Large Parlour, Kitchen, Larder and Scullery on the Ground Floor while on the First Floor there are 5 Bedrooms.

The Outbuildings comprise of:-

Scullery Closet Large Warehouse with Kiln and Store Room. There is also a Barn with Carpenters Shop, and Builders Yard with Large Corrugated Shed.

Apportioned Land Tax £1 17s 6d

The adjoining owners are:- Messrs:- A S Bush, W F S Humphreys, Evans and Adams.

This is sold subject to a Cart Road from the Hinton Road into field 337, which has been granted to the Daventry Rural District Council.

Notes by J.R.

The Barn with Carpenters Shop and Builders Yard with large Corrugated Shed, referred to above, would later be used from 1928 to 1946 by Harold Catlin, who was a Woodworker and Undertaker.

The Inclosure opposite Church House on the right side of the road was allotted in 1779 to the Rector and is the site of a building always known as the Tithe Barn **(see Map Seven point of interest 15).** The building was never used as such; some buildings that had previously been on the site probably had in fact been tithe barns. In fact the National school was built on this site and completed in 1780; records show the school was opened on June 26th 1780 by Jeremiah Tomalin, who died in 1838 aged 76. The facts are confirmed from maps, on the 1779 Enclosure Map which indicates a "U" shaped building, one leg of the "U" running along the roadside and the open end towards the rectory. The National School shown on the 1882/3 Ordnance Survey Map is not "U" shaped and is not on the same footprint. The position of the building on this Ordnance Survey Map indicates the same detail as it was when it was demolished in the 1960s. This National School was used for vestry meetings (parish administration before parish councils) and to discuss village matters. When parish councils were established in 1894, Byfield Parish Council held its meetings there.

Byfield Parish Council.

The very first meeting of the parish council was held in the "Boys School" on Tuesday 1st of January 1895. (details from parish records).

The building was used by the Church Sunday School, for choir suppers, for visiting clergy for robing, by the Mother's Union, the Boy Scouts, Guides and Brownies, for wedding receptions and for village dances. The building and surrounding areas were used in conjunction with various fetes, especially the annual church fete when it was the venue for the refreshments.

The school was rebuilt in 1842. Details dated 1847 show that the school was funded by voluntary subscription and the teachers were: 1847 – John Jenson as school master and Miss Maria Anna Bennett as mistress, (1851Census shows Ann Maria Jenson as school mistress); 1861 – James Hutchinson as Master; 1865 – William Bottomley as master and Miss Brew as mistress.

The National Education Act was passed in 1870 making education compulsory.

Detail from a contemporary encyclopaedia states:
With the Education Act of 1870, (W.E. Gladstone, 1809 – 1898, was then Prime Minister) the bill was presented by W. E. Forster (1818-1886). This first great national movement in England for the reform of schools made education compulsory, and every child had to attend school. The existing schools were totally inadequate in size and number, and money was voted for new ones. In every area bodies of men were elected to look after this development, and these were known as School Boards. The new schools were called Board Schools to distinguish them from the "British" and "National" already existing. Their maintenance was charged to the local authority in part, and this amount was increased by government grants paid each year after the schools had been inspected and reported upon by government officials. The Act of 1870 was the Magna Carta of education.

In 1874, due to a lack of space, the infant class was transferred to the building on The Green which is today the Byfield Conservative Club.

The 1885 Kelly's Northamptonshire Directory states: Parochial Church School for 113 pupils, average attendances 65. The teachers were: 1890 – William Bottomley schoolmaster and Miss Charlotte Marshall as mistress, who was the youngest daughter of George Marshall the first station master to serve at Byfield station. Charlotte was later to become Head Mistress at Dashwood Road School, Banbury, a post from which she retired. In 1895 William Bottomley died after serving as Byfield school master for thirty years. William Bottomley was followed by John Andrews, with his wife Mrs Ellen Andrews as Mistress. This building served as the school until January 14th 1907, when the children were transferred, with their teachers, to the new county primary school in Bell Lane.

National School placed under "County" control
October 9th 1903: The School having been placed under County Council control as a "Provided School", all distinctive Religious Teaching (such as Prayer Book and Catechism) has been discontinued.
(Details from Mixed School Log Book.)

John Andrews, before coming to Byfield, was Headmaster of Eydon school from 1882 to 1894. The building was then used as the Church Sunday school, social centre and meeting room. Another separate building on the site was used to stable the Rector's "pony and gig" and later, with the coming of the motor car, the stable was adapted into a garage for the Rector's car, specifically to accommodate the long bonnet of the blue Wolseley Fourteen, which belonged to the Reverend Rupert Bede Winsor, the first Rector to have a car (Rector 1945 to 1955).

Later this building was converted in 1983, using professional and voluntary labour, into a parish room and was named "The Bromley Room".

Ecumenical Bees! And the Bromley Room Roof
Part of the conversion and renovation was to inspect the condition of the building, including the roof. Fortunately the roof was in fair condition with the exception of the security of the ridge tiles, which needed re-bedding with mortar. J.R. agreed to take on this task, with the Rector supplying him with considerable quantities of mortar, J.R. sitting astride the ridge and Bill K.F. on top of the ladder. Both were stung twice by the Rector's Bees. "I have been stung," states J.R. (stronger language is not really allowed on church projects). "So have I," says Bill K.F. "I think we are on the flight path" says Bill K.F. "We are obviously on something," says J.R. "Hang on," says Bill K.F. and he disappears down the ladder into the Rectory and re-appears carrying two Beekeepers' hats and veils. On donning this anti-ecumenical-bee-protection-certified-equipment, it was not easy to bed ridge tiles or, in fact, to negotiate a ladder, due to a considerable amount of obscured vision. On realising what we would look like to a casual observer Bill. K.F. and J.R. exploded into hysterical laughter, Bill K.F. nearly falling off the ladder and J.R. needing to tighten the grip with his knees on the ridge of the roof to prevent him meeting terra-firma at an unreasonable speed! It is possible that even the bees were laughing!

The site was used as a billet and cookhouse in the Second World War.

The National School building continued to be used until the 1950s, when it became in need of urgent repair, especially the thatched roof. The incumbent, the Rev. David Henry Mould (Rector 1955 – died 1961), was reluctant to spend money on the building, as the parishioners were raising money to build a new village hall on the Brightwell field. Subsequently the building became unsafe and was pulled down in the 1960s. Obviously the loss of the Rector in June 1961, followed by a period of interregnum would not have been conducive to saving the building.

A new Rectory was built on this site in the 1980s by Martin Lilley, a local Byfield builder. The first family to live there was the family of the Rev. Kentigern-Fox, who brought with them, when they moved from the old Rectory, the telephone number which was originally Byfield 4 and is now 260204.

The next site on the right is the old Rectory, now named Church End House, and is now a private dwelling, owned by Mr and Mrs C Mann **(see Map Seven Old Inclosures/ Homesteads 135)**.

Falling Masonry
In 1947 during the deep snow and blizzards of that year, on March 17th one of the Rectory chimney stacks fell through the roof into an unoccupied bedroom, so fortunately no one was injured!

Recorded in the Causeway Charity records is the fact that the first meeting of the Causeway Charity was held in the "Parsonage House" in 1664, which it can be fairly accurately assumed was in the old Rectory, now only part of the present building, being the section on the south-west side, nearest and at right angles to the road, just behind the high stone wall.

In 1631 records show that the late incumbent, Thomas Knightley, laid out in his last will and testament, dated the thirteenth of June 1631, the sum of £1,000 in beautifying the Parsonage House. The house shown on the enclosure map of 1779 indicates a quite different outline from the 1882/3 Ordnance Survey Map, which shows an outline similar to that of today.

In 1688 a second Thomas Knightley, late incumbent, laid out in his last will and testament instructions that would become "The Thomas Knightley Charity".

The Thomas Knightley Charity (detail verbatim)
"Mr Thomas Knightley, the late Rector of this Parish, (besides five pounds to be distributed among the poor at his death) by his last Will and Testament dated the fourteenth of June 1688 gave the summe of Tenne pounds to be imployed as in these words therein expreet, viz.

"Whereas there are diverse Trustees, for the employing the rent of certain lands and houses to repair the Church wayes and other charitable uses in the parish, my further Will is that within three months after my decease my Executors shall pay the sum of Tenn pounds into the hands of the Trustees for the time being, and my will and request is that the said Trustees will take care to lay out the said ten pounds in buying hemp flax or wool to be sett forth for spinning unto the poorest of the said Parish, (who are the most impotent and unable for other works) and the said Trustees will take care of the sd. Hemp, flax and wool to spin to sell the same in yarn or otherwise to the best advantage for the paying such poor people as they shall think fit to imply and that they will lay out the remainder of the money to buy more hemp flax or wool and so yearly again sell the same to Spinning as aforesaid. And my further request is the said Trustees will yearly make up an accompt among themselves of what they have herein done in like manner as they do of the receipts and disbursements touching the repares of the Churchwayes in their Execution of the Trust concerning them". (Detail from Parish registers)

E. F. Poole in 1930 in his book "The Story of Byfield" adds the rider: "There was a definite constructive idea about this Charity, but its practical difficulties proved beyond the trustees, who had to resort to the usual method of distributing interest annually".

The field to the east of the Rectory was used by Byfield Cricket Club from 1947, when a wicket was cut out by soldiers returning from serving in the Second World War. These included Fred Tuckey and George Ellard. Cricket was played here until the mid-1980s **(see Map Seven point of interest 16)**, when the club moved to the Brightwell field.

Due to an assessment by the Rector and the Parochial Church Council that the churchyard was reaching a point when there would be no more room for burials, trial holes were dug in part of this field in 1960s, but the site was deemed unsuitable due to the fact that the ironstone was too close to the surface. **(see Map Seven point of interest 17)**.

It subsequently transpired that, with a change of Rector, to one who considered that it was possible to re-use the north-west side of the churchyard, the need for new ground for burials was therefore postponed until the 1980s.

The field further over to the east, right down to the parish boundary with Hinton (Woodford-cum-Membris), was allotted to the Rector for glebe, an area of 31 acres 1 rood and 26 perches **(see Map Seven Proprietors/ Owners 9)**, on part of which were 95 garden plots let for garden ground. The dividing paths between the rows of "plots" are clearly shown on the 1882 Ordnance Survey maps. **(See Map Seven point of interest 18.)**

Back to the road, the next land on the left was an Inclosure allotted in 1779 to a William Bloxham, an area of 1 rood 28 perches **(see Map Seven Old Inclosures/ Homesteads 124)**, the west boundary at the time being the Cornbrook stream. Prior to this, records show previous owners: 1776 – John Bainbridge, gentleman of Upper Boddington; July 1776 – William Chauncy of Edgecote (Lord of the Manor); April 7th 1779 — William Bloxham, who in the same year was allotted the Inclosure by the Overseers; 1811 – Susanna Bloxham; 1821 – William Thornton; 1842 – Edward and Joseph Watkins; 1867 – Martha Saul.

Malt Kiln property in Byfield (today 30 Church Street)
This Inclosure is referred to in a document dated April 1779 and the property is described as:

A Messuage or Tenement with malt kiln, orchard yard and backside there adjoining and belonging with their appurtenances situate and standing and being in Byfield.

Of the owners and tenants, William Bloxham, Edward Watkins and Martha Saul's husband John, are all listed as maltsters.

Malt (Mault).
Barley or other grain steeped in water, fermented, and dried in a kiln.

This site was also the location of the business of William Kerrod (1824–1883) a builder, wheelwright and millwright recorded in the census of 1881. The house was used by Miss Caroline Strange as a school from 1903 to 1910, and between 1925 and 1946 was the dwelling and business premises of Harold Catlin (1884–1946), who was a Woodworker and Undertaker. On the death of Mr Catlin his wife had a new house constructed on the site. This is now in the ownership of Mrs Liz Kemp.

On the right of the road at this point is a brick cottage built on an Inclosure which in 1779 was allotted to a Simon Gibbs, an area of 23 perches **(see Map Seven Old Inclosures/Homesteads 136)**. Prior to that it was owned by a William Bradshaw. The Gibbs family owned it until they sold it to a Thomas Lucket. The ownership, tenancy and/or occupancy up to 1939 are too complicated to be detailed here. In 1939 the property was conveyed from a Thomas Cary to Hester Maud Alice Lines (1878–1965), and at that point was known as "The Haven". Mrs Lines was a piano teacher and confirmation of this was on the gate of The Haven where A.L.C.M. was proudly displayed. Yes, Mrs Lines was an Associate of the London College of Music.

The Byfield W. I. was very active in producing and performing plays and "Lottie" Lines was one of the stars. After Lottie died in 1965, aged 87, her two single sons, both Byfield postmen, lived in the Haven until their demise and it was again sold on, finally to a developer who has built another house on the garden ground of The Haven.

Moving on down the road, on the left standing back was a small cottage which is shown on the 1779 enclosure map as being in an allotment of 31 perches allotted to an Ann Goldicutt **(see Map Seven Old Inclosures/ Homesteads 123),** and the outline of the cottage on the 1882/3 Ordnance Survey map shows it has not altered. Latterly it was lived in by the Potter family, the last two being Miss Molly Potter and her sister Miss Betty Potter, the family, as previously stated, being a large and eminent part of Byfield life over a fairly long period.

The 1779 enclosure map shows the next three Inclosures on the left are on very small plots, the first on an Inclosure allotted to a Mary Bilson of 8 perches **(see Map Seven Old Inclosures/Homesteads 122),** the second marked "Town Houses" of 7 perches **(see Map Seven Old Inclosures/Homesteads 121),** and the next to a John Saul of 12 perches **(see Map Seven Old Inclosures/Homesteads 120).** The land to the rear of these plots was allotted to a Thomas Cox, an area of 1 rood 18 perches **(see Map Seven Old Inclosures/Homesteads 119),** and by the present day this area had become one holding. Prior to this in the 1920s and through to the 1940s one of the small plots had become a shop owned by a John Innes (1876–1953) with his second wife Lily. It was a general store selling a wide range of merchandise, including paraffin. Unfortunately the other entire stock including foodstuff always smelt of paraffin.

On the opposite side of the road the plot on the right is an Inclosure which was allotted to a Thomas Orton, of 1 rood 9 perches **(see Map Seven Old Inclosures/Homesteads 137).** The first house on the top of the plot was built in the early 1900s and became known as Rutland House. Records show that in 1906 the village doctor Adam William Hope lived there, followed by the Eatock family. On June 3rd 1914 Miss Eatock married John Adams who then became sole proprietor of the grocery shop in the High Street; 1914 – Rev. Sidney F. Pilchard (who had taken the Curacy at Byfield, previously he had been a curate at Leamington Spa); 1920s – James Over; 1941 – Mrs Nellie Over (1883–1974); 1970s – the Bernie family; 1980s – the Jones family; the house is now the home of Mrs Mullins.

Further on the same site is a stone house with its gable end to the road. This house was later to be named Deene Cottage. It has a "Date stone" on the west gable with the letters M H E and a date of 1708, the 6th year of the reign of Queen Anne; this is possibly the year when the cottage was built. The building is clearly shown on the Enclosure Map of 1779, the outline being similar to that of today. Latterly the Haynes family lived here, Miss Canning the first student teacher at Byfield School lodged there, as did Miss Scott in 1932 who was also a teacher at the school.

A number of postmen lived here, including the Jones and Barratt families and a certain Mr Williams.

A "Ghostly" shock to the Postman.
When the graves were being dug in the 1920s adjacent to the central path of the Churchyard, an inebriated parishioner on his way home from one of the licensed liquor houses within the parish fell into an open grave. It was a warm summer's evening and being unable to extricate himself from the open grave he fell peacefully to sleep. A Mr Williams, a local postman, was on an early shift and walking from his home, Dean Cottage in Church Street, to the post office in High Street. On passing the open grave the then not so-inebriated parishioner looked up from within the grave and asked, "What's the time?" Mr Williams did not reply at what seemed to him to be a spiritual happening, but took to his heels and ran.

The first of the brick built houses on the left opposite was built in the 1950s by a Miss Horton, and the second in the 1990s.

The last house side-on to the street on the right is named "Wren Cottage"; the allotment in 1779 on this site was shown on the enclosure map as "Town houses", a plot of 28 perches. To the side and through to the back and at right angles to Wren Cottage was a row of six cottages. **(see Map Seven Old Inclosures/Homesteads138).** All of these houses on the site prior to the late 1920s were named "The Jetty" and were owned by the Causeway Charity, as was the "Town house" previously referred to further back on the other side of the road. Some had earth floors, and the condition of the houses became such that they were considered to be unfit for human habitation, were condemned and pulled down. Fortunately, with the efforts of Byfield Parish Council pushing for modern housing provision, (well documented in the parish council minute books) and the cooperation of the housing authority, Daventry Rural District Council, the first twelve council houses were built on Woodford Road in 1928. These charity-owned houses served for many years as what today would be called "starter homes". They also served as homes for others with limited incomes. Families such as the Hartwells, Eyles, Tomalin, Franklin, Harris, Maud, Wadsworth, Batchelor, Hirons and many others made their homes here. Wren Cottage itself was a little bit unusual in as much, in years gone by, within the front door were stone stairs and a pump. Two families used the same stairs to get to the bedrooms. Another unusual aspect was the fact that the garden of Wren Cottage was on the other side of the road. At the time when the Reverend Charlesworth was the Rector, (1919 to 1945), this cottage housed both his cook and gardener, namely Mr and Mrs Joe Brown (1878–1954) who were both the last full-time servants to be employed by any of the Byfield Rectors.

Mr Joe Brown (1873–1953) held a number of posts within the parish including that of parish council chairman, church clock winder, tower captain, trustee of several of the parish charities and in 1910 he held the post of parish constable.

Moving on, to our left is a site of twenty three relatively newly-built houses named Becketts Close which were completed in 1972. The first builders were a company named Finsons Ltd; unfortunately they went into receivership and the contract to build the houses was taken on by Andrews Carvell Building Ltd of 104 St. James Road, Northampton.

The houses were built on an Inclosure allotted in 1779 to Thomas Orton, on a relatively large tract of land of 3 acres 18 perches previously described as an L-shaped piece of land off the High Street (see Map Five Old Inclosures/ Homesteads 107). The part of the land stretching along Church Street was low-lying and liable to flooding, and in fact was wet for most of the calendar year (see Map Seven point of interest 19). Prior to building 30,000 (yes, thirty thousand!) tons of graded stone was delivered by the lorries of C & W Knight of Fenny Compton and was spread across the site of all the houses, which were built on concrete rafts. At the south end of the site is a pathway through to The Green; this pathway was requested by the first occupants of the houses. To allow a footway access to the village centre, a panel was left out of the boundary fence erected by the builders to provide this facility. The interesting fact is that this is not a definitive footpath but is from the culverted stream through and over the triangle of land past the houses towards the centre of the village is registered Village Green.

The row of modern houses was built on what was known up to the building of these houses as "Alley Close"; this was always the village sledging field.

As we reach the only bungalow on the left, this was built by "Baker Smith", a bachelor, for his retirement. As the name implies, he had been one of the village bakers. The bungalow was the first dwelling built in this end of Church Street; this part of the plot was known as "Rough Piece" and was at the bottom end of land owned by the Smith family, the top of which went through to the High Street. On the right side of the road at this point is a new Medical Centre (see Map Seven point of interest 20), built in the 1980s to serve the Byfield area. It was built on part of an Inclosure that in 1779 was allotted to Thomas Orton; an area of 2 acres 2 roods 31 perches. (see Map Seven Old Inclosures/Homesteads 139).

The roadway to the side of the Medical Centre today leads to a new housing development Knightley Close, named after the Thomas Knightley Charity previously detailed. This site was built by Billong Ltd in the 1980s. At first they wanted to build houses in an all-brick construction and at full height, that is without utilising the roof space for the bedrooms. A site meeting was requested by Byfield Parish Council which resulted in the planning authority, Daventry District Council, requesting that the front face of the houses be finished in local stone and that the height of the houses should be reduced by half a storey by utilising part of the roof space for the bedrooms.

Previously this site had been part of the farm yard of Manor Farm, as had stone barns on the roadside, now good quality homes. The dwelling which today is named Manor Arch has a date stone on the front dated 1844. These barns were converted by the local family firm of Furmor, with just one new stone house built on the north end of the row to complete the development.

This is a photograph of the Medical Centre built in Church Street in 1981, photograph taken by Peter Stevens.

This photograph is annotated AS243 in the Byfield Photo Museum. Lender Peter Stevens.

The archway through to the rear of Manor Arch was, before the conversion, a barn doorway, and the barn door hinges were stamped with the name of Thomas Mason (a photograph of the stamped hinge is in the Byfield Photo Museum). Thomas Mason was recorded in the 1847 Kelly's Northamptonshire Directory as a Byfield Blacksmith. It can be presumed with a degree of accuracy that these barns were built for the farmer William Barnes (see following details of the occupants of the manor house) in the 1840s, with local labour being used to provide fitments for the buildings.

The site was a part of the allotment previously referred to, land allotted to Thomas Orton in 1779. On the left side of the road at this point was the site of the old village hall, a wooden frame asbestos-clad building on brick pillars. Linked to it nearer to the roadside was a Nissen hut which acted as a kitchen; the main hall was built in 1925 and later added to **(see Map Seven point of interest 21)**. This building from 1925 was the main venue for dances – weddings – parties – social events – W. I. plays – harvest suppers and harvest produce sales – youth club and scout groups. One especially happy occasion in 1946 was when the village celebrated the return of "our lads" as they returned from service in the Second World War. Food and drink were donated by the village, joyous and relieved to see them return home.

Money raised especially from "the shilling and tanner dances" contributed to the funding of the building of the new village hall on The Green, which was built in1960, after which this old hall was dismantled and sold. The build-ing was used for a billet and mess rooms and the Nissen hut was used as a kitchen during the Second World War.

This whole Inclosure, including the Rose and Crown public house, was in 1779 allotted to Thomas Cox, an area of 2 roods 21 perches; obviously Thomas Cox was the landlord. **(See Map Five Old Inclosures/Homesteads 104.)** Thomas Cox was also allotted the next land on the left, which would become the site of Byfield cattle market **(see Map Five Proprietors/Owners 101)**.

On the last piece of land on the right, before reaching the crossroad and adjacent to the road, stands the Manor House. This is on an Inclosure allotted in 1779 to William Henry Chauncy the Lord of the Manor, being an area of 1 acre 1 rood 13 perches, **(see Map Seven Old Inclosures/ Homesteads 140)**. The Lord of the Manor was allotted this land yet he did not live in any dwelling on this site. but resided in the ancestral family seat at Edgecote House.

Sir Nikolaus Pevsner (1902 – 1983) the well-known writer on art and architecture, in his book "The Buildings of England" writes of the Manor House at Byfield: "Five bays, two storeys quoins. Doorway with an open segmental pediment. A small cherub's head in the opening. Probably early C18."

To the rear of this land the Lord of the Manor was allotted the first of a number of enclosures allotted to him, this first one consisting of 3 acres 2 roods **(see Map Seven Proprietors/Owners 14).**

On the east side of this allotment was a private roadway used by the Rector **(see Map Seven point of interest 22)**.

This photograph is of a partly completed Knightley Close and was taken in 1986 by Rex Partridge.

This photograph is annotated RP269 in the Byfield Photo Museum. Lender Rex Partridge.

This is a photograph of the inside of "The Old Hall" in Church Street in the late 1950s. The occasion is obviously some sort of show, as piano accompaniment is being provided by Frank Brookes from Woodford. The photograph is unusual as it is obviously taken from the stage, which gives a good indication of the identities of the large number of Byfield people attending.

This photograph is annotated JR1005 in the Byfield Photo Museum. Lenders Mr & Mrs Jim Buckle.

Survey of allotments.

In 1778/79 a complete survey of the parish of Byfield was made, the two surveyors appointed were as previously stated
- *Edward Linnell of Thorpe - Manderville.*
- *George King of Daventry.*

They surveyed all the land in the parish, thus enabling the Commissioners to allot land with the aid of an accurate and detailed map. The heading on the plan was (verbatim):

A

PLAN

And

SURVEY

of the ALLOTMENTS at

BYFIELD and WESTHRUP

In the county of

NORTHAMPTON

as made by the commissioners

for Inclosing the Fields

in the year 1779

and alfo of

TRAFFORD GROUND

and of the TOWNS of

BYFIELD and WESTRUP

Surveyed by

Geo. King.

The map is signed by Henry Homer – Thomas Bazely – John Chamberlain – James King – John Watts.

Notes by J.R.

A survey of the old inclosures and homesteads includes:

1. *The name of the person the land was allotted to.*

2. *The size of the allotment in Acres, Roods and Perches.*

3. *The total acreage of the entire centre part of the village being 80 Acres 1 Rood 67 Perches.*

4. *The land at Trafford Grounds, belonging to William Henry Chauncy, of 337 acres 1 Rood 33 Perches.*

A survey of the allotments as they were awarded includes:

1. *The Proprietors' names.*

2. *The size of the allotments in Acres Roods and Perches.*

3. *The value of the land allotted.*

4. *The total amount of land within the parish boundaries, excluding those in the centre part of the listed above, including the roads; a total of 2,613 Acres 24 Perches.*

The Manor House we see today was built around 1840. The footprints of the buildings on the site as shown on the 1779 enclosure map, are different from those shown on the 1882/83 Ordnance Survey Map.

The occupants or owners are shown as: 1841 – William Barnes; 1851 – Edward Barnes; 1881 – William Owen Cole; 1884 – Thomas Jones; 1890 – John Barratt; 1894 – Charles W Barratt; 1898 – James Rand; 1904 – James

Tack (died 1947); 1924 – Geoffrey Treadwell; 1947 – Darbishire Farms Ltd (occupant Mr Virtue); 1970s – David Green; then sold as a private house and the adjacent farm yard and buildings sold to two separate developers.

The 1861 census records that the amount of land farmed from Manor Farm was 293 acres. The 1881 census records that the amount of land farmed from Manor Farm was 416 acres. This would be Manor Farm at 293 acres together with Dodds Farm at 123 acres.

The house was used by the Conservative Club in the Second World War, due to the fact that the then Conservative Club on the green was commandeered by the Army and used as the N.A.A.F.I.

We have now reached the Five Ways Crossroads.

MAP EIGHT

THE TWISTLE

The BLACK NUMBERS are from the survey of Old Inclosures and Homesteads in the centre of the village.
The BLUE NUMBERS are Tracts of Land allotted to Proprietors and Owners in the rest of the parish.
The RED NUMBERS denote points of interest along the route.

This map is 1900 with some boundaries taken from the 1779 Enclosure Map of Byfield.

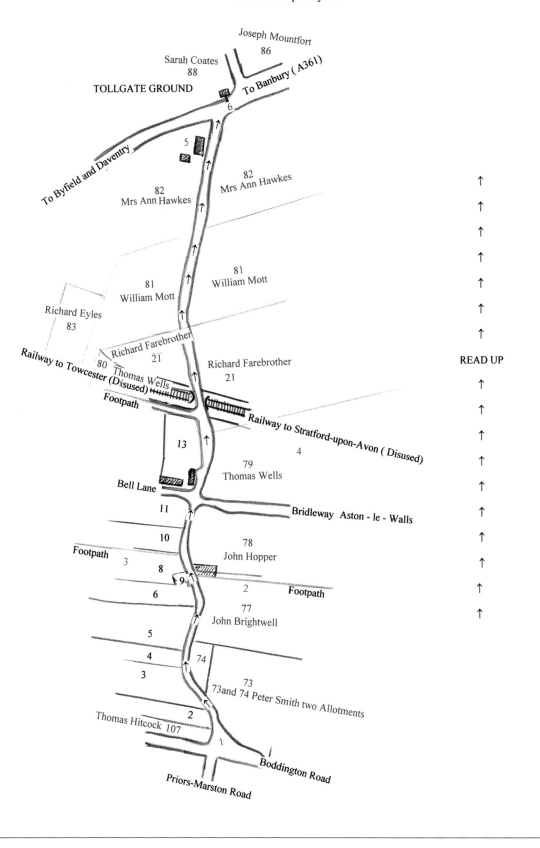

Joseph Mountfort
86

Sarah Coates
88

TOLLGATE GROUND

To Banbury (A361)

6

5

To Byfield and Daventry

82
Mrs Ann Hawkes

82
Mrs Ann Hawkes

81
William Mott

81
William Mott

Richard Eyles
83

Richard Farebrother
21

Railway to Towcester (Disused)

80

Richard Farebrother
21

Thomas Wells

Footpath

Railway to Stratford-upon-Avon (Disused)

13

4

79
Thomas Wells

Bell Lane

Bridleway   Aston - le - Walls

11

10

78
John Hopper

Footpath

3

8

9

2

Footpath

6

77
John Brightwell

5

4

74

3

73

73and 74 Peter Smith two Allotments

2

Thomas Hitcock 107

1

Boddington Road

Priors-Marston Road

READ UP

62

CHAPTER SIX

THE TWISTLE

(See Map Eight)

Starting at the cross roads at the southern end of the Priors Marston road, we continue entering Byfield from a northerly direction, into The Twistle. **(See Map Eight point of interest 1.)** From this starting point to the corner of Bell Lane there were no substantial buildings before the 1930s; all of the land plots and the buildings and services appertaining to them were on Westhorpe Lane or Boddington Road.

An interesting aspect of this part of the Twistle is that most of the plots had changed very little between the 1779 Enclosure Map and the 1882/3 Ordnance Survey Map, with only small changes in overall plot outline and, apart from minor internal divisions, it is the same up to the present day.

Moving forward, immediately on the left is a piece of lane allotted in 1779 to Thomas Hitchcock, an area of 1 rood 36 perches **(see Map Eight Proprietors/Owners 107)**. This land has now a detached brick-built house on the plot built in the 1990s. The second piece of land on the left is an Inclosure allotted to William Edwards of 2 roods **(see Map Eight Old Inclosures/Homesteads 2)** which has now on it a detached house built by the

Steel family. When George Edward Steele (1886–1965) died his address was given on the Byfield Burial Records by the old Byfield name of "Spinneys End". Later, from the late 1960s, it was lived in by Mr and Mrs Fred (Bolchin) Tomalin. Fred was one of Byfield's well-known characters.

Continuing on the left the next two Inclosures were allotted in 1779 to Richard Farebrother (1728–1795); the first is one of 1 acre 1 rood 7 perches **(see Map Eight Old Inclosures/Homesteads 3)**. This was sold by James Yorston in 1925. Today it has on it a detached house named Hill Crest, built by Douglas Russell (1908–1968) in 1934. It was rented off the Russells by George Palmer (1879–1953) and his wife Sarah (née Russell) up to 1953, later to be purchased by Arthur Johnson (1901–1974) and his wife. Their daughter Margaret still lives in the house today.

Adjacent to this house are two detached houses, built in the 1980s on a former paddock attached to Hill Crest. Also on this plot is a house built by the Allen family, relations of the well-known Batchelor family, and again built in the 1930s.

This photograph of The Twistle was taken in the 1950s, and shows the two houses built in the 1930s by the Russell family and the Allen family.

This photograph is annotated JR860 in the Byfield Photo Museum. Lender Margaret Johnson.

The second Inclosure allotted to Richard Farebrother of 2 roods 10 perches **(see Map Eight Old Inclosures/Homesteads 4)** has on it a bungalow built in the 1970s by Woodford and Upfield for Brian and Cathy Barnes. It was later purchased by Mr Neil Wyatt, who at the time lived at Iron Cross, for housing his employees.

Opposite these Inclosures on the right were two plots of land allotted to Peter Smith; one of 3 acres 2 roods **(see Map Eight Proprietors/Owner 73)**. Encroaching into the allotment was a smaller allotment on the roadside of 1 rood 35 perches **(see Map Eight Proprietors/Owners 74)**.

Of the next three Inclosures on the left after negotiating the right-hand bend, the first was allotted to John Brightwell (1745–1824) an area of 1 acre 4 perches **(see Map Eight Old Inclosures/Homesteads 5)**; the second to Richard Dodd, of 2 roods 33 perches **(see Map Eight Old Inclosures/Homesteads 6),** and the third small allotment adjacent to the road to John Thornton, 14 perches **(see Map Eight Old Inclosures/Homesteads 9)**. A number of modern detached dwellings are built on the left with their frontages on to the Twistle, as far down as the Bell Lane junction.

On the right hand side of the road the land was allotted to John Brightwell, an area of 7 acres 1 rood 23 perches **(see Map Eight Proprietors/Owners 77)**. On the Enclosure Map of 1779 is shown a definitive footpath to Boddington which originally ran diagonally across the plot **(see Map Eight point of interest 2)**. We immediately realise that the ground level is lower in this allotment; this is due to iron ore extraction but not to any great depth.

The reason for this is probably that the mining was in the early days, not long after Mr Payne had opened the Byfield Ironstone mines in 1915, and would have been dug by hand, or at least without the use of modern machinery as was used later by the successive mining companies.

When the land was reinstated and again producing crops, those crops were of garden produce, as this was garden ground let in plots, mostly to the people of Westhorpe.

The footpath was used by local men working on the Ironstone as it was the shortest route to the engine sheds; especially by driver George Batchelor who lived off the Twistle in a small holding on the opposite, left side of the road to that of the footpath, on land allotted to John Bromley, an area of 3 roods 12 perches **(see Map Eight Old Inclosure/Homesteads 8)**. An interesting aspect of the small holding is that a concrete-framed asbestos-roofed building, used to house animals, was purchased from the Byfield P.O.W. camp, after closure, by Jim Jordan **(see Map Eight point of interest 3)**. This building was used as a store by Mr Tom Upfield until very recently. It was removed to provide sufficient room for a bungalow to be built on the site.

The Inclosure next to this on the left was allotted to

This photograph is of the early days of the Ironstone Mines in Byfield. The topsoil and overburden are being removed by hand or at least with a limited amount of machinery. This would be not long after 1915.

This photograph is annotated BH2 in the Byfield Photo Museum. Lender Mr Dick Haynes.

Chapter Six: The Twistle

John Bromley, an area of 3 roods 12 perches (see Map Eight Old Inclosures/Homesteads10).

Again on the left, on the corner of the Twistle and Bell Lane, was an Inclosure allotment to John Hopper of 3 roods 39 perches. This was later in the 1970s called "Green Acre", and most of the bungalows were built over the years by the Green family. (See Map Eight Old Inclosures/ Homesteads 11.) The area was of a similar size as the allotment to John Hopper in 1779, being a difference of only 1 square perch (Square measure: 4 roods to the acre, 40 perches to a rood, 30.5 square yards to a perch).

On the right before Pit Lane, the plot allotted to John Hopper was an area of 16 acres 10 perches (see Map Eight Proprietors/Owners 78). The 1777 Militia List shows John Hopper as a Farmer.

On the left, past the entrance to Bell Lane, stands a stone cottage. The 1779 enclosure map shows a building on this footprint which is larger than the existing. The 1882/83 Ordnance Survey Map shows a footprint similar to that of today. The Inclosure, an allotment in 1779, was to William Henry Chauncy, Lord of the Manor, an area of 3 roods 18 perches (see Map Eight Old Inclosures/ Homesteads 13). This plot of land ran southwards along the Twistle to the private road that today heads east alongside the disused railway.

Sale of the Manors of Byfield and Westrop

In January 1758 Miss Anne Hitchcock of Daventry sold the combined Manors of Byfield and Westrop to Richard Chauncy esq. of Edgecote (detail Baker). By 1778 at the time of the enclosure the Chauncy family owned the combined Manors of Byfield, Westhrop also Trafford and West Warden. William Henry Chauncy was a direct descendant of Richard Chauncy.

The owner of this land and cottage from the 1930s to May 1956 was Charles Gardner (1876–1956). By this time the cottage had been named "West View". Charlie was a character. He boasted of having two birthdays, one on the day he was born, and one on the day that his birth was registered. Charlie was known for a number of things; he was a roadman (a lengthman), and a very good one at that! All the roadside grips (country term for drainage channels from roadside to ditch) were clear; no standing water if possible, certainly no rubbish on his length, and roadside grass mown with a scythe. He was a master with a scythe. In his younger days he would mow with the rhythm of a master because that was what he was, mowing to a standard of equal length of finish that a mechanical mower of today would be proud of. The acres mown in a day when Charlie worked on the land in his prime it would seem to us an impossible area to mow by hand. A historical article in the Northampton Chronicle and Echo dated July 9th 1954 states that at the age of 13 Charlie scythed two large fields in less than a day, much to the amazement of his employer the farmer.

Charlie was also a resolute practising non-conformist Christian, a Methodist, a disciple of John Wesley, as was his wife. He attended Chapel every Sunday, and sat at the back on the left of the wooden and asbestos building in Bell Lane, singing as loud as he could with feeling and faith!

What Charlie made of being a successor as a landowner to the Lord, not his Lord, but that Lord of the Manor, we cannot hazard a guess. Charlie also was a talker; was he a talker!! People reckoned if you walked along the road with Charlie he would keep talking and you could walk to Banbury and he would not notice.

From Charlie Gardner's cottage to the lane running alongside the railway there have been a number of houses, all built on Charlie's garden or orchard.

The second house to be built on this Inclosure was for Harry ("Shina") Green (1911–1971), another character, who ran a local plumbing business in Daventry with his brother. Harry was an avid cricket fan; a game he played and also umpired.

The third house to be built was on the top end of this Inclosure which became Charlie's orchard. It was built by George Farmalo and his wife, a bungalow to retire into. George was by trade a stonemason and some of his work can still be seen in the parish. The Farmalos had been market gardeners; they ran the nursery which was by the Bell Inn.

In recent times two more properties have in-filled the gaps between the houses.

Still on the left, we now reach the private roadway which serves one house and the rear of others, including Laurie's farm. The strip of land that is now a disused railway cutting was in 1779 an Inclosure allotted to Thomas Wells, an allotment of 1 rood 13 perches (see Map Eight Proprietors/Owners 80).

Also along this roadway is the start of a definitive footpath that winds on and over the Banbury road (A361) and on through to the Farndon road. On the 1779 enclosure map this roadway continues in the form of a track and appears to show that it goes through to the Turnpike, joining the turnpike road near the Westhorpe (Blindle) stream.

A detail of Public Foot-roads includes on page 84 of the Byfield Enclosure of 1779 a reference to this specific Public Foot-road, (copied Verbatim).

By the West side of Westhrop

One other public foot-road from and out of the said Turnpike Road, through and over an allotment to the said Ann Hawkes, the allotment to the said Richard Eyles, the allotment to the said William Molt and an allotment to the said Richard Farebrother and a second allotment to the said Thomas Wells, by the south side of the Inclosures of the Town of Byfield and of Westhrop into the said road on the west side of Westhrop.

Notes by J.R.

The detail above is describing the Foot-road from the Turnpike Road (A361) to the Twistle, i.e. the opposite direction to that as described in the script.

This Public Foot-road was slightly diverted towards the Westhorpe end from the line we walk today, when the East and West Junction Railway was constructed in the late 1860s.

Back to the road, the land on the right is an allotment of 16 acres 2 roods 1 perch to Thomas Wells (see Map Eight

Proprietors/Owners 79). This ground had within its bounds, adjacent to the appropriately named "Pit Lane", a stone pit shown on the 1779 Enclosure Map as being Stone Pit no. 2. This land was intersected by the railway when it was built. The land was further encroached by the construction of the railway sidings to accommodate the Ironstone ore wagons **(see Map Eight point of interest 4)**. The sidings were constructed very soon after the Ironstone mines were opened in 1915.

These sidings at the junction with the "Main Line" were used extensively, especially in the Second World War, when iron and steel production was at its height. The mined iron ore was taken from here to the various Iron Smelting Works. The sidings were built to receive the iron ore loaded wagons and to bring back the empty wagons to enable the production cycle to start again.

Stewarts and Lloyds were the last company to operate the mines, the last load of ore being dispatched in February 1965.

A short distance Stratford side of **point of interest 4** was the summit level at 513 feet above sea level, the highest point of the Stratford to Blisworth railway

---

The destinations for the iron ore from the Byfield mines

Sheltons Iron and Steel, Etruria

Frodingham, Scunthorpe

Normanby Park, Scunthorpe

Consett, County Durham

Port Clarance, Middlesbrough

Bell Bros, Tipton

Roberts, Tipton

Midland Coal, Coke & Iron Co Ltd, Apedale

The Scunthorpe traffic went via Woodford, whilst the Staffordshire traffic went via Broom. Business was so brisk that the sidings would overflow into Byfield goods yard. Another problem during the First World War was a severe shortage of wagons.

At times the iron ore receipts amounted to £1,400 per month. Some measure of the advantage of this traffic can be appreciated when it was known that the SMJ waited for the cheque for this traffic to pay the men's wages!

The next allotment to the right and to the left across the Twistle was allotted to Richard Farebrother; an allotment of 10 acres 3 roods 12 perches **(see Map Eight numbered on both sides of the Twistle Proprietors/Owners 21)**. This land was also intersected by the railway when it was built.

The next land again to the right and left of the Twistle was allotted to William Mott, an area of 12 acres 3 perches **(see Map Eight also numbered on both sides of the Twistle Proprietors/Owners 81)**.

We now reach the land of Mrs Ann Hawkes to the left and right **(see Map Eight again numbered on both sides of the Twistle Proprietors/Owners 82)**.

Later the land to the left was owned by the Checkley family. On the left, just before reaching the A361, was the site of the well known landmark in modern times of Checkley's barn, now demolished **(see Map Eight point of interest 5)**.

At the T-junction on our right on the turnpike would have been the toll gate **(see Map Eight point of interest 6)**.

CHAPTER SEVEN

BODDINGTON ROAD

MAP NINE

BODDINGTON ROAD

The BLACK NUMBERS are from the survey of Old Inclosures and Homesteads in the centre of the village.
The BLUE NUMBERS are Tracts of Land allotted to Proprietors and Owners in the rest of the parish.
The RED NUMBERS denote points of interest along the route.

A modern map with some boundaries taken from the 1779 Enclosure Map of Byfield.

Daventry Road
Cornbrooke Stream
Footpath
Woodford Road
40 John Hitchcock
Church Street
97
98
99
17
105 William Chambers
104 Mary Shaw
96 100
High Street
41 Thomas Wagstaff
Trustees of Drivers Children
16
42 Joseph Cox
39 John Hitchcock
43 Joseph Cox
33 John Bliss
15
14
Westhorpe Stream (Blindle)
34 John Bliss
44 James Smith
Bridleway
36 John Smith
45
45 James Smith
24
107 Thomas Hitchcock
The Twistle
Westhorpe Lane

24 John Bromley
in lieu of land
Purchased off Checkley
Footpath
75
James
Harris
76
Cresent
Boote
76
74
73
Two Allotments
Peter Smith
Priors-Marston Road
Pre.1940s
13
10
11
72 George Moor
108 William Edwards
62 John Edwards
12
71 Samuel Newbold
9
Post 1940s
Disused Ironstone Railway
"Middlegate"
The Rector
77 John Brightwell
25 John Bromley
78 plots of Garden ground
70 William Eyles
Footpath
for Tithes of the Field
37 John Smith
69
Richard Goodman
68 William Jordan
109 Samuel Jordan
8
67 Samuel Turner
66 Edward Brookes
61 Richard Hiccock
13 The Proprietors of the Oxford Canal
65 Daniel Bateman
Byfield Pool
7 The Rector
6
64 Job Allett
Byfield Parish
7
District and Parish Boundary
Canal Reservoir Feeder
3
Boddington Reservoir
5
Aston-le-Walls Parish
63 John Edwards
4
Canal Reservoir Feeder
2
4
1
District and Parish Boundary
Boddington Road
Boddington Parish

READ UP

BODDINGTON ROAD

(See Map Nine)

On this route, from the Boddington direction, the only one entering Byfield Parish from the west, the large expanse of water on the right is the Boddington Reservoir **(see Map Nine point of interest 1)**. On reaching the two brick pump houses on the right, **(see Map Nine point of interest 2)**, looking to the left is a stream, which is today used to supply water to the pumps to supplement the main reservoir feeder stream, which is further along the road. **(See Map Nine point of interest 3.)** The position of the culvert under the road at this point, before the reservoir was built, was spanned by a bridge named "Boddington Bridge".

At this point, before 1805, the view you would have seen to the left and the right would have been this stream meandering through the valley **(see Map Nine points of interest 4)**. The land on the right on the Byfield side of the stream in 1779 nearest to the road was allotted to John Edwards, an area of 11 acres 37 perches **(see Map Nine Proprietors/Owners 63)**. Today the whole of this allotment is submerged and is part of the reservoir. Moving downstream the next allotment was to Job Allett, an

area of 31 acres 17 perches **(see Map Nine Proprietors/Owners 64)**. Almost all of this allotment is under water and further downstream to the parish boundary was a large tract of land allotted to the Rector **(see Map Nine Proprietors/Owners 7)**; only a small percentage of this land was flooded when the reservoir was built.

One of the significant things is that this meandering stream which was, and is, the boundary between Boddington Parish and the Parish of Byfield, is also today the boundary between the districts of South Northamptonshire and Daventry. Obviously, since the land has been flooded, this boundary now runs through the middle of the reservoir. The records through the history of Banbury Sailing Club, which was formed in 1950, show the reservoir cost £20, 958.09 to build, being completed in 1811. One interesting detail from Byfield Parish records shows that in 1871, "ice on the pool was said to have been eleven inches thick in winter, where weeks of skating were enjoyed". In the Byfield Photo Museum we have a photograph of Denis Judd skating on the reservoir in 1929. Today people remember the nights when skating was

This photograph was taken on the 15th of February 1977 by Rex Partridge and is of the old bridge and weir at the outfall of Boddington Reservoir, before the present dam and new outfall system were installed.

This photograph is annotated RP5 in the Byfield Photo Museum. Lender Rex Partridge.

possible only when cars were lined up along the north bank, and their headlamps illuminated the scene to allow skating to take place. One may wonder about the duration of the light source as most of the cars would have 6 volt batteries, and hopefully a starting handle.

The reservoir has been extended twice; once in the early 1830s, the last time removing the Water Bailiff's house, the site of which is now part of the Reservoir **(see Map Nine point of interest 5)**. The old sluices from the south end of the reservoir were also removed.

A new dam and water outfall system were then built further downstream, increasing the size and also increasing the height of the water level. Byfield Reservoir is the largest of three supplying the summit of the Oxford Canal, the others being at Wormleighton in Warwickshire and Clattercote (Claydon) in Oxfordshire.

The 1828 Northamptonshire Directory records that Byfield Parish consisted of 2,714 acres of land and 46 acres of water. This shows that a considerable area of land located in Byfield Parish was flooded when the reservoir was built. The original area of land belonging to Job Allett, John Edwards and the Rector was flooded, and further areas have been flooded since **(see Map Nine)**.

Past water bailiffs who lived in the house were the Turner family. Mrs Turner used to serve tea in the summer on Sunday afternoons, charging 6d for the service. Sadly, one of the Turner sons was drowned when he was riding a bicycle round the bank of the reservoir in thick fog and was blown into the water. The Turner family were followed by the Hill family, and the last family to occupy the house, were the Parker family.

The water bailiffs today are "mobile" as against being resident on site.

In the Second World War, to prevent enemy sea planes landing on the water, telegraph poles were wrapped in barbed wire and floated on the surface of the water.

"The Pool" as it was always known by Byfield people, was used for swimming and was at its most popular in the late 1940s. A large number of people from all over the district used the facility of a "beach" and, in the centre of the east bank, an official swimming club was formed. After a time swimming was stopped due to a person contracting polio, which was deemed to have been caused by the unclean water.

A brief potted history of Banbury Sailing Club with additions by the Author.

In 1950 at the inaugural meeting twenty five people agreed to pay a fiver to start the club. The first Commodore of the club was J. H. Russell. (No relation to the Author.)

The gentleman who became the second Commodore, Mr Benyon-Brown, was a farmer. He brought a canvas shelter off a "tilt truck", pegged it down at the top of the dam and this, together with an army bell tent, formed the accommodation facilities of the newly-formed club. The few initial dinghies were picketed down along the top of the dam.

In about 1959, the boat parking became a problem so it was decided to move the club onto the centre of the east side of the reservoir. A road was constructed from the Boddington road to the new site, with many tons of railway ballast trans-

ported from Charwelton railway tunnel by local contractors. After much deliberation, approval was given by the committee to negotiate for a wooden pavilion that was on the market and belonged to Northampton Technical College. This was purchased with the proviso that it was sectionalised and delivered to the site. The new Clubhouse was erected together with the other necessary adjacent and constituent works, including a concrete ramp and mooring pontoons by volunteer members, some of whom, in addition to their own efforts, had very good contacts with people who had some of the necessary expertise needed.

*When the ramp was completed it was possible to think of moving the old clubhouse, which by then had become a green-painted aluminium corrugated building. It was found not to be possible to dismantle the building due to rusty bolts, and possible damage to the aluminium fabric if, in fact, the bolts were removed. It was decided to move the building in its entirety. The building was therefore released from its mooring on the south bank, manhandled on to pontoons powered by an Atco (Villiers) outboard motor, and moved to its new position on the east bank. On arrival at the east bank adjacent to the new site, the building was again manhandled, this time on to the ramp; about 25 to 30 members then entered the hut and lifted it bodily and carried it up the field on to its new foundations **(see Map Nine point of interest 6)**.*

As only the legs, not the bodies, of the members carrying it could be seen by spectators at the time, it was described by John Green as looking like some gigantic crustaceous millipede crawling in and then out of the water.

One problem the club regularly had in most years was a lack of water, especially in dry hot summers, and at times only very limited sailing was possible, and there were times when there was no sailing at all.

Note by J.R.

Reading "The History of Banbury Sailing Club" by John Green, written to celebrate fifty years since the initial formation of the club, 1950–2000, it is obvious that the club has been steered in a progressive, logical and efficient way by some very able members, and from within those members some sound elected officers. Together, and with the corporate spirit within the club, they have guided and extended both the sailing and competition side progressively over the years. It is obvious that the club has a stable and progressive future.

As well as some unusual visitors of the feathered variety, a much rarer visitor to Boddington was the arrival of a Tiger Moth Biplane numbered B-AIVW fitted with floats so that it could land on water. The aeroplane came past Boddington on three separate summers, first in the October of 1978 and subsequently in 1979 and 1980. Boddington was being used as a refuelling stop.

In 1984 British Waterways executed major work, costing £1,000,000, on raising and strengthening the southern dam, together with work along the reservoir bank. This did away with the road that used to service the cottage at the side of the dam.

In 1996 British Waterways undertook a study to increase the supply of water to the summit of the Oxford Canal, using the consultants Babtie from Glasgow.

The following details are from a presentation to Byfield

Parish Council by British Waterway Engineers.

The consultants were charged with examining these options:

Option 1: Drilling boreholes down to 300 metres into underground aquifers and transferring the water to the Oxford summit level.

Option 2: Pumping water from the south which would include water from the River Cherwell.

Option 3: To increase the size, extending the reservoir across the Boddington road into the valley on the other side, raising the water level by one and a half metres; originally a figure of two and a half metres was considered.

With the progression of time and with public consultation, further options were put forward.

Option 4: To increase the size of the reservoir, but by using two water levels on different sides of the Boddington road, this saving the cost of building a causeway to take the road. This would also save areas around the existing reservoir from being flooded.

Option 5: To pump water back to the summit from the north.

None of these options has as yet been utilised.

Subsequent to the consultation exercise, British Waterways have taken steps to facilitate the transfer of water from underground sources from the west of Birmingham via the canal system to the summit stretch of the Oxford Canal between Napton top lock and Claydon top lock. This system was first used in 1999 and resulted in the retention of good water levels at Boddington and no restrictions to date on the Oxford Canal.

Moving along the road towards the main feeder stream of the reservoir **(again see Map Nine point of interest 3)**, looking right over to the far end of the east bank is Byfield reservoir commonly known as "Byfield Pool". This reservoir was there before 1779, as it is detailed on the enclosure map as being allotted to The Proprietors of the Oxford Canal, an area of 8 acres 17 perches **(see Map Nine Proprietors/Owners 13)**.

A brief comment on the first of the English canals

In 1759 the Third Duke of Bridgewater (surname Egerton) built a canal between his coal mine in Worsley in Lancashire and Manchester, a distance of ten and a half miles. To build the canal he employed the famous engineer James Brindley (1716–1772) who supervised the work travelling on horseback.

The Duke had been influenced by canals he had seen on the continent. Obviously these canals were not the first to be constructed; there is evidence of the use of canals being built in China five hundred years before the birth of Christ.

The Bridgewater Canal was not only the first canal in England, but it was also constructed over the first aqueduct, a stone-arched structure 600 feet long, 36 feet wide and 39 feet above the River Irwell. Brindley had previously demonstrated to the Duke the use of "puddled clay" as a medium for water retention, using a model of the aqueduct, which was placed on the Duke's highly polished dining table and filled with water.

The result of building the Bridgewater canal was that it halved the price of coal into Manchester, which was now being transported from the Worsley Pit by canal rather than packhorses or horses and carts. Obviously the saving on transport costs using this form of transport resulted in canals being built all over the country; between 1759 and 1830 about 4,000 miles of canals were cut in England. One such canal was the Coventry to Oxford canal, by the Oxford Canal Company. Three Acts of Parliament were needed, in 1767, 1775 and 1786; this enabled initially the Coventry to Napton section to be completed in 1774, and extended to Banbury in 1778. Ease of construction was critical to avoid unnecessary locks, embankments and tunnels. By following the contours of the land, these early canals were known as "contour canals".

The eleven mile level section between Napton top lock and Claydon top lock needed a head of water. Byfield reservoir was built in 1774 at a cost of £1,373.0s.0d. To meet this demand, its capacity was expected to supply 35 locks of water per day in dry weather, but with a progressive increase in traffic this soon proved to be inadequate, and in 1787 Wormleighton reservoir was built to supplement the supply of water.

The Byfield old pool area is now a Northamptonshire nature reserve, but still supplies water, in conjunction with its bigger neighbour Boddington Reservoir, to the canal system. The Oxford Canal joined with other canal companies and with the river Thames. Coal was taken from the Warwickshire coalfields to such places as Banbury "Lectric Light" in Canal Street Banbury, as well as supplying coal to all those fireplaces in the Oxford colleges. The service provided by this new form of transport was such that, when the first boatload of coal arrived in Oxford from Coventry in 1790, the Church bells rang out all over the City, in celebration.

An idea of the cost of transport! 28 tons of coal transported for 22 pence a ton to Aynho wharf from the Coventry coal pit involves a round trip of three weeks.

When the "put-puts" came, which was a name given by the Bargees for boats with engines, the increased speed could not be used to its full potential due to the lack of water depth on "The Oxford", resulting in a lot of the Bargees transferring to the Grand Union Canal to earn their living. Obviously a big advantage of the "put-puts" was that the boat could be worked for longer hours, as the horse needed rest and the engine did not. The advantage of using the Grand Union Canal was that it was a faster, shorter route to London, the locks were double width and the canal was straighter and wider than the "contour" Oxford Canal.

Back to the road, we continue walking on past the main feeder, which has two main tributaries, both of which rise close to the Parish borders towards Priors Marston parish.

All the land on the left back to the Boddington boundary was allotted in 1779 to Richard Hiccock, an area of 110 acres 35 perches **(see Map Nine Proprietors/ Owners 61)**, subsequently divided into smaller plots. One plot, which was the field on the Byfield side of the feeder, was named Flat Ground. This was used in the 1940s by the inmates of the P.O.W. camp as a football field, playing against local village teams **(see Map Nine point of interest 7)**. The next field was divided into Cow House Ground and Lines Ground.

On the left at this point, half way up "Pool Hill", was

This is a photograph of Byfield Prisoner of War Camp in Boddington Road taken from the water tower, which is still there today. From the detail the photograph was taken around 1950, as it shows the inmates to be Displaced Persons, not, as previously, initially Italians followed by German prisoners.

This photograph is annotated JR148 in the Byfield Photo Museum. Lender Mr and Mrs J Buckle.

the first building; a worker's hostel in a complex of which by far the biggest part was a Second World War Prisoners of War Camp **(see Map Nine point of interest 8)**, part of which was built on Cow House Ground.

Byfield Prisoners of War Camp
1944–1949

The camp complex was constructed by the Banbury building firm of Hinkin and Frewin in 1944. The first building nearest the reservoir feeder stream was a hostel built to house mostly itinerant workers. Mrs Darby (1900–1966) was appointed to be the first warden of the hostel (a post that she applied for before the building was constructed). Mrs Darby was the mother of Mrs Jessie Jones, who later also worked in the hostel.

The main camp complex housed initially Italian Prisoners, who were transported to Byfield railway station and then marched to the camp via Church Street and Boddington Road (previously called "Back Way"), to be accommodated initially under canvas until the camp was ready for occupation. "Paddy" Kehoe, who would later marry a local girl, was one of the camp guards.

When the Italian prisoners vacated the camp they were replaced by German prisoners, who after a while formed a dance band; at the end of the war local people were invited to dances in the camp. Byfield Parish Council records show that at the council meeting of November 20th 1947, at the request of the Foreign Office P.O.W. section, German prisoners attended so that they might hear and see how an English

parish council meeting was conducted.

With the German prisoners repatriated, the camp was used to accommodate Displaced Persons, a rather bland title for those who had fought on the side of the Allies, and others who could not, or did not want to, return to their homelands.

The new occupants of the camp integrated very well into the local community, forming different sports clubs and pastimes, one being a very talented large choir which performed at venues over a large area. The abilities of all the occupants of the camp were many and varied. Some of the artistic talents were left behind as a legacy, and among them were various painting and murals on the walls of the buildings.

All of the occupants also worked within the local businesses and commerce of the area. They were transported by motor lorries, some owned by Denis Judd, and were supervised and organised by Les Dalton. Some of the men from the camp married local girls, and some became very valued members of the local communities.

1949 to date

After the camp had been derequisitioned, parts of it were dismantled and sold off.

The hostel was occupied by squatters, namely a family of husband, wife and two daughters with the surname of Rigby. Life must have been difficult, as the main services had been disconnected, with no electricity and no mains water, but probably the main drains still functioned. Luckily there was a strong, profuse spring in the roadway ditch nearby to supply the family with water. Mr Rigby became a well known character, he obviously was "an up-market sort of man" as is the description given in Denis Judd's book "Living in the Country". The tales of his escapades are better told by Dennis!

Later the hostel became the home of farm animals, specifically pigs, and still is today.

Between the site of the hostel and the main camp, the Northamptonshire County Council constructed a rock-salt hopper to store salt to treat the roads in winter.

Mr C. W. F. Laurie purchased the 20 ton public weighbridge from Towcester Station and installed it on the site.

The main camp has accommodated an array of businesses. Among them was a garage selling and repairing cars, a motor cycle workshop, Land Rover sales and service, a breakers yard for commercial vehicles for export, a scrap yard, a secondhand car parts outlet, and other small enterprises.

On the right side of the road, joining the allotment to Job Allett, were three plots: the first allotted to Daniel Bateman of 18 acres 3 perches (**see Map Nine Proprietors/Owners 65**), **the** second to Edward Brookes of 8 acres 3 roods 22 perches (**see Map Nine Proprietors/Owners 66**), the third to Samuel Turner of 4 acres 1 rood 11 perches (**see Map Nine Proprietors/Owners 67**).

Opposite the camp site on the right, the land had previously been allotted in 1779 to Samuel Jordan, an area of 1 acre 1 rood 30 perches (**see Map Nine Proprietors/Owners 109**). The next two plots on the right were allotted to William Jordan, of 5 acres 27 perches (**see Map Nine Proprietors/Owners 68**), and the second to Richard Goodman, 3 acres 2 roods 27 perches (**see Map Nine Proprietors/Owners 69**); these two plots together were later to be named Frenches Hill. All of these allotments were purchased by Mr C. W. F. Laurie in 1965.

We are now at the top of the hill, having travelled up 100 feet from the starting point at the boundary stream.

The next plot, still on the right, was a larger holding allotted to William Eyles of 30 acres 18 perches (**see Map Nine Proprietors/Owners 70**). The far end of this allotment was adjacent to "Byfield Pool".

The next allotment, of 139 acres 2 roods 17 perches, was a large tract of land stretching up and round to "Half Crown Corner" on the Banbury Road, which in 1779 was allotted to the Rector for Tithes of the Field (**see Map Nine Proprietors/Owners 7**). Parts of this allotment, adjoining Boddington Road, were the 78 garden plots on this site which were named "Middlegate". The holders of these garden plots would have to pay a Tithe to the Rector (one tenth of the value in cash or kind of the produce of the plot). This land was to become in the late 1990s "Crossings Farm" where occupiers were: 1940 – Ron Mold (a postman's son and would later become a postman himself) who purchased a mobile milking parlour, which was a phenomenon on the farming scene in those days; 1960s – Dennis Eyles; 1990s – Mr Slatcher, who sold it on to the Beech family.

Again on the right, the next allotment, to Samuel Newbold, was an area of 3 acres 2 roods 28 perches (**see Map Nine Proprietors/Owners 71**). **A**cross this plot, and across the road at this point, a level crossing was built in the 1940s for the Ironstone railway (**see Map Nine point of interest 9**). This continued across to the left of Boddington Road through a piece of land allotted to William Edwards, a plot of 1 acre 23 perches (**see Map Nine Proprietors/Owners108**). The railway then went across an allotment to John Edwards's allotment of 18 acres 3roods 4 perches (**see Map Nine Proprietors/Owners 62**) and on *under* the Priors Marston road (**see Map Nine point of interest 10**).

"She didn't blow"

The Ironstone railway system, even from the early days, always sloped down to the "Main Line". This had the advantage that the engine did not have to pull loaded wagons uphill; the disadvantage was that the loaded train had to be held back when coming down the incline.

Boys will be boys, and the railways have always had a fascination, so in the summer evenings, weekends and school holidays exploring the Ironstone workings was a must. There were always interesting things to see and to do, and the small bogies used by workers to move tools, bars, explosives etc. could be used for the boys to ride on.

On one such occasion, in the school holidays this time, with the men working, one lad released the brake on a wagon as it was on an incline. The wagon rolled, gathering momentum as it headed towards the Priors Marston road bridge. Normally, before getting to the Boddington road crossing, the engine driver would blow his whistle, but this time the runaway train coming over the hill did not blow the whistle as it was only a runaway wagon. The "Flag-man", Darky Henning, on hearing the rattle of iron wheels on rails, ran out of his little cabin frantically waving his red flag to stop any traffic. The wagon by this time was gathering speed, having negotiated the Priors Marston road bridge, and on reaching the crossing flashed past his nose, carried on under the Pit Lane bridge, crashing at the points adjacent to the Ironstone office and weighbridge.

The implications of the extreme danger of a runaway wagon out of control had the boys severely lectured by the Headmaster at Woodford School (the Byfield senior children by then attended Woodford School) on the dangers of playing games with full size trains. The perpetrator, although his identity was known to other boys, was never caught.

On the next plot on the right, allotted to George Moor, an allotment of 3 acres 2 roods (**see Map Nine Proprietors/Owners 72**), were sited the Ironstone Engine Sheds built in the 1920s (**see Map Nine point of interest 11**). Prior to the new route being built in the 1940s, the track to the Ironstone workings ran past these sheds and over the Boddington Road (**see Map Nine point of interest 12**) and also over the Priors Marston road (**see Map Nine point of interest 13**). The "Flag-men "over the later years of the operation were Benjamin James Wise, Jack Gregory and George (Darky) Henning.

"Flag-Men"

"Flag-men" was a "nickname" given to men who controlled the road traffic at "non-gated" railway level crossings, using red and green flags to ensure the safe operation of the crossing of the rail traffic over public roads.

The two allotments on the right, as the Boddington Road veers into the Twistle, were allotted to Peter Smith; one an area of 3 acres 2 roods and the other a smaller allotment of 1 rood 35 perches **(see Map Nine Proprietors/Owners 73 and 74)**.

After passing the crossroads, on the right the land was allotted to Thomas Hitchcock; a small plot of 1 rood 36 perches **(see Map Nine Proprietors/Owners 107)**.

The corner on the left, together with the roadway and further on, including an area on the right, was allotted in 1779 to Cressent Boote **(see Map Nine Proprietors/Owners 76)**.

Immediately as we pass a definitive footpath on our left, on the right, and on the far side of Westhorpe Lane standing back from Boddington Road, is the "Big Barn" with a date stone on the gable end in Westhorpe Lane of 1795, which was part of Home Farm but now has been converted into a desirable dwelling.

The next premises standing back, again a converted barn of Home Farm, is "Greenlands", now a private house but previously a restaurant specialising in Russian cuisine. All of this is part of an Inclosure as far as the Westhorpe (Blindle) stream which was allotted in 1779 to John Bromley; an area of 1 acre 16 perches **(see Map Nine Old Inclosures/Homesteads 45)**. Adjoining this Inclosure, on across the footpath, the roadway, which was all includ-

ed, together with the land on the left back to the Priors Marston road, was an allotment to John Bromley; a total area of 16 acres 13 perches **(see Map Nine Proprietors/ Owners 24)**. Additional detail on the Enclosure List gives "In lieu of land purchased off Checkley."

The Boddington Road
From the Boddington/Byfield Boundary through to the "Fiveways" crossroads, most of the enclosures were allotted on land up to the public road. The exception is the section of roadway between the two allotments to Cresent Boote and John Bromley; in both of these cases the roadway crosses, and is part of, their allotments and is not public road.

Because the roadway was on a gradient where it crossed the allotment to Cresent Boote this was known by the local people as "Boots Hill"

Moving down on over the Westhorpe stream (Blindle), from here on prior to street naming and numbering was known as "Back Way". The land immediately on the left, an area of 34 acres 10 perches, was allotted to James Smith, who is shown in the 1777 militia list as a farmer **(see Map Nine Proprietors/Owners 45)**.

The land immediately adjacent to the stream on the right allotted to John Smith, also shown in the 1777 Militia List as a farmer, was an area of 1 acre 3 roods 17

This is a photograph taken in the 1980s of "The Big Barn" in Boddington Road after it had been converted by John and Norah Frisby into a dwelling.

This photograph is annotated JR658 in the Byfield Photo Museum. Lender Mrs Pip Brimson

perches **(see Map Nine Proprietors/ Owners 36)**.

The next allotment on the right, allotted to James Smith, was an area of 4 acres 3 roods 20 perches **(see Map Nine proprietors/Owners 44)**, later to be part of a field which was to become known as Home Close **(see Map Nine point of interest 14)**. In the 1920s and 1930s there was both a tennis club and bowling club in Home Close, built by farmer Robert (Bob) Hutt.

Opposite on the left is a farm drive to a farmhouse that is now the centre of Beechcroft Farm, the owners of which are the Milnes family. Mrs Milnes is the youngest daughter of the late Bob and Ellen Hutt. A bridleway on the left leads through to Iron Cross.

Moving on, both allotments to the left and to the right were allotted to John Bliss; the land to the left being of 71 acres 31 perches **(see Map Nine Proprietors/Owners 34)**, later to be two fields named Pool Ground and Second Pool Ground. This land was one of two ironstone mining areas to be mined in Byfield before closure. The land to the right, an area of 2 acres 3 roods 33 perches **(see Map Nine Proprietors/Owners 33)**, was later named "Whitecroft". In the 1920s and 1930s there was a tennis court on "Whitecroft" built by W. H. Potter. The secretary of the club is shown in the Northamptonshire Directories in 1936 as Miss Betty Potter (W. H. Potter's great-niece).

Moving on again, both allotments to the left and to the right were to the same person. In this case they were allotted to Joseph Cox, the land to the left being 3 acres 2 rood 38 perches **(see Map Nine Proprietors/ Owners 43)**, later known as "Pump House Ground" due to the fact that within the field was a very strong spring which was used in conjunction with a force pump to supply drinking water. Today this water still flows but now discharges into the roadside ditch **(see Map Nine point of interest 15)**. This allotment is now the site of the Byfield Area Telephone Exchange. When telephones went on to the Subscriber Telephone Dialling system (S.T.D) gone for ever were the single digit telephone numbers – the Post Office Byfield 1(one), the Rectory 4, Russell's 6, Adams's shop 8.

The allotment on the right, again to Joseph Cox, was an allotment of 3 acres 1 rood 20 perches **(see Map Nine Proprietor/Owner 42)**, which is well known for specifically three things. It was known as the venue for the Byfield September "Colt Show", a well-attended area venue for horse colt and pony sales in the 1920s and 1930s; secondly for "Beastons Fun Fair", "set up" every year in the years before the Second World War; and thirdly it was chosen by Daventry Rural District Council as the site for the second development of municipal housing in Byfield, built in the 1930s and aptly named Jubilee Road. It was so named to commemorate the Silver Jubilee of King George V on May 6th 1935. (The King died in 1936.) With the advent of street naming and numbering in Byfield, this road was renamed Jubilee Close **(see Map Nine point of interest 16)**.

The next land on the left opposite Jubilee Close, an area of 32 acres 3 roods 7 perches, was in 1779 allotted to John Hitchcock **(see Map Nine Proprietors/Owners 39)**. On the roadside frontage of this allotment are today the premises of an agricultural engineering company housed in what was a redundant agricultural building, but which was converted to a workshop, stores and offices.

This photograph shows Jubilee Road from the Boddington Road in the late 1930s. It shows the estate not long after it was built.

This photograph is annotated JR743 in the Byfield Photo Museum. Lender Mr Donald Tomalin.

The eight newer houses in Boddington Road and Jubilee Close were built during the well-remembered very hard winter of 1946–47, when roads had up to six feet of driven snow blocking them. The construction of the houses was started in the autumn of 1946. Building was halted due to the adverse weather, and then completed in the spring of 1947.

As we reach the right hand bend, the land on the right was allotted to William Chambers, an area of 1 rood 34 perches **(see Map Nine Proprietors/Owners 105)**.

A very interesting entry in the enclosure documents refers to an area of land on the left on the apex of the bend. This was allotted to Thomas Wagstaff "Trustee for Driver's children" an area of 15 acres 26 perches **(see Map Nine Proprietors/Owners 41)**.

Entry in the enclosure documents re:
The Children of John Driver (Verbatim)

"To and for the said Thomas Wagstaff as Trustee for the said John Driver. Owners of one yard land given with common right there belonging to half a Lot of Bushes and half a plot of thorn and in lieu there of and all other their Estates rights and interest in and over the said open and common fields. One plot of land or ground containing fifteen acres and twenty six perches and now staked out and set exclusive of all roads and ways though and over the said same land of the annual value of sixteen pounds sixteen shillings and sixpence upon the Quality."

Notes by J.R.
Obviously John Driver had died, one would assume without a wife. And his children had inherited his rights in lieu of common that he held before the Enclosure Act of 1779. His children inherited this new allotment of fifteen acres twenty six perches under the supervision and protection of a Trustee, namely Thomas Wagstaff, as presumably they had not as yet "come of age".

Further round the bend, to the left before reaching the definitive footpath, was an Inclosure allotted in 1779 to Samuel Dumbleton, an area of 9 perches **(see Map Nine Old Inclosures/Homesteads 100)**. A building is shown on this allotment and also another building is shown on the 1882/83 Ordnance Survey Map, but not on the same footprint. The footprint on the second map coincides with the house that is now on the site and is today occupied by Mr and Mrs Greaves. Previous occupants in the 1930s and 1940s were Mr and Mrs E. Ward (grandparents of Mr Ken Lamb). Mr Ward was a founder member of "Byfield Cycling Club". Other occupants of the house were the Thompson family and Miss Hickcox.

Behind this land were two more plots, one allotted to William Dunkley of 3 perches, and one to George Turland of 7 perches **(see Map Nine Old Inclosures/Homesteads 96 and 97)**. These cottages were later referred to as Manor Farm Cottages. Some of the occupants over the years were: Mollie Adams; Eddie Barnes, William Eyles and

This photograph is of South View Cottage in Boddington Road at the time it was occupied by Miss Hickcox, in 1974

This photo is annotated JR652 in the Byfield Photo Museum. Lender Mrs Pip Brimson

his son Harry; the Turberville with the West Family. The present owners of Manor Cottage are the Cousins Family. The property has been extended and altered and an additional driveway has been provided, accessed from the Daventry Road.

Mollie Adams and the Lantern.

The late Cyril Nichols (1905–2001) related a story of one Mollie Adams who lived in Byfield next to Manor Cottage. Cyril had an aunt, a Mrs Tack, who was the wife of James Tack who farmed Manor Farm. Mollie used to visit Manor Farm, and on most occasions was given a "nip" of gin by Mrs Tack. Apparently Mollie was very partial to her "nip" of gin, so much so that when she was issued, as were all the other elderly parishioners in the parish prior to any form of street lighting, with a candle lantern, Mollie sold her newly acquired lantern to buy another "nip" or two of gin.

However! When details of the sale of the lantern became public knowledge a small community can be very cruel. Mollie became known as "Mollie swallow the lantern".

The large stone house on the left was once the farm house to Butterwell farm. The Inclosure of 2 roods 34 perches was allotted to John Hitchcock **(see Map Nine Old Inclosures/ Homesteads 99)**, as was the allotment adjoining, an area of 1 rood 3 perches **(see Map Nine Proprietors/Owners 40)**. The house and barn on the site today is shown on the same footprint as shown on the 1779 enclosure map and the 1882/83 Ordnance Survey Map.

The occupants of the house were: 1847 – Edmund Potter (1804–1879); 1866 – George Farebrother; 1871 – William Potter (1828–1869, father of W. H. and J. E. Potter); 1881 – John Edmund Potter (grandfather of Molly Potter (1908–1998), and Betty Potter (1912–2002); 1898 – Thomas H Brightwell; 1914 – George Ford (1861–1926); 1928 – William Ford; 1940 – Edward Thompson. The property then became a private house purchased in the 1960s by Doctor Tom and Mrs Winifrith, followed by Mr and Mrs O Tynan, in the 1970s.

Pretty Onions

Tom Winifrith, a lecturer at Warwick University, on passing the garden of Fred Hutt's house in Potters End on his way home, looked over the wall and spotted Fred in the garden planting his onion sets. On enquiring what they were, he was informed by Fred about the species and the planting

This photograph could have been of that very lantern, as it was owned before his demise by Cyril Nichols.

This photograph is annotated JR516 in the Byfield Photo Museum. Photo taken by Marion Eyles in 2001. Lender Marion Eyles.

This is a photograph of Butterwell Farmhouse, taken in the 1950s.

This photograph is annotated JR149 in the Byfield Photo Museum. Lender John Russell.

procedures. "I have some of those at home," said Tom and he duly went home and planted his "onion sets" as per Fred's instructions. Tom's onion sets grew, but Tom was a little surprised to find blooms appearing. He had selected the wrong species of "onion sets"; he had in fact planted Gladioli corms!

The next two modern brick-built houses on the left are on the same allotment; the first was built by Maurice Shepard in the 1980s and the second by Richard Lockyer in the 1990s.

The land with the cottages, on the left down to the bridge parapet, was part of the previous allotments to John Hitchcock. The cottages were built by James Hutt (1836–1885) between the very late 1850s and 1864 (**see Map Nine point of interest 17**).

James Hutt was the first of the well known Hutt family to settle in Byfield. He came to Byfield from Kidlington, Oxford and married a Byfield girl, Jane Carvel, on April 8th 1858. He was a carpenter and a wheelwright as well as being a farmer. His grandson, the late Fred Hutt, records that James Hutt worked on the restoration of Byfield Church in 1877.

James Hutt's Lathe

Victor A. Perry, grandson of James Hutt, has in his possession, handed down, a small rectangular table; the spindle/bobbin legs having been turned on a lathe in a small workshop adjacent to the bridge parapet, on the corner of High Street and Boddington Road. The lathe connected through to a waterwheel powered by the water flowing though a venturi built within the Cornbrook stream which ran through the premises. In living memory people remember the workshop

and have seen a lathe powered by a flywheel.

Notes by J.R.
It is highly likely that this lathe was started by using this flywheel, with the original inertia provided by hand or foot, and then the power to the lathe being supplemented by the flow of water.

James Hutt also built "Cosy Corner", the house on the "island" on the right around 1880. The premises remained in the Hutt family until the death of James Richard Hutt in December 1941. Various people rented the property, as accommodation was scarce, until council housing became available in the early 1930s. Mr Doug Hartwell and his wife rented one of the cottages at "Cosy Corner" before moving into No. 1 Jubilee Road in 1935. In 1942 Tom Lamb (1898–1956) controlled a taxi and carriers business from here; a business Tom had started originally from a base in Woodford when he was demobbed from the army after the First World War. Tom rented the larger of the two cottages, the other cottage being rented at the time by Mrs Bazeley. Later Tom Lamb purchased the cottages and converted them into one dwelling. His vehicles were not based at "Cosy Corner" but were garaged in a premises in Banbury Lane. Tom was followed in the Taxi business by his son Ken.

Mr and Mrs Herbert Eichler purchased the premises in the 1950s and ran a newsagent's business, at the same time that Mr Hebert Eichler ran a motor cycle repair operation from the old P.o.W. Camp. Mr Eichler is referred to in the Byfield Church Memorial book as being a Professional Soldier, who after internment and release made his home in Byfield.

This aerial photograph is of Cosy Corner taken in 1986 by Mike Bosley.

This photograph is annotated AS165 in the Byfield Photo Museum. Lender Mike Bosley.

Bridge Cottage is on the corner of what was Back Way and the Turnpike and was part of Potters End. today is on the corner of Boddington Road and the Main A361, and not part of Potters End. Bridge Cottage and the other buildings in the row were built by James Hutt. The photograph shows "Great Grandma" who was Jane Elizabeth Hutt (nee Carvel 1831- 1921) wife of James Hutt she is photographed with Bessie!

This photograph is annotated JR5 in the Byfield Photo Museum. Lender Mr & Mrs J.R. Hutt.

Today this land has roads all around it, but in 1779 there was no road. Where Potters End is today, the area is shown as a public open space.

The cottages built by James Hutt included a building that was later to be used as a garage. In the late1920s Denis Judd started his cycle repair business in these premises. He also rented one of the cottages. Life around the fireplace in the recession of the 1920s and 1930s is vividly recalled in Denis Judd's book "Living in the Country". The 1931 Northamptonshire Directory shows "Denis Allen Judd, cycle and motor cycle agent, and repairs". The cottage nearest the bridge was always known as "Bridge Cottage" and was occupied by William Eyles in 1881, and by Mrs Ellen C. Bagge in 1901. The building had a lean-to exten-sion added at a later date. This was used in conjunction with the house, but later was rented out to others, the last tenants being hairdressers, a Mr Andrews followed by a Mr Pratt. On the gable end of the house, over the top of the lean-to-extension, in the 1930s was an advertisement "J. R. Hutt The People's Outfitters". As the property was owned by the Hutt family they obviously had taken the opportunity to advertise the draper's shop in High Street. This was followed by another advertisement, this time for spares for "Durrant" cars. All of the cottages and outbuildings, including "Cosy Corner", are now used as private dwellings.

* * * * *

We have now reached the Five Ways cross roads.

CHAPTER EIGHT

POTTERS END

The BLACK NUMBERS are from the survey of Old Inclosures and Homesteads in the centre of the village.
The BLUE NUMBERS are Tracts of Land allotted to Proprietors and Owners in the rest of the parish.
The RED NUMBERS denote points of interest along the route.

Tracing from the 1779 Enclosure Map of Byfield with the road included and dotted outlines of more recent buildings .

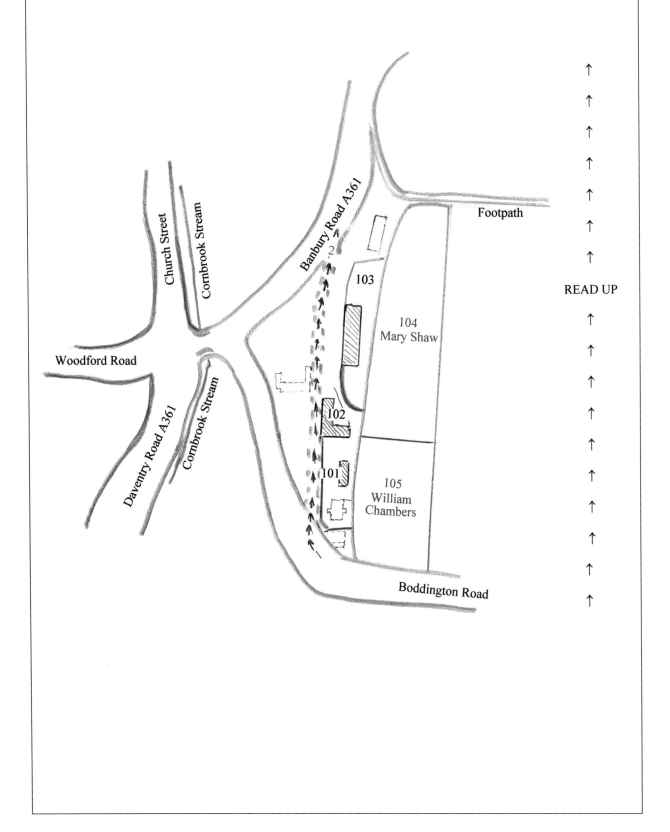

POTTERS END

(See Map Ten)

On the Enclosure Map of 1779 the roadway which today is named Potters End had not as yet been constructed. This roadway **(see Map Ten points of interest 1 to 2)**, is shown superimposed on the copy of the 1779 map. The first map to show a roadway is the 1882/83 Ordnance Survey Map.

We start walking along the roadway today known as Potters End from Boddington Road. The first Inclosure on the right, as shown on the 1779 Enclosure Map, was allotted to Richard Hiccock, an area of 19 perches **(see Map Ten Old Inclosures/Homesteads 101)**. Richard Hiccock was a farmer who was also allotted a large tract of land on Boddington Road.

The 1779 Enclosure Map shows one small building on this Inclosure, the footprint of which is not shown on the 1882/83 Ordnance Survey Map, but the property today known as "Turvins" is shown.

Records indicate that some of occupants included: 1866 – "The Fowke Doctors"; 1920 – Captain Cecil Fowke; 1924 – Mrs Mary Russell; – 1936 – Miss Helen Russell; 1945 – the Turberville family. It is interesting to note the Christian names of Mr Turberville: they were "George Noah Sollis"! 1950s – the Clare family, followed by the Linsey family.

The Fowke Family
The Northampton Directories record that from 1866 a Frederick Gustavus Fowke esq. lived in Byfield; 1874 – Frederick William Fowke M.D. surgeon; 1877 – Fowke and son surgeons; 1884 – Frederick William Fowke surgeon; 1906 – Frederick William Fowke is recorded as a "Private Resident"; 1920 – Captain Cecil W. Fowke.

The second Inclosure on the right was allotted to Samuel Lawrence, an area of 11 perches, **(see Map Ten Old Inclosures/Homesteads 102)**. The 1779 Enclosure Map shows an "L-shaped" building covering most of this allotment. The 1882/83 Ordnance Survey Map shows a building on some of this footprint. In living memory there were two semi-detached brick cottages on this site which were demolished in the 1950s. The last occupants were the Eyles family. The 1901 census shows a William Eyles and his wife Harriott living in Potters End. In the 1930s a family with the name of Butler lived in the cottage nearest the road, as did a character named Alfie Mold.

The 1777 militia list shows Samuel Lawrence as a mason. This list also records two more masons with the surname Lawrence! The Northamptonshire Directories, together with the Byfield censuses of 1871 and 1881, also give the detail that the Lawrence family lived in Potters End, with some listed as stonemasons.

It is interesting to note that, in the Causeway Charity records, a Thomas Lawrence supplied "stone for highways" on April 26th 1736 at a cost of £1-2s-0d.

The next Inclosure was allotted to Thomas Reynolds, an area of 19 perches. This included a building the footprint of which is shown on the 1882/83 Ordnance Survey Map. This footprint is an almost identical footprint of what today are two semi-detached stone cottages **(see Map Ten Old Inclosures/Homesteads 103)**.

The 1777 militia list gives Thomas Reynolds junior as a carpenter. The Byfield burial records show that Thomas Reynolds was buried in Byfield Churchyard in 1843 aged 86. This would make him twenty years of age when he was on the militia list, and twenty-two years of age when he was allotted the Inclosure. The 1841 Byfield Census shows a number of carpenters with the surname of Reynolds living in Potters End.

There would be a need for stonemasons, carpenters and other trades in the village at this time, between 1870 and 1874, and again in 1876, due to a large programme of remodelling, renovation and restoration to Byfield Church.

Byfield Church and a brief description of the work on the structure in the 1870s 1870–1874

- *Extensive repairs were completed on both the internal and external stonework.*
- *The chimney was removed from the south-west angle of the Chancel, and the adjacent low side window opened out and the area cleaned of soot.*
- *Wood floors were re-laid and ventilated.*
- *A roof of a new design was built in the Chancel, and the Nave roof was put back to its original pitch, which was then covered with slates instead of lead.*
- *The seats were extensively repaired.*
- *The old tombstone was removed from the east wall of the porch.*
- *Both the south and west galleries were removed and the tower arch opened out by removing the old brickwork.*
- *The "Three Decker" pulpit was taken out.*
- *The Reredos was taken out.*
- *The East Window, which had been covered by the Organ Chamber for the Barrel Organ, was opened up and the Organ Gallery taken down.*
- *With the money that was found to be surplus to requirements, the Spire was restored and a new lightning conductor fitted.*

1876

The whole of the north wall of the Chancel was pulled down, together with the Vestry which was on the north east corner. An Organ Chamber and a new Vestry were formed as an extension to the existing North Aisle, joined by a stone archway. All materials where appropriate were reused, including the windows, which were positioned to give the Chancel a more balanced appearance. The front of the organ when fitted would be in an archway between the Chancel and the Organ Chamber.

Other occupants of these cottages were: 1920s – Sergeant Judd, the Village Policeman, with his wife and young son Denis; this cottage was a billet for the local policeman.

When the police moved into the purpose-built house on the Woodford Road in the 1930s, Harry Ricketts (1887–1961), a porter at Byfield Station, and his family moved into the vacated cottage. In the 1940s Fred Hutt, well known long-serving churchwarden, bell ringer and chorister and his wife Janet, who was a daughter of Harry Ricketts, moved into the other cottage.

A list of Byfield's Police officers from the inception of the Northamptonshire County-funded Force up to the Second World War.

1881 – Police Constable Thomas Henshaw; 1894 – Police Constable Joseph Cottingham; 1898 – Police Sergeant Henry Tebby; 1903 – Police Sergeant Arthur Haynes; 1910 – Police Sergeant William Elliott; 1914 – Police Sergeant George Hardy Woodraffe; 1924 – Police Sergeant William Allen Day; 1926 – Police Sergeant Horace Allen Judd (1887–1961) who had served in the R.G.A. in the First World War as a Sergeant Major.

The number of Parish Constables from James Eyles and Robert Lord in 1852, up to William Edmunds in 1942, was a total of fifteen. It was at a Parish Council meeting in 1942 when Byfield Parish Council decided that there was no longer a need to have a Parish-funded civil Constable, as the size of the parish did not warrant his employment. (William Edmunds's remuneration at that time was one pound per annum).

Aspects of the duties of a Parish Constable in 1609

Constables shall search out rogues in each parish, apprehend vagrants, and take them before the Justices who shall commit them to a House of Correction.

When the roadway today known as Potters End was constructed it formed "an island of land" to the left side of Potters End, and two cottages were built on the island by James Hutt in the 1880s.

Continuing we now reach the High Street (**see Map Ten point of interest 2**).

A photograph of Hill View Cottage in Potters End in the 1920s showed when it was used as a Police House, complete with the Northamptonshire Police insignia over the door.

This photograph is annotated JR174 in the Byfield Photo Museum. Lender Mrs Janet Blake.

Street naming and numbering

Street naming and numbering in the parish of Byfield as we know today was only completed around 1960. Old names where applicable were used, new names were used where appropriate. Byfield Parish Council requested that all newly-built developments should be named after local Village Charities, hence the names Causeway, Lovett, Fessey, Curgenven, Thomas with Edwards, Greenwood, Knightley, Farebrother and the one just completed, Clock Meadow.

Other names that have been deemed appropriate and have been used include: Hutts Close, Becketts Close, Westhorpe Mews, and Whitecroft Lane.

Prior to the late 1950s and earlier we had names of streets, cottages, and areas which have long gone: Hitchcock's Shepherds Cottage: New Inn: Toll House: Old Banbury Turnpike: New Street: Crook Alley: Smiths Yard: Connecticut Row: Townsend Yard: Oxford Row: Barrack Row: Hopley's Yard: Tomalin's Yard (later to become Post Office Yard): Church Lane: The Jetty: Lower Green : Westhorpe End: Spinneys End: Boots Hill: Back Way: Station Fields: The Bell Inn: The New Bell Inn: (yes there were two Bell Inns both recorded on the 1901 Census!): Dolls Hill: Back Way: The Bridge: The Cattle Market: The Pound: Blacksmiths Yard: Bank Cottages Cross Street: The Yard Cross Street: Cross Tree Cottages (nicknamed by the residents as "Hell Yard"!): Alley Close: Tan Yard: Tanners Town End: Gooseberry Lane: School Hill: Cross Street (later to be Banbury Lane, so called because it crossed Main Street): Main Street (later to be Bell Lane and New Terrace).

One anomaly is Potters End, in that the roadway was named Potters End in the late 1950s but prior to that the title covered houses in what has been called "Back Way", now Boddington Road. The 1871 Census of Byfield shows thirteen dwellings with the address of Potters End. This is substantiated by the number of buildings shown on the 1882/83 Ordnance Survey Map.

The naming of a street or an area after a family name sometimes meant that they were the most prominent family by status, or by numbers of families with the same name in that area, hence Tomalin's Yard or Hopley's Yard. The reason why the name Potters End was used in 1871 was that the most eminent family in the area, living in one of those thirteen dwellings, were the Potter Family. The 1847 Northamptonshire Directory shows Edmund Potter (1804–1879) Farmer and Grazier; 1871 Census shows William Potter (1828–1869) Farmer of 61 acres employing two men, and the 1881 Census shows John Edmund Potter Farmer of 85 acres employing three men and two boys.

So "Potters' End" was the end of this part of Byfield where the eminent Potter family lived and the area was named on that basis.

MAP ELEVEN

WOODFORD ROAD

The BLACK NUMBERS are from the survey of Old Inclosures and Homesteads in the centre of the village.
The BLUE NUMBERS are Tracts of Land allotted to Proprietors and Owners in the rest of the parish.
The RED NUMBERS denote points of interest along the route.

Tracing from the 1779 Enclosure Map of Byfield with overlays with more modern additions.

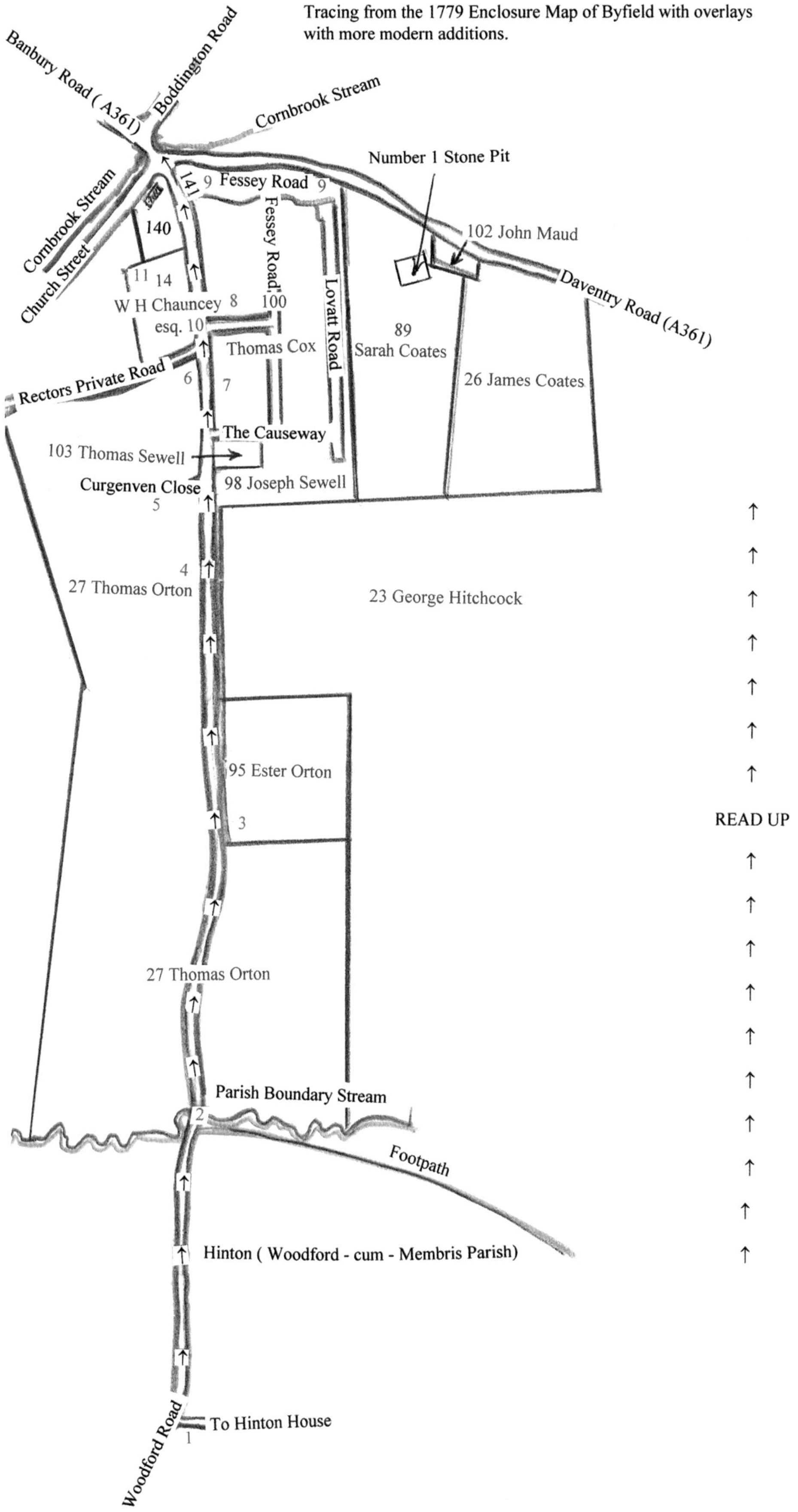

Banbury Road (A361)

Boddington Road

Cornbrook Stream

Cornbrook Stream

Number 1 Stone Pit

141
9 Fessey Road 9

140

102 John Maud

Church Street

Fessey Road

Cornbrook Stream

Lovatt Road

Daventry Road (A361)

11 14

W H Chauncey esq. 10

8
100

89
Sarah Coates

26 James Coates

Thomas Cox

Rectors Private Road

6
7

The Causeway

103 Thomas Sewell

Curgenven Close

98 Joseph Sewell

5

4

27 Thomas Orton

23 George Hitchcock

95 Ester Orton

↑
↑
↑
↑
↑
↑
↑

READ UP

3

↑
↑
↑
↑
↑
↑
↑
↑
↑
↑

27 Thomas Orton

Parish Boundary Stream

2

Footpath

Hinton (Woodford - cum - Membris Parish)

Woodford Road

To Hinton House

1

CHAPTER NINE

WOODFORD ROAD

(See Map Eleven)

Starting towards Byfield with the Gate-House to Hinton House on our right, **(see Map Eleven point of interest 1)**, as we move forward Hinton House itself is further over on our right; both buildings were built by Charles Cunningham Church around 1900.

On this route we are entering Byfield from the east; the 550 ft. (168 metres) contour crosses this road immediately before it descends into the village. When the east wind is blowing no snow collects on Woodford Road, as the road runs east to west. As we move towards the village the area is deemed to be "two overcoats colder" than down in the village.

Back to our journey, moving forward we come to "The Dip" **(see Map Eleven point of interest 2)**, so named by locals because the road dips, twists to the right, goes over the culvert of a stream and then twists to the left whilst rising sharply up again. The stream is the boundary between the parishes of Woodford-cum-Membris and Byfield.

Immediately we cross the Parish boundary the long strip of land on the left, reaching down to the Manor House Grounds, was allotted to Thomas Orton in 1779, an area of 59 acres 2 roods 18 perches **(see Map Eleven Proprietors/Owners 27)**. This was later named "Woodford Road Ploughing". This allotment joined the Inclosure which Thomas Orton was also allotted of 2 acres 2 roods 31 perches land in Church Street; the land on which Deene Cottage stands. It is likely that he lived in Deene Cottage. It is recorded in the 1777 militia list that Thomas Orton was a farmer.

The allotments along the Woodford road **(see Map Eleven Proprietors/Owners 27, 95 and 14)** were later part of Manor Farm and were owned and/or rented by: 1841 – William Barnes; 1851 – Edward Barnes; 1881 – William Owen Cole; 1884 – Thomas Jones; 1890 – John Barratt; 1894 – Charles W Barratt; 1898 – James Rand; 1906 – James Tack; 1924 – Geoffrey Treadwell; 1947 – Darbishire Farms Ltd; 1970 – David Green of Staverton; 1974 – E .W. and R. W. Watts.

The land on the right immediately over the boundary stream allotted in 1779 was also part of Thomas Orton's allotment **(see Map Eleven Proprietors/Owners 27)**. This is followed on the right by an allotment of 6 acres 1 rood allotted to Ester Orton, later to be named "Old Hester" **(see Map Eleven Proprietors/Owners 95)**. The part of the field abutting the right hand hedge of the Woodford road was, in the 1930s, the Byfield village football ground. In this spot was also a low area which in the winter was flooded and was used by the village children as a sliding and skating playground **(see Map Eleven point of interest 3)**.

The next allotment on the right was allotted in 1779 to George Hitchcock and was bounded on the east by the Hinton Lordship and on the west in part by the Daventry road (A361). This allotment was an area of 106 acres 2 roods 26 perches **(see Map Eleven Proprietors/Owners 23)**. On the left hand side, about halfway between the Parish boundary and the village, between the late 1940s and the late 1980s was the football ground of Byfield Athletic Football Club **(see Map Eleven point of interest 4)**.

A notable aspect of this area, together with the cricket field one field over, was the stratum of the ground which, with ironstone being close to the surface, gave it the ability to drain freely. On very few occasions after heavy winter rainfall was the football pitch in such a condition that the match had to be called off.

The fact regarding the stratum of the ground was borne out from the detail entered onto some Ordnance Survey maps of the time, which had inscribed across the whole area: "Area subject to Mineral Rights for future ore extraction".

Of the next two small allotments on the right, the first was allotted to Joseph Sewell and the second to Thomas Sewell; one being an allotment of 2 acres 3 roods 27 perches **(see Map Eleven Proprietors/Owners 98)** and the other of 2 roods 27 perches **(see Map Eleven Proprietors/Owners 103)**.

The houses on the left, opposite these two allotments, were built in the 1990s by a Housing Association, primarily as "Starter Homes" so that young couples in the parish could have the opportunity to buy a share in their first home **(see Map Eleven point of interest 5)**. Unfortunately, even when purchasing on a shared equity basis, the houses were too expensive for young couples to afford. Subsequently only three of the houses were sold and seven rented through the Housing Association. The development was named "Curgenven Close" after the Reverend Francis Henry Curgenven, the Rector of Byfield from 1872 to 1901, who was also the inaugural Chairman of Byfield Parish Council in 1894. He is interred in Byfield Churchyard in a grave on the south side of the chancel.

The next house on the left was built by Mr and Mrs Jim Smith in the 1930s and was used as a shop which was run by Mrs E. D. (Daisy) Smith, whose husband Jim was the manager of the Byfield Ironstone Company until its closure in 1965.

On the closure of the shop, the premises became a private house, which was purchased and extended by Mr and Mrs Colin Cooknell, **(see Map Eleven point of interest 6)**.

The next allotment on the right was the allotment in 1779 to Thomas Cox, an area of 12 acres 1 rood 30 perches **(see Map Eleven Proprietors/ Owners 100)**. This land was later, in the 1920s, owned by the Lord of the Manor A. R. T. Cartwright and farmed by J. R. Hutt. The land was listed at the April 19th 1925 meeting of Byfield Parish Council as a suitable site for local authority housing. The site was purchased by Daventry Rural District Council in the late 1920s to enable them to build local authority housing.

At the meeting of the Parish Council on September 25th 1925, a circular was received from the "House Town and Planning Committee", regarding the provision of local housing. A resolution was passed by the meeting that 12 houses as a minimum were required; 8 of Non- Parlour type and 4 of Parlour type. It was suggested that the maximum rent should be 4/6 a week plus rates.

The first 12 houses to be built, in 1928, were on the Woodford Road. Almost immediately there was a damp problem with some of these houses, especially those exposed to the weather with rain beating on outside walls. This ingress of water through the nine inch solid brickwork, was rectified by the landlord, Daventry Rural District Council.

On the east end of the row of these first twelve houses, in the early 1930s, the Northamptonshire County Council built a detached house for the village constable **(see Map Eleven point of interest 7)**.

Occupants were P.C. Lee : P.C. Jarratt : P.C. Grey : P.C. Brown : P.C. Dexter : P.C. Makepeace : P.C. Stroud and a second P.C. Lee. The house was sold off in the1980s to become a private house. The rest of the houses in Woodford Road were built together with houses in Fessey Road; the later ones built in the early 1930s had external cavity walls.

The Wartime Constable

The first P.C. Lee served as the local Policeman in the Second World War. P.C. Lee had to enforce wartime regulations, one of those being the "Blackout" conditions, which were that no light should be shown at night that would in any way assist German aircraft. This was rigidly enforced by P.C. Lee. As he was keen and, some would say, rather devious in his methods, he was always known as "Leery Lee". Many a household has been alarmed by the loud incessant knocking on a door or window followed by the words "Put that b— light out! Don't you know there's a war on."

All of these houses had piped water and flush toilets prior to the village being on a supply of mains water. This was achieved by sinking a well, on a site situated to the rear of what today is number 22 Woodford Road, and pumping water into a water tower to give the head of water pressure, **(see Map Eleven point of interest 8)**. The well was capped after mains water became available in 1937, and eventually the water tower was dismantled.

This is a photograph of the purpose-built Police House on Woodford Road; the photograph was taken by Cameron Fraser. The position from where the photograph was taken is on the site of the Woodford Road end of a thirty feet wide private road to the Rectory, which was constructed for the use of the Rector John Knightley after the Enclosure of 1779.

This photograph is annotated AS118 in the Byfield Photo Museum. Lender Cameron Fraser.

This photograph taken in 1971 is of "the road with no name"; it is in fact the link road between the Woodford Road and Fessey Road. The photograph shows the water tower which was built to give a head of water to the estate before the provision of mains water.

This photograph is annotated AS117 in the Byfield Photo Museum. Lender Mr Cameron Frazer.

To extend the existing Council Housing stock provision on this site, further land was purchased in the early 1950s consisting of part of what was **98 and 103** on Map Eleven. The houses in "The Causeway" were built and named after the oldest of the Byfield village charities. Followed by the houses on the left side of Lovett Road, again named after a Byfield village charity, the other houses in Lovett Road were built in progression after that.

When the main drainage was being installed to service these houses, the trenches were at a considerable depth below ground level. The site looked like a stone quarry due to the stratum of the ground being made up of large quantities of ironstone.

All of these houses were at first issued with the address of "Dolls Hill" and numbered to around 100. Later, with street naming and numbering in the late 1950s, houses were numbered in individual streets.

The private housing estate at the west end of Fessey Road was built by or through Donald Cugini in the 1980s, **(see Map Eleven points of interest at 9)**.

Fessey Road (Notes by J.R.)

Most new housing estates in Byfield are named after the village charities, Fessey Road being one of them. In February 1914 the Rector, who was at that time Rev. W. H. Rankin, considered there was a misunderstanding regarding the intentions of Joseph Fessey, the benefactor of the charity. So the Rector decided to clarify the situation with an article in the Church Magazine.

Fessey Gift (copied verbatim): "As misunderstanding has been sometimes found to exist with respect to the intentions of Joseph Fessey when he bequeathed a sum of money for investment, the annual interest of which is called the "Fessey Gift", it may be useful to give here an extract from the will of the Benefactor. 'I direct my Trustees to purchase the sum of £1,200 two and a half per cent Consols, and to transfer the same into the names of the Charity Commissioners for England and Wales, to be held by them in Trust for the Incumbent and Church Wardens for the time being of the parish of Byfield, to be applied by them for the benefit of the aged, infirm and deserving poor of that parish. I direct that they should apply the annual income in giving on Saint Thomas Day 10/- to each such poor inhabitants as they, or a majority of them shall in their discretion select. I desire that each charitable donation shall be denominated the "Joseph Fessey gift".'

"It is to be noticed here that no special mention is made of Widowers or Widows as such. Who are to have the preference are the aged, the infirm and the deserving. Widowers and Widows would often be found among these. The money must be given as far as it is possible to those who have one of these qualifications, who are aged, or infirm, or deserving without being aged or infirm."

The road serving this private housing estate was not put forward for adoption to the Highway Authority by the developer and as such is a private road.

On the left, before entering the site, a shop was built in the 1970s by Mr and Mrs Tom Davies. They named the shop "Handy Stores". This is today a private house.

Back to Woodford Road, opposite the entrance into the housing estate. At the request of the occupants of the estate, a brick and tiled-roof bus shelter was built by voluntary labour, with materials provided through Byfield Parish Council, **(see Map Eleven point of interest 10)**.

A private road was constructed in 1779, from the left side of what was then the public road from Byfield to Hinton, (today would be Byfield to Woodford), across to the Glebe land adjacent and to the east of Byfield Rectory, **(see Map Eleven)**. This roadway is clearly marked on the 1779 Byfield Enclosure Map. Today the position of the entrance to this road would be opposite number 32 Woodford Road.

References to the detail of the Enclosure Act 1779 and the allotments specifically in this case private of roads Private Roads for the Rector
(Details copied verbatim)

One private road or way of a width of thirty foot from the north part of the allotment to the said John Knightly, for his glebe through and over an allotment to the said Thomas Orton and by the East end of the allotment to the said William Henry Chauncy, into the said public road from Byfield to Hinton. For the use and convenience of the said John Knightly and his successors Rectors, as aforesaid and his and their friends, servants, agents and workmen from time to time and at all times hereafter to pass and re-pass on foot or on horseback or in their carriages, wagons and carts, excepted upon all his and their necessary occasions, he and they, from time to time and at all times forever hereafter and his and their own costs and charges funding repairing and keeping, in repair the gates and the gate posts between the allotment for his glebe and the allotment to the said Thomas Orton.

The said John Knightly having made such recompense and satisfaction in land out of the said Glebe lands to the said Thomas Orton, as we the said commissioners have thought a fair and adequate compensation for the same.

Notes by J.R.

This roadway, long gone, is now indicated by a wide gap on the Woodford road (not Hinton as in the above) opposite number 32 Woodford Road and adjacent to Dolls Hill Cottage. The roadway would have entered the Rectory grounds in what today is the second paddock east of the Rectory walled garden.

Obviously Thomas Orton agreed, with the authority of the Commissioners, to allow this private road across his allotment on receiving recompense, by way of a portion of the glebe land which was allotted to the Rector John Knightley in the Byfield Enclosure.

On the east side, on land on which the present Manor House stands, was a rear entrance to Manor Farm leading to a large stone barn built on an allotment to William Henry Chauncy on an area of 3 acres 2 roods **(see Map Eleven Proprietors/Owners 14)**.

In the 1960s Darbishire Farms Ltd operated a large deep-litter poultry unit on the site, which sadly ended when the flock contracted fowl pest and had to be slaughtered, **(see Map Eleven point of interest 11)**.

Continuing towards the centre of Byfield, halfway down the hill, towards the road junction, was a small Inclosure on the right allotted in 1779 to Richard Sewell, an area of 19 perches **(see Map Eleven Old Inclosures/Homesteads 141)**. The 1901 census indicates that a house had been built on this site and named "Mount Pleasant", which was occupied by Helen Sicar. In the 1950s and 1960s it was occupied by a Mr Benson. The footprint shown on this site on the 1779 Enclosure Map is of a similar size as the footprint of the house today, but is "side on" to the road. The footprint shown on the 1882/83 Ordnance Survey Map is similar to the footprint of the house today.

We have now reached the Fiveways crossroads.

CHAPTER TEN

THE PRIORS MARSTON ROAD

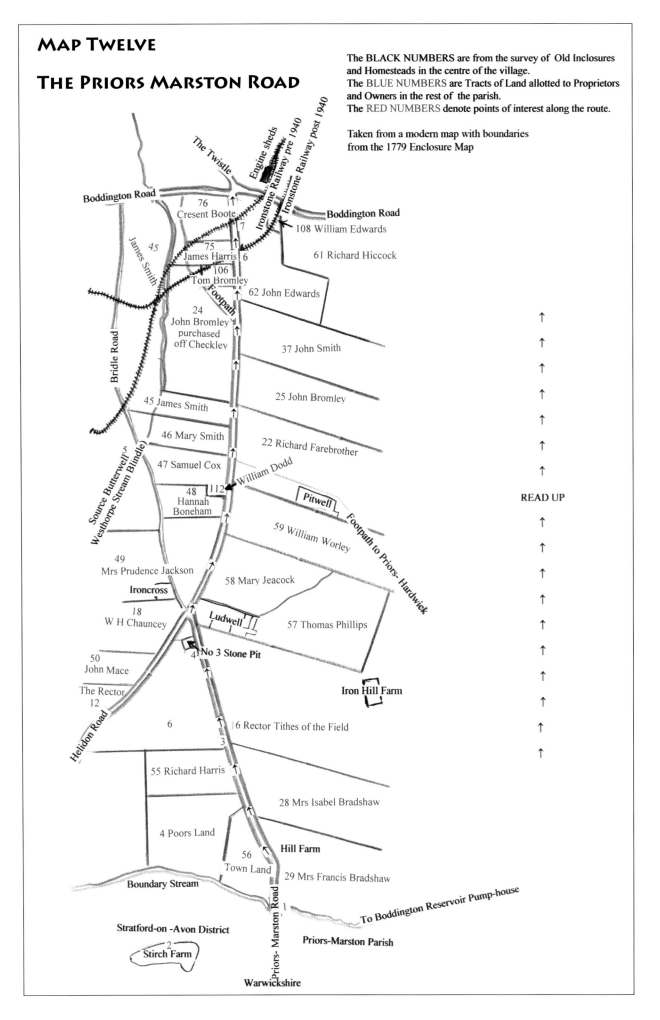

Map Twelve

The Priors Marston Road

The BLACK NUMBERS are from the survey of Old Inclosures and Homesteads in the centre of the village.
The BLUE NUMBERS are Tracts of Land allotted to Proprietors and Owners in the rest of the parish.
The RED NUMBERS denote points of interest along the route.

Taken from a modern map with boundaries from the 1779 Enclosure Map

The Twistle

Engine sheds

Ironstone Railway pre 1940

Ironstone Railway post 1940

Boddington Road

76 Cresent Boote

7

108 William Edwards

Boddington Road

James Smith

45

75 James Harris 6

61 Richard Hiccock

106 Tom Bromley

Footpath

62 John Edwards

Bridle Road

24 John Bromley purchased off Checkley

37 John Smith

25 John Bromley

45 James Smith

46 Mary Smith

22 Richard Farebrother

Source Butterwell

Westhorpe Stream Blindle

47 Samuel Cox

William Dodd

48 Hannah Boneham

112

Pitwell

Footpath to Priors-Hardwick

59 William Worley

49 Mrs Prudence Jackson

58 Mary Jeacock

Ironcross

18 W H Chauncey

Ludwell

57 Thomas Phillips

No 3 Stone Pit

50 John Mace

The Rector

12

Iron Hill Farm

Helidon Road

6

16 Rector Tithes of the Field

3

55 Richard Harris

28 Mrs Isabel Bradshaw

4 Poors Land

56 Town Land

Hill Farm

29 Mrs Francis Bradshaw

Boundary Stream

1

To Boddington Reservoir Pump-house

Stratford-on-Avon District

Priors-Marston Parish

Stirch Farm

2

Priors-Marston Road

Warwickshire

READ UP

Chapter Ten

The Priors Marston Road

(See Map Twelve)

On this route, one of two routes from the north entering the parish of Byfield, the bed of the stream at the bottom of Holcombe Hill marks the divisions between the counties of Warwickshire and Northamptonshire, the districts of Stratford-on-Avon and Daventry and the parishes of Priors Marston and Byfield **(see Map Twelve point of interest 1).**

Immediately on the right is Hill Farm, which at the time of the Enclosure in 1779 was made up of two plots of land of almost equal size. The first, abutting the stream, was allotted in 1779 to Mrs Frances Bradshaw, an area of 55 acres 2 roods 7 perches, **(see Map Twelve Proprietors/ Owners 29)**, and the second to Mrs Isabel Bradshaw, an area of 58 acres 3 roods 24 perches **(see Map Twelve Proprietors/ Owners 28)**. The Bradshaws also owned property in Westhorpe Lane which today is owned and occupied by Peter and Joan Bickley. They owned some other property in Bell Lane.

Previous to the Enclosure, Aholiab West Bradshaw of Priors Marston owned the holdings. He bequeathed them to Isabel Bradshaw, his mother, and Frances Bradshaw, his wife, in his will dated 1769. All of the property owned by the Bradshaw family was sold by auction, at the Wheatsheaf Hotel Daventry, on Wednesday 16th of August 1828, at 4 o'clock in the afternoon. The purchasers would have been the Thellusson family, either at the auction or a short time after.

The Farmers at Hill Farm were: 1841 – Thomas Fancott (born in 1805, died in 1845 having been killed in an accident, using a young horse and being trapped between the shafts of a cart and a gate post); 1845 – Harriett Fancott (1806 – 1889); 1863 – Richard Bilson; 1890 – Henry Fancott; 1891 – John H. Turner; 1901 – George Smith; 1924 – John and Charles Oliver; 1936 – John Oliver; 1942 – John Spencer, whose family still own and occupy the farm. Farmers are not necessarily owners, and some farms, land and/or houses are sub-let.

Hill Farm and the Thellusson ownership

The Northamptonshire Directories within the preamble of the script for each Parish give a list of principal land owners. The Byfield pages of the 1869 and 1874 Directories refer to a Lord Rendlesham, the 1877 refers to a C. S. A. Thellusson, together with other members of the Thellusson family up to and including the 1919 entry, with an address of Brodsworth Hall, Doncaster, as being principal land owners in Byfield.

Obviously it was something of a mystery as to why a family living so far away should own land in Byfield. On the way north journeying to a Northumberland holiday the author

paid a visit to Brodsworth, now owned by English Heritage, and discovered that Lord Rendlesham was a member of the Thellusson family, and the Thellusson family were Huguenot (Protestant) landowners in the Lyons area of France, who fled to Switzerland to escape religious persecution in the mid-sixteenth century. The family always showed great financial acumen. Theophile Thellusson (1645 – 1705) established a financial business, which his son Isaac turned into a bank, and Peter Thellusson (1735 – 1797) amassed a huge fortune. At his death it was estimated at around £700,000, or approximately £34 million at today's prices. The terms of his will were unusual and caused an immediate sensation, with his family contesting them in the courts. It has been famous ever since.

After bequests to his family of £100,000, the remainder of Peter Thellusson's fortune was left in trust to accumulate during the lives of any of his sons, grandsons and great-grandsons who were alive at his death.

On the death of the last of these, the estate would be divided between "the eldest male lineal descendants of my three sons left living". If there were no such descendants, it was to be used to pay off the National Debt! There were widespread concerns that fortunes of this size, accumulated for so long and concentrated in the hands of a few individuals, might be so vast as to disturb the economy of the whole country.

Thellusson's immediate family disputed the will in court soon after his death, but in spite of severe criticism it was upheld. Because of the serious issues involved, in 1800 Parliament passed the Accumulations Act, often called the Thellusson Act, which limited the time property could be left to accumulate to a period of no more than 21 years.

At the time of Peter Thellusson's death, nine of his sons and grandsons were alive. With the death in 1856 of the last of them – his grandson Charles – the long period governed by the will eventually came to an end. The final court judgement declared that the inheritance should be shared by two people, Frederick George Thellusson, the fourth Lord Rendlesham, (1825 – 1896) and Charles Sabine Augustus Thellusson, (1822 – 1885). There are parallels with the case of Jarndyce v. Jarndyce in Dickens's "Bleak House". Dickens himself said his novel reflected various celebrated cases of the day.

Lands held as part of Charles Sabine Augustus Thellusson's inheritance include land in Yorkshire 8,800 acres, (Brodsworth Hall being by far the largest landholding of 8,000 acres), Durham 810 acres, Hertfordshire 685 acres, Warwickshire 1,496 acres, and Northamptonshire 295 acres.

The Northamptonshire land holding was: Byfield Hill Farm – tenant in 1863 Bilson, £100 P.A. rent, 115 acres, house and buildings, arable and grassland; and Clem

Vengeance Farm Charwelton – tenants Frederick G. and H. H. Fowke, £130 P. A. rent, 180 acres, arable and grassland. The Fowke family originated from Priors Marston

With regard to the Thellusson family ownership of the farm, and the contacts that the author has had with English Heritage, a member of staff from Brodsworth Hall visited Byfield in 2004, and was shown around the farms in the area that had been owned by the Thellussons, one of course being Hill Farm, Byfield. The reason for the visit was to see if the architecture, model and style of the house and farm buildings were the same as those around Brodsworth Hall in Yorkshire. The result of the viewing was that Hill Farm is of the same model, style and architecture as the buildings around Brodsworth Hall; so it is now known that the farm house and buildings were built by the Thellusson family in the 1860s.

Immediately on entering the parish, over the boundary stream, to the left is a plot of land marked "Town Land", having been allotted to the Trustees of Byfield and Westhrop Land. This was an area of 10 acres 2 roods 26 perches **(see Map Twelve Proprietors/Owners 56)**. This was later to be called "The Causeway", as the rent from it was used for the upkeep of the Causeways (roads) and other charitable causes. It is the oldest recorded parochial charity in the Parish of Byfield, dated the sixth day of January the thirteenth year of the reign of Henry the Eighth.

Some details of the records and financial ledgers of the Charity make interesting reading.

A meeting is recorded to have been held at "The Parsonage House" on the 25th day of April 1664, which was the day set aside in the Church Calendar to celebrate the Feast of the Evangelist Saint Mark. A meeting was held every year on this special day.

Date	Item	Amount £-s-d
Some Expenses Recorded		
April 26th 1736	Thomas Lawrence stones for Highways	£1-2-0
1831	Work on poor houses in the Jetty Glazing	£2-6-2
1831	Work on poor houses in the Jetty Tar Cord and Gas Tar	£0-6-0
1831	Work on poor houses in the Jetty Mr Tew Bricks and Lime	£0-7-6
1831	Work on poor houses in the Jetty Richard Reynolds Window Frame	£0-6-6
1831	Work on poor houses in the Jetty Rob Douglas for Thatching	£3-3-6
1832	Ann Gardner for Beer	£0-1-3
1840	Beesoms (Brooms)	£0-8-0

Date	Item	Amount £-s-d
1843	Westhorps Well, Bricks	£11-0-0
1846	Property Tax	£1-6-4
1855	Rates for Cottages	£0-9-0
1858	Fire at Jetty cottages, men working Fire Engine	£0-10-0
1868	J. Hutt two new gates and sheep pens	
1868	Railway carriage to Fenny Compton	£3-0-0
1868	Mr Hardy, Nuneaton, for Bricks	£44-5-0
1868	Mr. Botterill, carriage to Marston Dolls	£17-3-9
1874	G. Elkington and J. Burbidge, mounding and hanging gates	£3-18-9
1877	G. Brown, coal	£5-9-2
Some income recorded		
1747	Rent for School House	£1-0-0
1757	"The Town Houses": rent	£0-18-0
1855	Rates for cottages	£0-9-0

The Causeway Charity

In the book "The Story of Byfield" written by a Byfield Schoolmaster, E. F. Poole, in 1930, the section headed Byfield Charities states (copied verbatim):

"The earliest charity recorded is that known as the "Causeway" Charity.

" 'Thomas Shaw of this parish by deed dated the thirteenth year of the reign of King Henry the Eighth gave a messuage and appurtenances in this prsh. to repair ye common wayes in Byfield and for other charitable uses there.

" 'The appurtenances of this messuage may be supposed to be ye arable land at this time in the occupation of Peter Pressidge ye tenant holding ye same of the present Trustees. [The names follow.] … as by deed … dated the First day of June in the Fourth year of the reign of King James 2nd may appear.' "

"A later hand has inserted the word 'church' between 'common' and 'wayes'.

"A blessing upon the bones of Thomas Shaw! His was a sane and practical benefaction. Possibly he lived far enough from the church to find the ways a handicap in winter. Roads, ill-made and badly kept, were rutted with quagmires. With Tudor foresight he made it possible to walk dry-shod from one end of the village to the other."

The next plot of land on the left, also a "Charity field", was allotted to The Rector, Lord of the Manor, Church Wardens and Overseers of the Poor of Byfield, having an area of 17 acres 2 roods 34 perches. **(see Map Twelve Proprietors/Owners 4)**. This charity was to become known as

"The Poors Allotment". The revenue from the rent was apportioned to the poor, initially in coal, but during the Second World War, because coal was in short supply, the charity distributed money. This situation lasted until 1953, when the charity once again distributed coal. In later years, when the use of coal fires diminished, other forms of benefit within the spirit of the charity were used.

Byfield Land Letting – Notes by J.R.

Both the Causeway Charity and the Poors Allotment were let on the first Friday after Easter, according to recognised custom, by auction. The manner and system of the auction was unique, in as much as the auctioneer accepted a bid, he placed his index finger in the centre of a small round table, and proceeded to walk around the table in an orderly fashion three times; after the third time he made for the door again in an orderly fashion, and if he managed to get through the door and close it behind him the bid was accepted; if not the whole procedure started again.

The yearly auction was held in one of the village public houses, each one taking it in turn; obviously being establishments which sold intoxicating beverages, normality of the proceedings was hard to maintain! The auctioneer's gyrations around the table became slightly less orderly with the effects of good beer and multiple bids.

The charities records show that in 1960, with the well known auctioneer Bert Wingrove(1909–1973) officiating, for the Causeway field, 33 bids were received; with 87 walks round the table and the closing bid of £74, the land was "knocked down" to Mr Joe Spencer of Dodds Farm (brother of John Spencer, who farmed Hill Farm). For the Poors Allotment 63 bids were received, with 126 walks round the table, and with a closing bid of £144 the land was "knocked down" to Mr Jimmy McKeen of Stirch Farm. **(see Map Twelve point of interest 2)**.

The last auctioneer before the fields were sold was Mr Tim Hutt, a member of the old family of Hutt, a branch of which had been associated with the administration of the Byfield Charity fields for a considerable number of years.

Conditions

"The conditions of letting the Poors Land in the Parish of Byfield was from April until March the following year containing 17 acres 2 roods 34 perches or thereabouts.

"The land is not to be ploughed or mown but grazed and the thistles and nettles kept down and the manure broken.

"The rent to be paid to the Trustees on or before the end of September next.

"The person who shall take this lot will be required at the time of letting to find a responsible person jointly with himself to become security for the payment of the rent when due.

"Thistles to be mown by 7th day of August."

In 1953 the land letting was recorded on radio, and at a later date was shown on television.

In the late 1990s both of the charity fields were sold to Mr Peter Hazlewood of Stirch Farm, just over the border in Warwickshire. His farm was directly adjacent to the Causeway field and to Poors Allotment on the other side of the boundary stream! The money was invested and the interest is still used for charitable purposes in Byfield Parish. The only thing that has been lost is the cut and thrust of that "Eastertide unique table-walking auction"!

Still on the left, the next allottment was to a Richard Harris, an area of 12 acres 3 roods 3 perches; this was later named Holcombe Hill Ground **(see Map Twelve Proprietors/Owners 55)**.

In our mind's eye we have travelled up this steep escarpment, from the boundary stream to this point now on level ground, a rise of some 134 feet (as a comparison this would be roughly the height of Byfield Church from churchyard to the gilded cockerel) **(see Map Twelve point of interest 3)**. Looking first left and then right there is a large tract of land of 181 acres 2 roods 12 perches which in 1779 was allotted to the Rector for "Tithes of the Field" **(see Map Twelve Proprietors/Owners 6)**. It ran from the Hellidon to Byfield Road, across this, the Priors Marston to Byfield road, and down to the Boddington parish boundary to the west. This later became Iron Hill farm. One of the farm barns has a "date stone" on it showing details of 1780 I. K. One can safely assume that the rector had the barn built (possibly by I.K!) after the allotment of the land in 1779.

This holding of 181 acres was the acreage of the largest of the Tithes of the Fields allotments. It was farmed by John Barratt in 1841. Subsequent farmers were: 1849 – John Harris; 1871 – Joseph Holden (1816–1888), shown in 1881 to have retired into a cottage in "Church Lane Byfield"; 1881 – John Hammond; 1891 – Edwin Ward (died in 1919 of an epidemic of "Spanish Flu", which "raged throughout the World"); 1920 – Mrs E Ward; 1924 – Mrs E Ward and son; 1928 – Thomas Kenneth Ward (1901–1961); 1961 – Mrs M D Ward; followed by Mr and Mrs B Deacon, (Mrs P Deacon née Ward), whose family still own and live in the farm.

On the left, just before we reach the road from Hellidon, the 1779 Enclosure Map shows a public stone pit, shown as No 3 Stone Pit, known as "Grindall Pits" **(see Map Twelve point of interest 4)**.

The 1871 census shows that the amount of land farmed from Iron Hill was 340 acres.

The next allotment on the right was to Thomas Phillips, an area of 31 acres 2 roods 2 perches **(see Map Twelve Proprietors/Owners 57)**; the adjacent allotment was to Mary Jaycock of 17 acres 3 roods 14 perches **(see Map Twelve Proprietors/Owners 58)**. These two allotments were later to become the property of William Harris Potter. When the two allotments were divided up, the fields became named Ludwell, Bottom Ludwell, Middle Ludwell and, the field fronting the road, Potters Byfield Field.

Ludwell is deemed to mean "Loud Spring", written Lodewell in 1247.

William Harris Potter became an eminent land owner. In 1926 he decided to build himself and his wife Mary Ellen a stone house on the right, to be named Ludwell.

Ludwell was very deliberately built exactly 100 years after his paternal grandfather, John Harris, had built a house "over the road" to our left, and named it Iron Cross House in 1826.

This is a photograph of "Ludwell" built in 1926 for Mr William Harris Potter by Kenches of Eydon. This photograph was taken on the completion of the building of the house.

This photograph is annotated JR1045 in the Byfield Photo Museum. Lenders Mr and Mrs Harris-Watson

This is a photograph of the house built by John Harris in 1826. This shows Lord and Lady Innes-Kerr sitting under the awning, just before the First World War.

This photograph is annotated JR87 in the Byfield Photo Museum. Lenders Mr & Mrs Harris-Watson.

To construct Ludwell a lot of the building materials, including the stone, the front door and two bay windows for the house, were obtained from a large house being demolished in Ashby St. Legers, and were transported by horse and cart.

William Harris Potter never lived in the house, because his wife Mary Ellen was reluctant to leave "Whitecroft", a house she loved which is in what is now Banbury Lane. Ludwell was let for a period to James C. H. Blyth, after which the Potters' daughter Audrey, who had married in 1927 to become Mrs W. H. Watson, moved into Ludwell in 1934. Mr Walter Herbert Watson F.R.C.O., L.R.A.M. was a composer and organist. The family line still continues, as the youngest son of Mrs and Mrs Watson, namely Keith Harris-Watson, and his family still live in the house his grandfather built!

The "house over the road", namely Iron Cross House, is now to the left. In 1779 the allotment of the land was to Mrs Prudence Jackson, an area of 35 acres 2 roods 38 perches (see Map Twelve Proprietors/Owners 49), later on to be named "Iron Cross Ground" – "Old Barn" – "House Ground" and "Slade". This allotment has a definitive bridleway diagonally across it, starting along the drive of Iron Cross House and entering Byfield village on the Boddington road.

As previously stated, the house was built by John Harris in 1826 when he was a fairly young man of 26. He lived in the house until he died in 1871, at which time the farmed acreage was 149 acres.

The John Harris Trust
*When John Harris died in 1871 the Northamptonshire Directories record that he left his estate in trust. It is indicated in the list of principal land owners that the trustees of the late John Harris were trustees in 1877 and up to 1906, a period of 29 years. This time span would **not** have been possible due to the Accumulations Act (Thellusson Act) of 1800, which limits the time that property could be left in trust to a period no longer than 21 years (see page 93). One can only assume the time interval from the facts being obtained to their entry into the directories, being printed was a discrepancy. The actual dates need to be further researched from other sources if detailed accuracy is required.*

The following occupants were: 1881 – John Oliver Band, who had married Esther Adelaide (always known as Lucy), the fourth daughter of John Harris – the last Miss Harris, Emma, died at Iron Cross in 1908; 1909 – Lieut. Col. Lord Charles John Innes-Kerr (relation to Lord Roxborough of Kelso in the Scottish borders) on lease; 1920 – Suffragan Bishop of Woolwich (surname Leeke); 1924 – Mrs J. C. Leeke; 1936 – Brig-Gen. Edward John Russell Peel, the great-great-grandson of Sir Robert Peel (founder of the modern police force); 1940 – Mrs Peel. (The house was sold out of the Harris Family in 1946)

There was a dispute in the Second World War with regard to the name of the property – "Iron Cross" – which was deemed by some to have some sort of allegiance to Germany, and they thought the name should be changed. The name, of course,

refers to the crossroads and to the abundance of ironstone in the area.

Other occupants were: Captain and Mrs Blyth: 1950 – Mrs Scott; 1980s – Mr Wyatt; 1990s – Mr Green.

Ties with Royalty
Captains Blyth's wife was related to the well known Mitford family whose nanny was Miss Lightbody, later to be employed by the Queen as nanny to Prince Charles.

The allotment on the left was to Hannah Boneham, an area of 8 acres 3 roods 8 perches, later to be named "Top Shirley" (see Map Twelve Proprietors/Owners 48). Encroaching into this allotment, adjacent to the roadside, is a small allotment to William Dodd of 1 rood 35 perches (see Map Twelve Proprietors/Owners 112), the same family with the name Dodd from which the name of the well in the grounds of the house on The Green was derived.

The next allotment on the left was to Samuel Cox, an area of 8 acres 2 roods 39 perches, later to be named "Middle Shirley" (see Map Twelve Proprietors/Owners 47). Further over in the next field is the source of the Westhorpe stream in a field named Butterwell Top Ground (see Map Twelve point of interest 5).

The driveway on the right, opposite the division between the allotments on the left, "Top Shirley" and "Middle Shirley", is to Pitwell farm. Pitwell was written Polewell in 1285, (see Map Twelve), together with an old land measure "Pittalls Furlong".

Furlong
Furlong, derived from Furrow-long, denoting the length of Furrow which could be conveniently ploughed by one man; forty poles, or one eighth of a mile.

In 1779 the first allotment on the right was to William Worley, an area of 39 acres 15 perches (see Map Twelve Proprietors/Owners 59), later to be four fields from the road named "Ploughed Barn Ground", "Barn Ground", "The Gogs" and "America". The second allotment on the right, to Richard Farebrother, was an area of 101 acres 2 roods and 37 perches (see Map Twelve Proprietors/Owners 22).

The farmers of Pitwell were: Pre-1779 – Richard Farebrother (1728–1795); 1796 – William Farebrother (1766–1838), who in 1796 married Mary Bromley (1775–1857), both William and his wife have memorials to them in the Trafford Aisle in Byfield Church; 1838 – William Farebrother (1799–1852); 1852 – George Farebrother, gent (1809–1892), together with his cousin, John Bromley "of Pitwell" (1803–1892); 1871 – John Bromley; 1890 – Percival Reading; 1910 – Mrs John Tew; 1912 – Edwin North (1862–1933); 1933 – Mrs Annie North; 1936 – Alfred North (Alfred North shot himself on the farm); 1957 – Watson/Kemp; 1996 – David E. and Mrs Noden.

Records from the 1871 Byfield Census show that the acreage farmed by John Bromley of Pitwell was 140 acres.

This photograph was taken in the early 1960s and is of workmen on the Ironstone laying explosives which were used to blast and loosen the rock to allow for easier digging of the iron-ore. The machine in the foreground is the drill; the men in the photograph are, left to right, Albert Wheeler, Bill Mitchell, and George Thornton. The photograph was taken by Gratton Darbishire.

This photograph is annotated JR840 in the Byfield Photo Museum. Lender Richard Watts.

On the left of the road opposite Pitwell, in the field, there was a secure brick building, now demolished. This was built in the 1940s, well away from any other buildings, and was where the Ironstone dynamite and fuses were stored. These explosives were used to loosen the ironstone rock before it was mined.

At this point, looking forward and across, around the south side of Red Hill, is the village of Chipping Warden. At night the lights of the village can be clearly seen, especially the security lights of the "Old Aerodrome Site", which is now an industrial estate employing many local people. The old World War Two hangers and other buildings are clearly visible and still in use. On the left side of the road entering Chipping Warden from Byfield is a building which was constructed as the sick quarters, mortuary and barrack accommodation for staff, when the site was an operational airfield. This building is now Chipping Warden County Primary School!

Chipping Warden Airfield
This section has details recorded in a book "A Village in Wartime" by Air Commodore Dennis Reader, with additions and interventions by the author. The airfield site was on an area of flat land to the north of Chipping Warden village, immediately to the south of the village of Aston-le-Walls, and a distance of two and a half miles south-west from the centre of Byfield.

The book gives details of the construction of the airfield itself, with its ancillary and constituent parts that were all around the actual operational area. The Air Commodore then gives details of its role when it became an operational W.W.II Aerodrome.

The aerodrome at Chipping Warden was built with many others in an emergency second phase, within a crash programme of airfield construction in a period of eighteen months in 1940 and 1941. Obviously this affected people in the surrounding villages, including Byfield, especially in the availability of work and trading opportunities for local businesses. With the influx of construction workers and Royal Air Force personnel came the uplift in the social life of the local communities. The aerodromes within this emergency construction programme would not be graced by simple and elegant buildings as pre-war aerodromes had been, but this would be the era of Nissen huts, single-brick-thickness structures, corrugated iron roofs and wooden dormitories! However miserly the budget for general construction, these airfields were to have concrete runways capable of taking the heaviest aircraft.

The domestic buildings (messes, barrack blocks etc.) were well removed from the technical site. In fact there were 13 such sites scattered across the countryside and among the villages and local farming communities.

At its peak there were about 1500 airmen and airwomen on site. Most were billeted there but some, mostly officers with their families, were "billeted out" in the homes of people in surrounding villages, a number of them in Byfield.

This O.T.U. was No 12 Operational Training Unit sent to Chipping Warden from RAF Benson near Oxford, with the task of training crews for Bomber Command. The aircraft principally used for this training was the Vickers Wellington.

The Vickers Wellington Bomber, because of its rather corpulent profile, had the affectionate nickname "The Wimpy", after Popeye's pal J. Wellington Wimpy – he with the addiction for hamburgers. By 1941 the Wellington Bomber was beginning to be phased out as an operational squadron aircraft, but it was a good, simple aircraft for the basic training of pilots, observers/navigators, wireless operators and gunners.

As a training aircraft the Wellington had much strength, from the geodetic structure, a design based on the principle of diamond-shaped small units. When the aircraft sustained damage to the structure, if not too severe, the diamond shape would still be retained, but in larger diamond shaped units, enabling the aircraft to be able to survive a greater degree of damage than most other types of construction. The geodetic structure was designed by Barnes Wallis who obtained special benefits with this design, as it gave great strength on the fuselage, even though it was covered only with fabric.

The crash rate on the Wimpy was quite high. At the beginning they crashed all around the local area, including Byfield. Locals remember one crashing close to the Farndon road, and being guarded by troops to prevent people getting too near, because of the danger of unexploded munitions. One Saturday night another Wimpy taking off "fully bombed up", using the airfield's south to north runway, failed to gain enough height and crashed onto the Manor Farm house which is next to Boddington Church. The impact alone caused devastation on the immediate site, killing the bomber crew and three occupants of the house, ironically the family of an airman serving at Chipping Warden. Obviously local people visited the scene on the following Sunday morning, and most were devastated by the sight of the carnage and damage that greeted them.

A contributory factor that could have been a reason for the aircraft not attaining sufficient height, was that aircraft based at airfields used by operational training units usually had de-rated engines. When Air Marshal A. T. Harris succeeded Sir Richard Pierse as C in C Bomber Command, the numbers of bombers used to bomb German cities increased, from a maximum of 228 against a single target, to a force 1000 strong. The first 1000 bomber raid was on the 30th of May 1942. It is little wonder that the C in C became known as "Bomber Harris". It was on these raids that all available aircraft were used, including those based at O.T.Us. This included the crews based and being trained at Chipping Warden.

Many people can remember very badly damaged Wimpies, which were on the last leg of the north west route back from Germany, struggling to get back to base, and making "belly landings" on or just outside the airfield, especially in the Chipping Warden garden allotments, near the main road, finally falling short of the south/north runway.

But without the design and strength of the Barnes Wallis structure they would not have made it home at all!

There were normally 32 aircraft based at Chipping Warden, but at any one time 12 O.T.U. possessed up to 60 Wel-

lingtons, plus the Ansons and Martinets used for navigation training and target-towing. All operational stations had satellite airfields due to the density of traffic. Gaydon (later to become a base for "V" Bombers in the 1950s during the "Cold War") opened as Chipping Warden's satellite on November 11th 1941. Normally half the aircraft were housed there; Turweston became the satellite in 1942, followed by Edgehill (Shenington) in 1943, until the end of the war.

A large number of all types of aircraft were diverted to other airfields for a number of reasons, but mostly because they could not land at their home field due to adverse weather! One night Chipping Warden was home to 14 Lancasters!

With all the aircraft movement, the skies over south Northamptonshire were constantly filled with noise of aero engines, and the villagers, including those living in Byfield, became accustomed to living with a constant reminder that we were without doubt fighting a war!

As a rider to this, there is a small "Wellington Museum" on the Evesham road just out of Moreton-in-Marsh.

Ironically, this flat land around Chipping Warden, from where war planes went to war in the 1940s, was also the site on which the Royalist army camped before the battle of Edgehill in 1642.

Continuing along the Priors Marston road, the next land on the left was allotted to Mary Smith, an area of 8 acres 2 roods 14 perches **(see Map Twelve Proprietors/ Owners 46)**.

Marital status and allotments

The details within the Enclosure indicate that when females were listed as Proprietors/Owners of land, or were separately listed in the detail of Old Inclosures or Homesteads, their title if unmarried was their Christian name only; alternatively, if they were married or widowed, their title was Mrs followed by their Christian name. This obviously makes the historical investigation of accession easier to follow, but still in some cases difficult to unravel.

A good example of this is in the case of Hill Farm and the relationship between Mrs Frances Bradshaw and Mrs Isabel Bradshaw; one being the mother of Aholiab and the other his wife; both bequeathed property/rights in his will dated 1769, Aholiab having died before the Enclosure. The detail of the will was assessed by the Commissioners in 1779 at the time of Byfield's Enclosure, leading to the situation that both Mother and Wife received almost equal allotments of land within the conditions of the Enclosure Act.

The land adjoining Mary Smith's allotment was to James Smith, an area of 35 acres 10 perches, later to be purchased in 1929 by J. R. Hutt from the Cleaver family, **(see Map Twelve Proprietors/Owners 45)**. To date we do not know if there is a connection between these two Smiths

The next land on the right is an allotment in 1779 to John Bromley of (1726–1805) of 87 acres 1 rood 12 perches **(see Map Twelve Proprietors/Owners 25)**.

Continuing forward, the next land on the right was allotted to John Smith, an area of 46 acres 2 roods 11 perches, **(see Map Twelve Proprietors/Owners 37)**. When divided the fields were named "Gospel", "Bankey Ground",

"Smiths Meadow", "Nether Furlong", "Pen Ground" and "First Water Furrow". The last four of these fields were sold out of the Bromley family in 1925 with the death of Mrs Mary Elizabeth Bromley.

Another allotment on the left was also to John Bromley; an area of 16 acres 13 perches of land purchased from Checkley, **(see Map Twelve Proprietors/Owners 24)**. The name of this field is "Blindswell" (Blindle), with a date on the map of field names of 1657. The Ironstone track bed ran down across this field, continuing across two more allotments still on the left side of the road. The first was allotted to T. Bromley, an area of 1 acre 1 rood 11 perches, **(see Map Twelve Proprietors/Owners 106)**, the second to James Harris, an area of 3 acres 2 roods 23 perches **(see Map Twelve Proprietors/Owners 75)**.

A Lease to the Northamptonshire Ironstone Co, copied verbatim.

A portion of the field called Top Slade, 15 feet wide and 313 feet long, is subject to a Lease, dated 12th of July 1917, to James William Pain trading as Northamptonshire Ironstone Co.(which has been assigned to the Northamptonshire Ironstone Co. Ltd.) for 30 years from the 25th of March 1917, on payment of:

(1) A Yearly Surface Rent of £10

(2) A Minimum Yearly Way leave Rent of £50

(3) A Way leave or Royalty Rent of Three Farthings for every Ton (of 2,240 lbs.) of Ironstone carried over the said Land; credit to be given for the minimum Way leave Rent in calculating the said Way leave or Royalty Rent.

On the left and the right, adjacent to the road, are the safety railings of the Ironstone railway bridge built in the Second World War, together with the track bed, by Italian prisoners of war interned in Byfield P.O.W. camp on Boddington Road. The track continued under the bridge **(see Map Twelve point of interest 6)** over two allotments, one to John Edwards, an area of 18 acres 3 roods 4 perches **(see Map Twelve Proprietors/Owners 62)**. This allotment was also to be purchased by J. R. Hutt in 1929, the other ran on over an allotment to William Edwards, an area of 1 acre 23 perches **(see Map Twelve Proprietors/Owners 108)**, continued on across the Boddington Road, down under Pit Lane bridge, over the weighbridge and on to connect to the "Main Line."

Of the last field on the left before the cross roads, it is recorded in 1738 that the land was owned by John Eyles of Husbands Bosworth in Leicestershire, who sold it to Thomas Heath. It was then purchased by Cressent Boote (Yeoman) on December 29th 1755. Because Cressent Boote was the owner of this land at the time of the Enclosure in 1779, the Commissioners allotted it to him in lieu of this previous holding, an area of 7 acres 1 rood 28

This photograph is of Nicholas and Victor Perehinec on the east side of the Priors-Marston Road leaning on the safety railing of the Ironstone Railway Bridge in 1955.

This Photograph in annotated JR791 in the Byfield Photo Museum. Lenders Mrs and Mrs Perehinec.

perches, **(see Map Twelve Proprietors/Owners 76)**. This included the adjacent part of the Boddington Road and a small piece of land on the far side of the road. The field is still known as "Bootes Ground". In his will, in 1802, Cressent Boote bequeathed the allotment to his son John Boote (who is shown in the property deeds as a "Cooper" living in Mollington Warwickshire). The ownership came to Thomas Boote, who sold it to John Gardner of Edgehill Oxfordshire. William Bromley (1800–1879) purchased it, and it was bequeathed to John Henry Bromley (1837–1916). On the death of his wife, Mrs Mary Elizabeth Bromley (1856–1924), it was purchased at auction by James Richard Hutt (1864–1941) in 1925. By then the field had been separated from the land on the other side of Boddington Road, as is shown by the acreage of the field being recorded as 6.986 acres. The field was then passed to his son, James Robert Hutt (1907–1999), and on to his daughter, Josephine Milnes (née Hutt), in whose family ownership it is today. In the 1920s this was the Byfield village football ground.

The first Ironstone railway track pre-1940 was routed down across Bootes Ground over the Priors Marston Road, **(see Map Twelve point of interest 7)**, and, as with the later route, ran across the John Edwards allotment on the right side of the road, going on over the Boddington Road. The line then ran past the Engine Sheds **(see Map Twelve)**, under the Pit Lane bridge, and again over the weighbridge to the "Main Line".

The "Marston road", as it has always been known, is the road in Byfield that dries out the quickest after rain! That is why people remember mothers pushing their high "Silver Cross" prams along here in the 1930s.

More famously, being a "north/south road", it filled with snow when that arctic east wind sent the blizzards from the Woodford direction. During the big snow of 1947, you could walk on top of the snow over the hedges and not know they were there. A number of village people had their photographs taken against the wall of snow at the cross roads. In 1962 and 1969 the snow was not as deep, but still this snow-trapping road was impassable.

On more sunny days it was also the "speed track" of Byfield where vehicles, and especially Motor Cycles, were "Tested". It was the first site and the first time that in the 1950s the author reached a speed of 100 miles per hour on his 500 cc Triumph Tiger 100.

We have now reached the cross roads.

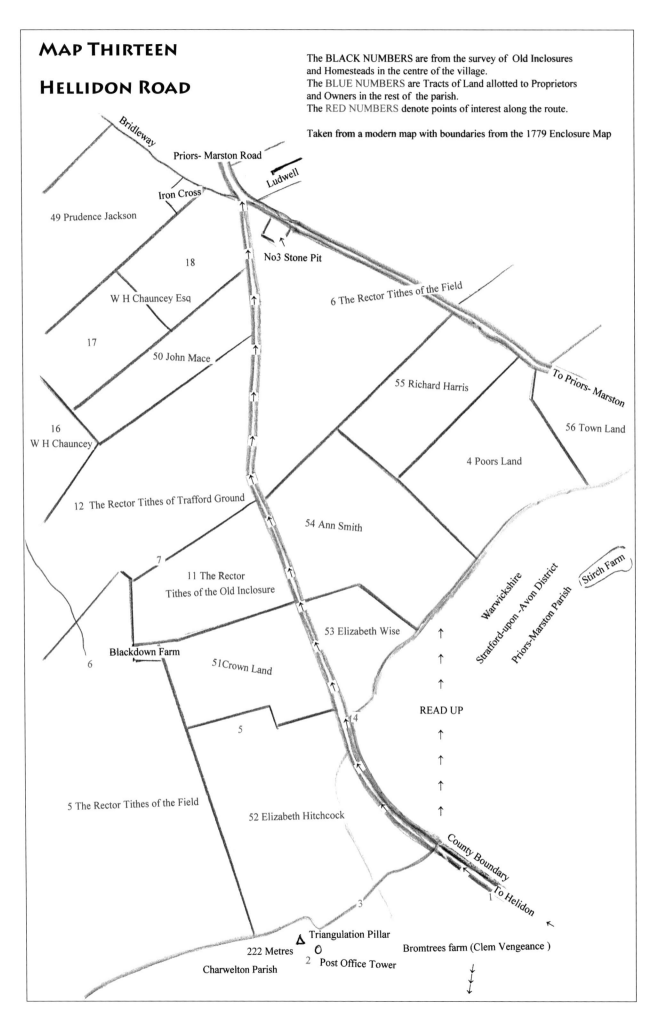

MAP THIRTEEN

HELLIDON ROAD

The BLACK NUMBERS are from the survey of Old Inclosures
and Homesteads in the centre of the village.
The BLUE NUMBERS are Tracts of Land allotted to Proprietors
and Owners in the rest of the parish.
The RED NUMBERS denote points of interest along the route.

Taken from a modern map with boundaries from the 1779 Enclosure Map

Bridleway

Priors- Marston Road

Ludwell

Iron Cross

49 Prudence Jackson

No3 Stone Pit

18

6 The Rector Tithes of the Field

W H Chauncey Esq

17

To Priors- Marston

50 John Mace

55 Richard Harris

56 Town Land

16
W H Chauncey

4 Poors Land

12 The Rector Tithes of Trafford Ground

54 Ann Smith

7

Stirch Farm

11 The Rector
Tithes of the Old Inclosure

Warwickshire

Stratford-upon -Avon District

Priors-Marston Parish

53 Elizabeth Wise

Blackdown Farm

6

51 Crown Land

READ UP

5

4

5 The Rector Tithes of the Field

52 Elizabeth Hitchcock

County Boundary

To Helidon

1

3

Triangulation Pillar

222 Metres

Post Office Tower

Bromtrees farm (Clem Vengeance)

2

Charwelton Parish

CHAPTER ELEVEN

HELLIDON ROAD

(See Map Thirteen)

This route and the road from Priors Marston are the only two entering Byfield parish from the north. Starting the journey from the Priors Marston to Charwelton road heading towards Byfield, **(see Map Thirteen point of interest 1)**, we have passed the farm on the left which is in Charwelton Parish. This was named "Bromtrees" by a Mr Brown of Hellidon who purchased the farm from the Thellusson family estates.

The Thellussons came from Brodsworth Hall near Doncaster (see page 93). The farm at the time was called "Clem Vengeance Farm", a holding of some 180 acres. Mr Brown purchased it in July 1914 for the sum of £3,000 (detail from Thellusson Family Estates records).

Prior to this, again from Estate records: the land owned by the Thellusson family in 1863 in Charwelton parish was Clem Vengeance Farm and the tenants were Frederick G. and H. H. Fowke. The Northamptonshire Directories of 1866 and 1869 show a Frederick Gustavus Fowke as a surgeon (the doctor for the local area) living in Byfield.

Continuing along the road described in the 1779 Enclosure Act as "The Freeboard", on the far side of the right hand hedge of the road is initially the County boundary between Warwickshire and Northamptonshire, the District boundary between Stratford-upon-Avon and Daventry and the Parish boundary between Priors Marston and Charwelton **(see Map Thirteen)**.

On the left, rising from its base height 727 feet (222 meters) above sea level, is the 400 foot high Post Office Tower, built in the autumn of 1962 and the spring of 1963, construction being held up by a considerable depth of snow. The tower was originally built to beam television signals over this high point **(see Map Thirteen point of interest 2)**. This tower is now genuinely multipurpose, being fitted with more and more dishes and aerials; only the main operator would know what they are all for. Let us hope that with the extra equipment fitted the height will not cause a danger to aircraft, as the tower has already been struck by an American F111 aircraft flying from its base in Germany. Luckily the aircraft remained in the air and, apart from minor damage, the tower remains standing.

Just in front of the tower, not visible from the road, is an Ordnance Survey Triangulation Pillar. As we look up towards this Pillar we are looking along the line of the parish boundary between Charwelton Parish and Byfield Parish **(see Map Thirteen point of interest 3)**. Moving forward along the road we are now in Byfield Parish.

The land on our left allotted to Elizabeth Hitchcock was an area of 33 acres 1 rood 38 perches **(see Map Thirteen Proprietors/Owners 52)** and was later divided into two

and named "Top Byfield Field" and "Byfield Field".

Further on to the right is a culvert with a stream going down towards Stirch Farm. This stream marks the line of the County, District and Parish boundaries **(see Map Thirteen point of interest 4)**. As we pass this point Byfield Parish is now also to our right as well as to our left.

The land on the left is marked on the map as Crown Land and was allotted to the King and John Caldicott. An acreage of 15 acres 1 rood 14 perches **(see Map Thirteen Proprietors/Owners 51)**, it was named King's Piece.

Crown Land

"The King" at the time of the Enclosure of the land in Byfield was George III and the custodian of the land and the King's "agent" was John Caldicott. One would assume that the Crown had incurred, or would incur, certain expenses within Byfield Parish, probably to do with the actual Enclosure of land within the Parish . This allotment of 15 acres 1 rood and 14 perches could have been allotted to offset these expenses.

Between the allotments of Elizabeth Hitchcock and the Crown Land was a Spinney named Blackdown Covert. This was later removed to allow cultivation of the land **(see Map Thirteen point of interest 5)**. Further over in 1779 was an allotment to the Rector of 101 acres 2 roods 17 perches for Tithes of the Field **(see Map Thirteen Proprietors/Owners 5)**. The source of the Cornbrook stream is on this allotment **(see Map Thirteen point of interest 6)**.

Moving on again, just past the position of the Covert is Blackdown Farm **(see Map Thirteen)**. This is again on this large tract of land allotted to the Rector.

The farmers were: 1866 – George Hitchcock; 1881 – William Hatt (Farmer's son); 1911 – Thomas Russell (Tenant); followed by William Arthur Spencer (Tenant); 1943 – Joseph William Shaw (1888–1963). In the 1962 winter the snow made the Hellidon and Priors Marston roads impassable. Mr Shaw needed urgent hospital treatment and he was taken by helicopter, which was a very unusual occurrence in those days.

On Blackdown Farm in the 1940s lived an old character known to all in the neighbourhood as "Titanic Tom". He lived in an old tumbledown barn. He could be seen every morning, coming into the village with his tea can and long ash walking stick, stepping out briskly and making his regular house calls. He would ask politely for some boiling water for his tea can, and if possible a pinch of tea and a spoonful of sugar. Tom claimed he was a survivor from the sinking of the Titanic. He reflected on the experience with conviction; but as to the truth we can only hazard a guess! I wonder where Tom actually was on that day in 1912, when the Titanic struck the iceberg? A photograph of Titanic Tom is in the Byfield Photo Museum.

The land to the right of the road just over the boundary allotted to Elizabeth Wise was an area of 7 acres 26 perches (see Map Thirteen Proprietors/ Owners 53), later to be named Dead Man's Pits.

Moving further on again, on the right allotted to Ann Smith was an area of 22 acres 3 roods 37 perches (see Map Thirteen Proprietors/Owners 54). Later it was divided in two and named "Watts Barn Ground" and "Siden".

Across the road to the left was an allotment to the Rector, which is marked on the Enclosure Map "The Rector for Tithes of the old Inclosure" and is an area of 6 acres 23 perches (see Map Thirteen Proprietors/Owners 11).

The adjacent allotment was also to the Rector and marked on the Enclosure Map "for Tithes of Trafford Ground", an area of 54 acres 37 perches (see Map Thirteen Proprietors/Owners 12). The owner of Trafford Grounds was the Lord of the Manor William Henry Chauncy. The land was allotted to the Rector in lieu of "such great and or small tythes, moduses or compositions due issuing or payable from or out of the estate called Trafford" (detail copied verbatim).

Meaning of ancient terms and words used in the enclosure documents,

Some of these old words are not found in modern dictionaries. Research by John Roddis from "A Pocket Dictionary or complete English Expositor" dated 1765:

Tythes (more modern spelling "tithes"): A tithe is a tenth part, and was originally a tenth part of the produce of the soil within the parish, due to the ministers of the church for their maintenance.

Moduses: A compensation for tithes; a moderate equivalent in money, given by the owner of land in lieu of tithes.

Compositions: This was when an agreement was made between the owner of lands and the incumbent, with the consent of the ordinary and the patron, that the lands should for the future, be discharged from the payment of tithes, by reason of some land or other real recompense given in lieu and satisfaction thereof.

The Hamlet of Trafford

Trafford is a hamlet containing one farmhouse and 325 acres of land.

The estate in 1778 belonged to William Henry Chauncy, Lord of the Manor, and is recorded as being an area of 337 acres 1 rood and 33 perches. At that time it was bounded by the Lordships of Chipping Warden to the west and to the north, Eydon to the north-east, Culworth to the south-east, and Edgecote to the south.

Trafford house is three miles due south of the centre of the village of Byfield.

Part of the area around the house is shown on Ordnance Survey Maps as being the site of the Medieval Village of Trafford.

By Local Government Order 15,251, dated March 24th 1884, Trafford was transferred from Byfield to Chipping

Warden, in the Banbury Union. The Lord of the Manor was then Richard Aubrey Cartwright, the Lordship having passed down the lineage through the Chauncy, Carter and the Cartwright families, both through the male and female lines.

There is in Byfield Church a side aisle on the south side of the church named "The Trafford Aisle". It can probably be assumed that in the days of the Lord of the Manor, prior to 1884, the workers on the Trafford estate would attend Byfield Church and sit in this side aisle.

To the right of the road was another allotment to the Rector for Tithes of the Fields, which went as far as the Boddington/Byfield Parish boundary, a total area of 181 acres 1 rood 33 perches (see Map Thirteen Proprietors/ Owners 6).

The triangular field between the Hellidon to Byfield road and the Priors Marston to Byfield road was later named "Iron Cross Ground".

The land allotted to the Rector, Reverend John Knightley in 1779

The total amount of land allotted to the Rector John Knightley in Byfield Parish was:

One allotment for Glebe, an area of 35 acres 1 rood 26 perches (see Map Seven Proprietors/Owners 9).

One allotment for "Tithes of Trafford Grounds" with an acreage of 54 acres 37 perches (see Map Thirteen Proprietors/Owners 12).

Two allotments for "Tithes of Old Enclosure", one with an acreage of 6 acres 23 perches (see Map Thirteen Proprietors/Owners 11), the other with an acreage of 5 acres 2 roods 30 perches (see Map Seven Proprietors/Owners 10).

Three allotments for Tithes of the Field, one with an acreage of 101 acres 2 roods 17 perches (see Map Thirteen Proprietors/Owners 5), one of 181 acres 1 rood 33 perches (see Map Twelve Proprietors/Owners 6), and the other of 139 acres 2 roods 17 perches (see Maps Four and Nine Operators/Owners 7).

This made a total area of land allotted to the Rector of 524 acres 23 perches out of the total acreage of the land allotted outside the centre of the village of 2569 acres 3 roods 29 perches. Almost a fifth of the total land allotted in the Byfield Parish in 1779 was to the incumbent Rector, John Knightley.

The allotment on the left was to John Mace, an area of 10 acres 3 roods 20 perches (see Map Thirteen Proprietors/ Owners 50). Detail on the map of field names records that in 1702 the field was given the name of "Sharpland".

At the point where the Hellidon road joins the Priors Marston road, records show that in 1771 these crossroads were called "Iron Stone Cross". The land on the left was composed of two allotments to the Lord of the Manor W. H. Chauncy Esq. The two allotments were of almost equal size; one of 10 acres 1 rood 6 perches (see Map Thirteen Proprietors/Owners 17) was later named "Rough Piece", and the other, of 10 acres 23 perches, (see Map Thirteen Proprietors/Owners 18), was later named "Iron Cross Ploughing". These fields, together with others in a block of land, the total area of which is 129.811 acres, are still today in the ownership of R. W. Watts of Manor Farm! This area of land was the area from which the last loads of iron ore were mined before the Ironstone closed in 1965 **(see Map Thirteen point of interest 7)**.

Land allotted to The Lord of the Manor W. H. Chauncy Esq. in 1779

The Lord of the Manor was also allotted a considerable amount of land in Byfield Parish in 1779, six Allotments, five smaller areas but one was a considerable tract of land, an acreage of 256 acres 2 roods 18 perches; the total area of these six allotments being 286 acres 2 roods 32 perches.

As "Trafford Grounds" was included in Byfield Parish within the Act of Enclosure, W. H. Chauncy Esq. was also allotted an additional area of 337 acres 1 rood 33 perches, which was the total allotment of Trafford Grounds.

We have now reached the Priors Marston Road.

The BLACK NUMBERS are from the survey of Old Inclosures and Homesteads in the centre of the village.
The BLUE NUMBERS are Tracts of Land allotted to Proprietors and Owners in the rest of the parish.
The RED NUMBERS denote points of interest along the route.
Detail taken from the 1779 Enclosure Map.

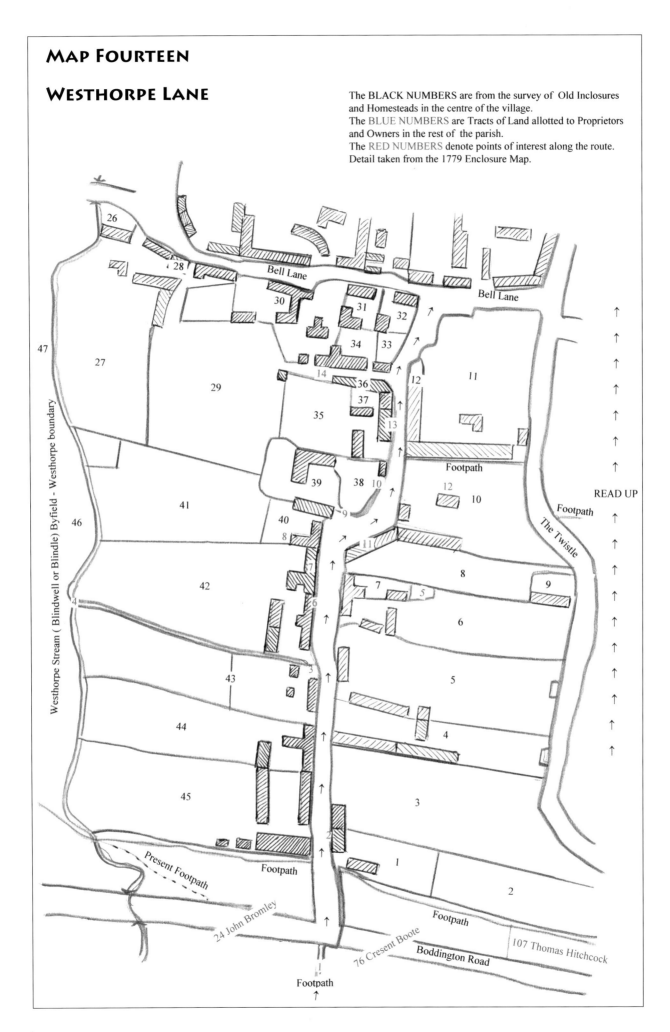

Bell Lane

Bell Lane

Footpath

READ UP

The Twistle

Footpath

Westhorpe Stream (Blindwell or Blindle) Byfield - Westhorpe boundary

Present Footpath

Footpath

24 John Bromley

76 Cresent Boote

Boddington Road

107 Thomas Hitchcock

Footpath

Footpath

Chapter Twelve

Westhorpe Lane

(See Map Fourteen)

This lane runs from north to south linking Boddington Road and Bell Lane. Starting the journey from the definitive footpath on the far side of Boddington Road opposite Westhorpe Lane, **(see Map Fourteen point of interest 1)**, the first Allotment on the right includes the roadway and the land on the corner of the Priors Marston Road and Boddington Road. In 1779, 7 acres 1 rood 28 perches **(see Map Fourteen Proprietors/ Owners 76)**, were allotted to Cressent Boote, who was also allotted the next Inclosure on the right, an area of 38 perches "within the Township of Westhrup" **(see Map Fourteen Old Inclosures/Homesteads 1)**.

Allotment Proprietors/Owners 76 and Old Inclosure/ Homesteads number 1 "within the Township of Westhrup"

The property was described in March 1738 before the Enclosure of Byfield and Westrup and would have included additional land other than that indicated which was allotted to Cressent Boote in 1779. One messuage, one cottage and one garden; one orchard twelve acres of land; three acres of meadow, eight acres of pasture, one acre of furze & heath and common of pasture for all cattle with appurtenances.

In the 1600s the property was in the possession of Daniell Righton, who sold it to Samuel Gardner, a weaver.

1700: it was purchased by Benjamin Eyles, yeoman, for £53.0.0. On his death it was bequeathed to John Eyles, yeoman of Husbands Bosworth.

1738: it was purchased by Thomas Heath for £60.10.0.

1755: the property was sold to Cressent Boote, yeoman of Westrup for £57.0.0.

In the 1779 Byfield Enclosure, Cressent Boote was allotted (**Proprietors/Owners 76**) and the Inclosure **Old Inclosures/Homesteads 1**.

The description of the parcels of land, plants and land boundaries at the time of the Byfield 1779 Enclosure.

Meadow *A piece of land where grass is mown or cut down rather than grazed;*
Pasture *Grass for grazing.*
Furze *The win or gorse; a prickly evergreen bush with papilionaceous yellow flowers.*
Heath *Barren open country, heather.*
Fern *A plant with leaves usually like feathers, having seed or spores on the back.*
Bushes
A thicket, a collection of trees or shrubs, thickly or closely set.

Open and Common fields *A tract of open land, used in common by the inhabitants of a Town or Parish.*
Mound *An artificial bank of earth or stone; an artificial mount.*

1802: on the death of Cressent Boote, the property was bequeathed to John Boote, who was a cooper of Mollington. Other children of Cressent are Thomas Boote, Sarah Gardner, and Elizabeth Boote, a spinster living in the Westrup cottage.

July 1829: John Boote died intestate and his property passed to his son Thomas his heir-in-law.

1846: John Gardner, yeoman of Edgecote, purchased the property for £950.0.0.

1849: William Bromley, purchased the property for £1,000.0.0.

1879: William Bromley died and the property was willed to John Henry Bromley.

1916: John Henry Bromley died and the property was left to Mary Elizabeth Bromley (née Tew).

August 6th 1924: Mrs Mary Elizabeth Bromley died.

18th June 1925: Mrs M. E. Bromley's estate auctioned by Midland Marts Ltd of Banbury.

12th October 1925: the property which was **Old Inclosures/Homesteads 1** with an area of 38 perches, which had become known as "The Firs", was purchased by Thomas Henry Brightwell on behalf of Mrs Mary Bromley-Young (the wife of Thomas Young, carter of The Cottage, Church Road, Byfield).

1931: Mary Bromley-Young sold "The Firs" and the adjoining field to Arthur Russell (grocer) for £450.

1942: "The Firs" and orchard are sold to William Arthur Russell the Postmaster for £400.

1945: "The Firs" was sold to Mrs Doris Francis Knott, wife of Horace James Knott of Wormleighton.

March 22nd 1960: "The Firs" was sold to Sydney Owen Norman Garland and his wife Betty Garland.

1974: Mrs Garland sold "The Firs" to Mr S. D. Fennell.

August 1977: "The Firs" was sold to Mr and Mrs Norman David Blundell.

The site was divided into what was to become 39 and 41 Westhorpe Lane.

1987: Mr and Mrs J. D. Roddis purchased 39 Westhorpe Lane.

This does illustrate the complexity of property sales, and the bequeathing of property, and also how property is transferred when there is no will (intestate). It also shows the position when the owner of a property or of land is allotted that which he owned or an asset of equal value and quality in lieu (within the allotments by the Commissioners of the terms and conditions of the 1779 Enclosure Act.)

Some other previous occupants were as follows. In 1903 George Dester (carrier) was tenant, and by 1910 a Mr Yorston, also a tenant, is listed in the Northamptonshire Directories as a Carrier, Coal Merchant, News Agent, Book Seller and Waste Material Merchant, who retired but was still the sitting tenant on the 18th June 1925 when the property was sold. The property was then described as comprising: a substantially built stone and thatched house consisting of sitting room, range parlour, and entrance hall, plus three bedrooms, a thatched barn and stabling with a corrugated wagon hovel.

Local Carriers

Carriers' carts brought in country people and their produce to the towns and distributed merchandise from the towns to agricultural districts.

An idea may be formed of its commerce by the fact that records show that in 1854 nearly 300 carriers attended the weekly market in Banbury. Many of them visited on other days of the week, and also attended other markets on a regular and routine basis.

Details from the Northamptonshire Directories from 1847 to 1940: the carriers that served the village of Byfield.

1847 to **Banbury**, *John Brightwell (1796–1873) and William Gardner(1805–1880) – Mon & Thurs;* **Daventry** *– Wed & Sat.*

1849 *Ditto with an additional service to* **Leamington***.*

1854 to **Banbury**, *William Gardner – Mon & Thurs (at 9 am returning about 4 aft).*

1866 to **Banbury** *and* **Daventry***, W. Gardner and Levi West.*

1869 to **Banbury**, *W. Gardner and Levi West – Mon & Thurs;* **Daventry** *– Wed & Sat;* **Leamington**, *Levi West – Frid.*

1884 to **Banbury**, *John Allen (and farmer) – Mon, Thurs & Sat; Robert Howes – Mon & Thurs;* **Northampton**, *Sat. James Smith Mon & Thurs,* **Daventry** *Wed & Sat, Levi West Mon & Thurs* **Daventry** *Wed.*

1885 to **Banbury**, *James Smith and Levi West – Mon & Thurs; John Allen – Mon, Thurs & Sat; to* **Daventry**, *James Smith – Wed & Sat; Levi West – Wed;* **Leamington**, *Levi West – Sat.*

1903 *To* **Banbury**, *George Dester – Mon &Thurs (at 9 returning about 7), and to* **Daventry** *– Wed.*

1906 *Ditto with the addition of Marlow from Woodford, to* **Daventry** *– Wed & Sat.*

This photograph is taken in the 1950s from the north end of Westhorpe Lane. It shows The Firs on the right and Home Farm on the left, which was obviously a working dairy farm, hence the milk churns adjacent to the roadway. Yew Tree Cottage can be seen further on the right, as can the stone house on the far left; this dwelling is now known as "Sundial Cottage".

This photograph is annotated BH40 in the Byfield Photo Museum. Lender Mrs Janet Blake.

*1910   to **Banbury**, James Yorston – Mon, Thurs & Sat;
Daventry – Tues & Sat; Anderson from Woodford
– Wed & Sat.*

*1920   to **Banbury**, James Yorston – Mon, Thurs & Sat.*

*1924   to **Banbury** (motor), James Yorston – Mon, Thurs
& Sat; Thomas George Lamb – Mon & Sat, and
to **Northampton** – Wed & Sat (Passengers and
Goods). Note: The demise of the horse.*

*1928   to **Banbury** (motor), Thomas George Lamb – Mon
& Thurs; to **Northampton** – Wed & Sat (Passengers
and Goods); Snape Woodford Halse to **Banbury**
passing through Mon. Knight from Hellidon to
Banbury – Thurs. The Midland Red ran a motor
omnibus service to **Banbury** – Thurs, Sat & Sun,
and from **Daventry** to **Leamington** – Thurs.*

*1940   to **Banbury** (motor), Thomas George Lamb – Mon
& Thurs, and to **Northampton** – Wed & Sat
(Passenger and Goods). Snape from Woodford Halse
passes through Thurs; George Page **Daventry** passes
through Sat & Mon.*

Later, The Firs house was occupied in the 1940s by the White family, then by their relations the Sykes family. Descendants of these families still live in Byfield. The buildings had become derelict and were pulled down.

In the early 1900s the Foresters Fete procession started from here, **(see Map Fourteen point of interest 2)**, and progressed to the Rectory grounds via Westhorpe Lane, Bell Lane, Banbury Lane, High Street and Church Street (which then would have been Westhorpe End), Main Street, Cross Street, High Street or Turnpike, and then into Church Street. The procession was always led by a band, either the local Byfield Band (known as "the beer and bacca band"), or the Long Buckby Band. People dressed up in appropriate attire for the occasion There are photographs of these occasions in the Byfield Photo Museum.

Retracing our steps back onto the definitive footpath opposite Westhorpe Lane **(point of interest 1),** and again looking into Westhorpe Lane, the land to the left including the roadway and the first plot of land on the left on entering Westhorpe Lane allotted to John Bromley was an area of 16 acres 13 perches **(see Map Fourteen Proprietors/Owners 24)**. He was also allotted the adjacent Inclosure, an area of 1 acre 16 perches **(see Map Fourteen Old Inclosures/Homesteads 45)**. Within the Enclosure documents this was named "Home Close", obviously part of "Home Farm". The house has on it a "Date Stone" dated 1714, on the front wall. The building has a cruck beam construction, which would indicate that it is one of the oldest houses in the parish. Recently completed alterations located a large underground water reservoir, possibly there to store water to extinguish fire in the thatched roof if one occurred. This was possibly a requirement specified by the insurance policy covering the building. Some of the footprints of the buildings differ from those on the site now. Various structures have been built, reflecting the changing needs in farming and in domestic use. One of

them was a large barn with a date stone on the gable showing a date of 1795; probably indicating that John Bromley built the barn after the allotment.

This barn was converted by an ex-postmaster, Mr Frisby, and his wife in the 1980s into a very desirable dwelling.

These allotments were held in the Bromley family for over 200 hundred years. Occupants were pre-1779 – John Bromley; Thomas Bromley (1773–1825); William Bromley (1800–1879); 1877 – John Henry Bromley (who later moved to Church House); 1928 – Septimus Harold and Humphrey Bromley; 1940 – Septimus Harold Bromley; 1973 – Mrs Doris Bromley.

Records from the 1871 Byfield Census show that in 1871 William Bromley farmed 163 acres.

Home Farm
A description of Home Farm in 1925 when it was sold on the death of Mrs Mary Elizabeth Bromley at an Auction Sale on the 18th of June 1925.

The Dwelling House, which is known as "Lower House", is built of stone with a thatched roof and contains:

On the ground floor: Parlour, Sitting Room, Kitchen, Larder Lobby with Copper, Dairy and Wash House.

On the First Floor: 4 Bedrooms, Box room, (and above) 2 Attics.

The Outbuildings comprise:

Thatched Wool Room, Wood Barn and Closet. A range of Brick-built and Slated Piggeries.

Thatched Open Hovel and Loose Box with Granary over. Large Stone and Slated Barn.

Range of Stone-built and Thatched Buildings comprising: Mixing Shed, Cowhouse for 12 Cows, Stabling for 6 Horses, Nag Stable, and Harness Room with Loft over. 3 Thatched Loose Boxes with enclosed Yards.

The Coates/Bromley family, being an old and relatively large Byfield family, have a large number of graves and memorials in the Church and Churchyard. These include the seven white marble gravestones adjacent to the north door of the Church, also the upright family gravestone and a separate gravestone adjacent to it, situated opposite the south door of the Church. The last of the Bromleys are buried in the 1933 Churchyard extension (consecrated in 1936) to the north-west of the Church. The land in which they are interred was purchased from the Bromley family. In the Church, two stained glass windows have been erected in memory of members of the Bromley family. The one in the west wall of the tower is in memoriam to John Bromley, known as "John of Pitwell", and his wife Sarah. The second window is in the centre of the wall of the North Aisle, in memoriam to Richard Bromley and his wife Sarah. Richard Bromley was the son of "John of Pitwell".

The Coates – Bromley – Farebrother Family.
The Coates – Bromley – Farebrother family tree records the first Bromley as Thomas Bromley, born in 1689.

The Bromley lineage ended in Byfield with the death of the only son of Septimus Harold Bromley and Mrs Doris Bromley.

Douglas Peter Bromley was returning home on his motorcycle from a night at Brandon Speedway, the track of the "Brandon Bees", the Coventry Speedway club, on May 22nd 1949, when he was tragically killed in an accident at the Staverton turn on the Daventry to Banbury road.

The loss of Peter, as he was always affectionately known, at the young age of 21 was a tragic blow to all, especially to his parents.

The next Inclosure on the left, with buildings abutting the Bromley ground, allotted in 1779 to John Smith, was an area of 1 acre and 4 perches **(see Map Fourteen Old Inclosures/Homesteads 44)**. The 1882/83 Ordnance Survey Map shows this land as an orchard, and in fact the site nearest the road was later to become the Bromleys' garden. Today it is the site on which has been built a modern detached house.

On the other side of the road, the Inclosure allotted to Richard Farebrother, was an area of 1 acre 1 rood 7 perches **(see Map Fourteen Old Inclosures/Homesteads 3)**. Today, at the bottom end of it in Westhorpe Lane, are a number of brick-built dwellings, including a row of bungalows. Such is the steepness of the escarpment, in this part of Westhorpe Lane, that the garages to these bungalows are in the basements at a level with the line of the roadway.

Moving on, the adjacent Inclosure, again allotted to Richard Farebrother, was an area of 2 roods 10 perches; the building gable on to the road is now known as "Yew Tree Cottage". The 1779 Enclosure Map shows the footprint on which the present dwelling stands to be much longer, with the east end abutting the road **(see Map Fourteen Old Inclosures/Homesteads 4)**. The Hartwell family lived there from just after the First World War up to the late 1940s. There was Henry James Hartwell (1871–1942), followed by Wilfred Henry Hartwell (1894–1945), who was the manager of Adams Store in the Byfield High Street.

In the 1980s this house was owned by a lady living away from the village, and was left fully furnished for a considerable time. In as much as it was considered to have become a danger as the building was not secure, the Local Authority set in train procedures to secure the building and to contact the owner. This resulted in the house being sold renovated and restored into a desirable dwelling.

Over the road on the left of this Inclosure an allotment to William John Eyles was an area of 1 acre 10 perches **(see Map Fourteen Old Inclosure/Homesteads 43)**. Within the curtilage of the allotment adjacent to the roadside is "Westhorpe Well", one of the public wells in the Byfield parish. This water supply is fed by a strong spring, **(see Map Fourteen point of interest 3)**, the overflow of which runs into the Westhorpe (Blindwell or blindle) stream **(see Map Fourteen point of interest 4)**. A thatched cottage was on this site up to the 1960s, adjacent to the roadside. This is shown on the footprint on the 1779 Enclosure Map and the 1882/83 Ordnance Survey Map. This cottage was last lived in by the Batchelor

This photograph is of the barrel-vaulted roofed bungalow in Westhorpe Lane which was named "Grandon". The photograph was taken by Rex Partridge in 1998.

This photograph is annotated RP469 in the Byfield Photo Museum. Lender Rex Partridge.

family until it was pulled down. This made way for a rather unusual bungalow, the construction of which consisted of a copper-covered barrel-vault roof. Latterly this was lived in by the well-known First World War veteran and local poet Norman Hurst and his wife Sybil.

Norman and Sybil Hurst

Norman and Sybil moved to Byfield in 1975, and soon became integrated into the community. Norman was born with a twin brother in 1899; both his parents were teachers. The family moved to Berkhamstead where Norman won a scholarship to Berkhamstead School.

In 1917 he joined the Army, and was sent out to the Front as a young subaltern in the Worcestershire Regiment. Within three months he was badly wounded in both legs by a shell. His right leg was amputated, and he spent several years in and out of hospital in Oxford. During this time he managed to gain an M.A. in Literature at Wadham College, Oxford.

Norman obtained a teaching post in South Africa, but while he was waiting to sail he took a temporary position at Burford Grammar School, where the Headmaster's niece, one Sybil Piggott, caught his eye. Norman proposed on their second meeting. They were engaged and married in four weeks, as the boat to South Africa was already booked. It is quite amazing that Sybil's Guardian should agree to her being married and whisked off to the other side of the world in such a short space of time! The decision was a right one, as they were happily married for 71 years.

After a short period at Vryheid High School in Natal, they moved to Stellenbosch near Cape Town, where Norman became a Lecturer in English at Stellenbosch University. In 1936 Norman obtained his Ph.D. Around this time the couple had two children.

In 1961 Norman retired and the family home was sold; both Sybil and Norman devoted the next fifteen years of their lives to the World Prayer Movement, which entailed living in different parts of the country from Kent to Scotland.

On finally retiring to Byfield, Norman's love of literature, specifically his zest for writing poetry, and the couple's continuing love of gardening, travelling and walking kept them busy. Their faith in the Lord was manifested on a daily basis with a period of prayer and meditation every day at 11 a.m. The Hursts were looked on with much affection and respect by all. They are sadly missed!

After the death firstly of Sybil, and then later Norman, both at the age of over 90 years, this bungalow was in turn pulled down and a large modern brick house built in its place.

Opposite the well in the 1950s was a stone barn with its double doors opening onto the road. This was on an Inclosure allotted to John Brightwell, an area of 1 acre 4 perches (see Map Fourteen Old Inclosures/Homesteads 5). The barn was part of a farm. The farmhouse was located on the boundary of the previous allotment. This was later to become known locally as "Cleavers Farm". Owners: Pre-1869 – Richard Cleaver; 1885 – Alfred Cleaver (1852–1914); 1914 – William Richard Cleaver; 1924 – Richard William Cleaver (1884–1965) up to the late 1940s.

Subsequently, the local builders Woodford and Upfield bought the site in the 1980s, and constructed two substantial detached stone bungalows, using the stone from the demolished house and buildings. The next Inclosure on the right is shown on the 1779 Enclosure Map as having a narrow entrance, which leads into a large plot on which are shown two buildings. The allotment to Richard Dodd was of 2 roods 33 perches (see Map Fourteen Old Inclosures/Homesteads 6). Richard Dodd is recorded in the 1777 militia list as being a farmer. In the 1940s and early 1950s the cottage on the roadside was lived in by Benjamin James Wise (1880–1960) and his family. In the 1940s Ben was a "Flag Man" on the Byfield Ironstone railway, controlling the road crossings. His son, William Wise, lived with his family in the cottage at the back.

The site was developed by Doctor and Mrs Morrison in the 1970s.

The next plot also had a cottage on the roadside adjoining together with the previous cottage making a pair, semi-detached. This Inclosure was allotted to John Howe and was an area of 17 perches (see Map Fourteen Old Inclosures/Homesteads 7). The cottage was occupied from the late 1800s, up to his death in 1931, by James Turner (1843–1931), an expert thatcher. James Turner was renowned for his work, and as such was photographed with a number of prizes he won over the years for his expertise in the art, most being at local agricultural shows, such as the annual show at Woodford Halse. He was also a Byfield Church bell ringer. In 1932, on the death of James Turner, the property was purchased by Leslie Edwin Russell and his wife Dorothy as their first home, for the princely sum of £135. Later it was sold to John Francis (Frank) Holmes and his wife Margaret in 1945 for £300. Frank worked for the Russells in their General Store in Bell Lane for forty two years. As a widower, Frank lived in the cottage until his death on 19th February 2000 at the age of ninety one. The house has since been much altered and extended.

In the 1930s, on a site behind this property, was built a "prefabricated bungalow". This is shown on some aerial photographs in the Byfield Photo Museum (see Map Fourteen point of interest 5). It was lived in initially by Miss Scott, a teacher at Byfield Primary School in the 1930s. When subjected to a storm and strong winds the rather frail structure failed, and the roof was blown completely off. After repair and renovation, further occupants were: 1940s – Mr Ivens; 1950s – Mr and Mrs Bill Evans.

The larger Inclosure on the opposite side of the road on the left was allotted in 1779 to Mrs Isabel Bradshaw and Mrs Frances Bradshaw, an area of 1 acre 2 roods 7 perches (see Map Fourteen Old Inclosures/Homesteads 42). As previously described, they had also been allotted the land, in two almost equal plots, which became Hill Farm on the Priors Marston Road (see Map Twelve Proprietors/Owners 28 and 29).

This Inclosure is bounded on the north by the overflow stream from the "Westhorpe Well". Previous to the Enclosure in 1779, Aholiab West Bradshaw of Priors Marston owned the holdings. He bequeathed them to Isabel Bradshaw, his mother, and Frances Bradshaw, his wife, in his will dated 1769. All of the property owned by the

Bradshaw family was sold at auction at the Wheat Sheaf Hotel, Daventry on Wednesday 16th of August 1828 at 4 o'clock in the afternoon.

Particulars of the Land Sale Auction (copied verbatim)

Freehold and Tithe-free
ESTATE,

BYFIELD, Northamptonshire.

To be SOLD by AUCTION,

BY JOHN DUMBLETON

On WEDNESDAY the 6th Day of AUGUST, 1828,

At four o'clock in the afternoon precisely,

Unless previously disposed of by private contract, of which due notice will be given,

LOT 1. ALL THAT

MESSUAGE OR TENEMENT,

With the Yard Stable and Hovel, and a close of Land or Orchard immediately adjoining, situate in WESTHUP, in the Parish of BYFIELD and continuing about one Acre, in the occupation of Mr Henry Thornton, who will show the Premises.

LOT 2. All those FIVE several INCLOSURES of capital ARABLE, MEADOW, AND PASTURE LAND,

Situate and being at WESTRUP, in the Parish of BYFIELD afore-said, late the Estate and in the occupation of AHOLIAB BRADSHAW, Esq. Deceased, and containing, by Admeasurement, 115A. 2R. 16P.

VIZ.

	A	R	P
Ox-house Meadow.........	11	1	15
Lower Meadow..............	11	3	25
Great Meadow	48	3	12
Lower Close (Pasture).....	20	0	31
Upper Close (Arable)......	23	1	15
	115	2	16

(possession may be by Michaelmas next).

The above Estate is Freehold and Tithe free, within a ring Fence. well fenced timbered and watered, and on which is a capital Ox-House.

Byfield is nine miles from Banbury seven miles from Daventry, and eighteen miles from Warwick To view the Estate apply to Mr BOLTON. Priors Marston, Warwickshire; and for further particulars and to treat for the purchase, to Mr VANDERPLANK, Long Buckby, Northamptonshire; to Mr Freeman, Solicitor, 21 Bartlet's Buildings London; if by letter Post paid.

8th July 1828. (Dicey and Smithsons, Printers Parade Northampton)

In 1779 this Inclosure had two blocks of buildings that make up almost the entire roadside frontage. Photographs show some of them as cottages, but it is said that this was the site of a public house named "The Blackbird". As yet no evidence has come to light to substantiate this **(see Map Fourteen point of interest 6)**.

The house now on the site was built by Jim Jordan in the 1934, from stone taken from the cottages on the site that had been demolished. The property was purchased on their marriage in the 1950s by Peter and Joan Bickley. The house has since been extended.

The last building along the road on this Inclosure, is said to have been used by "The Knackerman" Tommy Major in the 1930s. This was later used by the Bickleys as a store and garage, but has since been purchased and converted into an office by Mr Paul Upfield **(see Map Fourteen point of interest 7)**. The land at the rear of this building, down to the Westhorpe stream, was part of the area purchased, and a stone detached house has recently been built on the site.

Knacker (detail from a contemporary dictionary)
Knacker-man, one who buys and slaughters old horses.

The building adjoining the previous property, situated on the left before the corner, was in 1779 on an Inclosure allotted to William Nicholls, an area of 25 perches **(see Map Fourteen Old Inclosure/Homestead 40)**. The 1882/83 Ordnance Survey Map shows a number of cottages joined to the back of the house **(see Map Fourteen point of interest 8)**. The house itself is on the same footprint today as is shown on the 1779 Enclosure Map. In the Second World War the Seath family were evacuated from London into these cottages, at a time when the Batchelor family lived in the main dwelling.

In the 1960s Mr and Mrs Alec Robinson lived in the House. Mr Robinson served the village as Church Treasurer; he was also Chairman of the Parish Council. Together with his wife he was also responsible for starting the Byfield Over 60s Club in 1968.

The land between this allotment and the Westhorpe stream was an Inclosure of 1 acre 6 perches, allotted to William Molt **(see Map Fourteen Old Inclosure/Homestead 41)**. This area today is part of "Greenwood Close".

The house on the site on the apex of the bend is now the home of Mrs Sheila Dexter. It was originally on an Inclosure allotted to Edward Thornton, an area of 1 rood 9 perches **(see Map Fourteen Old Inclosures/Homesteads 39)**. The 1777 militia list gives Edward Thornton as a surgeon. On the 1779 Enclosure Map this site is seen to accommodate a number of cottages in an "L–shaped" footprint at the back of the site. The same footmark is shown on the 1882/83 Ordnance Survey Map. The Steel family lived in some of these cottages.

The 1891 census of "Westrop End" shows nine members of Henry Steel's family living in one dwelling, and six members of Silvanus Steel's family in another.

Some cottages were situated across what is now the entrance to the site. These were lived in during the 1930s by the Lines and the Gare families **(see Map Fourteen point of interest 9)**.

As the road bears round to the left the Inclosure on this corner was allotted to John Bromley in 1779, an area of 28 perches **(see Map Fourteen Old Inclosures/Homesteads 38)**. It shows one small building side-on to the road.

In 1925, on the death of Mrs Mary Elizabeth Bromley, the Inclosure had two cottages built on it, and was sold out of the Bromley ownership at auction. The cottages were described as "Two well-built stone and thatched cottages with 'Tudor windows', containing Kitchen, Pantry and 2 Bedrooms." It can be assumed that this Inclosure was in the Bromley family ownership from the Allotment in 1779 to the sale in 1925. The occupants at this time were Mrs Rose Emma Stone (1868–1955) – Mrs Stone married twice; the first marriage to George Gardner in 1892 – and Mr Eyles in the other cottage. The Gardner family have been one of the families to occupy these cottages over the years, one of whom sadly ended his own life in the 1940s, in the lean-to barn on the end of the house, **(see Map Fourteen point of interest 10)**. Later this cottage was lived in by the Ayres family, and later in the 1950s the occupants were again the Gardner family with Bert Gardner, a local "Roadman". Later in life he built a modern bungalow in the garden. This is now occupied by Mr and Mrs Maurice Smith. The two cottages, now one dwelling, today are lived in by Mr and Mrs Fred Snook.

On the outside of the corner, to the right of the road, was a long building clearly shown on the 1779 Enclosure Map. On the 1882/83 Ordnance Survey Map this map indicates that the footprint was much smaller and shows two cottages on the site. These were on an Inclosure allotted again to John Bromley, an area of 1 rood 34 perches. This land was accessed from the Twistle **(see Map Fourteen Old Inclosure/Homesteads 8)**.

When these cottages were demolished, one was converted into a garage, **(see Map Fourteen point of interest 11)**, where Mr L. E. Jackson the School Headmaster (1943–1964) kept his 1935 Ford 10, which was of the relatively rare "C" model, nicknamed the "Barrel" because of the bulbous shape of the body.

Early Fords of Great Britain and the Model "C"
(Detail from a Car Encyclopaedia)

Until 1932 British-built Fords were assembled at Trafford Park, Manchester, and were Anglicized versions of the American models T and A. However, with the building of the vast Dagenham factory, opened in 1932, Ford of Britain was able to produce models specifically designed for use in the U.K. The first model to emerge from the new factory was the famous 933 cc 8 hp Model Y, with the simple side valve engine, three-speed gearbox and transverse leaf-spring suspension. The car, a full four-seater, was made in two- and four-door form,

and the two-door model became the first full-sized four-sized saloon to be sold for £100, in late 1935. In the same year, the 1172 cc 10 hp Model C was introduced, an attractive car with flowing bodywork lines.

The Model Y was replaced in August 1937, by the 7Y or "New Eight", which featured more rounded styling, "easy-clean" disc wheels. and doors hinged from the front – unusual in the 1930s. In the same year the Model C was replaced by the 10 hp 7W, with similar bodywork as for the 7Y.

The next Inclosure on the right was again allotted to John Bromley, an area of 3 roods 12 perches **(see Map Fourteen Old Inclosures/Homesteads 10)**. Today the first stone house, adjacent to the road on the corner of the north of the site, is on the same footprint as the dwelling is on both of the 1779 Enclosure Map and the 1882/83 Ordnance Survey Map. This map shows four cottages on the footprint. These cottages were later converted into one larger dwelling, and some farm outbuildings, by Jim Jordan, who moved into it in the 1950s. Other parts of the property were extended. This was then a working farm. An interesting building on the site was one purchased in the 1950s by Jim Jordan from the P.O.W. Camp, just down the Boddington road.

Frederick Batchelor, who is shown in the Byfield Memorial Book as being a smallholder and platelayer, built a new brick-built house in the 1920s. The Northamptonshire Directory of 1924 and those up to 1940 give Frederick Batchelor (1873–1953) as a smallholder.

The 1779 Enclosure Map also shows some other cottages on this site **(see Map Fourteen point of interest 12)**. They were accessed from the definitive footpath which ran along the south side of the site, between the Twistle and Westhorpe Lane, in the 1930s. Some of the people who lived there included Annie Douglas and relatives of the Smith family.

Part of the property was purchased in the 1970s by Mr and Mrs Tom Upfield as well as their home; the site became the administration base of the building firm Woodford and Upfield. The next plot on the right on the other side of the definitive footpath, was an Inclosure allotted to John Hopper, area 3 roods 39 perches **(see Map Fourteen Old Inclosures/Homesteads 11)**; this plot had a building running for almost the full length of the footpath. On the right, encroaching into the Inclosure to John Hopper, was another building abutting at right angles, and along the roadside. This building was also of considerable length and capacity, covering almost all of an allotment to a Josiah Boneham, which was an area of 5 perches **(see Map Fourteen Old Inclosures/Homesteads 12)**.

Opposite the site of these barns, on the left of the road, was an Inclosure allotted in 1779 to William Jordan, an area of 2 roods 2 perches **(see Map Fourteen Old Inclosures/Homesteads 35)**. Adjacent to the roadside there was a row of cottages occupied in the early 1930s by the Barnes, Wingrove and Freeman families, and others **(see Map Fourteen point of interest 13)**. The cottages have since been demolished, but today the position of some of the doorways can still be seen in the front roadside garden wall.

The property now known as "Wisteria Cottage" was previously known as "Bottomley's" after the School Headmaster who lived there. The house is shown in the 1881 Byfield Census as being occupied by Richard Bilson, a retired farmer who had previously farmed Westhorpe Farm in "Main Street", later to become Bell Lane. He is shown in the census as head of the household. Living with him were his daughter and his son-in-law William Bottomley (1844–1895), and two infant daughters. William Bottomley was the school headmaster at the National School in Church Street (1865–1895). The property is recorded as being owned by a Mrs Bottomley in 1925.

The house had a glass-roofed passageway from the house to another building to the rear of the property; this was the venue for the Victory in Europe Day celebrations after the Second World War, when all the school children in the Westhorpe area were entertained and given a high tea.

Other occupiers were: 1930s – Mr John Oliver; 1940s – Mr and Mrs Ted (Flip) Smith; 1950 – Mr Arthur John Evans and his two daughters; and in the early 1960s Mr and Mrs Andrew Bone, whose son Adam attended Byfield Primary School and who has returned to the parish to become one of the local doctors. Mr and Mrs Thomas now live in the house.

The next Inclosure on the left, allotted to James Riddle, was an area of 10 perches (**see Map Fourteen Old Inclosure/Homesteads 37**). In the 1930s Mr and Mrs

Owen Roberts built a new detached brick house on this site. Mr Roberts (1890–1969) had retired from his post as a schoolmaster in London and came to retire in Byfield. But Mr Roberts did help out by teaching for a few months in 1941 in the school.

He is best known for his compilation of the Byfield "Book of Remembance" which continues to be kept in the church and is continually updated.

Byfield Book of Remembrance (a newspaper report from the Banbury Guardian November 12th 1959 verbatim).

"In the presence of a large congregation, which included members of the British Legion and the St. John Ambulance Brigade, the Bishop of Peterborough on Sunday dedicated the Byfield Book of Remembrance in Byfield Church.

"This handsome book – the fruit of tireless work by the former Rector, the Rev R. B. Winsor and Mrs Winsor – contains the names of Byfield men who fell in the two World Wars and a record of 185 parishioners who died in the twelve years 1945–1956.

"With these are memorials to the late King George VI, and the two former Bishops of Peterborough, Bishop Blagdon and Dr. Spencer-Leeson (who wrote the foreword for the book). Also included are the names of the Rectors of Byfield since 1242.

"The Bishop, the Right Rev. R. Stopford, also dedicated a glazed oak case, craftsman-made by Mr Bird of Woodford in which the book will be displayed.

This photograph is of the collapsed cottage in Westhorpe Lane. The photograph was taken by Mike Bosley on the 1st of May 1983.

This photograph is annotated AS520 in the Byfield Photo Museum. Lender Mike Bosley.

"Bound in brown morocco leather tooled in gold, the pages of the book have been hand lettered and illuminated in gold and glowing colours by H.O. Roberts a retired schoolmaster living in Byfield.

"In his foreword Dr Spencer-Leeson wrote: The book is not only a Book of Remembrance but it is also a beautiful work of art. For both of these reasons it will be cherished in years to come – and as I turned over the pages I was conscious of the presence of a great family, not of the living and the dead, but those here and those beyond.

"The dedication took place at the Service of Remembrance at Byfield Church. Assisting the Bishop was the Rector the Rev. D. S. Mould. The Rev. Winser and Mrs Winser were also present."

The house has been purchased by Mr Mike Ward, who has modernised and extended it to make it a very desirable dwelling.

The next Inclosure is shown as backing on to and adjoining the previous plot. The 1779 Enclosure Map shows there is no additional land other than that covered by the footprint of the building **(see Map Fourteen Old Inclosures/Homesteads 36)**. This was allotted to Thomas Bromley, an area of just 2 perches. The building is shown on the 1882/83 Ordnance Survey Map as three cottages.

The roadway on the left, running in front of these cottages, was the access to an Inclosure; an allotment to John Gibbins of 1 acre 1 rood 19 perches. This land today is part of Greenwood Close, **(see Map Fourteen Old Inclosures/Homesteads 29)**.

As part of the planning conditions for the housing complex in Greenwood Close, this access was blocked off at the Greenwood Close end, still giving access to the other adjacent users of the roadway. This roadway was deemed to have been a "Pound" **(see Map Fourteen point of interest 14)**.

A definition of "A Pound" as in to confine straying animals (Oxford Dictionary verbatim)

"Pound" – to shut up or confine, as strayed animals; an enclosure in which strayed animals are confined; poundage, a charge made for pounding stray cattle.

Back to Westhorpe Lane, the next Inclosure on the left was allotted to Josiah Boneham, an area of 2 perches **(see Map Fourteen Old Inclosures/Homesteads 33)**. The 1882/83 Ordnance Survey Map shows a cottage on the site. One unusual feature of this cottage was that it had a stone winding staircase.

Occupants were: the Thornton brothers; then in the 1950s – Mr and Mrs Billy Edmunds; 1970s – Mr and Mrs Freeman. In the 1940s Muriel Smith had a small wooden building in the garden of the cottage from which she sold sweets. The cottage was sold in the1980s. The new owner was "working" on the cottage when it "fell down". Two new houses have been built on the site.

The Thornton Brothers

The two Thornton brothers, "nicknames" Do-Da and Nogger, lived in the cottage with the "stone stairs". It is said that all their possessions were on the kitchen table; "a loaf of bread", a "bowl of fat", "a candle in a bottle". The cottage had a chimney corner and the fire was such that Do-Da stoked his side of the fire, Nogger stoked his, never the twain shall meet. If a knock came at the door, Do-Da said "Your turn Nogger" "No! your turn Do Da!" and folklore has it that they never did answer the door.

The Inclosure behind the cottage was allotted in 1779 by the Commissioners to the Crown, an area of 28 perches **(see Map Fourteen Old Inclosures/Homesteads 34)**. The 1779 Enclosure Map shows that there was a fairly substantial building on the site, fronting onto the roadway/pound, only part of which is shown on the 1882/83 Ordnance Survey Map.

The last Inclosure on the left is referred to under Bell Lane **(see Map Eighteen Old Inclosures/Homesteads 32)**.

MAP FIFTEEN

BANBURY LANE

The BLACK NUMBERS are from the survey of Old Inclosures and Homesteads in the centre of the village.
The BLUE NUMBERS are Tracts of Land allotted to Proprietors and Owners in the rest of the parish.
The RED NUMBERS denote points of interest along the route.
Detail taken from the 1779 Enclosure Map.

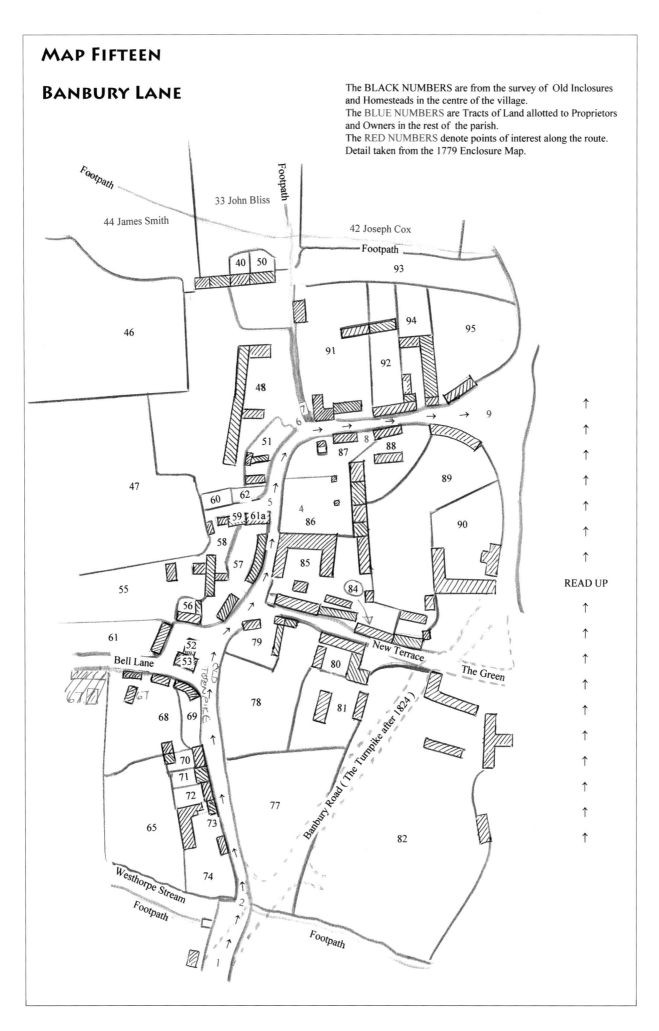

Footpath

44 James Smith

33 John Bliss

42 Joseph Cox

Footpath

40 | 50

93

46

94

95

91

92

48

7

6

9

51

8

87

88

89

47

60 | 62

5

59 | 61a

4

86

90

58

85

57

55

84

56

New Terrace

61

Bell Lane

52

53

79

The Green

80

67

67

78

81

68 | 69

70

71

72

77

82

65

73

74

Westhorpe Stream

Footpath

2

1

Footpath

OLD TURNPIKE

Banbury Road (The Turnpike after 1824)

READ UP

CHAPTER THIRTEEN

BANBURY LANE

"THE OLD TURNPIKE"

(See Map Fifteen)

The journey is started by walking down into the village from the direction of Banbury, on the "New Turnpike Road" (A361), with its prescribed width of 60 feet between the hedges. This is the measurement as was required within the 1779 Enclosure Act, **(see Map Fifteen point of interest 1),** a dimension that it was then, and still is today.

After crossing the Westhorpe (Blindwell or Blindle) stream and turning left onto the Old Turnpike, we see a narrow roadway which is now Banbury Lane. The traveller would have to be alert, especially if he was using a vehicle that was unusually wide, **(see Map Fifteen point of interest 2).** The road forward did not follow the line it does today until after 1824.

After negotiating the left turn into Banbury Lane, the first Inclosure on the left was allotted in 1779 within the

Enclosure Act to John Spicer, an area of 1 rood 9 perches **(see Map Fifteen Old Inclosures/Homesteads 74).** John Spicer is shown in the 1777 Militia list as being a collar maker!

The next Inclosure on the left, allotted to Jonathan Franklin, was an area of 1 perch **(see Map Fifteen Old Inclosures/Homesteads 73).** This would have been just a small building of thirty and a half square yards. The footprints of these two inclosures are shown on the 1882/83 Ordnance Survey Map, and they show different outlines from those on the 1779 Enclosure Map.

Both of these allotments were to come, by 1889, under the ownership of Benjamin Checkley (1861–1949), Farmer and Farrier, who was the son of Silas and Sarah Ann Checkley of Charwelton, where the family produced medication for animals. The 1903 Northamptonshire

This is a photograph of Banbury Lane, Byfield, showing the orchard on the left and a complete row of houses. At the top of the picture is Haycock and Russell's shop and to the left, further on, what today is 30/32 Banbury Lane and which is still known today as "The Pottery". This house would not have been visible after 1913, due to three stone cottages being built in front of it. The detail from Haycock and Russell's shop, and the cottages being built, date this photograph between 1903 and 1913, which is endorsed by the fact that the postmark on the photograph is July 25th 1913.

This photograph is annotated BH10 in the Byfield Photo Museum. Lender Mr Dick Haynes.

Directory records that he has expanded his business to become "Benjamin Checkley: Veterinary Surgeon & proprietor of the infallible ointment for human beings, also for cattle & horses; established since 1652."

The situation apparently was, from details of which were handed down by word of mouth, that Benjamin Checkley elevated himself to the rank of veterinary surgeon, and was notified by the Royal College of Veterinary Surgeons, "that this was not technically the correct procedure". This was reflected in the 1914 Northamptonshire Directory, where he is entered as Benjamin Checkley, cattle and horse medicines; the Directories up to 1940 show similar entries. The title given in those days when referring to a person who was treating animals but was not a qualified veterinary surgeon was that of "Horse Doctor". So in essence Benjamin Checkley was a Horse Doctor. It was said by his customers that he had an aptitude for treating animals. It is interesting to note that in the Byfield Memorial Book in the Church there is an entry which reads "Benjamin Checkley; Veterinary Surgeon"!

The Checkley family also kept animals on a number of small landholdings. After the death of Benjamin Checkley, his wife Charlotte Anne and daughter Elsie continued to farm the land until Mrs Checkley died in 1951. From then Elsie continued until her own demise in the 1980s.

In the 1920s and 1930s, Elsie Checkley ran a private school from the house. Some of the pupils were: Rupert Hornsby, Lillian Rand, Mollie and Betty Potter, Tom Montgomery, Peter Bromley and others.

The dwelling lived in by the Checkleys had a cottage attached to it on the north side. This was last lived in by the Waite family. When the Waites moved out around 1940, Benjamin Checkley pulled the house down to prevent any further occupation. After the death of Elsie Checkley, the land on which this specific house had stood was sold to a local builder, Will Montgomery, who constructed a small detached house on the site. Also, a new house, "a self-build", was built by the Bygrave family on what had been the Checkley's orchard.

On Miss Elsie Checkley's death the main house was purchased by the Gill family. It was then modernised and extended. Modernisation was needed, an example being that the house had never had running water installed, or indeed a connection to the main sewage system; these amenities were in an outside lavatory in the yard. In 1991 the Gill and the Bosley families "swapped houses". The Bosleys still live in the house today.

As we move from the big house, continuing on the left was a line of three terraced cottages, which in the early 1900s were all owned by the Maycock family.

The first of these cottages was on an Inclosure allotted in the 1779 Enclosure Act to Thomas Boneham, an area of 9 perches (see Map Fifteen Old Inclosures/Homesteads 72). The last occupants were Walter and Lottie Clegg, with their daughter Beatrice (Beatie) and her husband Fred Tuckey. In the 1940s and 1950s the Cleggs brought up a number of Doctor Barnardo boys, among them Jim and Tom Buckle and later Maurice Hanley.

The cottage was purchased from the owners, the Maycock family, in 1959 by John and Jill Russell, who owned the half acre paddock behind the site. The cottage was pulled down and a bungalow built on the paddock, with this plot being used as the access from Banbury Lane into the site. The half acre of land referred to is shown on the 1779 Enclosure Map as being of 2 roods 11 perches, and was allotted to Thomas Wells (see Map Fifteen Old Inclosures/Homesteads 65). The area is still the same today.

The second cottage is on an Inclosure allotted in 1779 to Daniel Treadwell, an area of 6 perches (see Map Fifteen Old Inclosures/Homesteads 71). This cottage was lived in by members of the Maycock family for a number of years, including Herbert Maycock after he married. He had previously been brought up in the adjoining third cottage owned by the Maycock family. Other occupants were: the Barrell, Bruce, Bailey, Clark and Miall families, and today the Jones family.

The third cottage was on an Inclosure allotted in 1779 to George Wilcox, an area of 20 perches (see Map Fifteen Old Inclosures/Homesteads 70). This larger plot, as shown on the 1882/1883 Ordnance Survey Maps, probably reflected that the buildings were more than a dwelling. This is shown as being so, for in the Northamptonshire Directories and ratified in the 1901 census the premises are shown as a shop. The 1901 census records that the head of the household was Thomas Maycock, a "House Agent"; one would presume that this occupation would today be described as an estate agent. His wife Emma was the shopkeeper, and son Walter at the age of fifteen is recorded as a "Newsagent" (alongside this entry is an unofficial note "Hawk"! made by the Enumerator Thomas Andrews, Byfield schoolmaster, which indicates that Walter was a Hawker). The census also records two more children, both at school. Mrs Emma Maycock (1860–1945) is recorded as a shopkeeper up to and including the Northamptonshire Directory of 1931.

Hawker

A contemporary dictionary, states that a hawker is: one who carries about goods for sale; a pedlar;
Hawk: *to carry about for sale; to cry for sale.*

Leslie Russell (1902–1987) often recalled, when he was a lad, having purchased 1d worth of sweets from the shop, also when required he was sent to purchase a new cap by his mother. These two items indicate the diversification of merchandise stocked in this small shop.

This propery was owned and occupied by members related to the Maycock family until the 1960s, when, after the demise of a female member of the family line Mrs Elsie Yandle, it was sold to the Pereira family. A wooden chalet was erected in the garden for use as a bedroom, as Mr George Grovenor Pereira (1906–1953) sadly suffered from tuberculosis. (Fresh clean air was recommended at the time for people suffering from this complaint).

The house was then sold to Colin Pilditch, who was a celebrity! He was a dancer and choreographer working for the B.BC. He is specifically remembered performing with the "New Generation" dance group who danced in a programme screened in the early evening on a Saturday. Colin lived with Karen his partner, later to become his wife. Karen bred pedigree long-haired cats as a hobby. They were housed in a special heated cat house in the garden. Karen was also proud of the fact that she had appeared in a certain tabloid newspaper "on page three". To prove it she had photographs in the appropriate non-attire hanging in the house.

The house is now lived in by the Broad family, who have extended the house and garden.

The Inclosure to the right of the lane, opposite these cottages, was allotted to Joseph Mountford, an area of 3 roods 16 perches (see Map Fifteen Old Inclosures/Homesteads 77).

The adjacent Inclosure on the right was allotted to John Edwards, an area of 2 roods 25 perches (see Map Fifteen Old Inclosures/Homesteads 78).

The area covered by the housing estate which today is known as Farebrother Close includes 77, part of 78 and part of 81 (see Map Fifteen). This land until the 1990s was owned by the consecutive breweries who owned the public house known as the Cross Tree. Prior to that it was known as the New Inn. Farebrother Close was named after the Farebrother family.

This area was used between 1911 and 1959 for the venue of the Byfield Pig Club's Annual Show.

The Byfield Farebrothers

The Farebrother memorials are in the Trafford Aisle of Byfield Church, and the interred remains of some of the family are in graves readily recognised as those having large flat raised memorials, in the churchyard to the south of and adjacent to the window in the Trafford Aisle.

The oldest entry on the Farebrother family tree shows Richard Farebrother (1728–1795). The Byfield Enclosure Map details also show Richard Farebrother being allotted four separate plots of land in 1779, which made up a considerable acreage. Richard's son William (1766–1838) married into the Bromley family, and this is the part of the Farebrother family that is commemorated in Byfield Church. One of the sons of William Farebrother and Mary Bromley was Thomas Farebrother (1807–1896) whose memorial is in the church. He was an ordained Anglican priest but was not an incumbent of the Byfield living. The 1869 to 1885 Northampton Directories also give the Rev. Thomas Farebrother as a principal landowner in Byfield. On his death the land ownership was inherited by a Miss Farebrother, whose address is given as Church Walk, Oxford, and is recorded in the Northamptonshire Directories as being a principal land owner up to the 1940s.

The land allotted to Richard Farebrother in the Enclosure Act of 1779 was obviously the land in part, or maybe the whole of the four allotments, that was passed down through the Rev. Thomas Farebrother to Miss Farebrother of Church Walk, Oxford.

The next Inclosure on the left. on the corner of Banbury Lane and Bell Lane, was allotted in 1779 to William Gibbins, an area of 15 perches (see Map Fifteen Old Inclosures/Homesteads 69).

The present owner, Bryan Martin, has completed a historical investigation into the property and its past own-ership and occupancy, the detail being too complex to record here. But to summarise: the building was extended in the mid-1700s with a new front door to Banbury Lane. In 1863 Samuel Gardner sold the cottage to John Smith and others for the erection thereon of a chapel or meeting place and school. In 1883 the cottage was sold to William Kerrod, a builder. In 1888 William Booth (1829–1912), founder of the Salvation Army, bought the adjacent property. The signature of William Booth is on the property deeds. Between 1888 and 1891 a Salvation Army barracks was built, attached to the western gable of the cottage. In 1894 the cottage was sold by William Kerrod to Frederick Turvey, Letter Carrier, for £80. (Frederick Turvey was also a Churchwarden, Sexton and bell ringer at Byfield Church). In 1916 John Andrews, Schoolmaster, bought the Barracks and sold the front three bays of the five bay building to Frederick Turvey (1858–1947) for £50. In 1949 the cottage and part of the Barracks was sold to George Henry Plummer for £900. In 1950 George Henry Plummer sold the cottage and part of the Barracks to Frank Raymond Ellington Monk "Gentleman" of 150 Watling Street, East Towcester for £1,100. In 1951 Frank Raymond Ellington Monk sold the cottage and part of the Barracks to Catherine Mary Prichard and Gertrude Mary Allison Prichard both of Hill Barn, Icomb near Stow-on-the-Wold, Gloucestershire for £2,850 (an astonishing profit margin of £1,750 on an outlay of £1,100 in just eleven months); did this reflect actually just how much of a gentleman F. R. E. Monk was, or was he just a profiteer? In 1992 the cottage and part of the barracks were sold to Bryan Martin who is the present owner and occupier. living there with his wife and daughter. At some time during the life of the cottage it became known as "The Gabled Cottage".

"The Gabled Cottage" Detail of some of its occupiers, its life and times (Verbatim).

1887 – Lieutenant Colonel John Toomer (1866–1943) of the Salvation Army (Detail verbatim from "Exile Always at Home" by Cyril J Barnes)

John's next appointment was to take charge as a Captain, of the Corps at Byfield, Northamptonshire. He travelled by slow train, arriving late at night in pitch blackness. Even the station boasted but one paraffin lamp, and that had a smoky chimney. John waited alone not knowing how to find his Quarters. Presently he heard voices. 'Can anyone direct me to the Salvation Army?' he called. And in a moment he was surrounded by half a dozen jolly young fellows who offered to act as guides and carriers. After a long and tiring walk one of the party announced: "Here you are Captain; goodnight!" The Box was dropped on the doorstep and the lads went off laughing. Next morning John discovered that his cottage was a few moments walk from the Station; he had been taken through every street in the village.

Despite a day spent visiting the soldiers, nobody arrived at the "Welcome Meeting", so by the time it was due to begin, John proceeded alone. He strapped the drum to his chest, took a stick with his left hand and a cornet with his right and marched towards the village green playing "We're the army that shall conquer". After he had spoken about the love of

God he asked if there was anyone who would like to be saved. A young woman knelt and prayed for forgiveness of sins at the drum, which John had laid down to act as a Penitent-form. She was the first of many to seek salvation during the months of his command.

Regarding the first weekend in Byfield, and when he had forgotten the loneliness of his arrival and another young officer had been sent to help him, John wrote to the War Cry: "Byfield Salvationists and friends, both saved and unsaved, gave us an encouraging welcome. When we arrived to take charge, we very soon felt at home. Sunday morning we assembled together to get filled with the Holy Ghost. A poor backslider came home to a loving God and found him ready to receive him. Hallelujah!

"We marched upon the villages of Hellidon and Charwelton and had some splendid times, getting back to Byfield for the evening meeting. We managed to pack in fifty people into our little cottage. We had a rather warm time, besides having to turn away a great number for want of room. On Monday night a young woman boldly took up her cross and came and sought salvation. Glory to God!"

A fortnight later a visiting officer reported: "Hello what is that?" The band! Heads are pushed out of the windows, doors opened, children running. It is the Captain taking a march all to himself, blowing his cornet and beating the drum at the same time. "Who's that shouting?" It is the Hallelujah Fishmonger acting as town crier. "What is he saying?" Come and have a cup of tea at the Salvation Army Barracks. About fifty people accepted the invitation. (John's only barracks was his cottage) People walk for miles from villages around anxious to hear our testimonies and never tiring of the story of Jesus.

In November John Toomer was able to turn over to his district officer the work he had commenced in Culworth, one of the surrounding villages.

Notes by J.R.

1891 Census shows that in "Barrack Row" there were six dwellings. The name is only used in this census. We must presume that these were cottages adjacent to the Salvation Army Barracks due to the location of the six dwellings as arranged within the 1891 Census, and also in one of the dwellings it names.

Pattie Pritchard is shown as Head of the household aged 27, and is listed as "Salvation Army Captain".

Alice Hunt, shown as companion aged 25, is listed as "Salvation Army Lieutenant".

***Backslider**: One who backslides; an apostate, a renegade, one who renounces or is false to his principles.*

Progressing forward past the turning to the left into Bell Lane. **(see Map Fifteen point of interest 3)**, then passing the village green, on which in 1779 shown on the Enclosure Map we see two Inclosures, one allotted to John Jones, an area of 2 perches **(see Map Eighteen Old Inclosures/Homesteads 53)**, and the other to William Turner, an area of 3 perches **(see Map Eighteen Old Inclosures/Homesteads 52)**.

The next Inclosure on the right was allotted to Jane Townend, an area of 24 perches **(see Map Fifteen Old Inclosures/Homesteads 79)**; on the Enclosure Map of 1779, just one building is shown, sited at an angle on the

corner of Banbury Lane and New Terrace. This building is not shown on the 1882/83 Ordnance Survey Map.

The row of three stone houses that are there today in Banbury Lane, and another row of five of the same design in New Terrace, were all built by a Mr Bartholemew of Blakesley Hall in 1913.

They have been occupied by a number of well-known local families; both Sgt. Judd and his son Denis lived there at different times in different houses. The families of Dugan, Eyles, Callow, Parkes, Kenyon and Sargeant, and others, all lived there.

The Inclosure opposite on the left, still known as "The Pottery" but now not used as such, was allotted in 1779 to Richard Davies, an area of 39 perches, and the Enclosure Map shows two buildings on the plot, both on the roadside. The first, the smaller of the two, is on the same footprint as the building that is there today. The map shows a gap between the first and second building which appears roughly twice the length of the other as it continues up bending to the left in a line with the road contour, **(see Map Fifteen Old Inclosures/Homesteads 57)**. The second building is not shown on the 1882/83 Ordnance Survey Map; it had obviously been demolished. In the 1950s a stone bungalow was built on this site by the well-known local builders, Thomas Kench of Eydon, for Mr and Mrs Hodgekins, a retired dentist, and his wife, followed by Mrs Irene Phyllis Russell until her demise in November 2000.

The first house which was to become "The Pottery" was obviously built before the Enclosure. The 1849 Northamptonshire Directory gives a William Samuel Sedgwick (1802–1895) as a draper and is shown in the Directory of 1874 as being draper and clothier and agent for the Manchester Fire and Life Office. The 1885 Directory expands to: "William Samuel Sedgwick linen & woollen draper, haberdasher, hosier & clothier, family mourning, carpets, hats, caps, bonnets, stays, flowers, boots and shoes". William Samuel Sedgwick was also the Enumerator for the Byfield 1891 census.

Haberdasher
A seller of small wares, as ribbons, tape etc.
Stays
A kind of stiff inner waistcoat, worn by females; corsets!

In 1893 the property was sold by Mr George Sedgwick to Mr William George Sedgwick (1852–1935).

Sale of Valuable Business Premises (detail from the Auction particulars)
Particulars and conditions of sale of Valuable Business Premises. To be sold by auction by Mr George Castle, Auctioneer at the Rose and Crown, Byfield.

On Tuesday November the 28th, 1893 at 4 for 5 o'clock in the afternoon.

A valuable Freehold Dwelling House and Business Premises containing Sitting Room: 3 Clothiers Shops: 4 Bedrooms and 3 Attics: Underground Cellar: Detached Kitchen with 2 Rooms Over: Brush House, Stable with loft over: Coach House, and Capital Piece of Garden Ground: the whole being pleasantly situated and adjoining the Village Street.

The property is held by Mr George Sedgwick, Draper and Clothier, under a lease for 17 years from 25th of March 1887 expiring on the 25th of March 1904 at a yearly rent of £30.

An excellent trade has been conducted on the premises for many years.

Land tax 10s 4d

Sold to William George Sedgwick of Byfield, Draper for £ 625.

Rose Emma Withers came from Tittleshall, Norfolk to train as a seamstress at the Sedgwicks in the 1890s. She was later to become Mrs Rose Emma Russell when she married Arthur Russell, and went on to have four children and six grandchildren.

The business was continued by William George Sedgwick until his demise in 1935. The property came into the ownership of Miss Jane Sedgwick and Mrs Mary Jane Farebrother. William's son Gerald Thompson Sedgwick, who had been trading on his own account as a light leather goods manufacturer, continued in the premises until 1936.

The premises were rented by Percy Thomas Jarvis in 1937, moving from the premises in Banbury Road from which he had been trading since 1923.

Percy continued as saddler, tennis racquet maker (restrings and repairs), radio dealer and a dealer in bicycles, but extended his business into charging up accumulators for radios, operating an exchange service. His recharging service also applied to the large lead acid batteries used to start the Byfield Ironstone navvies, the navvies being equipped with electric starter motors, but with no charging system to recharge the batteries. In fact Percy was quite an entrepreneur.

After Percy retired to a house on the Woodford road, the premises were purchased by a succession of potters and a kiln was built in one of the outhouses. The last three potters whose families lived in the premises were the Maund family (Mrs Maund was a teacher at Byfield School), the Kedros family, and the Buchanan-Wollaston family.

Nigel Buchanan-Wollaston produced a particular form of stoneware and was producing pottery in 1977 at the time of the present Queen's Silver Jubilee. The children of Byfield who were in full time education were presented with Commemorative Jubilee Mugs, suitably inscribed, that were unique, in as much as they were produced by the skilled hand of the local potter, namely Nigel Buchanan-Wollaston. The number produced was in excess of four hundred.

One would imagine that, by the time the Queen celebrated her Golden Jubilee, the mugs made by Nigel Buchanan-Wollaston had been distributed over a wide area, as the children who on that Silver Jubilee celebration day, in June 1977, had received those locally made mementos grew into adults and moved away, some to far away places.

Moving up the lane, and as the roadway narrows, the Inclosure on the right was in 1779 allotted to Thomas Cox, an area of 2 roods **(see Map Fifteen Old Inclosures/ Homesteads 85)**. Several large buildings are shown on the 1779 footprint; one adjacent to the roadside being in

a "U" shape, the open end facing back down the lane. By 1882/83 the only side of the building to remain was the part adjacent and side-on to the lane. Later these were to become known as "Blacksmiths Yard", as the first of the cottages was a blacksmith's, with the forge in an outhouse opposite the back door of the cottage, and this building is shown on the 1882/83 Ordnance Survey Map and on a photograph in the Byfield Photo Museum. The 1900 Ordnance Survey Map shows the map marked "Smithy" and indicates that it was of a considerable size. The blacksmiths shown in the 1847 Northampton Directory were John Samuel Townsend (1785–1852) and William Townsend (1808–1856), but only one John is in the 1849 directory. However, a John Townsend (1837–1909) is recorded as a Blacksmith until 1910, but as his death is recorded in 1909 the records after that could apply to his son Arthur John Townsend (1870–1938), who is also recorded in the 1901 census as a Blacksmith.

Mr Knightley's bill from Thomas Townsend, Blacksmith dated November 24th 1695 to April 30th 1696

Listed are 25 items some for goods, other work done which included "parts and labour" the total amount was £ 1-5s-3d.

The Church records show a Joseph Townsend as churchwarden in 1725. This together with the detail above indicates that the Townsend family were a longstanding Byfield family.

The row of cottages known as Blacksmiths Yard was purchased by the Byfield Ironstone Company between the First and Second World Wars. A number of well-known Byfield families lived there, some being employed by the local ironstone company; among them were the Haynes, Henning, Tomalin, Michell, Maycock, Batchelor, Maud, Seath, and other families.

At this point within the narrow confines of this lane, in September 1949, a member of the local Tomalin family, Barrington Charles Tomalin, always known as Barry, lost his life when he fell from the horse he was riding.

The next Inclosure, on the right, in 1779 allotted to Hannah Boneham, was an area of 1 rood 35 perches **(see Map Fifteen Old Inclosure/Homesteads 86)**; the 1777 militia list shows a Thomas Boneham as a weaver.

The cottages to the rear of the site were later to become part of a row of seven or eight cottages to be named "Cross Tree Cottages" and nicknamed "Hell Yard". These are shown on the 1882/83 Ordnance Survey Map. The families that lived there included the Tomalin, Burt, Brown, Steel, Stevens, Haynes, Webb, Douglas, Marriott and other families. The nickname of Hell Yard was probably given to the dwellings by the occupants, reflecting the standard of accommodation. The cottages were pulled down before the Second World War. Traces of the stone window frames can still be seen today in the remaining walls.

In the early 1800s a row of brick cottages was shown on the 1882/83 Ordnance Survey map as being seven. These cottages were named "Bank Cottages", obviously because of their elevated position, **(see Map Fifteen point of interest 4)**.

Some of the occupants were: Buckland, Marriott, Humphrey, Smith, Devonshire and Allen. One family, the Wrights, were grandparents of the Jones family of today; Mr Wright had an unusual job, that of a "Well-sinker". A sad and unusual set of circumstances occurred. Mrs Allen and her mother Mrs Wright were both living in this row of cottages when Mrs Allen died on March 5th 1950. Such was the trauma and shock to her mother that two days later she also died. Mother and daughter were buried in Byfield Churchyard on the same day, March 9th 1950. Mrs Winifred Elizabeth Allen was 55 years of age and Mrs Jane Wright was 80.

On the opposite, the left, side of Banbury Lane from the footpath to these cottages, is a house now named "Kings Farthing". Previously named "Fern Villa", its gable to the road, the plot on which the house stands is about the size of the area of the Inclosure, 2 perches allotted in 1779 to Mary Coates (**see Map Fifteen Old Inclosures/Homesteads 61a**). Another owner was Mary Lawrence. The property was let to Samuel Townsend; 1835 – John Owen; 1841 – William Gazey (junior); 1856 – Robert Austin (Yeoman); 1865 – Charles Dodd (grocer); 1881 – Sarah Dodd and Sarah Bloxham Dodd. (In 1938 Benjamin Checkley (1861–1949), at the age of 77, was asked to make a declaration that he had been sent by his father at the age of eight or ten to collect cattle medicines and drugs from a Charles Dodd, a Chemist. This would be in 1869 to 1871, when obviously the grocer had become also a Chemist). 1901 – Richard Bromley (1839–1919, (he married a Sarah Dodd in 1886). He is listed as a shopkeeper and grocer. Richard Bromley was the Byfield Parish Clerk from 1885 to 1906; he was also related through the lineage of the Coates/Bromley families, and he was the third son of John Bromley of Pitwell. Further occupants were: 1919 – Sarah Bromley; June 1928 – Percy Bloxham; July 1928 – Miss Ellen Margaret Garrett. In 1938 Miss Garrett purchased Inclosure number 60 from Annie Treadwell, and parts of Inclosures marked 57 and 59 from Jane Sedgwick and Mary Jane Farebrother. 1950 – Reverend Thomas Wilson, a retired Methodist Minister, and his wife Ethel; 1971 – Barry and Valerie Tarling; 1978 – Charles and Alison Burger; 1982 – Martin and Clare Bull; 1994 – Jasper Hope and Nicola Clarerton; 1999 – land registered in the name of Michele Hopley.

Valerie Tarling's Historical Research

Valerie Georgina Tarling researched and collected a huge amount of data about the history of Byfield, collated in date order. The work runs to four hundred pages or so. Not all are full of script, but the information contained within these pages is invaluable when researching Byfield's history. Sadly, Valerie died in 1981 at the age of 41. It was quite a while before the people interested in the history of Byfield realised what priceless work she had done over a long period with so much dedication. Valerie was interred in Byfield Church Yard on February 13th 1981.

As we pass the gable end of Kings Farthing, we could in 1779 have turned left into a cul-de-sac (**see Map Fifteen point of interest 5**). Further in, on the left in the cul-de-

sac, joining Kings Farthing is another cottage. The plot on which this cottage stands, again is on an Inclosure of 2 perches allotted to William Burbage (**see Map Fifteen Old Inclosures/Homesteads 59**).

Moving on again, the buildings on the left and the ground behind are on an Inclosure allotted to John Thornton (1730–1818), an area of 12 perches which would later become part of the "Pottery" (**see Map Fifteen Old Inclosures/Homesteads 58**).

On the other side of the cul-de-sac are two plots. One of 4 perches was allotted to William Burbage, which was opposite his other allotment, (**see Map Fifteen Old Inclosures/Homesteads 60**). The other plot of 3 perches was allotted to Mary Coates. Again it is opposite her previous allotment (**see Map Fifteen Old Inclosures/Homesteads 62**).

Carrying on along Banbury Lane, the next Inclosure on the left was allotted to Richard Townsend, an area of 11 perches. On the Enclosure Map is a building at the south end of the site (**see Map Fifteen Old Inclosures/Homesteads 51**). On the same site the 1882/83 Ordnance Survey Map shows two brick-built semi-detached cottages with the gable end adjacent to the road. These cottages were built in the mid-1800s and were pulled down in the 1950s. The last occupants were the Haynes family.

Getting to the acute right-hand bend, again on the left, is an entrance into a housing estate of three detached stone houses built in the 1990s and named "Hutts Close" (**see Map Fifteen point of interest 6**). In 1779 this was the entrance to a farm and farmyard. This was part of an Inclosure to James Smith, an area of 1 acre 1 rood 22 perches (**see Map Fifteen Old Inclosure/Homesteads 48**). To the west of this Inclosure is another allotment to James Smith of 2 acres 3 roods 24 perches (**see Map Fifteen Old Inclosures/Homesteads 46**), also with an allotment of 4 acres 3 roods and 20 perches (**see Map Fifteen Proprietors/Owners 44**). The land from the farm extended to the Boddington Road. James Smith is shown in the 1779 Enclosure List as a farmer of a total of 42 acres and 36 perches.

The farm and farmyard off Banbury Lane includes, as shown on the 1779 Enclosure Map, a very long building, which contained from south to north a brew house, the dwelling house, small store houses, a milking parlour, the farm's large barn-store and a small barn. The building which we see today is only part of this original building. This house has cruck beams within its construction, indicating that this house is one of the oldest dwellings in the parish. The house and adjacent farm were at some stage named Beechcroft Farm. The owners were: pre-1779 – James Smith; 1841 – James Smith (born 1796); 1869 – Richard Cleaver; 1881 – Lucy Cleaver; 1911 – James Richard Hutt; 1932 – James Robert Hutt. They did not all live at what became known as Beechcroft; records show that from 1912 to 1928 Frank Abbott lived there.

By the time the land came into the ownership of the Hutt family, the holding around the farm buildings included the plot originally allotted to Samuel Cox, an area of 2 acres 2 roods and 9 perches (**see Map Fifteen Old Inclosures/Homesteads 47**).

This is a photograph of Beechcroft Farm house taken around 1920.

This photograph is annotated JR24 in the Byfield Photo Museum. Lender Mr & Mrs Harris Watson.

This is a photograph of Hutts farmyard in Banbury Lane taken in 1971, and shows the herd of Ayrshire cattle in the milking yard. Ayrshires went out of favour as a breed but appear to be making a come back. H.R.H. Prince Charles has a herd at Highgrove.

This photograph is annotated AS125 in the Byfield Photo Museum. Lender Mr Cameron Frazer.

Plots 44, 46, 47 and 48 formed an area of 10 acres 1 rood and 13 perches, which became known as "Home Close" and still is today, and is still owned through the lineage of the Hutt family. When James Robert (Bob) Hutt was a young man in the 1930s he formed both a private Tennis Club and Bowling Club in Home Close; also comic cricket matches were held, Ladies versus Men, which were always followed by a communal tea.

Further on the left, next to "Hutts Close", is the start of a definitive footpath **(see Map Fifteen point of interest 7)**. The first part of this path is routed between two stone walls and is the access to six brick-built slated roofed cottages formerly named "Whitecroft Cottages", but since street naming and numbering in the 1950s now known as 14 to 24 Banbury Lane. The cottages were built in the early 1900s, but not on the footprint of previous buildings on the site. Occupants of these cottages included the families of Davies, Mold, Maycock, Clegg, Steel, Haynes, Porter, Thornton, Haslop, Tipler, Bristow, Bruce and others.

The 1881 census only records one dwelling on this site. The 1882/83 Ordnance Survey Map shows a large building with some smaller buildings on the site. The 1901 census only shows one family living there, that of Harry Maycock, his wife, three sons, one daughter and two "Boarders", one being a John Lines, bricklayer's labourer, and most likely to have been the husband of "Lotty" Lines and father of Reg and Bruce, late of The Haven in Church Street. The 1779 Enclosure Map shows a row of four buildings. The first one in from the footpath is an Inclosure allotted to John Bliss, an area of 39 perches **(see**

Map Fifteen Old Inclosures/Homesteads 50). The land behind the buildings up to the Boddington road was also allotted to John Bliss, an area of 2 acres 3 roods 35 perches **(see Map Fourteen Proprietors/Owners 33)**. This field was named "Whitecroft" in 1702. John Bliss also had a larger tract of land allotted to him on the north side of the Boddington road (opposite allotment 33); this was an area of 79 acres 31 perches.

The second cottage from the footpath is in an Inclosure allotted to William Nicholls, an area of 25 perches **(see Map Fifteen Old Inclosures/Homesteads 40)**.

The other buildings are within the curtilage of the Inclosure allotted to James Smith, number 48.

The Inclosure on the left of Banbury Lane on the right side of the wall of the definitive footpath was allotted again to John Bliss, an area of 2 roods 22 perches **(see Map Fourteen Old Inclosures/Homesteads 91)**. The "L-shaped" building shown on the 1779 Enclosure map is on the same site, but not the same footprint, as the building on the 1882/83 Ordnance Survey Map, which is the same as the house is today. This house is named "Whitecroft". It would have been built in the early 1800s, probably by the Farebrother family. There are now four new houses built on this allotment to the north of the site, on what was the farm yard when the site was a working farm. This development has been named "Whitecroft Lane".

The interesting aspect of the plots allotted to John Bliss, namely 50, 33 and 91, is that they, with the 74 acres 31 perches to the north of the Boddington road, make up the holdings which would become the "Whitecroft Farm"

This photograph is of the stone-built Whitecroft Cottages in the 1890s.

This photograph is annotated BH49 in the Byfield Photo Museum. Lender Mr Horace Aston.

unit, within one curtilage. Until the house and farmyard were sold in the 1990s, this remained as a unit; additional land was added, but all the farming was controlled from this base.

The parish record of 1803 lists a William Bliss as Churchwarden.

In 1919, when sites were being discussed for Local Authority rural housing, "Whitecroft" was a suggested site. In the Byfield Parish Council Minute Book, records show that the land was owned by the Farebrother family and was in the occupation of W. H. Potter.

Occupants were: 1901 – W. H. Potter; 1929 – Mrs M. E. Potter; 1940 – F. Over; 1949 – Edward Thompson; 1990 – Mrs Evelyn Thompson.

William Harris Potter (1862–1929)

W. H. Potter was born in Byfield, the second son of William and Catherine Potter, and married Mary Ellen Hall (1880–1940) at Shuckburgh in Warwickshire in 1900. William Harris Potter's grandfather on his father's side was Edmund Potter, and on his mothers side was John Harris. Both were eminent farmers, both born in Byfield.

W. H. Potter is listed in the Northampton Directories as being a farmer in 1890. The entry in 1903 shows him as "Farmer and forage contractor, Gentlemen's stables and

Newmarket trainers supplied"! He also sold forage and co-ordinated supplies to the Military during the 1914–1918 War. The use of steam-driven threshing machines, and other powered farm equipment, also reflected the fact that he was an entrepreneur.

As well as being an arable farmer and a land owner, he was also a well-known cattle breeder, winning numerous awards for the quality cattle at a number of shows, against other national recognized breeders.

Records show he was a generous and gregarious person; his involvement in the local community is legendary. He was the local band leader in the late 1800s and early 1900s; a member of the Church choir; a village Overseer from 1896 to 1903; a Local Tax Assessor in 1909; he was also a County Councillor.

He is shown in photographs as a leading member of the Byfield Football Club and of the Cricket Club. He promoted the laying down of a tennis court at Whitecroft. He is shown as being the leader in the celebration of national events such as organising the building of a huge bonfire in 1911 to enable Byfield folk to celebrate the Coronation of King George 5th.

His grandfather, John Harris, built Ironcross House in 1826; W. H. Potter built Ludwell House exactly 100 years later in 1926, laying down the gardens four years prior to building the house, but never lived there. His daughter

This photograph is taken in the farmyard at Whitecroft and shows the process of cutting hay "out of the rick" and carting it, probably for sale, as W H Potter who is sitting on a bale in the photograph, obviously supervising the work, was a farmer and forage contractor.

This photograph is annotated JR33 in the Byfield Photo Museum. Lender Mr & Mrs Harris-Watson.

This photograph was taken at Banbury Stock Yard with W.H. Potter's prize bull, with Ted Smith and William Eyles. Fond memories of Christmas past! An article from the Banbury Guardian December 20th 2001: "Equally popular was the Banbury Fat Stock Show. It first took place in 1880 and was a street phenomenon until 1925 when Midland Marts Ltd offered the new sale ground in Grimsbury. This occasion was specially remarkable because W. H. Potter of Byfield swept the board of prizes. He claimed 110 awards for fat cattle. In class seven, first place went to his animal which was later to cost Mr Jeffs the local butcher £54."

This photograph is annotated JR86 in the Byfield Photo Museum. Lender Mr & Mrs Harris-Watson.

Audrey married and became Mrs Watson, and started married life living in Ludwell; their younger son Keith Harris-Watson and his family still reside in the house.

William Harris Potter and his wife Mary Ellen are interred in Byfield Churchyard. They are also commemorated in Byfield Church in the form of a stained glass window in the east end of the north aisle.

In 1911, on the 22nd of June by kind permission of Mr W. H. Potter, the celebrations commemorating the coronation of King George V were held in the Whitecroft Grounds.

In the 1950s, when Edward Thompson was working the farm, there was a milking parlour on the site and other farm buildings. Some of these buildings were not needed for farm use, and so were let to Tom Pollard and Claude Webb, who were partners in a retail garage business.

Prior to moving to "Whitecroft", Edward Thompson farmed from Butterwell, and was one of the first milk producers to deliver pasteurised milk in the area in bottles. Edward was a true servant of Byfield; he served as a special constable, he was Chairman of Byfield Parish Council, he served as the elected Rural District Councillor on

Daventry Rural District Council, he was also a long-serving Church Warden for 28 years, and a member of the Byfield Charities committee.

Pasteurize (detail from a contemporary dictionary)
Pasteurize (from Pasteur, a French scientist) to sterilize Milk, etc. by heat.

Opposite Whitecroft, on the right side of Banbury Lane, located on the inside of the sharp right hand bend, is an Inclosure allotted in 1779 to Joseph Mountford (**see Map Fifteen Old Inclosures/Homesteads 87**). The two cottages now on the site are in the same position, but are now "L-shaped" as they also were on the 1882/83 Ordnance Survey Map. Occupants of these cottages included Mr and Mrs Trenfield. Mr Frederick Trenfield (1884–1962) was Station Master at Byfield Station from 1914 until 1949.

Other occupants included Mrs Irene Phyllis Russell, Mr and Mrs Harry Leigh, Mrs Jennings, Mr and Mrs Reynolds and others.

The entry immediately on the right past these cottages gives access to the rear of these cottages, together with

"Bank Cottages" and, when they were there, access to "Cross Tree Cottages" (Hell Yard) (see Map Fifteen point of interest 8).

Over the boundary wall from this entry, the next Inclosure was allotted to Richard Harris, an area of 32 perches (see Map Fifteen Old Inclosures/Homesteads 88). The 1777 Militia list shows Richard Harris as a farmer; he was also allotted in the Enclosure 12 acres 3 roods and 3 perches on the Priors Marston road next to "The Poors Allotment", later to be named Holcombe Hill Ground. The footprints of the buildings in Banbury Lane shown on the 1779 Enclosure Map, are shown as altered and enlarged on the 1882/83 Ordnance Survey Map, and again altered to form the buildings that are there today.

The Inclosure to the rear and to the side of this property, fronting on to Banbury Lane and further on to High Street, (see Map Fifteen Old Inclosures/Homesteads 89), was allotted to George Hitchcock, an area of 3 roods 16 perches. He was also allotted land off the Woodford road of some 106 acres 2 roods 26 perches, a considerable landholding, later to be named "The Big Field". The plot on the right corner of Banbury Lane and High Street is shown on the 1882/83 Ordnance Survey Map as an orchard. By the late 1880s allotments 88 and 89 became one and this was later known as "The Lawns"; it had an entrance into the orchard from High Street. In 1923 the owners became Herbert Travelyn Monroe (1868–1945) with his wife Dorothy. There is a photograph in the Byfield Photo Museum of Herbert on a fishing expedition to the local reservoir holding a pike which, because of Herbert's small stature, is almost as long as Herbert is high. Mrs Monroe is remembered as a smart, gregarious, forceful lady who organised fetes at the "Lawns", normally in aid of the Red Cross.

In the early 1950s "The Lawns" was sold to Gratton and Dorothy Darbishire. Gratton was a professional photographer and also a director of Darbishire Farms Ltd., who farmed Manor Farm, then around 295 acres. Mrs Darbishire was by profession a nursing sister, who had worked in a remote Mission Hospital on the north-west frontier of Pakistan. The Darbishire family became very involved with village life – Dorothy in various organisations, especially the village drama groups; Gratton serving on several village committees including Byfield Parish Council, and also serving on Daventry Rural District Council. The orchard was later sold and was to have two dwellings built on it; the first a bungalow built in the 1960s by Martin Lilley for his own use. Later occupants were Colin and Greta Thornton and their family, followed by Percy Blake and his first wife, and later with his second wife Janet. Since Percy's death Janet still lives there. The second dwelling, on part of the orchard, was built recently.

In the late 1970s the Unification Church was using The Lawns with the blessing of Gratton Darbishire as a recruiting centre.

The effect of the Unification Church coming into the rural community of Byfield.

In the late 1970s "The Lawns" became a refuge for newly-recruited members of the Unification Church, commonly known as "The Moonies". The recruits changed every two weeks so there was a considerable throughput; this disturbed the village community, and some people thought the recruits looked and acted "different" from the normal villager.

There was concern that people, especially young people, would be persuaded to become involved. Because of this the village people probably overreacted, and letters were written and verbal representations made, by both individuals and village organisations, to Byfield Parish Council, Daventry District Council, the local M.P. etc.

One problem that befell the Byfield Parish Council, and especially its Chairman, was the considerable national media interest. As the problem was of a civil as well as an ecumenical nature, the civic authorities could deal with the enquiries into the civil implications of the problem, but did not have the specialist knowledge to comment and deal with the ecumenical aspects. The problem was exacerbated by the fact that the Byfield parish was in an interregnum and had been for a number of months.

The Byfield Parish Council sought the help of the Vicar of Woodford, who fortunately was pleased to help. The media was then dealt with by the Chairman and members of the Parish Council dealing with the press on the civil aspects of the problem, and the Vicar of Woodford dealing with the ecumenical aspects.

The Parish Council was concerned that the Anglican Church, having become involved at a higher level through the media interest, was condemning the actions and teachings of the Unification Church without putting forward the Christian teachings of the Anglican Church. In short, their stance was negative rather than positive! The Parish Council Chairman contacted the Archdeacon of Northampton, making the Council's point that these actions were not allaying the fears of the people of Byfield. "What do you want me to do?" was the Archdeacon's question. "Come and preach to the people of Byfield to allay their fears" was the reply!

The Archdeacon came and preached at evensong in Holy Cross Church Byfield. This did a lot to calm the situation and went some way to allay the parishioners' fears.

Fortunately a new Rector was appointed, and he was seriously concerned to the extent that he found it necessary to excommunicate one of the leading members of the sect from using the Parish Church.

With the involvement of the Daventry District Council, the Planning Authority, and again through the amount of media interest, the owner of the property was advised that, with the numbers of people being housed in the Lawns, planning permission was needed. Obviously the owner of the property was aware that considerable expense would be incurred to make the property conform to enable it to be used for such multiple occupation, and that perhaps the buildings were not conducive to such alterations that would be necessary to make them comply anyway.

The use of the property by the Unification Church ceased, and the concerns and worries of the people of Byfield regarding the members of the sect living within their midst were alleviated.

The ironical aspect of the newly recruited members being looked on as "different" was that, with the considerable persuasive methods of such organisations when recruiting new members, we were probably all at risk to some degree, and might have found ourselves in a communal dormitory in a building being used for "multiple occupation".

A Jogger's story

As a jogger and his red setter dog were doing their normal keep-fit run through the disused Byfield Station, on the derelict platform were four people standing facing inwards towards each other praying! The jogger, who was a bit of a "wag", continued on his way. On reaching home he decided to put the story round the village, that he had seen these people praying and had stopped and advised them that it was no use praying; the train would never come; they "took" the lines up in 1965.

At this point, on the left side of Banbury Lane opposite The Lawns, was an Inclosure allotted in 1779 to Joseph Cox, an area of 1 rood 3 perches **(see Map Fifteen Old Inclosures/Homesteads 92)**. The 1779 Enclosure Map shows a long building parallel with the road. The footprint of the building on the 1882/83 Ordnance Survey Map shows a larger differently-shaped building.

The 1849 Northamptonshire Directory shows Robert Lake Lord (1823–1875) as a butcher and baker, and the 1849 Directory shows Mrs Sarah Ann Lord (née Newcombe 1826–1891) as a straw-hat manufacturer. But with the death of her husband from a stroke, which in those days was called "apoplexy", she is shown in the 1877 through to the 1890 directories as a baker and butcher, and the 1881 census also shows a Sarah Ann Lord, a widow, as butcher and baker, in the Old Turnpike Road. The other interesting aspects are that the census records Bessie Lord aged 18 as a Pupil Teacher, and her sister Edith aged 13 as a Stipendiary Monitress (Classroom helper). The girls would by then have been attending the National School in Church Street. Also recorded is that a visitor in the household was a retired Inn Keeper, a Mary A. Newcombe. Mrs Newcombe had previously been Landlady at the Bell Public House.

The 1894 and 1898 Directories show a James Lord as butcher. The 1903 Directory shows Arthur J. Montgomery as a butcher. The 1901 census shows that the premises was a butcher's; Thomas H. Montgomery recorded as a retired farmer, and his wife Elizabeth as a butcher together with Arthur J. her son. Another son, Herbert H., and an employee, a Herbert J. Green, were also butchers but listed as "Journeymen". The number of butchers indicates a fair volume of trade on the premises. The 1903 through to 1920 Directories show Arthur J. Montgomery (1867–1926) as a butcher. With the demise of Arthur J. Montgomery the butchers business moved into Byfield High Street to use the same premises as an off-licence; the butcher's business being run by Mrs Louisa Montgomery and the off-licence being run by William Montgomery.

Journeyman

Journeyman: one who works by the day; any hired workman.

The premises today, under the arch of the gateway, still has the large pulley wheel that was used to hoist the animal carcases up into a vertical position to enable the butcher to dissect the carcase into more manageable joints.

In 1920 Thomas George Lamb (1898–1956) operated a carriers business here. At this time his parents rented the property. The property was later to be named "Chimneys". On leaving the army in 1918 after serving in the First World War, Tom started initially operating in Woodford, but in the 1924 Byfield entry of the Northamptonshire Directory Thomas George Lamb is shown as a carrier of both passengers and goods to Banbury and Northampton. He is also shown as a "Fruiterer", progressing in the 1928 Directory as a carrier, fruiterer and motor engineer with cars for hire. Later directories also show Tom Lamb as an omnibus proprietor.

Just before the Second World War Tom purchased the property; however he still did not live there but at "Cosy Corner" in Potters End. It was obvious that Tom Lamb was another of Byfield's entrepreneurs.

Later, due to pressure of work, Tom's mother Mrs Clara Lamb is shown as having taken over the running of the fruiterer's business; Mrs Clara Lamb's father was Thomas Wright, a miller at Farndon Mill.

When Tom's son Ken was demobbed from the Royal Air Force in 1953 he operated up to five taxis from Chimneys.

Miss Margaret Lamb lived in the house with her mother and ran a hairdressers business; she also dealt in small antiques and curios from the premises. In the Byfield Photo Museum we have photographs of Margaret previously working in a mobile hairdressing salon in an adapted Pantechnicon lorry.

With the death of Miss Margaret Lamb in 1990 and her mother Mrs Irene Lamb in 1991, the premises were sold and used as a private house.

The next Inclosure on the left was allotted in 1779 to Elizabeth Wise, an area of 39 perches **(see Map Fifteen Old Inclosures/Homesteads 94)**, the footprint of the main building is the same as we see today. Records indicate that the property was owned by the Brightwell family in the 1880s, further owners were: 1886 – W. H. Potter; 1910 – John Jones; 1925 – Mary Pilcher; the Reverend Sidney F. Pilcher retruned to Byfield where he had previously been Church Curate from 1915 to 1918. Sadly, on retiring in Bristol he died as a result of a road accident in July 1953. 1952 – the Vereker family (Mr Vereker was Treasurer of the Village Hall when it was opened in 1960); 1982 – Dr McAvoy and family; 1984 – John and Janet Dunlop. The property was requisitioned in the Second World War by the Military and was used as an Officers' Mess.

Maurice Charles Prendergast Vereker (1884–1963) is recorded in Byfield records as a farmer. During his service in the British Army he was awarded the Military Cross. His wife's surname before marriage was Fiennes, of the well-known acting family, by which connection he was related to Lord Saye and Sele of Broughton Castle near Banbury.

Continuing on the left, the next Inclosure was allotted to Samuel Batchelor an area of 2 roods 1 perch. This plot also included a property known as "The Hollies" **(see**

This photograph is of Chimneys, the Lambs' fruit and sweet shop in Banbury Lane The photograph was taken in 1926 and shows Mrs C. Lamb and Mrs T. Lamb with Margaret and her "Hobby Horse".

This photograph is annotated KL23 in the Byfield Photo Museum. Lender Ken Lamb.

This cottage was named Japonica Villa, today it is number 4 Banbury Lane, which was previously the Old Turnpike, and the photograph is of John Jones the Byfield Postmaster. The photograph was taken around 1910.

This photograph is annotated JR23 in the Byfield Photo Museum. Lender Mr & Mrs Harris-Watson.

Map Fifteen Old Inclosures/Homesteads 95). The 1777 Militia list records Samuel Batchelor as a servant. The footprint of the two semi-detached cottages that are now on the site is the same as shown on the 1882/83 Ordnance Survey Map but larger than the footprint shown on the 1779 Enclosure map.

The occupants of these cottages were: John Jones Postmaster, 1890 to 1912; Mr and Mrs Mee; Miss Tottenham; Mrs and Mrs Bill Knight; Mrs and Miss Linlaw; more recently Mr and Mrs Bob Lowe.

The strip of land to the rear of the Inclosures numbered 91, 92, 94 and 95 was allotted to Joseph Cox, an area of 1 rood 37 perches (**see Map Fifteen Old Inclosures/ Homesteads 93**); this strip joined his previous allotment numbered 92.

* * * * *

This brings us to the junction of Banbury Lane and High Street (**see Map Fifteen point of interest 9**).

CHAPTER FOURTEEN

THE GREEN

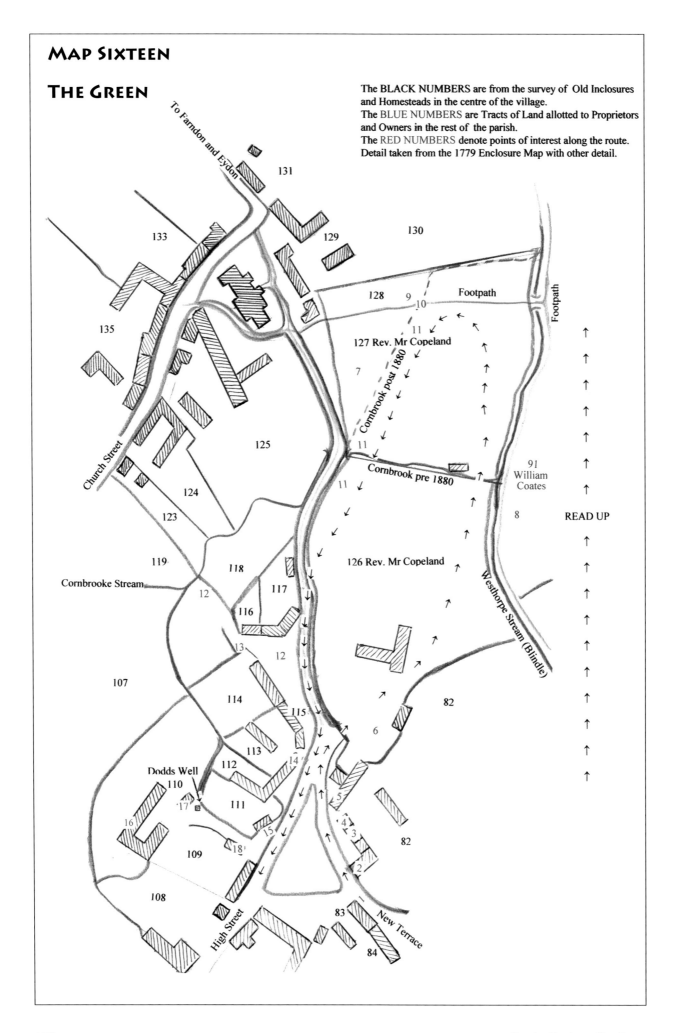

Map Sixteen

The Green

The BLACK NUMBERS are from the survey of Old Inclosures and Homesteads in the centre of the village.
The BLUE NUMBERS are Tracts of Land allotted to Proprietors and Owners in the rest of the parish.
The RED NUMBERS denote points of interest along the route.
Detail taken from the 1779 Enclosure Map with other detail.

To Farndon and Eydon

131

133

129

130

Footpath

128   9
10   Footpath

135   11

127 Rev. Mr Copeland

7

Cornbrook post 1880

125   11

Cornbrook pre 1880

91 William Coates

124   11

123   8   READ UP

119   126 Rev. Mr Copeland

Cornbrooke Stream   118   12

117

12   116

13

12

107   114

115   82

6

113

112   14

Dodds Well
110   5

17   111

16   4   3

15   82

18

109   2

108

High Street   83   New Terrace

84

Church Street

Westhorpe Stream (Blindle)

Chapter Fourteen

The Green

(See Map Sixteen)

We are now moving east out of New Terrace from the side of Flora Innes House **(see Map Sixteen point of interest 1)** and over the main road. All of the stone houses on the right were allotted in 1779 to George Hitchcock, an area of 2 acres 2 roods and 38 perches **(see Map Sixteen Old Inclosures/Homesteads 82)**. The extent of allotment included what is now part of the main road (this was prior to the Turnpike road being redirected along its present route). It also included the slaughter house, and all of the land on which Edwards Close is built down to the Westhorpe stream.

The first house with its gable facing The Green, has now a window on the ground floor; this was originally a doorway **(see Map Sixteen point of interest 2)**. Photographs show that it was a shopfront showing the sign J. H. Warr Saddler. This is confirmed by the Northamptonshire Directories, which detail John Henry Warr, saddler in 1894 and 1903. The 1901 census shows that John Henry Warr was born at Buckingham, his wife Alice in London, and together they lived with their two children aged 4 and 6; both born in Byfield. There was a lodger, a 19 year old John Alfred Witherby, also a saddler, who was born in West Haddon. Others who lived there were: 1943 – Miss Mary Edith Billson (1886–1960, eldest daughter of Thomas R J Billson of Westhorpe Farm); 1960 – Cecil Cockerill and family; 1980s – Mr and Mrs Robert (Bill) Johnson to the 1990s.

The house in the middle of the three facing the Green, now number 12 **(see Map Sixteen point of interest 3)**, was occupied by: 1881 – Samuel Bush (grocer); 1891 – Anne Fenemore (caretaker); 1901 – John E Potter. (An occupant of the house at this time as a lodger was Frederick Lawlor, the Byfield Station Master). The property was used by the Byfield Conservative Club for accommodation of Club officers and staff. The property on the bottom end of the row, now number 11, was used as a Conservative club, **(see Map Sixteen point of interest 4)**. The accommodation within the club was a large club room on the first floor, built over a lounge bar and skittle room.

Some of the officers from the club's inception were:
President: 1890 – J. H. Bromley; 1914 – Sir C. V. Knightley, Bart.
Chairman 1914: J. H. Bromley.
Secretaries: 1890 – W. H. Potter; 1894 – William Kerrod; 1903 – Henry Goodland; 1906 – William Waite; 1928 – Gerald Thompson Sedgwick; 1940 – Frank H. Over.
1914 – there was a change of title to Byfield and District Working Men's Conservative Club!

1928 – again a change of title, to Byfield Conservative and Constitutional Club!

Details from a contemporary encyclopaedia show:
The word Conservative as a title first came into use in 1830.

The club was used by members and guests, and it is also recorded that it was used by the Mothers' Union for meetings. The premises also accommodated wedding receptions. The building was used in the Second World War as a N.A.A.F.I. Canteen, used by troops billeted in a variety of accommodation in the village.

The N.A.A.F.I.
The N.A.A.F.I. was the Navy, Army and Air Force Institute providing canteen facilities for local servicemen and women.

After the premises had been derequisitioned, they were rented by Harry Stockley, who was a printer, and subsequently by Colin Thornton, also a printer.

Just before the First World War the site of these properties, including the field on which Edwards Close is built, came into the ownership of James Tack (1863–1947), a farmer living at the Manor. On his death, it was passed to Mrs Emma Tack (1864–1950), who was living in one of the properties at the time of her demise. The whole holding was then bequeathed to Cyril Nicholls, who was Mrs Tack's nephew.

Later the site was purchased by a Miss K. R. Ponting, a member of the family running the London store of Pontings, well known for its specialist mail order outlet.

The rural news reporter from the local
Banbury Guardian.
When the Pontings London store closed, Miss Ponting acquired some of the stock; large wooden boxes of fabrics etc. One of the boxes contained a large number of bottles of eucalyptus oil. Miss Ponting was very fond of cats and kept several. They were house cats and used cat trays in the house. To offset the odours from the cat trays, Miss Ponting used what she had the most of and that was, in this case, eucalyptus oil! These trays were emptied outside the back door of the house. After a time there was an accumulation of a strong-smelling heap of eucalyptus-oil-impregnated mixture. Such was the strength of the odours, that it was obvious even from the adjacent public pathway and roadway.

On the regular monthly meeting of Byfield Parish Council, a young reporter from the Banbury Guardian came to do a feature on Byfield Parish Council. One of the first subjects under discussion was a complaint through the local doctor, who was also a councillor, who stated "What are we going to do about this smell of eucalyptus oil?" The local reporter sat back looking rather puzzled, but not being able to ask a question because the council was in closed session. The meeting continued, and had within its membership older village people who referred to people and places by nicknames or names long lost in history, and who also expressed strong opinions when details from the past were called into question. The young reporter wrote nothing or very little. He must have gone back to his editor complaining of being sent to a village whose language had little resemblance to the English he had been taught, and being asked to report on people, places and situations completely unknown to all others beyond a select few from the village "out in the sticks"; a place called Byfield. Obviously no article from this reporter about this specific Parish Council meeting, in this strange place, ever appeared in print.

The slaughter house and adjacent buildings are shown on the 1779 enclosure map, virtually on the same footprint as they are today **(see Map Sixteen point of interest 5)**. The slaughter house is now a dwelling and the adjacent buildings that were byres are now garages. When the slaughter house was in use, up to and including the 1930s, Harry Hyde, the knacker-man, slept in the loft.

The stone houses and the slaughter house were sold off. The land to the south was sold to a developer, who built there what is now Edwards Close **(see Map Sixteen Old Inclosures/Homesteads 82)**.

Continuing in an anticlockwise direction around the Green, the next building on the right is the new Village Hall **(see Map Sixteen point of interest 6)**. An article in the Northampton Mercury and Herald dated June 10th 1960 indicates the intention of Byfield residents to build a new hall.

Byfield Village Hall, The Green Byfield
(copied verbatim)
The seed was sown on Queen Elizabeth II's coronation day, June 2nd 1953, when on the Brightwell Recreation Ground in the middle of the village two stones were laid to mark the site of the new Village Hall.

These two stones were laid by Mr Alfred Brightwell, at 91 the oldest inhabitant in the Village, the brother of the donor of the playing field. Because of a difference of opinion with the Town and Country Planning Committee, the Byfield Village Hall New Management Committee had to move the site of the Hall a few yards from where the stones had been placed.

Now the stones have been incorporated in the front of the new building. Surrounded by old stone-built cottages, with the Parish Church in the distance, the Recreation Ground is a picturesque setting. The overall cost of the hall will be £4,684, of which £ 4,128 has already been raised, the most recent of which being a fete on Saturday which added £65 to the total.

The Village itself has raised £1,417 and there are firm promises of another £50. A Ministry Grant of £1,561 is assumed, while bonds of £800 raised by the British Legion for a Hall some years ago have been handed over. The Recreation

Ground Committee has donated £ 200 and a further £150 banked from the old Village Hall fund.

At present Village activities take place in a forty year old, wood and corrugated iron hut, given to the Village by the British Legion some 9 years ago. This will be sold and it is expected that a sum nearing £200 will be obtained.

The New Hall has been designed to cater for all tastes among the village's inhabitants. It is 82 feet long by 26 feet wide. When all the appointments and furnishings are complete there will be an auditorium 41 feet by 24.

Beneath the stage will be dressing rooms, while at ground level are cloakrooms, toilets and kitchen space. The dance floor will be made of hardwood blocks.

The full history of Byfield Village Hall can be found in Chapter Nineteen.

The next facility, continuing again anticlockwise around the Green, is the Recreation Ground, the first section of which was a gift of land in 1944 by Thomas Brightwell in memory of his son who had been killed in action in the First World War. Additional land has since been purchased by Byfield Parish Council and the area extended.

The Enclosure Act in 1779 shows the original land, which was located between what are now the Westhorpe and the Cornbrook streams, as two Inclosures of land separated by the Cornbrook stream which then flowed across what would now be the centre of the field and joined the Westhorpe stream.

These two Inclosures, were numbers 126, an area of 2 acres 3 roods 10 perches, and 127, an area of 2 acres 22 perches, **(see Map Sixteen Old Inclosures/Homesteads 126 and 127)**. Both plots were allotted to the Reverend Mr Copeland, the Byfield Rector's Curate. The field name was Dove House Close, known locally as "The Duffus", when the plots subsequently became one. Allotment 127 also included in 1779 what was to become by the Ordnance Survey of 1882/83 part of the churchyard **(see Map Sixteen point of interest 7)**.

Know your place!
The Reverend Mr Copeland was the Rector's Curate. It is apparent that the Rector John Knightley at the time of the Byfield Enclosure was reluctant to let his curate be Reverend Copeland. The serious pecking order of the day must be maintained! There was to be only one Rector and the Rector's curate would be known by the title of "Reverend Mr".

Note by J.R.
This order of rank is further illustrated by Gilbert Gilbert (Christian and surname the same) who in the middle of the 1800s was the Byfield Church Clerk. He also was an Ordained Priest, but he seriously had to "know his place".

The Enclosure Map again shows the land to the south-west of the Westhorpe stream. This was initially, at the time of the Enclosure, part of a much larger landholding, and included further to the south-west an allotment of 22 acres 1 rood and 22 perches allotted to William Coates **(see Map Sixteen Proprietors/Owners 91)**. When the railway was built in 1866 a part of this allotment between the Westhorpe stream and the railway became known as

This is a photograph of the occasion on June 2nd 1953 when Mr Alfred Brightwell, the oldest resident in the parish at the time, laid the foundation stone that would later be part of the construction of the New Byfield Village Hall. The other people attending were, left to right, George West, George Farmilo and Fred (Dink) Haynes.

This photograph is annotated JR548 in the Byfield Photo Museum. Lender Mr Derek Thornton.

the Shoulder of Mutton because of its shape. Later, in the 1980s, it was to become known as "William's Field", after a much loved Byfield horse that grazed there **(see Map Sixteen point of interest 8)**.

The full history of the Brightwell Recreation Ground can be found in Chapter Eighteen.

At the bottom of the Recreation Ground, overlooking the area, is a cottage which is now numbered 42 Church Street. As the Cornbrook stream flows through the property it is appropriately named Brook Cottage **(see Map Sixteen point of interest 9)**. This cottage was originally two dwellings; these were the last cottages situated in the bottom end in what was then "Gooseberry Lane". The cottages are not shown on the 1779 Enclosure Map, but the Inclosure was allotted to "Gibbs" (no Christian name listed), an area of 1 rood 10 perches **(see Map Sixteen Old Inclosures/Homesteads 128)**, and the cottages are shown on the 1882/83 Ordnance Survey Map on the same footprint as they are today. Occupants of the cottages were: 1940s – Mr and Mrs Frank Walters (Frank Walters (1882–1963) worked at Byfield Woodyard); the McKenzie family with "Granny" Rainbird being evacuated here in 1941; 1970 – the Sampford family; 1980 – Mr and Mrs Rod Healey.

Getting the Message to the Customer

When Granny Rainbird was preparing the family's meal in Brook Cottage, it would almost certainly consist of fruit and vegetables in season; the skins and peelings were put in a bucket! At the time Stan Checkley was renting the Brightwell Field from the Parish Council. Stan kept a pig in the field, a black and white saddleback sow. Granny, standing at the field fence, would hit the bucket with a stick; immediately "the customer raced to the product"! This must be the ultimate method of advertising!

The definitive footpaths in this area today are shown on the Enclosure Map of 1779.

We continue in an anticlockwise direction around the area towards a concrete slab which forms a bridge across the Cornbrook stream. The top of this slab was the datum used when the Brightwell was levelled and developed in the 1980s **(see Map Sixteen point of interest 10)**. Turning and moving up a line of Lime and Poplar trees, that follow the line of the stream in the Brightwell Field, these trees were planted in 1962 by the "Byfield Preservation Group" (since disbanded). The trees are actually planted directly over the main sewer which flows from north and east end of the parish. One would presume this was an oversight; obviously the pipes are deep enough under so as not to be affected by the tree roots. To date the system is still working! **(See Map Sixteen points of interest 11.)**

The next cottage on the right is "The Old Thatch", one of the oldest cottages in the parish and clearly shown on the 1779 Enclosure Map; an Inclosure that was allotted to John Serjeant (1731–1814) of an area of 33 perches **(see**

Map Sixteen Old Inclosures/Homesteads 117). George Marlow (1809–1884), a retired rope maker, is shown as living there in the 1881 Census. He was also shown to be the Independent Chapel Keeper in 1884. Records also show that the well-known character Dick Haynes was born in "The Old Thatch" in 1909. Later Edward Matthews (1876–1945) lived there, and in the 1940s and 1950s a Miss Smart, living with her uncle Reginald Edward Bernard Phillips (1882–1970). People remember his two cars; one a Rover coupe and the other an Austin 10 coupe, both of which were rare models.

The adjoining cottage, on an Inclosure allotted to Peter Smith, an area of 13 perches **(see Map Sixteen Old Inclosures/Homesteads 116)**, was later known as "Knowle Cottage". Occupants included Frederick William Hutt (1874–1935), a wheelwright, and his wife Constance (1880–1975), who outlived her husband by 40 years; the Russell family; and the Haynes family. The cottage is now owned by the Moran family.

The tongue of land down the side of this cottage is shown on the 1779 Enclosure Map as an access through to Church Street, in part passing along the bed of the Cornbrook stream. In living memory it was said that the "Knacker Cart" used to be driven through the stream to wash the blood out and off it!

In 1972 parish councils were advised by Central Government to register all common land not in private ownership as Village Greens. A number of parcels of land were registered by Byfield Parish Council. Among them was the triangle of land in front of these cottages, registered as a Village Green, as is the tongue of land leading from it ending at the stream **(see Map Sixteen two points of interest 12)**. This led to an ownership dispute.

A dispute over land ownership

Within the Local Government Act there are the powers given to Parish Councils to register land as village greens. There is within the act, as there is in all such acts, a procedure of appeal to enable persons disputing the legality of the registration to appeal against the registration of the land, as a whole or in part.

In this case, two of the adjacent property holders separately appealed against part of the registration of this specific village green. The outlines of the land in the individual appeals in fact overlapped.

The Commissioner hearing the appeal was The Right Honourable Sir Reginald Manningham-Buller M.P. The result was that the Commissioner ruled that the whole of the land had been correctly registered and was "Village Green".

One of the appellants appeared not to accept the initial registration, or indeed the decision of the Commissioner on appeal, that this area was in fact Village Green, because he erected a fence to prevent free passage across the green!

The Parish Council took legal advice though the Association of Local Councils and were advised that solicitors should be employed to get the obstruction that had been erected removed.

This photograph of The Green was taken from the Church Tower in 1962 by Fred Hutt it shows the extent to which the area has changed from what it is today.

This photograph is annotated AS254 in the Byfield Photo Museum. Lender Tim Hutt.

The Parish Council Chairman was instructed to liaise with the Council's Solicitor. On outlining the problem the Solicitor agreed to take on the case, stating that the Parish Council had a good case and the dispute should go in the Council's favour. However, litigation would impose a certain amount of cost on the Council, and hence onto the Ratepayer. This was relayed back to the Council who realised that the registration had been the subject of an appeal that had been turned down, and that the council had an open and shut case.

It was pointed out that whatever litigation was used (and even if it went to the House of Lords) then in the end someone would have to physically take down the obstruction! It was then decided by the Council to reverse the process and pull the fence down first!

The police were contacted and they sent an officer to prevent a breach of the peace. The Chairman, flanked by two Councillors, went to the house of the perpetrator, and stated "You have erected a fence on a registered village green. If you do not remove it within seven days we shall dismantle it." The fence was not removed so, after the seven days had expired, the members of Byfield Parish Council dismantled and removed the fence, again with a police officer in attendance. The constituent parts of the dismantled fence were placed on land the perpetrator owned.

The perpetrator then erected another fence, this time surrounding the posts with concrete; the Parish Council followed the same procedure again. The Chairman took two different councillors to prevent accusations against individual councillors. This time the posts had to be "removed" using a Tractor.

Yet a third obstruction was built on the registered Village Green. This time it was a shed! The same procedure was followed by the Council; the Chairman taking two more different councillors. The shed was not removed within the specified time, so again it was dismantled by Councillors!

The "saga" ended when the perpetrator moved away from the village.

Obviously reversing the procedure in this specific case saved a considerable amount of public money that would have been spent on litigation and also saved a considerable amount of time, even though the procedures adopted were rather unpleasant for the Councillors involved.

The next house, moving again anticlockwise round the Green, is Farndon Cottage, which in 1779 was an Inclosure allotted to William Sewell (who was buried in Byfield Church Yard on July 10th 1813) with an area of 1 rood 10 perches (see Map Sixteen Old Inclosures/Homesteads114). The land and the footprint of the building were then as they are today.

In the 1930s and to 1987 the house was lived in by the Merivale family and is now occupied by Mr and Mrs Walden and family.

Further on, the adjoining property as shown in 1779 is listed in the Byfield Enclosure details as a "School House" with an area of 3 perches. This would be the area of the "original building" as it is today, when it is the local Conservative Club (see Map Sixteen Old Inclosures/Homesteads 115). In 1779 the building was owned by the

This photograph was taken around 1928, showing Farndon Cottage today number 8 The Green. It also shows Miss Molly Potter standing on what was later to become in 1972, a registered Village Green.

This photograph is annotated J.R/303 in the Byfield Photo Museum. Lender Betty Potter.

Causeway Charity and was let to the School Master, and the rent was given to the poor. The 1777 militia list gives an Edward Harris as a School Master who was most probably teaching in this building.

Parish records details show that the children moved from this Schoolroom (these would be children of all ages) to the National School in Church Street when it was built in 1780, (rebuilt in 1842).

In 1870 the Education Act made education compulsory, and this obviously increased the number of children attending. The infants moved out of the National School on July 6th 1874 back to this building, due to insufficient space within the National School. Records show that Miss Clara Stanway was the Mistress.

It is interesting to record that there were no mains services to the building. Lighting would have been by oil lamps, water would have been fetched from the public well down on the Green. Round the corner from the well were the "Privies" – earth closets, used by the children and the staff, **(see Map Sixteen point of interest 13)**.

A new County Primary School was built in Bell Lane in 1906 and was the first County Primary School to be built in Northamptonshire. On the 14th of January 1907 the infants from this school and the children from the National School marched to the new school. This was

often vividly recounted by Leslie Edwin Russell, who was one of those infants and was aged five at the time.

The use of the building after it was vacated by the school is unclear. There is a reference, after the First World War, that at a Council meeting of April 19th 1919 a working party of Councillors had been requested to ascertain the conditions in which people in the parish were living. When they reported back to the Council, one situation was that a family of three were living in the disused School Room and there was only one room and no inside accommodation.

Later the building was used by the Byfield Boy Scouts, when the Reverend Pilcher the Church Curate was scoutmaster for a time.

The Boy Scout Movement in Byfield (A report in the Byfield Parish Church Magazine in December 1911, abridged version)

A meeting for starting the Boy Scout Movement in Byfield was held in the largest room of the School. On Friday November 24th 1911, Mr C. W. Emlyn of Culworth Hall, the organising and inspecting Commissioner of Scouts in this part of the World, came to explain the subject and lead the way in any application of the movement to Byfield which the meeting might occasion. Mr Hatwell of the Post Office was

This photograph was probably taken in January 1907. The children are photographed outside the Congregational Chapel on The Green which was next door to the Infants School. The board displayed showing the class "Infants Byfield Group 2" is identical in script to other boards displayed with groups of children being photographed outside the new County Primary School into which they are all about to move. The detail in the Northamptonshire Directory of 1903 records that the Infants School (which is today the Conservative Club) was built in 1842 for 50 children, that the average attendance was 54 and Miss Mary Baiden was the mistress.

This photo is annotated BH54 in the Byfield Photo Museum. Lender Horace Aston.

appointed the Byfield Scout Master and his assistants were Messrs Arthur Watt and Gerald Sedgwick.

Notes by J.R.
The school referred to is the present County Primary School.

Mr Hatwell was the Postmaster in the Post Office from 1911 to 1926, which was on the site of the Post Office today.

The building was used from 1924 by the newly formed Byfield Women's Institute up to the Second World War, when it was requisitioned by the army and used as a billet.

It is interesting to note that records show that the metal from the school bell was used when melted down to assist the war effort in the Second World War.

A Village Dispute
A complaint was lodged by the Women's Institute at the Annual Parish Meeting of March 29th 1945, under the heading "Causeway Charity", to the effect that when the army authorities derequisitioned the old infant school it should have reverted back to them, instead of which the Trustees had let it to the Conservative Club.

The following resolution was put forward by Mr S. Merivale (who actually lived next door to the premises): "That this meeting of Parishioners condemns the action of the Causeway Charity Trustees, in the letting of parish property to the Conservative Party, to be used as a licensed Conservative Club, as such premises are totally unsuitable for such a purpose; having no sanitation, no water and no drainage. And also this meeting also requests that the Conservative Club give up the premises as early as possible, and that the tenancy revert back to the former tenants, namely the Woman's Institute, who had prior claim.

"Further to this meeting that the Trustees are not in order in the manner of the letting as several of the Trustees are leading members of the Conservative Club.

"That a copy of this resolution be sent to the Ministry of Health, the Charity Commissioners, the Chief of Police for the County of Northampton. The resolution was proposed by P. Barnes seconded by L .E. Jackson (husband of an eminent member of the Women's Institute)".

Details from the Parish Council minute book.

Note by J.R.
Obviously the correspondence with its representations had little effect, as the Conservative Club continued to occupy the premises and eventually purchased them. The Conservative Club is still using the building today.

The building was purchased from the Parish Council (as the administrator of the Causeway Charity) by the Conservative Club in 1951. The trustees of the adjacent Independent Chapel sold the Conservative Club 25 square yards of ground to the rear of the Club in 1952, as well as other ground in the 1980s. It has since been altered and extended; the most significant change is that the building has been adapted and modified to form two storeys, with a rotunda built in place of the old wood and asbestos-clad porch.

In the rotunda is a spiral stairway to access the first floor, and there is also an emergency escape route via an emergency doorway from the rear of the building. The Chapel trustees also licensed the continuation of the escape route over their property to the Conservative Club Committee. The use of the additional first floor is primarily to accommodate a full size snooker and billiard table. On the ground floor a cellar has been added to the west side and there are improved toilet facilities, together with a small extension to complement the main ground floor club room on the north side.

Moving on, the next Inclosure on the right, allotted to Thomas Hitchcock (1732 – 1818), was an area of 36 perches **(see Map Sixteen Old Inclosures/Homesteads 113)**. The Enclosure Map of 1779 shows a small building abutting the west side of the previously described Conservative Club, and of a scale of about half the floor area of the Club.

The site was purchased by members of the Independent Chapel, with the help of donations from others, in 1826. The earlier building previously described was pulled down and a Chapel built in 1827.

The Twenty Six Founder Members of the Byfield Congregational Church
Robert Devonshire; William Barnes; John Harbidge; William Gardner; Abraham Devonshire; Richard Eyles; John Cadd; William Cave; Mary Austin; Mary Barnes; Susan Harbidge; Ann Eyles; Ann Grey; Mary Cadd; Sarah Austin; Elizabeth Devonshire; John Gardner; Susanna Gardner; Margaret Saul; Hannah Lawrence; Samuel Bush; Mary Bush; Elizabeth Gare; May Jeffrey; John Rosomond; Thomas Jeffrey.

The first Minister was the Rev. John Grey (minister 1827 – 1830).

This Independent Chapel was later to become a Congregational Chapel and then a United Reformed Church. When an inspection of the fabric of the building was carried out in the late 1990s, defects were found; the first floor balcony and the roof were considered to be unsafe, and the building was condemned for church use. This, together with an ageing stewardship and a gradually diminishing and ageing congregation, meant that to rectify and to continue to maintain the building was impossible. The situation had become untenable.

The last service was on Sunday 19th of September 1999 at a United Harvest Festival, together with friends from the congregation of Byfield Holy Cross Church.

It was regretfully decided to apply for planning permission to convert the building into a dwelling and sell the site, thus ending 173 years of Christian witness.

The Chapel was purchased in 2000 by a developer, and was converted into a house, retaining a lot of the character of the original building; it was then sold in 2002.

The next building is the Chapel Cottage being No. 6 The Green. The cottage has a date stone dated 1679 **(see Map Sixteen point of interest 14)**. The enclosure map of 1779 shows the cottage on the same Inclosure on which the Chapel was built in 1827.

Records indicate that this cottage was rented for chapel meetings and worship for three months in a room fitted out for the purpose, prior to the new Independent Chapel being ready for use, in 1827. The cottage was also used to accommodate the "Chapel Keeper". In 1876 records show a Mrs Devonshire-Lawrence as "Chapel Keeper", and she was accepted as tenant for the cottage. Later keepers became caretakers, and one of the caretakers in the 1920s was Mrs Sarah Clegg.

In the 1940s the cottage was occupied by Mr and Mrs Bert West and their son George, and was later to be bought by Mr and Mrs Fred Adams. It is still owned by their son, Doctor Stuart Adams. This cottage was at the south end of a terrace of cottages, of which the next adjoining cottage was within an Inclosure to Mary Jaycock, with an allotment of 16 perches **(see Map Sixteen Old Inclosures/Homesteads 112)**. Records show her cottage was used for Nonconformist meetings prior to any purpose-built Chapels being erected. This cottage was lived in in the1940s and 1950s by Miss Chadbourne (1884–1974), and later by Mr and Mrs Vokes (née Walters).

Moving on again, the next cottage in the terrace was in the 1950s lived in by Fred and Lillian Gates, and next door was the Bull family (William Bull 1845–1944). In 1959 Fred and Lillian purchased the other cottage, demolished both of the cottages, and built a new house on the site, using the stone from both of these cottages.

The Chapel Manse was built on the next Inclosure on the right which, in 1779, had been allotted to Elizabeth Gee with an area of 30 perches **(see Map Sixteen Old Inclosures/Homesteads 111)**. Records show that prior to 1834 there were two cottages on this site facing the Village Green. The enclosure map of 1779 only shows a footprint of a building in this position **(see Map Sixteen point of interest 15)**. These cottages were used to house some of the village poor. It is suggested they might have been part of a nunnery which is thought to have existed on this site.

After the introduction of the Poor Law Amendment Act in 1834, the cottages were purchased by Thomas Lake from the Guardians of the Poor of the Daventry Union, the Church Wardens and the Overseers of Byfield.

Ownership: 1834 – Thomas Lake; 1872 – Robert Lake Lord (who was the Village Constable 1853–1869); the cottages were pulled down and the house built; 1875 – Sarah Lord; 1886 – Trustees of the Congregational Chapel, purchased at a price of £330, the house then became the Chapel Manse.

Occupying Chapel Ministers: 1887 – Rev A. Taylor; 1868 – Rev H. Beamish; 1872 – Rev Charles Brown; 1882 – Rev John Adams; 1892 – xxxxx; 1898 – Rev Eli T. Sanders, (Eli Thomas Sanders was also a County Councillor and Alderman for 33 years); 1928 – Rev E. W. Checher; 1932 – Rev Walter Harrison.

The official residence of the Ministers was transferred to Weedon Bec Manse. The officiating Minister was the Rev George Hooper, who held the post for some 40 years.

This photograph is of the Chapel Manse on The Green, taken in 1927.

This photograph is annotated AS228 in the Byfield Photo Museum. Lender Mr Dennis Watson.

Further occupants: 1930 – Sgt Judd; 1940 – Alice May Baroness d'Aulnis de Bourouill.

Ownership: August 14th 1957 – Harry Blanchett; 1975 – Peggy Blanchett; 1979 – Charles Rake; 1987 – Peggy Rake.

The Poor Laws

Overseers (a superintendent; an officer who has the care of the poor) were established by the Poor Law Act of 1597/98 and made obligatory on parishes by the Poor Relief Act of 1601. Under these laws, parishes were held responsible for their own paupers. This often meant buying plots of land and building cottages.

The Poor Law Amendment Act 1834: *This Act was introduced on April 17th 1834 by the Chancellor of the Exchequer, Lord Althorpe. It repealed or amended 500 existing acts. The Act wound up the old Parochial system and caused the establishment of Guardians of the Poor Unions and District Workhouses. Parishes were compulsorily amalgamated into Unions, the whole system being centralised under the control of a body of Poor Law Commissioners.*

The Byfield poor were sent to Daventry, where a workhouse to house 230 destitute people was built in 1837 outside the then Town boundary (the building is now part of the Daventry Hospital complex and is well within the present expanded town boundary).

The new system meant that many villages had surplus cottages for which they had no use. Some landowners who had built the cottages simply pulled them down. Other parishes *had to apply to the Poor Law Commissioners, via the district Board of Guardians, for permission to sell.*

The private roadway next to the Manse leads down to "Dodds Well", a public well on private property!

This Inclosure, allotted in 1779 to William Dodd, was an area comprising 3 roods 29 perches **(see Map Sixteen Old Inclosures/Homesteads 110)**, hence the name of the well. There are on the current Ordnance Survey Map a house named Dodd's cottage and a Dodd's barn just off the Daventry Road on land that in 1779 was allotted to the Lord of the Manor, William Henry Chauncy.

There are two dwellings off this private driveway; the first one is on part of the footprint of the building shown on the Enclosure Map **(see Map Sixteen point of interest 16)**, the 1779 footprint with more of the building extending towards the west in an "inverted horseshoe shape". This dwelling is now known as "Brookwell".

Owners/ Occupants: 1681 – Henry and Joyce Adkins; 1704 – Robert and Israel Thornton; 1738 – Robert Thornton (son of the previous owner); 1764 – Thomas Brightwell (son-in-law of Robert Thornton); between 1768 and 1888 there were three generations of William Dodds; 1889 – Frederick William Fowke (surgeon); 1908 – James Henry (Jim) Over (1880–1941), the 1906 Northamptonshire Directory shows James H. Over as a beer retailer; 1942 – Mrs Over; 1945 – Edwin Allen; 1950 – Eustace and Alice Partridge; 1951 – "Fayre Lady Cottage" (central part of the main premises) sold to Victor

This is a photograph of the roadway to Dodds Well taken at the time around 1910 when Jim Over was in residence. In fact that is him in the doorway of what came to be known as "Brookwell". Also in the picture is the rear entrance to the Post Office, also the stone cottage which was pulled down in the 1950s.

This photo is annotated JR584 in the Byfield Photo Museum. Lender Mr John Litchfield.

and Iris Gutteridge; 1957 – John Baines Colton; 1964 – Michael Terrance and Patricia Ann Mahoney; 1969 – Gervase Alan Drake-Brockman; 1971 – George Graham and Helen Patricia Wesley Cole; 1980s – Russ and Margaret Mallace and family; 1990s – Ian and Victoria McAllister and family.

On the enclosure map there is another building not far from the Public Well which, in the time of Jim Over, was the stabling for up to five heavy horses used at the Byfield Woodyard **(see Map Sixteen point of interest 17)**. Mr Over was initially a partner and later the sole proprietor of the Woodyard.

Parish records show that there was a complaint lodged to the Byfield Parish Council with regard to the state of the well when at one point was made that there was a manure heap within 25 yards of the well.

The second building on this driveway is a modern bungalow built by Anthony McCaughey, later, in 1969, to be purchased by Doctor and Mrs Holland. This is on the other part of the "inverted horseshoe footprint" previously described.

Moving back up the private driveway, on the right, adjacent to and near to what today is the rear of a Co-op shop and Post Office, was the site prior to the 1950s of a thatched cottage **(see Map Sixteen point of interest 18)**. This cottage, shown on the 1779 Enclosure Map, was in the curtilage of an Inclosure allotted to Henry Thornton, an area of 1 rood 9 perches **(see Map Sixteen Old Inclosures/Homesteads 109)**. The cottage was last lived in by the Beazley family.

* * * * *

We have now reached the High Street (A361).

CHAPTER FIFTEEN

PIT LANE

Map Seventeen

Pit Lane

The BLACK NUMBERS are from the survey of Old Inclosures
and Homesteads in the centre of the village.
The BLUE NUMBERS are Tracts of Land allotted to Proprietors
and Owners in the rest of the parish.
The RED NUMBERS denote points of interest along the route.
Detail taken from a modern map some detail from the 1779
Enclosure Map with other detail added.

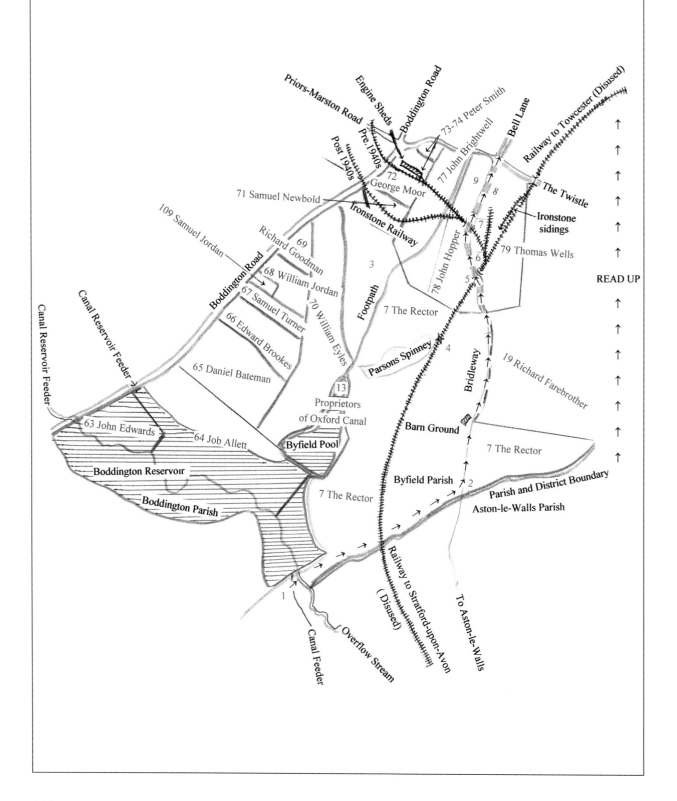

CHAPTER FIFTEEN

PIT LANE

(See Map Seventeen)

Before starting the journey into Byfield along the bridleway from Aston-le-Walls, we start our walk at the dam of Boddington Reservoir and stand adjacent to the canal feeder and the overflow stream running from it **(see Map Seventeen point of interest 1)**. We are standing in the lowest part of Byfield parish, 377 feet (115 metres) above sea level. The highest point in the parish is close to the post office tower at 727 feet (222 metres), a height difference of over 350 feet (107 metres).

The overflow stream which, prior to 1805, ran right up through the valley, is the boundary between Boddington parish and Byfield parish. This boundary is now through the middle of the reservoir. Downstream from the dam to the hedge, this is the point where Boddington, Aston-le-Walls and Byfield parishes meet. Turning up the hedgerow towards Half Crown Corner, to the point where it meets the bridle road from Aston-le-Walls into Byfield, we then turn on this bridleway to face Byfield **(see Map Seventeen point of interest 2)**.

Looking up to the right towards Half Crown Corner and the A361, sweeping down from that point across in front of us towards the Boddington Road, we see the large tract of land, some 139 acres, allotted to the Rector the Reverend John Knightley in 1779 for Glebe **(see Map Seventeen Proprietors/ Owners 7)**.

At the far end of this land, adjacent to the Boddington Road, were 78 plots of garden land known as Middlegate, **(see Map Seventeen point of interest 3)**. These plots of land were rented by Byfield people with the rent paid to the Rector, and are shown in detail on Map Nine.

In 1779 a small plot of land was allotted to the north of this Glebe land in the valley, where the water flow from streams was abundant; the Proprietors of the Oxford Canal were allotted 8 acres 3 roods 17 perches to provide a feeder reservoir for the newly built canal **(see Map Seventeen Proprietors/Owners 13)**. A further 10 acres was later purchased from the church.

We pass along the bridleway into "Barn Ground" which, as this name implies, was an area with a collection of barns, the last one recently demolished. This was part of Pool Farm, and the farmers up to the late 1950s were the Howes family. In the 1920s they were also landlords of the public house in Byfield called The New Inn. Yearly at harvest time a family of itinerant gipsies, by the name of Innes, set up camp here, to take on seasonal work on the farm.

Moving on towards Byfield, the field on the right was allotted in 1779 to Richard Farebrother, an area of 33 acres 11 perches **(see Map Seventeen Proprietors/Owners**

19). Up the slope in the same area in 1944, in a barn that is no longer there, Fred Brooks, a thatcher and a Byfield man, hanged himself. Before moving into the confines of Pit Lane, looking to the left we see a small wood. This is Parson's Spinney, so named because it was on the Rector's ground. On this side of the spinney we can see a bridge used by farmers especially to take stock under the railway from one side of the railway to the other. This bridge was also used by the Bicester and Warden Hill hunt **(see Map Seventeen point of interest 4)**. If we had been standing here in 1866 we would have seen the East and West Railway being built, and in 1873 we might have seen the first passenger train on this new line.

Forward into Pit Lane, the paddock on the left now belongs to Tim Hutt, the great-grandson of James Hutt, wheelwright and farmer, the first of the Hutt family to come to Byfield from Kidlington, Oxford. As we walk up the slope which was the approach to the now dismantled railway bridge, this bridge actually collapsed under the weight of a large six-wheeled motor lorry, which was bringing concrete preformed ring sections to form a well for the previous owner on what is now Tim Hutt's ground. The lorry came from Sittingbourne in Kent and was driven by a Mr Sid Reeves, who luckily was spared from serious injury **(see Map Seventeen point of interest 5)**.

The land to the right through to the Twistle Road now belongs to the Laurie family. In 1779 this was allotted to Thomas Wells and is an area of 16 acres 2 roods 1 perch and was later named Slade Bottom **(see Map Seventeen Proprietors/Owners 79)**. Around this area were public stone and gravel pits. Just to the right over the railway bridge the 1779 Enclosure Map shows the site of Public Stone Pit number 2 **(see Map Seventeen point 6)**. Just up the railway trackbed, to our left, there was a milepost indicated on the Ordnance Survey Maps indicating Towcester 11 miles.

Continuing on to the left to the land which now belongs to the Clayton family, we proceed through the gate round the right hand corner on to a "hump in the Lane". We are in fact standing on the railway bridge which was filled in after the ironstone works closed in 1965 **(see Map Seventeen point of interest 7)**. If we had looked over the bridge parapet to our right prior to this date, we would have seen the Ironstone Railway lines and the offices of the manager, the last one being Mr Jim Smith, (husband of Mrs Daisy Smith shopkeeper on Dolls Hill), together with his office staff, and the weigh bridge. Further down line was the gate which separated the Ironstone rail traffic from what the Ironstone staff called the "Main line", with its sidings to accommodate the ironstone wagons.

Over to the left side bridge parapet we would have seen, prior to 1965, a line bearing to the left which was the line to the Ironstone workings, and a line bearing to the right which went to the engine sheds, **(see Map Seventeen)**, which over the years had accommodated the James, Sir Barclay, Byfield No. 2, Avonside and Cherwell engines.

Fame in the Frame

The 0-6-0 railway engine "Sir Barclay", which was used on the Ironstone workings at Byfield, had its moment of fame when it was used in the famous film "The Railway Children". Details on the computer internet give specifics and also show two photographs of the engine; one outside the engine sheds, the other shows the engine in the background, with a group of actors in the foreground, one of whom is the lead actress in the film, Jenny Agutter.

Parts of the film were shot at Charwelton Station (detail Leicester Museum)

The Cherwell, with George Batchelor on the footplate, was the engine that delivered the final "clearing up" load of ore to the "main line" on the 12th of February1965. The original line to the ironstone workings went on past these sheds over the Boddington road and over the Priors Marston road, (not, as shown on some of the Ironstone maps, *under* the road), with the same flagman stopping road traffic on both crossings. The line bearing to the left, with high banks on the Boddington side, swept round to give a more gradual curve to allow the line to go under the Priors Marston road bridge. This new route and the bridge were constructed by Italian P.O.W.s in the 1940s. Continuing on, observing especially the left side of the road, we see evidence by the level of the field of a limited amount of ore extraction. To the right, ore extraction had taken place, but infill had taken place, firstly by the section nearest the lane being a domestic refuse tip, mostly of ashes from open fires, **(see Map Seventeen point of interest 8)**. This was initially collected on behalf of the Parish Council by a local farmer using local labour. The area used to self-ignite on a semi-permanent basis, and needed the regular attendance of the Woodford-based local fire brigade.

The whole area of the field on this side was infilled with material from the redundant factory site in Banbury of Automotive Products, previously Lockheed, now the site of Beaumont Road Industrial Estate. This infill brings the field back to its pre-ore-extraction levels prior to 1915, when Mr J. W. Payne had started commercial ore extraction.

Back to the left hand side of the lane, just prior to its junction with The Twistle, was an allotment to John Hopper, an area of 16 acres 10 perches **(see Map Seventeen Proprietors/Owners 78)**. In the late 1940s this was the site of Byfield football field. Woodford United played in a Byfield Bethel cup final here. This site was used by Byfield Athletic Football Club for a relatively short period **(see Map Seventeen point of interest 9)**.

We leave Pit, Tip, or Muddy Lane, Pit in fact being the correct name, taken from those old pre-Enclosure, stone and gravel pits.

We have now reached the junction with The Twistle.

CHAPTER SIXTEEN

BELL LANE

MAP EIGHTEEN

BELL LANE

The BLACK NUMBERS are from the survey of Old Inclosures and Homesteads in the centre of the village.
The BLUE NUMBERS are Tracts of Land allotted to Proprietors and Owners in the rest of the parish.
The RED NUMBERS denote points of interest along the route. Detail taken from a modern map some detail from the 1779 Enclosure Map with other detail added.

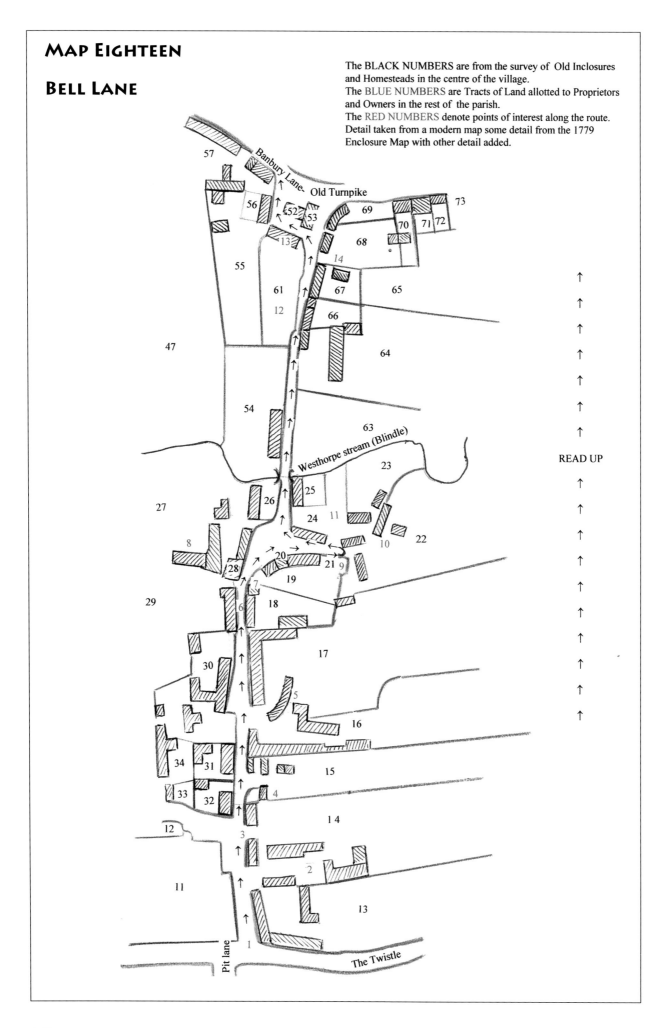

READ UP

Chapter Sixteen

Bell Lane

(See Map Eighteen)

We move from Pit Lane over into Bell Lane, named after the "new" Bell Inn public house built around 1900. This lane had been named over the years: Main Street; then School Street, and part of it School Hill after 1907 when the new County Primary School was opened **(see Map Eighteen point of interest 1)**.

Immediately on the right was an Inclosure, allotted in 1779 to the Lord of the Manor William Henry Chauncy, an area of 3 roods 18 perches **(see Map Eighteen Old Inclosures/Homesteads 13)**. Moving on we see the stone house, also on the right on the roadside in Bell Lane, which was built by Sam Gardner (1892–1963) and his wife, formerly Miss Searl, a Byfield school teacher. Both were leading members of the local independent chapel. The house was built on the site of three cottages which previously had been lived in by the Eyles, Widdows, and Gardner families. Sam and his wife named their new house "Stone-Leigh".

Moving along, still on the right, looking through an archway into what is today "Westhorpe Mews" we see a group of dwellings converted from former farm buildings. The archway was formed by Martin Lilley, without which the character of "The Mews" would not be the same.

The building on the roadside was formerly the farmhouse, most of the area having until December 31st 2001 been Martin Lilley's builders yard, the headquarters of a business started in 1958. This Inclosure was allotted in the Enclosure of 1779 to Richard Hitchcock, an area of 1 acre 1 rood 9 perches **(see Map Eighteen Old Inclosures/Homesteads 14)**. Later occupants were: 1849 – Richard Bilson; 1894 – Thomas Richard Jordan Bilson (1847–1934); 1936 – Frank Elkington; 1940 – William Elkington; in the late 1940s – Kilby Holtom followed by Cook, the last farmer to use the premises, and then Martin Lilley.

The whole of these premises today are quite similar in outline to the detail on the 1779 Enclosure Map, when what are now very comfortable dwellings were barns, pig sties and cow sheds; all the buildings you would find on a mixed farm in the 18th and 19th centuries **(see Map Eighteen point of interest 2)**. On the roadside adjacent to this Inclosure, opposite Westhorpe Lane, is a Victorian Postbox **(see Map Eighteen point of interest 3)**, into which Byfield people have been posting mail for well over 100 years. When this was to be re-sited it was in fact broken, and was repaired by Martin Lilley at his expense.

On the left today, between The Twistle and Westhorpe Lane, are a series of new bungalows built progressively over recent years. The original Inclosure allotted to John Hopper in 1779 was an area of 3 roods 39 perches **(see Map Eighteen Old Inclosures/Homesteads 11)**. The ownership until the individual plots were sold off goes back through the old Byfield family of Batchelor, of which the Green family became a part.

On the other corner of Westhorpe Lane and Bell Lane is the dwelling "Corner House", previously thatched and built in 1728. The footprint of the building is the same today as it was at the time of the Byfield Enclosure. This Inclosure was allotted in 1779 to Samuel Turner and was an area of 15 perches, **(see Map Eighteen Old Inclosures/Homesteads 32)**. Today it is occupied by Rosemary Johnson and Andrew Spackman.

Previous owners have been the Waterhouse family and Miss Phyllis Taylor, a well known local character, who had been a teacher, not only in this country but in the northern wastes of Canada among the Inuit people. Miss Taylor was a writer of poetry and hymns; she was also a keen amateur filmmaker and photographer.

Robert Eyles and his family lived in the cottage up to 1914. The Northamptonshire Directories from 1894 to 1914 record Robert Eyles (1854–1919) as a carpenter. Henry James Hartwell (1871–1942) and Sarah Hartwell lived there in the 1920s. The 1901 Census records that Henry was an agricultural labourer.

Jim Hodges (1873–1957) and his wife lived there in the 1930s, and their daughter Frances later became Mrs Davies. They also brought up Dr Barnardo's children, including the Ward twin brothers, Ted and Dick. Jim was a hay tier and smoked clay pipes, but not lit when tying the hay for obvious reasons. These clay pipes had broken-off stems caused by putting them in his waistcoat ("wescut") pocket and bending over.

Jim was also a member of the Band of Hope, and had "signed the pledge" which was to stay away from any form of alcohol.

Alcohol abuse was an acute problem then for families with low incomes.

The next Inclosure on the left had previously been thatched; the stonework on the west gable shows the angle of the pitch of the old roof. The footprint today is similar to that on the Enclosure Map of 1779 when the land was allotted to Thomas Ward, 16 perches **(see Map Eighteen Old Inclosures/Homesteads 31)**. The Byfield Photo Museum has just been lent a photograph of this cottage, dated around 1890. It has what appears to be a sign indicating that it was some sort of a shop. It is probable the slated roof was put on by the Gregory family, as until quite recently the building was two

This photograph is of Bell Lane taken in the very early 1900s and shows the typical dress of the period. The photograph was on a postcard postmarked September the 25th 1913. The script refers to army manoeuvres. One would presume these were the same manoeuvres that were attended by King George V which concluded on Sharmans Hill between Badby and Charwelton in the same year.

This photograph is annotated AS443 in the Byfield Photo Museum. Lender Mike Fennell.

cottages. Fred Gregory (1891–1960) is shown in the 1928 Northamptonshire Directory as being a newsagent, a business he bought from the Yorston family, who had also been carriers and coal merchants, with a yard at the end of Westhorpe Lane.

Mrs Gregory (1908–1962) was "in charge". She was willowy in stature, always wore an old beret, and was mostly seen on an old upright bicycle, and would normally be smoking her favourite brand of cigarette, a "Woodbine"! A harder worker you would not find. She rented a large garden at the top of Bell Lane in the grounds of the Methodist chapel. In the appropriate season she was always planting, hoeing or harvesting; we even have a photograph of her helping "in her spare time" with the harvest on Ken Ward's farm.

Colin and Greta Thornton purchased the newsagents business from the Gregory family in 1961, just prior to the death of Mrs Gregory, which was in March 1962.

Mr and Mrs Gregory lived in the larger of the two cottages and various people lived in the other, which was much smaller, including in the 1930s Harry Trustler, who married Eve French, bringing together two old Byfield families. Mr and Mrs Gregory's youngest son Jack was one of the "Flag Men" who worked on the Byfield Ironstone Railway road crossings, followed in to the cottage by Ted Ward and his wife before they emigrated to Australia.

The cottages were then purchased and converted into one house by Alan and Rita Hobday.

At this point, on the right side of the road, was a thatched cottage side-on to the road, which was demolished in the 1950s (see **Map Eighteen point of interest 4**). The cottage was on another Inclosure, an area of 2 roods 26 perches allotted to Mrs Isabel and Mrs Frances Bradshaw (see **Map Eighteen Old Inclosures/Homesteads 15**).

The cottage latterly was occupied by George Plummer (1882–1960), nicknamed "Dawdy", who is listed in the 1901 Census as being a carter on a farm. He played both football and cricket for the village. He was very proud of the fact that his nephew played professional football as a centre half for Leicester City in the 1950s, who were then in the old Second Division of the Football League.

Earlier the Plummer family had been tinsmiths and braziers over a number of years in Main Street, later Bell Lane. Those recorded are: George Plummer (1806–1881) and John Plummer (1840–1914). The next Inclosure on the right was allotted to Richard Farebrother in 1779, an area of 1 acre 2 roods 33 perches (see **Map Eighteen Old Inclosures/Homesteads 17**). The house which takes up most of the roadside frontage of the property was built as a Gentleman's residence and was named Westrup House. In fact, what became the cowshed, when it became a farm, originally housed the Gentlemen's carriages. The first gable of the house facing the road has a date stone marked H

M and dated 1715. This date would not be indicative of the age of the main structure, but could have been transferred from an earlier part of the building. A very interesting footprint of a "curved" building is shown on the 1779 Enclosure Map **(see Map Eighteen point of interest 5)**. This footprint is not shown on the 1882/83 Ordnance Survey Map. It would be interesting to know what building was on that footprint.

Further occupants were: William Farebrother (1766–1831); George Farebrother (1809–1892); and then 1894 – Matthew Hall (1840–1916, committed suicide); 1916 – Richard Haycock; 1936 – Cecil William Farrar Laurie, who initially rented the farm from Miss Farebrother, who is shown in the Northamptonshire Directories as residing in Church Walk, Oxford. The Farebrother family tree shows direct lineage from Richard Farebrother who was originally allotted the Inclosure.

The ownership line was broken when Cecil William Farrar Laurie purchased the farm as sitting tenant on the death of Miss Farebrother in the 1940s. The house has been sold out of the Laurie family ownership, but Cecil Laurie junior has been connected with this farm since he was two years of age. The family came from Oxfordshire, and prior to that came to the U.K. from Barbados in the West Indies. Brothers Cecil and Dick now run the farm,

Cecil William Farrar Laurie, as well as being a farmer, was a senior Maths Master at Wellingborough Grammar School.

Cecil William Farrar Laurie M.A. (1902–1977) was born in Lemon Arbor Sugar Estate, Barbados, West Indies. He obtained second class honours in Mathematics at Saint John's College Oxford.

We have photographs taken at the rear of the Westrup House of various village functions, May Day celebrations, Foresters' fetes etc. in the early 1900s.

What is now "Stepping Stone Barn" originally housed the Gentlemen's Carriages and for years was the farm's cowshed; the cows being taken from here to and from pasture along Pit Lane, until it was converted into a very desirable dwelling by the grandson of Cecil W. F. Laurie, Victor Perehinec. From this detail it looks as though there have only been four families who have actually owned the impressive stone structure of Westrup (Westhrup): the Farebrothers; Lauries; Reads; and the present owners, the Boddingtons.

Opposite Westrup House, on the left of Bell Lane, are two semi-detached cottages adjacent to the roadway; they were built by Mr C. W. F. Laurie in the 1960s. Originally this Inclosure was allotted to William Worley, shown in the 1777 Byfield militia list as a farmer. This allotment was an area of 2 roods 9 perches **(see Map Eighteen Old Inclosures/Homesteads 30)**. William Worley was also allotted a plot of agricultural land off the Priors Marston road.

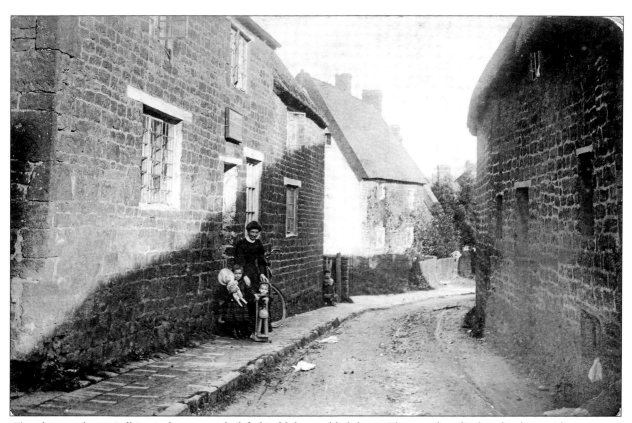

This photograph is in Bell Lane, showing on the left the old shop and bakehouse. The name board, when the photograph was computer enhanced, shows the name Mrs Ethel B. Lawrence. The 1906 and 1910 Northampton Directories indicate that Mrs Lawrence was the shopkeeper. The cottages on the right are still there today. The cottage on the left further on was demolished and is on the site of what is now the entrance to Greenwood Close.

This photograph is annotated JR216 in the Byfield Photo Museum. Lender Mr Maurice Smith.

The 1779 Enclosure Map shows, as does the Ordnance Survey of 1882/83 albeit on different footprints, that the site had previously contained what can only be described as a conglomeration of buildings. Six dwellings are shown on the 1900 Ordnance Survey Map on this footprint.

These dwellings over the years have been occupied by various people: the Freeman family; George Gare (1876–1944); Bill Garlic, (these two followed each other as the bakers at Russells Shop); Billy Edmunds (who was the coal carter for Russells); two single men, Daniel Douglas who lived with Alfred Brightwell, brother of the benefactor who gave the village the Brightwell Recreation Ground. Alfred Brightwell, being the oldest person in the village at 92 years, laid the foundation stone to the new village hall in 1953, the new hall being built seven years later.

As we go forward down the slope the next Inclosure on the left was allotted in 1779 to John Gibbins, a larger plot of land **(see Map Eighteen Old Inclosures/Homesteads 29)** consisting of an area of 1 acre 1 rood 19 perches. This land was later to have on it in the 1960s the houses of Greenwood Close. The stone building shown on the road side, the footprint of which is on both the 1779 Enclosure Map and the 1882/83 Ordnance Survey Map, was later to become a shop. The position of this building reduced the roadway width to only about 10 feet **(see Map Eighteen point of interest 6)**.

Records show that the shop in 1881 was occupied by Charles Johnson; 1906 – Mrs Ethel B. Lawrence; 1911 – Mr C. Batchelor; 1914 – Mrs Nellie Batchelor; 1931 – Teddy Gardner. All these were general dealers or grocers and bakers. This building was pulled down in the 1950s for road widening. Immediately to the right were a number of cottages, allotted to Thomas Richards in 1779, an area of 31 perches. Thomas Richards is listed in the 1777 militia list as a brazier **(see Map Eighteen Old Inclosures/Homesteads 18)**.

A Brazier: being a person who works with brass.

The first cottage, which can now be accessed only from the rear, was lived in by a Mrs Maycock in the 1920s, who was foster mother to Kathleen Fennell who later became a primary school teacher, Mrs Young. The bottom cottage was another shop; a general store, a brick-built extension to a stone cottage. From 1910 – Mrs Edwin Batchelor; from 1914 to the 1950s this was kept by Annie (Mary Anne) Batchelor, grocer, confectioner, tobacconist, and hardware dealer. Her wholesale supplier was Russells shop **(see Map Eighteen point of interest 7)**.

At the rear of Annie Batchelor's shop were two semi-detached thatched cottages. The last occupants before these cottages were demolished were the Stanley family, relations to the Eyles family, as was Annie Batchelor.

On the left was the old Bell Inn public house, (there were two "Bells" one on each side of the road). An Inclosure of only 4 perches was allotted to Thomas Furniss. On the 1779 Enclosure Map it appears that the Inclosure is just the footprint of the actual building **(see Map Eighteen Old Inclosures/Homesteads 28)**. The records of 1847 show Samuel Newcombe shoe maker and "Bell"; 1877

– Mrs Mary Newcomb (1806–1884); 1884 – Thomas Newcombe, Bell public house, and boot and shoe maker. There is no record after 1901 of this Public house, as it was said to have burnt down. The buildings alongside and adjoining and the buildings behind the Bell, were in 1779 on an Inclosure allotted to William Edmunds, a holding of 1 acre 1 rood 9 perches **(see Map Eighteen Old Inclosures/Homesteads 27)**.

One of these buildings was used from 1898 to 1928 as a Cycle Shop by Mr Henry (Harry) Whitmill **(see Map Eighteen point of interest 8)**.

Understanding signs
It is said that a sign was displayed on the outside of the cycle shop "H WHITMILL CYCLE DEPOT", and the tale is told that when a local was asked for directions to this establishment, he replied: "If you go down there past the school there is a building on the right with a sign, " H WHITMILL CIS-CILI- D-POT".

Interesting aspects of the Whitmill family which are recorded in the Byfield pages of the Northamptonshire Directories show that various members of the Whitmill family had varied and diverse occupations. Harry (1873–1958), the last recorded member of the Whitmill family, was not only running a retail cycle shop, but he also made up cycle frames and assembled them from their many constituent parts. When his workshop was locked up for the last time in the 1940s the area was left as it was. This was later discovered to contain numerous parts; tools, complete bicycles, and also a number of "belt-driven" motorcycles, with makes such as Douglas, Triumph, Rudge and Imperial, all left unattended; they were later to be acquired by others, one being Denis Judd the local garage proprietor.

Other Whitmills are listed as grocers and farmers. The 1874 Northamptonshire Directory records Miss Hannah Whitmill as a farmer or grazier; 1877 shows Mrs Ann Whitmill as a cow-keeper; 1884 as cottager and cow-keeper, and finally in 1885 as a farmer. Two Mark Whitmills, father and son, listed as Mark Whitmill Sen. and Mark Whitmill Jun. in the 1854 Kelly's Directory were plush weavers. Mark Whitmill junior was buried on April 6th 1892; the account of his death in the Byfield Burial Records contains an unofficial note: "Old Ringer muffled peal after the Funeral". This was entered by the officiating Rector at the time Francis Henry Curgenven, who obviously deemed that this detail should be recorded.

Plush and Plush Weavers
The making of Shags or Plush: a fabric with a double warp of two twisted threads of worsted or cotton, and a single thread of silk or mohair. The description of Plush in a contemporary dictionary is "cloth like velvet but having a longer pile".

Plush was used in upholstery, hats, and liveries. It was also used in the manufacture of other high quality fabrics.

Plush was sold on the international market. Plush Weavers worked on looms sometimes at home, but later on in factories where there were several looms.

The whole of this Inclosure is now the road into Greenwood Close; another housing estate named after a Byfield charity. This housing development was built in three phases by A. C. Lloyd of Leamington Spa in the 1960s, an established company still today based in Leamington Spa and still building houses.

Initially the houses cost £3,750.00 These houses were built on a very wet site; previously it had been the farm yard, buildings and paddock to Pool Farm, belonging to the Howes family. On the road frontage of the farm yard was a farm cottage lived in over the years by Mr Teddy Gardner, a milkman; the well known Haynes family which numbered eleven children; the Cranes; the Swifts, and the Garners. Later the Swifts and the Garners were to form a partnership in a building and decorating business.

The Greenwood Charity 1694 (Verbatim)
Memorandum that Samuel Greenwood of Westhrop in the parish of Byfield in the County of Northamptonshire, Hemp dresser, by his last will and testament dated October Ye 12th 1693. Gave the sum of three pounds yearly after the decease of his wife, for instructing the poor children in the parish of Byfield, charitable upon certain land in Byfield and other lands in the parish of Woodford as will at large appear by the same will proved at Northton A. D. 1694.
Notes by J.R.
In more modern times this charity was used to buy books and once was used to provide a television set for the County

primary school and later smaller items of equipment. As the value of the original gift became eroded with inflation, the charity was amalgamated with other village charities, with the blessing of the Charity Commissioners, to become "Byfield Combined Charities". This joint funding enabled more sizable sums to be provided for village charitable causes.

Definition of Hemp, and Hemp Dresser
Hemp
A nettle with a fibrous bark used for cordage, coarse cloth etc; the fibrous rind prepared for spinning.
Hemp Dresser
One who prepares the fibrous rind for spinning.

The next building on the right was the Bell Inn; built on what in 1779 were three small Inclosures (**see Map Eighteen Old Inclosures/Homesteads 19, 20 and 21**). One of 15 perches was allotted to Samuel Gardener, one of 1 perch allotted to William Eyles, and the other of 10 perches allotted to William Gardener.

The entry in the 1901 Census shows two Bell Inns, one to the left and one to the right of Main Street. The one to the right of the road, now known as Bell Lodge, is shown in the "building column" in the Census. This indicates that it was not completed and had not as yet been occupied.

The first indication of occupation is in Kelly's Directory of 1906 which records Thomas Richardson, Bell

This is a photograph of the members of the Causeway and Poors Piece Charity, about to commence the Auction of the Charity Fields in The Bell Inn. In the foreground, with his finger on the centre of the table, is the Auctioneer, Bert Wingrove; the other officers are L. to R. Cecil Cockerill, Fred Boddington, Fred Trenfield, Frank Howes, Alf Smith and Edward Thompson.

This photograph is annotated JR1069 in the Byfield Photo Museum. Lender Barbara Smith.

Inn and Cycle Agent; 1914 – James Trevor Smart; 1920 – George Clifford White; 1928 – Arthur Holmes; 1934 – Frank Maude (1898–1966); Mrs Maude until closure. The 1901 census records Frank Maude at the age of two having been born in Byfield, living with his parents in "Tomalin's Yard".

Two birds with one stone!
Frank Maude was married on February 24th 1934, and as a married man, took on the licence of the Bell Inn on that very same day.

After closure the premises were purchased by Alf Webb from the brewery for £4,000.00. The use of the building when it was a public house was diverse. It was used by the Ancient Order of Buffaloes, various village clubs and charities, including the annual Causeway and Poors Piece Land Auction. This auction was televised on one occasion from this venue, in the 1960s.

The Foresters also used the building, and the membership of the Foresters was such that they had an influence on the design of the building, inasmuch as Mr Hunt from the brewery was persuaded to increase the size of the function room on the first floor to the whole length of the building due to the very considerable membership of their organisation.

The Byfield Foresters
Records from 1908 show that the Byfield Order was shown on the Court Banner as "Foresters Court 3230 of the Ancient Order of Foresters". At this time Thomas Richardson, Landlord of the "Bell Inn", was a member of the Foresters.

This building was an army billet in the Second World War.

As we move down the narrow lane in front of what today is Bell Lodge Nursing Home, along on the right are some iron railings. These railings were erected in front of the Primitive Methodist Chapel, **(see Map Eighteen point of interest 9),** built in 1836, and initially had 24 members and was part of the Banbury Methodist circuit.

The Ex-Primitive Methodist Connection
Luther Brailsford, Banbury Circuit Methodist Historian, records that the Ex-Primitive Methodist Connection (P.M.C.) had a Society in Byfield previous to 1832 but, owing to threats of victimisation from work, eviction of tenants who opened their houses for services and other causes, the services were discontinued.

This building was also used as an army billet in the Second World War.

The two semi-detached cottages at the end of the lane, to the right, were allotted to William Molt in 1779 on an Inclosure of 2 roods 36 perches **(see Map Eighteen Old Inclosures/Homesteads 22)**. Detail of the ownership progression is broken, but the Eyles family owned the properties from before the Second World War up to the late 1990s, and lived in the larger of the two. Mr Eyles purchased the chapel when it closed and demolished it

after it was derequisitioned by the military after the war.

Arthur Holmes lived in the other cottage in the late 1920s before moving to the Bell Inn, followed by the Stowe family in 1936, and the well-known Grey family. In the 1940s, Mr Grey had been employed as a butler in service to the local gentry in the area, and his daughter Florrie became the second wife of Ted Lewis. The last occupant in this cottage was the equally well known Baroness, (Baroness Alice May d'Aulnis de Bourouill), until her death in 1975 at the age of 99.

We are told that within these premises was the "rope walk". In the Village records, John Harbridge was a rope maker in 1847, and George Marlow a rope and twine maker from 1860 to 1874. There is no evidence as yet that any other premises in the village were used for this purpose. **(see Map Eighteen point of interest 10)**.

Further round to the left is Bertie's Cottage; the origin of the name is unknown. The cottage is on an Inclosure allotted to a James Saul in 1779; an area of 1 rood 22 perches **(see Map Eighteen Old Inclosures/Homesteads 23)**. The 1777 Militia list shows the Saul family as coopers. The building is thatched and is likely to have been built in the early 1700s. The occupants from the First World War through to well after the Second World War were the Dowler family. George Dowler worked as a tailor's representative for A. J. Walker, who had a shop in Byfield High Street which today is a Co-op shop and post office. A. J. Walker also had a shop in Parsons Street in Woodford Halse.

Cooper
A Cooper was a person who made Tubs, Casks, or Barrels.

Moving back to Bell Lane turn right to continue along Bell Lane. On the corner is a stone house built on an Inclosure which, in 1779, was allotted to William Eyles, an area of 27 perches **(see Map Eighteen Old Inclosures/Homesteads 24)**. In front of this house was a thatched cottage, which is still shown on photographs in the early 1900s with the new Bell Inn.

Still on the right, the new red brick buildings further up Bell Lane are today three houses. These were built in the 1980s by Martin Lilley. They are within the curtilage of an Inclosure allotted to John Whitmill, an area of 10 perches **(see Map Eighteen Old Inlosures/Homesteads 25)**. Originally on this site on the roadside was a stone building that was demolished in the 1940s and stayed as a ruin until the site was developed.

Both the allotment above and this allotment were later to become part of a plant nursery **(see Map Eighteen point of interest 11)**; the glass-houses are clearly shown on the 1900 Ordnance Survey Map. The nursery was firstly owned by a Mr Henry Wilmot (1871–1940), who in the 1901 census is listed as a "retired coffee-house keeper" born in London. He also had garden land at the top of "Boots Hill", on the Boddington/Priors Marston crossroads, which produced fresh fruit and vegetables that were sold from the nursery premises. Mr Wilmot was followed in the nursery business by Mr Farmilo (1895–1963). He was also a stone mason, and was responsible for constructing various buildings in Byfield, quite a number being on the Brightwell Recreation Ground. He also set the two ancient crosses in the north aisle of the Church. He built a bungalow as a retirement home for himself and his wife in the Twistle.

Opposite, on the left hand side of Bell Lane, is Rose Cottage, on an Inclosure allotted in 1779 to Thomas Saul, an area of 15 perches. (see Map Eighteen Old Inclosures/Homesteads 26). It was lived in by the Townsend family and their relations, the Watts family, for a number of years. Records show that the Townsends were blacksmiths in the parish for at least one hundred and fifty years. Walter Benjamin Townsend (1875–1949), blacksmith and railway worker, was the last of the male line of family in Byfield who owned the property. The property was purchased by Mr and Mrs Peter Hince, who later purchased additional land to the rear of the property, but the original holding purchased in the 1950s was the same in size as that shown on the 1779 Enclosure Map.

There is a right-of-way to the well and use of water on this property by the occupants of adjoining properties, subject to the payment of one-half part of the expense of keeping the well in repair. Obviously the use of this facility was not needed after the availability of mains water. The stream is the Westhorpe stream flowing left to right; which is the boundary between Westhorpe and Byfield.

Within the history of Westhorpe in various documents it is spelt a number of different ways: Westrup, Westrop, Westhorp.

On the left just over the stream is shown on the 1779 Enclosure Map as being an Inclosure to Richard Eyles, an area of 1 rood 39 perches (see Map Eighteen Old Inclosures/Homesteads 54). The 1777 Militia list records Richard Eyles as a collar maker. Today the first building is a brick-built house, which was originally two cottages, probably built in the late 1800s. We have a photograph of Maurice Smith's grandmother at the door of the first cottage in the 1930s, with Maurice's first bike propped against the wall. It had wooden blocks on the pedals to offset little Maurice's lack of length of leg. In the 1940s George Brough and his family also lived there, followed by Mr Charlie Humphrey and his wife.

The second cottage of the two was lived in by Mr J. French in 1906, followed by the Maycock family. Herbert Maycock was an officer in the Independent chapel; he also was a "length man" (a roadman). Mrs Maycock brought up several foster children, who were initially fostered here, and later among them were Fred Pitman and Ron Sutton. Ron later died, still a young man, in a motor cycle accident. Auction details show that these cottages were owned by James Richard Hutt, and were sold on his death in 1942. They were then owned by Bill Russell and then Edward Thompson, who sold them to the Bartle family as sitting tenants and who converted the two cottages into one dwelling. This house is today occupied by the Dring family.

The next stone house on this Inclosure is shown on the same footprint as it is today; the 1882/83 Ordnance Survey Map indicates the building was four cottages. These premises were also sold at auction in 1942 with the death of James Richard Hutt, later to be purchased and lived in by the Stowe family for many years. It was by then two cottages, with Mr George Henry Stowe (1870–1958) and Mrs Stowe living in one, and son Arthur Stowe (1907–1989) and his family living in the other. George Henry is shown in the Byfield records as a Carrier and Smallholder. The house High Banks was built in the Stowes' garden. The house is now lived in by the Saunders family, and the house is now named "Waterfields" after former occupants; a very musical and scholastic family.

Some people will remember that one trick the children used to play on the residents in this house in the winter, was to roll two snowballs up to about 18 inches diameter, place one about 6 inches from the front door, and then place the other one on top of it leaning it against the door. The door was then knocked! When the door was opened, because there were a number of steps down from the road, the top snowball rolled onto the person who had opened the door and into the house.

The Inclosure opposite on the right is an allotment again to Richard Eyles the collar maker; an area of 2 roods 14 perches on the Enclosure Map of 1779. This shows no buildings on this plot (see Map Eighteen Old Inclosures/Homesteads 63). The two brick-built semi-detached houses now on the plot were built by the building firm J. T. Constable of Blakesley, in 1924. Their name is still on the manhole covers. The 1928 and 1936 Northamptonshire Directories show that Felix Robinson was the Byfield dentist. He lived in the first of these two houses, and Herbert Peake, a well known "not so gentle" Banbury dentist, also practised from here. The Northamptonshire Directory of 1924 also records that J. A. Wilson dentist, of the well known practice of Hudson and Wilson, practised in Byfield; but the location of their premises has yet to be determined. This was the district nurse's house in the 1940s; everyone loved Nurse Conway! Other owners were Walter Maycock (1885–1961) and his wife. Mr and Mrs Maycock fostered Margaret Fennell, later to marry Frank Holmes.

The Thornton family newsagents and printers purchased the property in 1961 at auction, on the death of Walter Maycock. Colin Thornton was later to become the Byfield Postmaster, who then with his family lived in the Post Office in the High Street.

The cottage was purchased by the well-known Byfield character Cyril Nicholls, who lived there until his death at the age of 94.

The second house was lived in by the Holton family. Mr George Holton was the last Byfield stationmaster before closure. The Holtons were followed by the Mitchell-Harris family, Mr Mitchell-Harris being a Byfield village schoolmaster. Other occupants were the Needle family, and, after their marriage, and a number of rented homes, it was purchased by Maurice and Rita Smith, Rita (née Stowe) then living opposite her old family home.

The next large stone building on the right is the local primary school, the first County Primary to be built in Northamptonshire, on an Inclosure of 1 acre 15 perches which in 1779 was allotted to Ann Hawkes. The Enclosure

Map shows a large building almost on the same foot print as the present school, (see Map Eighteen Old Inclosures/Homesteads 64). The boundary to this inclosure to the south was the Westhorpe stream. The school was built in 1906, to accommodate 120 mixed and 72 infants, a total of 192. The school cost £2,778-7-0 to build, with fixtures and fittings, and a 29 year loan was taken out to fund the building. It was built with outside toilets for the simple reason that main modern drainage would not be available in Byfield for another 25 years.

On January 7th 1907 the school was officially opened by Sir Charles Knightley, accompanied by the Chairman of the Education Committee of Northamptonshire County Council, and other dignitaries. The children marched from their previous schools; the infants from what is now the Conservative club, and the seniors and juniors from the National School, which was on the site on which the new rectory stands.

Mr John Andrews (1860–1938) was the school headmaster, moving with the children to the new school from the National School. He was Headmaster from 1895 to 1923). In around 1910 Mr John Andrews planted a number of lime trees around the school field; these are now mature specimens. In 1911 the school was fitted with a flag pole to commemorate King George V's coronation, which sadly has since been taken down and not replaced.

In 1925, triggered by the shortage of accommodation in the village, Byfield parish council requested that a house be provided for the Headmaster. The Headmaster's house was finally built in 1926 after much deliberation.

The Logic of the "Planning Process"

When L. E. Jackson decided he wanted a garage in the late 1940s at the School House, to garage his 1937 Ford 10, it was at the time the practice to garage your car. He purchased a "Banbury Buildings" concrete garage from their Adderbury factory. After "Batley", Banbury Buildings were an early manufacturer of concrete garages. These early garages were even fitted with a concrete interlocking roof.

The local Planning Authority was concerned about this new type of construction and its intrusion into the rural scene. So much so, that they went up the Banbury road to check the intended site and position of this intended "new white concrete structure".

In 1951 the Northamptonshire Education Authority constructed a huge Canteen, a "new white concrete structure" right in front of the School Headmaster's house, totally blocking a very pleasant southern aspect view from the house front windows. There were obvious alternative sites for this "new, very large white concrete structure".

On September 11th 1931 the school became a receiving school for "Chipping Warden Seniors". In 1938 the pump was removed from the school, mains water having been installed.

In the early part of the Second World War the headmaster was Frank Hodgkinson. When the evacuees started to arrive in any numbers, the school was closed for a week and made a rest home, being the only building in the village big enough with the appropriate services to cope with the numbers. Mrs Humphreys of Byfield House was in charge of the rest home, and Frank Howes was the billeting officer, allotting the newly arrived Londoners to appropriate village families. School records show an interesting detail, that with the arrival of the evacuees in 1940, 136 native + 75 evacuees = 211; three of them Russian children whose families were billeted with the Laurie family at Westrop Farm. Those of us who were at this school at the time remember the blast netting up at the windows. We also remember the Canadian troops outside the school in their Bren gun carriers, brewing up their coffee.

In 1942 Northamptonshire County Council officials inspected and measured the school, with a view to setting up an emergency kitchen should the threatened invasion take place.

Occupying Headmasters of the School House were: 1926 – Charles W. White; late 1926 – Edward F. Poole; 1933 – Raymond F. Wheatley; 1938 – Charles Eden; 1940 – Frank Hodgkinson; 1943 – Leslie Jackson (1903–1973); 1964 – Victor H. Dutton; 1968 – Cameron Fraser; late 1970s – Raymond W. Phizacklea, (died in Canada, 29th July 1979, and as a memorial the leaded panes in the windows were repaired or replaced in the Chancel of Byfield Church).

The school house was then sold and became a private house.

In 1979 the next school Head teacher was Mrs Chris Cross, who lived in a private house in Bell Lane.

The school canteen, now a school hall, was built in 1951, initially supplying school dinners to Byfield, and later to other schools in the area. Later it became the school hall, after the Northamptonshire County Council Education Committee had stopped the provision of school dinners to save money.

As the roadway narrows, the next cottage on the right is shown on the Enclosure Map as two cottages, on an Inclosure allotted to Thomas Wells in 1779, an area of 23 perches (see Map Eighteen Old Inclosures/Homesteads 66). In the 1930s the Mold family lived in the first one for a number of years, father Tom and son Ron were both Rural Postmen. Their relations the White family lived in the second cottage; Mrs Tom Mold was a member of the White family.

The next house adjoining was built by William Kerrod in the 1850s, on an Inclosure allotted to John Burbidge, an area of 16 perches (see Map Eighteen Old Inclosures/Homesteads 67). The adjoining buildings were used by Mr Kerrod as workshops and storage for his own use as he was by trade a builder.

Occupiers over the years included the Russell family, firstly from the late 1890s to the early 1900s, when both William Russell and Leslie Russell were born there. And later, in another period of occupancy from the 1930s, this time with Leslie Russell and his wife Dorothy purchasing the property from a Mrs Mumford, their son John Russell was born in 1936. Father and son born in the same house with broken occupancy is rather unusual. At some time the house was named "Ramblegarth".

On the left side of the road opposite "Ramblegarth" was an Inclosure in 1779 which was allotted to Samuel Cox, an

This is a photograph taken of the Methodist Chapel in Bell Lane, constructed in 1937, dismantled and sold in the 1980s.

This photograph is annotated AS133 in the Byfield Photo Museum. Lender Mr Cameron Frazer.

area of 1 rood 6 perches **(see Map Eighteen Old Inclosures/ Homesteads 61)**. In 1937 a new wooden-framed building with asbestos cladding was built on this elevated site. This was the new Methodist chapel, with a small anteroom used as a Sunday school **(see Map Eighteen point 12)**. Backed by a Banbury solicitor, a Mr Barfield, the chapel was built at a cost including fixtures and fittings of £524. Mrs Gardner, being the oldest member of the Chapel membership, was invited to be the first person to unlock the door! Mrs Gardner was the wife of the well-known Charlie Gardner, both being dedicated Methodists.

In the 1980s, the building was dismantled and sold to the Ford Motor Company as a sports pavilion, and was erected on the Ford Sports Ground at Daventry. One would hope that the words of the hymns sung by the new users were not too big a shock to the sensitive structure.

On the east side of this site was a large thatched house, which was probably more than one dwelling. This was pulled down in 1935. One of the workmen who assisted in the demolition was Bill West, the father of Mrs May Haynes. The site now has on it a pair of semi-detached houses and a detached house, all built by the local builder Martin Lilley **(see Map Eighteen point of interest 13)**.

On the small green opposite, it is a job to envisage that there were two small thatched cottages standing on this small area, but the layout of the roads was different and the roads were not as wide. These cottages were on two Inclosures, one allotted in 1779 to William Turner of 3

perches, and one to John Jones of 2 perches **(see Map Eighteen Old Inclosures/Homesteads 52 and 53)**. The 1777 militia list records William Turner as a servant.

An interesting entry in the Byfield Vestry minute book is regarding a motion in the meeting of May 13th 1864. With reference to these cottages, it was proposed by Mr Sedgwick that the three cottages opposite Mr Bush's shop be taken down. The proposal met with no seconder!

To the right of these cottages, down a narrow driveway **(see Map Eighteen point of interest 14)**, stands a detached house on an Inclosure that in 1779 was allotted to Peter Smith; an area of 36 perches, **(see Map Eighteen Old Inclosures/Homesteads 68)**. The Enclosure Map shows only a small footprint on what now is the site of the house. The 1882/83 survey shows a longer footprint, the size of the house as it is today, without the later brick extension.

The first people recorded who lived in the house we know today were the Probert family, who were locksmiths. Records show that the Probert family were living in the house in 1888, followed by the Andrews family, the head of which was John Andrews (1859 – 1938). He was the school headmaster from 1895 to 1923, having previously held a similar post at the village of Eydon from 1882 to 1894. John Andrews was also choirmaster and organist for a similar period in Byfield, and the Enumerator for the Byfield 1901 census! His wife Ellen Nellie née Lord, (1867 – 1950), was also a teacher at Byfield School.

The Probert family emigrated to North America and some served in the First World War in the Canadian armed forces. Some of the Probert family's descendants came back to visit the house, and specifically remembered the large sized interior door keys! They also enquired about their grandfather's "English Rose", a lady by the name of Elsie Checkley!

Denis Judd, son of the local police sergeant, then purchased the house in 1931. He was a local entrepreneur, owning, over a period, sweet shops, a cycle shop repair business, which developed into a motor garage and bus hire, and he later purchased the coal merchants business from Russells. Part of this property included 2/5ths of a Salvation Army barracks (the whole building was a "five bay" brick built structure). This building was unique in as much as the deeds of the property were signed by General Booth, founder of the Salvation Army. The other 3/5ths of the barracks is part of the property today numbered 38 Banbury Lane. Denis states in his book "Living in the Country" that the deeds of his house go back to 1753.

On the left side of the road stands a large building which is on the site of a plot of land allotted to Edward Bush in 1779, described then as "an house and yard", an area of 14 perches which is the area of the buildings and yard today **(see Map Eighteen Old Inclosures/Home-steads 56)**. It can be assumed that the "shop building" we see today was built by the Bush family around 1850. Ownership can also safely be assumed to be continuous within the Bush family from before 1779 to 1897 when the last of the Bush family, S. A. Bush J.P., died.

The premises were then taken over by J. Worley and sons to 1903, when it transferred to Haycock and Russell to 1917, when A. Russell bought out his partner and the shop continued in the name of Russell to 1969. It is interesting to note that, when telephones were made available in Byfield, this shop was Byfield 6.

S. A. Bush's shop in the 1870s, which was in Main Street at the time the photograph was taken; at some time it became named Central Stores. It is today 2 and 2a Bell Lane. One of the gentlemen by the horse and cart one would presume was Mr S. A. Bush; the two ladies in the doorway are the "Miss Masons", Ellen and Mary Ann. Using the detail on the 1851 census, their ages on this photograph would be 22 and 26, and they are pictured with the other members of the shop staff. Mr S. A. Bush had taken over the running of the shop on the death of his father Samuel Bush in 1871. Details from the Byfield Congregational Church Centenary Souvenir Booklet, dated 1927, show Mr Samuel Amos Bush as Deacon and Treasurer. Details in the Byfield Parish Council records show that Mr S. A. Bush put himself forward as a nominee to become a member of Byfield Parish Council on December 4th 1894, but he failed to get elected (Parish Councils were only formed earlier in the year). S. A. Bush J.P. was buried in Byfield churchyard on October 7th 1897 aged 63. He is believed to be the only Justice of the Peace buried in Byfield. With the death of Mr S. A. Bush in 1897 the ownership from the original allotment to Edward Bush in 1779 moved out of the Bush family.

This photograph is annotated JR1 in the Byfield Photo Museum. Lender John Russell.

This photograph of Russells shop was taken in 1917 at the time Arthur Russell had taken the shop over. In the photograph are W. A. Russell, L. E Russell and George Haynes, with D. B. Russell looking from the bedroom window.

This photograph is annotated JR49 in the Byfield Photo Museum. Lender John Russell.

Russells Shop "An Institution" (The memories of John Russell, grandson of Arthur Russell).

In 1917 the shop in Bell Lane was taken over by Arthur Russell, who had been initially a baker but later also became a grocer.

The shop in Bell Lane had been established for around seventy years when Arthur Russell became the proud owner of the business. He ran the shop until his death in 1943 at the age of 71, when the business continued until 1969 having been owned by Arthur's sons Douglas and Leslie Russell. At its height the business had around 1000 customers, and delivered to up to twenty surrounding villages, taking orders one day, and delivering the goods two days later, initially by horse and cart and later by motor van and motor lorry.

The diversity of merchandise and services provided was amazing. As well as a grocer, greengrocer, provision merchant, baker, wine and spirit merchant, coal merchant, dealer in patent medicines, hardware and paint, paraffin and lamp oils, chicken and animal feedstuffs, tobacco and cigarettes both wholesale and retail, Russells were also insurance agents.

The shop itself: The top shelf, which was up to the shop ceiling, stored the light packets of cornflakes, and the like. A "long arm", a pole with a hook on, was used to dislodge the specific package and this was then caught by the shop assistant waiting below.

Steps were used to reach the next tier of shelves of tea, jam, coffee, tinned milk, cordials, sweets, chocolates, and "patent medicines". These were brand-named products which were deemed to cure, or at least relieve, most common minor ailments. The author remembers one package in this section "De-Witts" backache pills, reading on the package that one side effect of taking these pills was that it turned the patient's urine vivid green. The author not actually suffering from backache decided to take a pill or two, and will be remembered by the lads as the only boy at Towcester Grammar School who gave coloured demonstrations of an art previously unseen in a part of the building not normally used for iridescent colour shows.

Various items were kept in the large drawers under the counter, one of them being bulk granulated sugar, which was always "bagged up" into blue paper bags on Wednesday afternoons. Currants and sultanas were also received in bulk and bagged up in the shop.

On one of the counter tops were cakes in glass cabinets, and by the window was the bacon-slicer. The speed with which some of the assistants sliced a side of bacon into rashers was an art. In front of the counters in boxes were stacked boxes of fresh fruit and vegetables.

In the windows were various displays to promote different merchandise, shaded in the summer by external white blinds, and inside there were always dozens of wasps attracted by the smells and tastes of the food on sale.

Behind the counter, near the door through to the house, was a wind-pipe connected to the office at the far end of the building. At each end of this pipe there was a plug which was a whistle. If a message needed to be passed along the pipe, the caller blew down the pipe, which blew the whistle at the other end and the message was relayed by speaking down the pipe; obviously it was essential to replace the whistle after use.

Another commodity sold on the premises was salt; it was delivered to Byfield Station in a special salt van, from Salt Union Bromsgrove, and was in big tapered bars in three ton loads. Normally it was fetched from the station using a pony and trap; the pony belonged to the Author whose father Les fetched the salt. Now Les could never load any vehicle he was using by half measure, so the trap was fully laden in a manner that the pony was almost lifted off the ground. This was rectified by the weight of Les when he sat on the driving seat on the trap. The very willing pony, when getting to the end of Church Street and into High Street, had great difficulty in obtaining traction between her hooves and the road surface but fortunately no problems ever occurred. The pony and trap was backed up to a first floor window over the ovens of the Bakehouse where the salt was stored in warm dry conditions. The salt was sawn into about 2 inch sections from the tapered bar, using a normal wood saw kept for the purpose in the salt store, and then these were sold by weight. This salt was used together with saltpetre (potassium nitrate) by customers for curing bacon from pigs that they had reared.

The shop area itself was a very busy place, not only with customers coming in but staff "getting up orders" to be delivered. Orders were placed on the counter and then checked off; one member of staff packing, one relating what was listed. Such shouts as "2 of gran – 100 Players – ½ of bacon – ½ of Priory – 1lb of Typhoo - packet of asprin" etc. would be heard, and the packer would pack them at an incredible rate in a cardboard box that had previously contained incoming goods from a wholesale supplier, fitting in each component as if the box was made for just that specific order. The box was then transferred by hand to the warehouse area ready to be loaded into the delivery vehicle.

The shop and office were heated by paraffin stoves in the middle of the floors. Health and safety; what health and safety? Later the heating system was updated and overhead radiant heaters were installed. The building basically consisted of the shop at one end and the warehouse at the other; in the middle was living accommodation.

The warehouse consisted of a ground floor, a first floor, and cellars. These were connected by a "crane"; the windlass was operated through a gear system by a large handle, and the cogs of the gears could be locked by a ratchet bar to hold a load in any position. The load-bearing pulley wheel of about two feet diameter was attached to a beam at ceiling height on the first floor over which a chain ran, one end attached to the windlass and another to the load! Between each of the floors were trap doors, each consisting of two upward-opening flaps with a hole for the chain to run through in the centre. This meant that a load coming up would automatically open the flaps, and when the load had passed through the flaps would close again.

Obviously this saved manual carrying of any kind of heavy crates, boxes and sacks, and this was even used for pigs that had been slaughtered to be hung in the cellar overnight prior to being butchered, the pig being held by a locking bar across the two flaps of the trap doors.

There was also an external set of trap doors from "the street", under which were two fixed lubricated skids angled down into the cellar down which beer barrels and the like were skidded. The floors were joined by two flights of internal stairs on the back wall of the warehouse; the cellars were also serviced by a set of internal stairs at the shop end, and a set of external stairs from the back of the building. The complex of interlinked cellars was sited under all of the building with the exception of the shop itself; two more cellars were sited under the yard outside.

The cellars stored potatoes, shoe, floor and other polishes, including black lead, beer both in barrels and in bottles, and cheeses (Russells purchased eighteen Canadian Cheddar Cheeses and matured them for twelve months prior to sale). There were also wines and spirits in racks in one of the vaulted cellars under the yard. The other cellar under the yard was used to process the curing of hams and bacon in lead-lined troughs; also, because of the cooler atmosphere, the bulk of the butter, margarine and lard was stored in there. The lard was purchased in 28lb packs, which were delivered in cardboard boxes and later "weighed up" into smaller pats for sale.

The ground floor of the warehouse consisted of one large room in which the windlass of the crane was housed. Stored in this area were all types of sugar, the granulated sugar in large hessian sacks; a vented safe in which sides of cured bacon were kept; bulk vinegar was stored in a barrel and dispensed from here; also large tins of biscuits and crisps were stored on shelves in here.

The small room was the office, the "control centre" of the whole operation. There was a small desk used by one of the office clerical staff who would be completing purchasing ledgers and sales ledgers; there was also on the wall, lit by the only window, a desk that was used by staff standing up! This type of desk was normally associated with the banking or legal professions. On this desk was the only telephone, the number being Byfield **6**, the sixth telephone to be connected to the Byfield manual exchange. In the corner of the office was the shop's safe; a large very heavy affair.

This office room was also in essence a warehouse, for in it were stored cigarettes and tobacco, with names not now common: Turf, Shag, Twist, Cut Golden Bar, Players Digger, Bells Three Nuns, Capstan Navy Cut, Gold Flake, Players, Craven "A", Weights, Senior Service, Kensitas, Woodbines, Churchmans, and also goods that were being promoted, especially at times like Easter and Christmas. The huge variety of confectionery, especially at Christmas, will always be remembered.

This was also a very busy area; customers coming to pay their accounts or change a cheque, some accounts were of long standing. Russells were very proud of the fact that they looked after their customers even to the extent of allowing local farmers twelve months credit even for bread, due to the fact that a lot of farmers received a large percentage of their income only after crops had been harvested, and also it has to be remembered that Arthur Russell was trading though the Depression of the 1920s and early 1930s.

This was also where the representatives of the wholesalers came to tout their wares. One gentleman especially remembered was the rep for Birds Custard, who appeared on a "two crossbar" upright bicycle, dapperly dressed in suit and bowler hat and bike clips, having ridden from Banbury where he had alighted from the Birmingham train. Birds were then based in Birmingham, later to relocate to Banbury.

The first floor of the warehouse was set out in a similar format, as was the ground floor with two rooms; a large one and a small one. The large room had shelves round the walls and large wooden bins complete with lids in the centre. As previously described, the big pulley wheel of the crane was attached to a beam in the ceiling of this room. The shelves stored a variety of stock and the bins contained such items as split peas, haricot beans, pearl barley, tapioca, mixed peel, rice etc. The small room contained shelves around the walls stocking all items of hardware and of paint. The hardware ranged from an eggcup to a dust bin, a table knife to a garden fork, from the smallest tin of enamel paint to the largest tin of emulsion (or, before emulsion, "whitening"). Candles, oil lamps, electric light bulbs (after 1928 when mains electricity came to Byfield), kettles, brushes, brooms, clothes baskets. If Russells had not got it they would get it!

Back to the building, attached to the rear of the shop main building was an older building, which appears on the 1779 enclosure map (the main building was built in the mid 1800s). The ground floor of this building contained the kitchen of the living quarters and also the Bakehouse, which had two large coal-fired ovens. There were two long dough "kivers", the sides and bottom each made out of a single piece of elm; these were placed at right angles to each other, each

placed against a wall. The dough was mixed and kneaded the previous evening, allowed to rise overnight, and baked the next day. This meant of course that the baker worked the dough even on a Sunday evening.

The bread produced in coal-fired ovens had a taste of its own, with the flame travelling from the fire along the side of the oven, hitting the back, travelling towards the oven door then exhausting up the chimney, with all the oxygen being drawn into the oven and some strategically placed loaves being nicely caught by extra heat and burnt on one side. It is no wonder that the modern fan-assisted gas-fired ovens cannot compete with the taste and texture of bread baked in bakehouses such as Russells.

All sorts of goodies were produced: pork pies made from good cuts of quality pork (nice textured meat not red meat bacon pies), the pig having been reared on the premises or locally, and dough cakes. These were two specialities for which people travelled quite long distances to purchase. The bakehouse also produced a fine variety of pastries and cakes; large slabs of fruit cake which later were cut into six sections for sale. This was always known as "Slab Cake". Seasonal items, such as hot cross buns at Easter, sold out very quickly.

There were two bakehouses in Byfield, Russells and Smiths, that offered the facility, because the ovens had always to be

This photograph was taken at the bottom of "School Hill" in the 1940s and is of a group of village men taking their Sunday roasts home having collected them from Russells Bakehouse. They are L to R: Arnold Watts, Charlie Gardner, Bert Gardner, Ted Eyles and George (Dawdy) Plummer.

This photograph is annotated JR878 in the Byfield Photo Museum. Lender: the Cross Tree Public House.

kept up to a certain temperature, for people to bring their Sunday roast dinners to the bakehouses to be cooked. It was said that dinners cooked in these ovens "tasted lovely"; the other reason that people brought the dinners to be cooked at the bakehouses was because to cook a dinner in a big enough baking tin to feed a large family was just not possible in a small cottage range. Also, of course, this was a social event for the men or boys of the house, who were normally tasked with the job, enabling them to meet people they would not meet at any other time, as most people worked long hours in their normal working week. These meetings were normally amicable until, of course, someone dropped their tin, or the dinners got mixed up, then the atmosphere was not quite as amicable.

On the first floor over the kitchen was the Flour store, all in two hundredweight and a quarter cwt sacks. There was no hoist in this part of the building; all had to be taken up on "somebody's back" and in fact down again! The floor over the actual Bakehouse, strangely enough, was used to store empty biscuit tins, of which there was a considerable number. Further on, over the ovens as previously described, were stored the three tons of bar salt.

Other buildings on the premises stored washing soap, washing powders, and other soaps – Sunlight, Hudson's, Lifebuoy, Oxydol, Surf, Persil, Tide, and Reckitts washing blue to add to the rinse to whiten the clothes!

In the yard there was a building housing a large paraffin tank and a drum of methylated spirits to supply customers for heating, lighting and cooking in their homes. There were also pig sties and stables for up to five or six horses, later to be converted into garages for motor cars, delivery vans and lorries.

The first motor van, a model "T" Ford, was purchased in 1921 and was driven by Les Russell. The reliability of this vehicle was, as one would expect in those early days, none too good. It visited Ewins garage in Banbury quite regularly (Ewins were the original Ford dealers in Banbury; the franchise was soon to be transferred to Sid Young and Ewins became the Vauxhall dealers). Mr Russell senior was surprised at the time and cost incurred, as he had been previously familiar with using horses, most of which he could use relatively trouble free, perhaps then even selling the animal for more than he bought it for. He soon realised this was not the case with this "new fangled motor". He informed his son Leslie, "Boy I think these things are sinking funds!" Little did he realise how wise a statement that was! His realisation of the cost of running and maintaining a road vehicle driven by an internal combustion engine has since been made painfully apparent to a very large number of people.

Over the road from the shop, in other premises owned by the Russell family previously described, were buildings which stored preserves, jams, marmalades and chutneys etc. Another building on this side of the road had a "stage", a raised section for storing animal feedstuffs, corn, bran, toppings, maize, hops sold by the bushel, etc.

Keeping of chickens, pigs and other animals by the average householder was commonplace, and a lot were fed by feedstuff from Russells.

Russells were also coal merchants; this part of the business was based at Byfield station. From the start it was apparent to Arthur Russell that it was advantageous for coal merchants to own their own coal wagons. The fact was that the "turn round

This photograph is of Byfield station in 1930, showing "Russell's Truck No 4" in the station sidings.

This photograph is annotated JR161 in the Byfield Photo Museum. Lender John Russell.

time" at the pitheads was faster, i.e. privately owned wagons were loaded before unmarked wagons. The result was that A. Russell purchased six coal wagons numbered 1 to 6. The coal was purchased from Baddesley Colliery at Atherstone, Ansty Hall Colliery at Stockingford Nuneaton, and Babbington Colliery, Bullwell Nottingham.

Over the years that Russells traded there were a number of characters who worked for them.

Billy Edmunds – Billy was the coal carter, using a horse and wagon. Billy had a special affinity with his horses, always keeping them in prime condition. It was said that he "borrowed" apples and pears and other titbits to give to his horse from the carefully stored produce of customers. Billy also had a reputation regarding his ability to consume quite large quantities of strong bottled beer, apparently with no effect on his ability to walk straight or talk straight! Billy's grandson tells of Billy in his last hours asking for a drink of beer.

Sammy Snape – Sammy was a coal carter, using Russells' first motor lorry, a two ton Bedford. Sammy was not a young man but he was fit; he had been a good footballer in his youth.

Thomas the Italian – he was followed by Freddy the German, both PoWs from the local Byfield camp. Freddy will always be remembered as a large, strong good-natured man; both men helped Sammy deliver the coal.

Frank Holmes – Frank worked in Russells' office. He was employed by them for forty two years with just a break for his wartime army service; a well-liked man of principle.

Alf Haynes – another long-serving employee working for Russells for nearly as long as Frank. Again he had a break for wartime army service. "Figgy", as he was nicknamed, was a good-natured man, definitely in the right job with his polite and affable manner. Alf's brother Tom had earlier worked for the firm, as did another brother Harold, who had the nickname of "Porky".

George Gare – was the baker before and during the Second World War, famous for his pork pies.

Bill Garlick – who followed George into the Bakehouse is remembered for his dough cakes.

Les Henning – followed Bill into the Bakehouse. Les was probably the most versatile workman Russells ever had; he had the ability to "turn his hand" to any job! Les, after being the baker, became the main delivery man. He was a very jovial bubbly character, who was very popular with customers and other staff alike.

The female staff, which included Rita, Esme, Joyce, Dorothy, Joan, Cynthia, Monica, Brenda, Joyce, Sheila and others, added a bit of glamour to the business. Hardworking and efficient, they all got on well with the customers and were certainly an asset to trade.

Harry Hinton – the van driver; when the throughput of the bakehouse was at its height, with the bread and other deliveries, Harry was a very busy chap who always had a smile for everyone.

The end of Russells came in 1969 when the stock, fixtures and fittings were disposed of and the premises sold. The closure of this institution was caused by a number of factors. The first was the death of one of the partners, Douglas Russell, in May 1968. This together with the fact that Leslie was past retiring age and also the threat of that North American institution the "Super Store" which was lurking round the corner. The future generations of Russells realised that the whole principle of shopping was going to change, from personal service to self-service, and that there would be no future for the local shop, at least one the size of the Russells' operation. This forecast has since been proven.

Whether in the fullness of time the situation will revert to this very personal level of service we can only guess.

An interesting coincidence! Within the Byfield Photo Museum is a photograph of Haycock and Russell's Shop. Arthur Russell is standing in the doorway of the shop in 1904. By his side is Frederick Lawrence, who also worked in the shop. Arthur Russell became the grandfather of John Russell, and Frederick Lawrence became the grandfather of John Hutt. John Russell and John Hutt worked together in the Banbury garage of Grimsbury Motors in the late 1950s. Prior to this working relationship the two Johns had never met.

The premises were later used over a fairly short period by: a wood worker; it then became a café; carpet shop; an interior designer's, and others, and was finally divided and became two private dwellings. The cottages behind the shop were probably built by the Bush family, on the site of older buildings which are shown on a similar footprint on the 1779 Enclosure Map.

In the 1930s William Steel and his wife and family lived there. The number of children was such that the girls of the family slept in the family cottage, and the boys next door with their uncle, Mrs Steel's brother, a Mr Bilson. One of the boys, Ben Steel, lost his life in the first week of the Second World War, when the warship Courageous was sunk by German U-boats in the Western Approaches. Other occupants of the cottages were a Mrs Coy and the Edmunds family.

The Inclosure around these cottages was an area of 1 rood 30 perches (**see Map Eighteen Old Inclosures/ Homesteads 55**), and it was allotted to John Maud; the one and the same who had with eight yeoman farmers planted the elm tree on the Cross Tree Green in 1753. Part of this site became part of Russells and is now a Motor Repair Garage operated by the McKenzie family. The largest of the cottages is now being tastefully renovated and modernised by Norman McKenzie. The other part of the site was the garden attached to the shop, and is now the site of a detached house built by Peter and Ann Codling. Ann is a descendant of the Hutt family.

Moving forward, Bell Lane (formerly Main Street) now joins Banbury Lane (formerly The Old Turnpike).

NEW TERRACE

The BLACK NUMBERS are from the survey of Old Inclosures and Homesteads in the centre of the village.
The BLUE NUMBERS are Tracts of Land allotted to Proprietors and Owners in the rest of the parish.
The RED NUMBERS denote points of interest along the route.
Detail taken from a modern map some detail from the 1779 Enclosure Map with other detail added including the " New Turnpike" built in 1824.

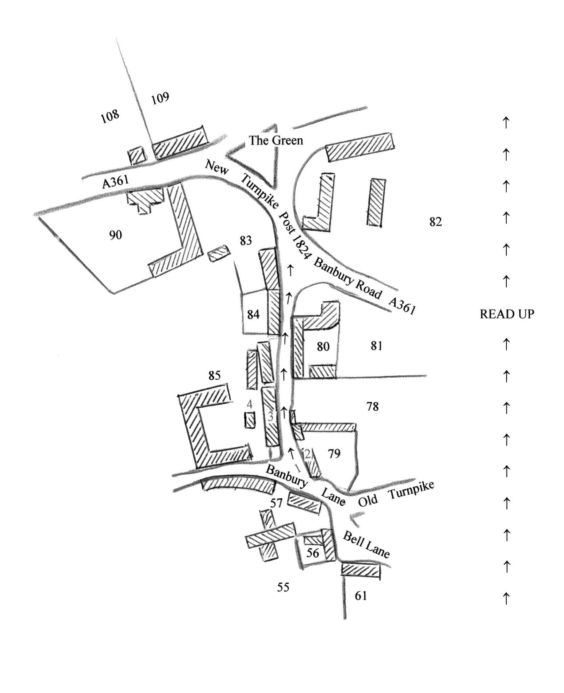

CHAPTER SEVENTEEN

NEW TERRACE

(See Map Nineteen)

Moving across from Banbury Lane into New Terrace, passing the stone-built cottages on our right, **(see Map Nineteen point of interest 1)**, these are similar cottages to those in Banbury Lane. They were all built by Mr Charles Bartholomew, of Blakesley Hall, in 1913.

The Bartholomew Gift

Charles Bartholomew (1851 – 1919) was bought by his father, who was a Victorian industrialist, who made his money from coal, the whole village of Blakesley in 1876! This included all of the houses; in fact he bought the lot, pubs, shops and all. Charles had been given a complete little world, for the village had butchers, coopers, wheelwrights, bakers and shoemakers. He was also given Blakesley Hall, an imposing country seat.

The Hall was connected to the Stratford Midland Junction railway "main line" by its own 15 inch gauge railway track; the engines of the system being made by Bassett Lowke of Northampton. The line conveyed both goods and passengers between the Hall and Blakesley Station. This would mean that there was a transport rail link between Blakesley Hall and Byfield.

Charles Bartholomew had two passions; one was railways, the other was an attraction to the opposite sex, none being safe from him. When children were born, Charles would accommodate mother and child in a house. Perhaps the words of Lord Acton (1834 – 1902) are apt. Power tends to corrupt and absolute power corrupts absolutely.

Perhaps it should not be mentioned, but why did Charles Bartholomew build these cottages in Byfield? Note: More details of Blakesley and the Bartholomews can be found in "The Green Lane to Nowhere: The Life of an English Village" by Byron Rogers.

These cottages were some of the first modern, well-appointed solidly-constructed homes for working class families built in the village of Byfield, some fifteen years before the first municipal housing was constructed.

They must have been a revolution at the time considering that a lot of village cottages were in a bad state of repair, some with earth floors.

The cottages were built on two Inclosures; an allotment in 1779 to Jane Townsend of an area of 24 perches, and

This photograph taken in the 1950s is of New Terrace, Byfield. The Bartholomew cottages on the right were built in 1913. The farm house on the left was taken down for road widening. "John's Cottages" can be seen further along on the left into New Terrace.

This photograph is annotated BH33 in the Byfield Photo Museum. Lender Mrs Janet Blake.

part of another allotment to John Edwards, an area of 2 roods 25 perches (see Map Nineteen Old Inclosures/Homesteads 79 and 78). Some of the occupants were: Goodland; Tomalin (later Buggins); Waite; Tuckey; Boddington; Wheeler; Phillips; Henning; Cross and others. An early photograph of New Terrace shows a single thatched cottage on the right at the bottom end near Banbury Lane, (see Map Nineteen point of interest 2). This cottage was demolished to make way for the Bartholomew Houses.

On the opposite side of the road, only about fifteen feet away from these cottages across a very narrow roadway, was a large farmhouse (see Map Nineteen point of interest 3). This site had previously had on it three cottages. This Inclosure was allotted to Thomas Cox in 1779, an area of 2 roods (see Map Nineteen Old Inclosures/Homesteads 85). He was also allotted various other land and inclosures, which included the Rose and Crown in High Street and the Inclosure which became Byfield Cattle Market.

This farmhouse was owned by the Howes family who, as you may recall, had a farmyard and buildings in Bell Lane and land along the end of Pit Lane from the 1860s. In the 1870s Samuel Howes (1821–1893) is recorded as a farmer. In 1894 – Mrs Mary Ann Howes and 1928 – Frank Howes, who lived until he was 90 (1880–1970). He was presented with a bakelite portable radio by Fred Hutt, Churchwarden, for being in the church choir for 70 years. One of Frank's employees was Fred (Dink) Haynes, who could be seen with a yoke across his shoulders carrying two pails of milk from the milking parlour in Bell Lane up past the school to the farm dairy (see Map Nineteen point of interest 4). The site of this dairy is today indicated by the gate posts of the lower of the two bungalows now on the site. The butter churn, now belonging to Byfield Parish Council, which was used in this dairy, has been taken to this gateway on the site where it produced the butter, and photographed, to be displayed in Byfield Photo Museum. This imposing farm house was pulled down in the 1950s for road widening; the present pathway is subject to sinking due to the fact that it is above the position of what were the farmhouse cellars. The farm yard, behind the house up to this time, was used by Mr Denis Judd who kept some of his buses there.

We move on to the two cottages on the left. The original Inclosure was allotted in 1779 to a John Burbidge, an area of 14 perches. It also shows a dwelling on the site at this time. This would be the area of the site today, (see Map Nineteen Old Inclosures/Homesteads 84).

Certainly the most renowned and interesting person to live there, from 1907 to her death in 1972, was Mrs Lily Maher, previously Mrs Lily Smith.

Lily Maher(previously Lily Smith)

Lily was born in Tanner Street Northampton in 1877. Her father worked on the railway; he was knocked down and killed, by a train in Hunsbury Hill Tunnel. On his death, her mother married the lodger, who was the same age as her eldest son. Lily was the youngest of four children; the other three were boys. When Lily was 3 or 4 her mother died of TB and Lily went to live with her aunt in Bedford. This did not work

out and Lily was sent back to her stepfather. Her stepfather left her food and she went to a neighbour to be dressed. She was sent to the workhouse and, after some other very disruptive moves, in 1893, then aged 16, she was offered a job as domestic help by the Sedgwick family and trained to become the family's cook. The Sedgwick family were drapers in what is now 32/34 Banbury Lane, Byfield (the old pottery) (see Map Nineteen Old Inclosures/Homesteads 57).

In 1895 at the age of 18 she married Mr John Smith. She had £7 in the bank! Her husband had no money and only had casual work, working one day at a time. She had a baby every two years until 1921, 11 children all born in Byfield.

They moved into New Terrace in 1907. In 1921 her husband died of Bright's disease (kidneys) and she was left with five children; four at school and a small baby not yet walking! She lived on 10/- from the government, 3/- from the Railway Orphan Fund, and the income from a little sweet shop she opened on the suggestion of one of her small sons. The old cottage was pulled down, and the two cottages we see today built with the insurance money paid on the death of her husband.

She married her lodger Michael (Mick) Maher (1878–1956), in September 1944; he worked as a porter on Byfield Station.

Lily Maher died in 1972 at the age of 94, and the burial records give her address as "John's Cottages", a quiet reminder of in whose memory the cottages were built.

A mother's devotion to a well-loved son.

Lily Smith's (later to become Lily Maher) second son Walter G. Smith, born 1899, enlisted when he was 17 into the Machine Gun Corps. He was awarded the Military Medal on September 31st 1918, wounded at Etaples in France and died of his wounds on October 21st 1918.

Lily, small in stature but stout of heart, fetched the wooden cross that had been placed on his grave in France. It was secured to the wall of the Independent Chapel in the village of Byfield until the chapel closed.

This cross now hangs in the Parish Church; a reminder to all of the dedication of a man who paid the ultimate price in the defence of his country, and of the dedication to that son sadly missed by a loving Mother, who visited his grave, retrieved the cross marking his final resting place and brought it home.

Lily Smith left her little shop when she retired and she moved into the other cottage next door. The shop continued and was first run by Joan and Denis Judd, later by Frances Davies (née Hodges) and then by Joan Gough (née Shenton) until it was once again used as a private house.

Barbara Smith was a daughter of Bill Smith and his wife Elsie; Barbara passed away in November 2004 at the age of 78. She was very proud of the fact that she was born in John's Cottages in New Terrace.

The last Inclosure on the right of New Terrace, allotted to John Gibbins, was an area of 16 perches. This allotment was to become part of the premises that would be the New Inn and later the Cross Tree Public House (see Map Nineteen Old Inclosures/Homesteads 80).

CHAPTER EIGHTEEN

THE BRIGHTWELL FIELD ENHANCED

THE BRIGHTWELL FIELD

This is a copy of a plan of the original suggested project drawn up in 1984, there are additional points of interest that have been added in RED.

The original was annotated "To all sports bodies in Byfield, this is only a suggested project. Please have sight of these details and then a meeting on site can be arranged, to discuss detail or any other alternative suggestions".

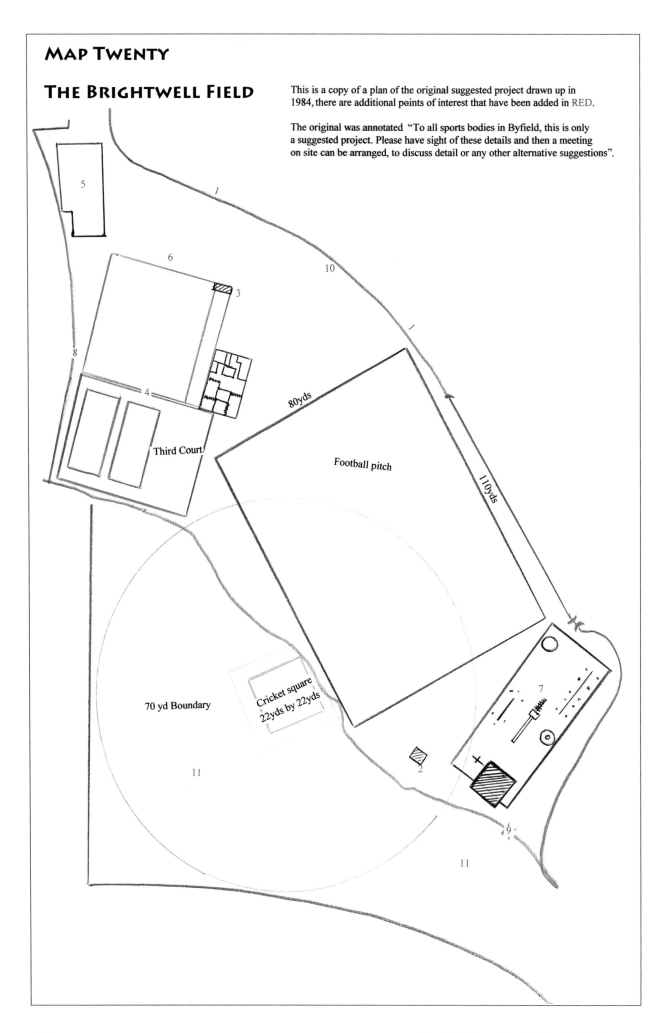

5

6

3

1

10

8

4

80yds

Third Court

Football pitch

110yds

70 yd Boundary

Cricket square
22yds by 22yds

7

11

2

11

9

Chapter Eighteen

The Brightwell Field Enhanced

(See Map Twenty)

Details from the Byfield parish records reveal that the first mention of Mr Brightwell's Field was at a meeting of the Byfield Parish Council on October 8th 1929, when it was rented as a Recreation Ground. The terms of an agreement were read and a sub-committee formed. Obviously the "ridge and furrow" field was not suitable for recreation, so it was sublet to a Mr Stanley Checkley, at an annual rent of two pounds ten shillings. This subletting continued until 1944 when details of a Parish Council meeting dated January 14th record important news from Solicitors Stops and Burton. This was the gift of a field to the Parish to be confirmed as "Dove House Close". The field was gifted by Mr Thomas Brightwell in memory of his son who was lost in the First World War.

A meeting of October 12th 1944 discussed the deed of conveyance of Dove House Close. A letter from Stops and Burton stated that the Brightwell family had lived in Byfield since the 18th century, and in view of this the Executors proposed that the field should be called "The Brightwell Recreation Ground". This was agreed and carried. At the following meeting Councillors W. F. Trefield and F. W. Boddington were nominated, in addition to Byfield Parish Council Chairman, Councillor J Brown, to sign the deed of conveyance.

In 1945, Mr Stanley Checkley, having been given due notice to vacate the field, put in a claim for disturbance, countered by a claim by the Parish Council for dilapidation. The dispute ended with Mr Checkley paying the Byfield Parish Council twelve shillings and six pence.

The Annual Parish Meeting of March 29th 1945 agreed that a committee of 17 should be formed immediately, with the Parish Council having powers to co-opt. The first Chairman of Brightwell was Leslie Jackson, Byfield School Headmaster. His title was Chairman of Brightwell Construction Committee.

Minutes of the meeting of May 15th 1945 record a demand from the Inland Revenue for land tax on the Recreation Ground. There is no record whether this demand was met or disputed. This meeting also contained a minute in which the Recreation Ground Committee made an application to the Parish Council, as custodian trustees, for a decision on whether the Recreation Ground should be opened on a Sunday.

The meeting of August 10th 1945 indicated an estimated figure of £1,000 for levelling the field. The ground would be on three levels; in addition there was a drainage system to consider.

At a further meeting Mr F. W. Boddington reported that grants could be obtained from the National Playing Fields Association. Also that the Local Education Authority, if satisfied by the conditions, would pay a small rent for the use of the field by children. It was also indicated that "The Village" will be expected to contribute substantially.

A letter was read from Norton Griffith (Plant) Ltd, a local company based at Hellidon, giving an estimate for levelling the Recreation Ground of £1,250. This price was thought to be rather excessive and it was decided to get three more estimates.

The meeting of November 8th 1945, indicated that the Parish Council had obtained another estimate to level the Recreation Ground, from Thomas Lowe and Sons of Uxbridge London of £1,000 to £1,200. The Annual Parish Meeting of March 11th 1946, indicated that £406-15-8 had been raised by the village.

The meeting of June 4th 1946 reflects the use of Prisoners of War as labour from the Boddington Road Camp, with a decision that an account for the work for drainage on the Brightwell field should not be paid, the hourly rate having been deemed too high.

The meeting of June 4th 1946 records an anonymous gift of £1,250 being offered provided that fund-raising accrued the balance of the total cost, estimated at £3,350.

Progression of the initial development.

The long wall between the Brightwell field and the footpath to the Church **(see Map Twenty two points marked of interest 1)** was taken down by Frank Holmes and Edward Thompson using Edward's horse and cart.

Subsequently some of the stone was used to build a shelter adjacent to the children's play area. The shelter had a plaque inside on the back wall in memory of Mr Wilfred Henry Hartwell **(see Map Twenty point of interest 2)**. Some of the stone was used to build a machinery store for the Byfield bowling club **(see Map Twenty point of interest 3)**, and the retaining wall between the bowling green and the tennis courts, **(see Map Twenty point of interest 4)**. All of these structures were built by Mr George Farmilo, a local stone mason. Some of the stone was stored and used to build the new Byfield village hall in 1960 **(see Map Twenty point of interest 5)**.

Regarding the landscaping, this was originally done by the Hellidon firm of Norton Griffith (Plant) Ltd using D2 Caterpillar crawler tractors and rope-controlled earth scrapers. Unfortunately the company went into liquidation and the work had to be completed by others.

During the landscaping work several aspects of the past use of the site were unearthed, one being a most beautifully constructed well. This was very well built using cut stone and larger in diameter than the normal domestic well **(see Map Twenty point of interest 6)**.

Perhaps this does indicate that this was the site of the Hospice of Saint John, as mentioned in Denis Judd's book "Living in the Country".

When the work on the field was completed, a Tennis Club and a Bowling Club were formed.

The main area was used for a very short time by the Football Club, but it was too wet for the purpose. One reason for this was that soil was taken from the main area of the field and used to elevate the site of the tennis courts and bowling green, for aesthetic effect.

The children's play area with its Wicksteed equipment was, by the request of parents, placed at the bottom end of the field; the reason given was that it would keep the children away from the roads **(see Map Twenty point of interest 7)**. The play equipment provision included two sets of swings, an ocean wave, a witch's hat roundabout, a merry-go-round, a plank swing and a 40 foot cabin slide, supplemented at a later date with a see-saw.

The old wooden building that had previously been used as a cobbler's shop by Ernest Victor Vine, in Smith the Baker's yard in High Street, was dug into the bank adjacent to the gate to the tennis courts and became the first tennis pavilion **(see Map Twenty point of interest 8)**.

The main area of the field was used by the children of the village for impromptu games, when the surface was dry enough for the purpose.

Sadly, in 1958 the Bowling Club folded, and the bowling green became defunct. The last demarcation of the area was when the split chestnut fencing was removed in the 1960s and used to provide the dividing fence between the Poors Piece and the Causeway Charity land on the Priors Marston Road.

The Tennis Club went from strength to strength, and in fact expressed a wish a number of times to build a third court and also a pavilion on the disused bowling green. Permission was refused for both the third court and the pavilion, the Parish Council being aware that the resurrection of the bowling green was always a possibility. Around this time the Brightwell Committee, which had started off as such a large and robust committee, disbanded, and the responsibility for the administration of the facility passed back to the Parish Council.

1960 onward

The Trustees of the Village Hall built a new village hall on the north (top) of the site in 1960 on Brightwell land, and at the time the disused water supply, that had serviced the plush Cumberland turf of the bowling green, was teed-off and used as the water supply for the new Village Hall.

Byfield Scout Headquarters Building

The Byfield Scout Group expressed a wish to build a Scout Headquarters building on the Brightwell field. This initiative was promoted and eagerly pushed forward by John

This photograph is of the Byfield Bowling Green in its original form of four rinks. The photograph was taken in the 1950s. The interesting aspects are the style of dress of the bowlers, and the fact that they are all men.

This photograph is annotated BH178 in the Byfield Photo Museum. Lender Brian Haynes.

This photograph, taken in 1980, shows the newly-constructed Scout Headquarters; also it shows the large number of volunteers resurfacing the then children's play area. One interesting aspect is that all the equipment and the tarmacadam surface would not be acceptable today on safety grounds.

This photograph is annotated AS440 in the Byfield Photo Museum. Lender Richard Tidmarsh.

Cook. Plans were drawn up by Michael Bartle, and the Parish Council was approached for permission to site it on the field. Obviously one problem was the actual position of the building, due to the very basic fact that, with any future development, the use of the field should not be impaired by the position of the Scout Headquarters. The Parish Council agreed that the building could be built on the field as long as it was positioned as near as possible to the bridge over the Westhorpe Stream, which was the route of the definitive footpath which continued across the bottom end of the Brightwell Field, and on towards the Church **(see Map Twenty point of interest 9)**.

The position of the building was reluctantly agreed by the Scout Group, who would have preferred it nearer the top end of the field.

The Scout Group had obtained a quantity of stone, which was stored on land adjacent to the Twistle Road railway bridge, on land belonging to Mr C. W. F. Laurie. This was to have been used to raise the Scout building to raise the slab base, but this was not used. Norman Contracts of Fenny Compton installed a ½ inch mains water feed across the field from a meter adjacent to the Village Green **(see Map Twenty point of interest 10)**. The building was connected to the main sewer, which fortunately ran adjacent to it.

The impending danger of the threat of loss of amenities

The Parish Council was acutely aware of the lack of longevity of tenancy of both Byfield Football Club and Byfield Cricket Club, the basic problem being that both of the fields the clubs were using were farmed by the same farmer, who had issued a notice to quit on both of the clubs. The cricket club was asked to vacate the ground after the 1986 season.

Fortunately the field used by the football club changed ownership, and the new owner stated "I will let you continue using the field. I would prefer it if you moved, but I will not turn you off". The Byfield Cricket Club wrote to the landowners of the cricket field, namely the Church Commissioners, who persuaded the tenant farmer of the land to let cricket continue to be played on the field. This he reluctantly agreed to do, albeit with a substantial increase in rental.

Land purchase

On a suggestion of Fred Tuckey, the Parish Council approached British Rail with reference to buying the land known as "The Shoulder of Mutton" or "William's Field" **(see Map Twenty, two points of interest 11)**, which was with the adjacent railway cutting an area of 2.9 acres. This was purchased in 1978 for £1,700, with legal fees and other costs a total of £2,000. Obviously there needed to be contact with Mr Dennis Eyles, the sitting tenant, regarding disturbance. This was done through the Council's Solicitors, Shoosmith and Harrison, and the problem resolved.

Importation of soil.
The Byfield Parish Council were aware of a road improvement scheme and road realignment one mile south of Byfield at "Half Crown Corner", and had approached the Northamptonshire County Council with regard to excess soil being available.

At this time the Byfield Tennis Club was requiring an additional court to bring the total of courts to three. An extra court was required to accommodate the demand from members for more court time. Also, the fact was stressed that league status could only be achieved with a minimum of three courts. The re-formed Byfield Bowling Club under the leadership of George Bell, a county standard bowler, were looking at resurrecting the disused bowling green. The Parish Council was aware that it was preferable that the four-rink green be increased in size to a six rink green, to enable bowlers to bowl both ways, not only up and down, but across. This was important, as in a wet season it reduced wear on the rink ends. Also, of course, it would accommodate far more bowlers.

Prior to the soil being imported, Thames Water decided that a new 18 inch sewer was needed from the Westhorpe Stream bridge in Bell Lane to the Sewage Treatment Works. This was routed along the right side of the stream, almost as soon as it entered Brightwell land. It discharged into a manhole and was then directed under the Westhorpe stream, continuing on diagonally across the site of the third tennis court into another manhole. It then ran directly in an almost straight line to the sewerage treatment works. The depth of the sewer under the surface of the Brightwell is approximately 16 feet.

A total of 1,500 tons of soil was imported from "Half Crown Corner" and was tipped directly alongside the two existing tennis courts. This raised the area to accommodate the third tennis court and for it to be at the same level as the two existing courts.

A further 600 tons of soil from the same source was imported to increase the size of the existing bowling green site to six rinks. Due to the very wet conditions, it was not possible to get the soil directly on to site, even using six-wheel drive Volvo dump trucks (this was due to the stratum of the ground at the top end of the Brightwell field having rock almost directly under the top soil). The soil was therefore delivered and stored at the top end of the site. A "Drott" bulldozer was employed to cut a step at the edge of the existing four rink green area and transfer the imported soil on to the site, compacting it in 10 inch layers for future soil stability.

The main aspects of the development of the site
The Tennis Club applied for and obtained grant aid of 55% for the additional court, towards a scheme with an estimated cost of £8,982; members of the Tennis Club funding the sponsors' share. This was the first improve-

ment at this time to any of the sports facilities on the site and was completed before any other facility.

In order to plan the progression of the development of the whole site, the Chairman of the Parish Council, Councillor John Russell, formulated a progress chart to enable all the integrated parts of the scheme to progress.

The chart started with the formation of a Burial Committee from within the Parish Council, with co-options including the Rector, the Rev. W. P. Kentigern-Fox. This committee was headed by Councillor Brighid Buchanan-Wollaston.

One of the most important items on the progress chart was to invite parishioners to a public meeting. The public meeting was held under the chairmanship of the Parish Council Chairman on May 22nd 1985. The attendance was 97 parishioners, out of these 54 voted to develop the field, 20 voted against and 9 abstained; obviously some others also abstained. Also a suggestion for the building of a multi-purpose pavilion on the "field side" of the bowling green site was put forward, but did not find favour with the majority of persons attending.

The meeting felt that decisions made were not conclusive enough, and a proposition from the floor for a referendum was requested and was agreed by those attending. This referendum was organised and a number of questions were put. The main one recorded from questionnaires returned indicated that 61% were in favour of developing and levelling the area for sport and recreation.

More soil importation.
In the intervening period the contractor who had delivered the soil from Half Crown Corner, for the provision of the third tennis court and the bowling green extension, contacted the Parish Council Chairman (who was also chairman of the Brightwell committee), with an offer of 2,500 tons of soil, 1,000 tons of which was top soil. This soil was from a mature garden in Daventry, in an area which was to become an extension to Daventry New Street car park. This offer was accepted, the top soil being delivered and stored on the Old Woodyard area for future use.

The remainder was levelled, and graded with a bulldozer over the old station and Woodyard. This was to enhance the area, and commence the process of making the majority of it into a mini country park, which had been requested by the majority though the referendum.

With regard to the original estimate of 2,500 tons, the lorries kept coming. "How much more is there?" was the question asked. "Not more than 3,000 tons" was the reply, but the lorries still kept coming, and soon the area had been enhanced as much as was required. "Tip the rest behind the Scout Hut" was the instruction! The six-wheeled tipper trucks, reversing in, kept getting bogged down. To alleviate this, the contractor sent loads of hard core and spent tarmac; thus making a hard road.

The final amount of soil imported from the Daventry site was approximately 4,000 tons, including the stock of about 1,000 tons behind the Scout hut. The total amount of imported soil onto the entire site, including that for the third tennis court and the extension of the bowling green, was in excess of 6,000 tons.

The only expense was the hiring of the "Drott" bull-dozer to get the soil from the top of the field on to the site of the bowling green extension; the cost of this amounted to £300. All of that soil and a hard road constructed free!

Phases of the development.
With regard to the development of the Brightwell area, estimated costings were obtained for the whole scheme. This included levelling the field, culverting the intervening stream, and providing drainage to the site.

For providing a six rink bowling green, a purpose-built cricket wicket, and a car park at the top end of the site, the estimated cost was £109,000.

On consulting the possible grant aid providers – the Sports Council, the Northamptonshire County Council and the Daventry District Council – it was stated that it would not be possible for them to assist with outright grants on this relatively high figure, but could the development be phased? Accordingly the scheme phases were defined:

Phase one of the scheme was to level the field, culvert the intersecting stream and drain and seed the whole area;

Phase two was to provide a six rink bowling green on the site of the original four rink green, provide a purpose built cricket wicket, and provide a car park at the top end of the site.

After various meetings the Brightwell Recreation Grounds Association (BRGA) was formed, with all interested parties, i.e. users or future users plus two lay representatives. The composition of the committee was as had been determined by the Trust Deed, the details of which had been seen and approved by Solicitors. The initial drafting of the documents had been piloted by Martin Bull and Chris Cross.

Consultants were appointed, namely Brian Cole Associates of Wellingborough.

Quotes were obtained, together with the consultant's estimate.

It was obvious to all of the committee members that the quotes being received were far too high. The Chairman was aware of a company from Shipston-on-Stour, namely D. W. Clark Land Drainage Ltd. The consultant was instructed to obtain a quote from this company; the price quoted by the company was exactly £64,500. This quote was far lower by a considerable margin than any other quotes and indeed much less than the consultant's cost estimate. These being the facts, the contract was awarded to D. W. Clark Drainage Ltd.

A case was then made for grant aid, and the prepared paper was submitted to the prospective grant providers. Its format drew favourable comments from the recipients. This was mainly due to the expertise of Oliver Tynan, in the professional manner in which the case was presented.

The application for grant aid for the scheme was successful.

Note: In most cases, and definitely in this case, provision of grant aid from individual providers depends on them agreeing to support the project and being sure of the project's viability.

Grant aid awards were:

Grant awarding body	% of total cost	Grant
Northamptonshire County Council	27.5%	£17,500
Daventry District Council	27%	£17,500
East Midland Region of the Sports Council	20%	£12,500
Total grant aid		**£47,500**

This left the Sponsor to raise £16,000. It was realised that if 100 people could be persuaded to donate £120 on covenant this would realise the sum required.

Calculated as such: £120 x 1.33 (income tax was 25 pence in the pound) rounded up = £160. £160 x 100 people = £16,000, this being the sum required.

Also, the Sports Council offered a £5,000 interest-free loan, which was gratefully accepted. The obvious advantage of this was that it improved the cash flow situation and therefore brought the start of the project forward!

Obviously money-raising continued during this period, including in the summer of 1986 a three day festival which was led by Russ Mallace. This festival raised a considerable amount of money for the scheme. A big Christmas draw, and a barn dance in Richard Watts's barn were among many other fund raising-efforts.

Suitable covenant forms were produced. People who had expressed a wish to contribute financially to the project on the referendum questionnaire were approached. Almost all of the participants agreed to donation by standing order, most covenants were either for £1.25 a month or £15 a year.

Note: The legal minimum covenant is four years. This was deemed perhaps to be too costly, and so this was extended to eight years. £120 over eight years equates to 29 pence a week, which was considered an amount of financial contribution that would be difficult to refuse, against setting an amount that was assumed people could afford.

It must be said that this magical marketing figure was arrived at by accident.

In all around 150 people gifted money to the scheme, not all on covenant, and in differing amounts. The first covenant was taken out on November 16th 1986. Some covenants by the Tennis Club were received using the Brightwell Charity status, and used specifically to fund the third tennis court.

These covenants are not shown in the above figures, the reason being that the third tennis court provision was administered entirely by Byfield Tennis Club and was the subject of completely separate funding, separate contractor, namely Fosse Contracts Ltd of Leicester and, as previously stated, another successful grant application by the Tennis Club.

This photograph is of the commencement of work on the Brightwell Field by D. W. Clark Drainage Ltd in August 1987. The photograph was taken by Mike Bosley; it shows the initial task of removing and burning unwanted trees and shrubs.

This photograph is annotated AS497 in the Byfield Photo Museum. Lender Mike Bosley.

Practicalities of the Recreation Ground Re-formation

On the main scheme, initially sixteen or so trees, some "scrub" but some quite nice mature trees, along the Westhorpe stream, were felled prior to the contractor coming on to the site, and the timber was sold to various villagers.

D. W. Clark Drainage Ltd started work on phase one. The first day of commencement of work the Brightwell Chairman thought he had better visit the site before going to work. On walking on to the site he could hear trees being ripped out, he approached the operator and stated "You will get me shot for two reasons; one, certain people do not like mature trees being up-rooted, and two, you are starting in the wrong place. You are not even on the site!"

The site was prepared, trees and fences removed, topsoil stored on site and the main area levelled by moving approximately 10,500 tons of soil from "William's Field" on to the formerly bequeathed Brightwell area. Also a small amount was used to bring the old railway cutting up to the finished level. The thousand tons of imported soil stored behind the Scout hut were also utilised in the levelling process.

The practical levelling of the site was completed using a Caterpillar bulldozer compacting the soil in ten inch layers for future ground stability, the finished gradient being a metre fall across the site. Finished levels were determined using a laser receiver attached to the bulldozer blade.

The intersecting Westhorpe stream was culverted using a 900 mm reinforced concrete pipe, the size, gradients, inlet and outfall specifications having been previously agreed with Thames Water.

The field was drained using two drainage grids; one on either side of the 900 mm culvert. The drains were 80 mm set at 450 mm depth on 5 metre centres, feeding into 100 mm interceptors with outlets into the 900 mm culvert at the downstream end. The drainage pipes were filled over with pea shingle to ground level. The depth and gradient of the drainage pipes were determined using a laser receiver on the drainage machine.

Note: D. W. Clark Land Drainage Ltd advised that they considered that 35 mm pipes on 1 metre centres at a depth of 300 mm would be more efficient across the whole of the site, and especially on the "cut" i.e. William's Field side of the site. This was rejected by the Turf Research Institute who were the advisors to one of the grant providers, namely the Sports Council. One reason given for this was that on their trial site they did not have this type of drainage, and therefore they had no practical knowledge of the efficiency of it.

An additional 250 mm drain at a depth of 1.5 to 2 metres below the finished level was installed across the old railway cutting at the north end, to act as a "French Drain" to pick up the water coming into the field from the adjacent filled cutting. This drain was connected to an underground manhole on the field side "east" of the old railway cutting, running down the side of the cutting. This connected into an existing ex-British Rail 10 inch glazed drainage pipe, which passed though an inspection manhole where it was diverted to outfall into the adjacent stream. The drain was a considerable depth below the main field surface drainage grids and was therefore not part of the surface drainage system.

At this stage the Committee decided to dispense with the services of the consultants. A meeting was arranged between Derek Clark, Managing Director of D. W. Clark Drainage Ltd, and the Chairman and Vice Chairman of Brightwell regarding progress of the scheme! Derek Clark announced that the cost of the scheme to date was £47,500, priced on labour and the amount of material used to date. It was immediately apparent to the Brightwell contingent that to spend only this sum was not advantageous due to loss of grant aid that the £63,500 would attract. So it was decided to bring phase two of the scheme into phase one. The problem with this was that it would be very difficult practically, and in the necessary time scale, to go out to tender to specialist providers.

It was apparent that the only way forward was to ask D.W. Clark Drainage Ltd to "buy in" the necessary expertise to complete phase two.

With regard to the progression of the revised scheme, the Chairman of the Brightwell Committee John Russell formulated a second updated progress chart dated June 12th 1988. This enabled all of the new and existing aspects of the scheme to go forward.

The grant providers were not happy, but consented to continue to support the whole scheme, realising that they were not being asked to contribute any extra money.

With regards to the bowling green, the result was that the preformed ditch sections were laid to the wrong levels, that is the existing levels rather than to actual levels. Some soil used was more subsoil than topsoil.

Derek Clark agreed to rectify the anomalies, and did so to the satisfaction of the Chairman of Brightwell. But not necessarily to the satisfaction of some members of the Bowling Club!

It was decided by the Brightwell Committee that, because the bowling green was elevated, it was obvious that it would drain readily. It was therefore decided to install a Cameron pop-up bowling green irrigation system. This was funded from Brightwell funds, and was an extra cost over and above the amount attracting grants.

The irrigation system had a 1,000 gallon storage tank feeding an electric pump. The pressurised pipes from the pump were then linked to the four Cameron pop-up sprinklers. These pressurised pipes were installed under the ditches and under the drainage pipes; the outfall of the drainage system was into the top end (upstream) end of the 900 mm culvert.

A considerable amount of hard work by members of the Bowling Club ensured that the bowling green surface was brought up to such a standard that, in a relatively short period, it was then inspected by County Green Assessors, and given a "B" grade marking, shortly afterwards to be elevated to "A" grade.

The specification regarding the cricket wicket was to:

1. Remove 200 mm of soil from the cricket square as per drawing, fit 80 mm peripheral drains and

2. Connect into the existing drainage system. Prepare stone base finish with a cover of topsoil to the finished level, seed with a pre-agreed mixture, provide Boughton loam. The top soil to be used was that stored previously on the old station area.

3. To provide a water supply to the cricket square.

The car park at the top end of the site was formed with graded stone and raw ballast, compacted with a roller and with a finished surface of tarmac. The drainage system was a French drain on the bowling green side piped into the top end of the playing field side ditch drain of the bowling green.

Consequently, water running off the car park ran through and into the top (upstream) end of the 900 mm culvert in common with the bowling green drainage.

Prior to the car park being laid, the water supply to the bowling green (which from 1960 had been used to supply the Village Hall) was renewed. This old pipe was of black iron which had failed a number of times previously and was therefore replaced with polythene piping.

Financial assistance of £1,000 was given by Byfield Conservative Club towards the provision of car parking on the top of the site; this generous gesture was gratefully accepted. This sum of money, as well as assisting to provide the extra parking provision, had the advantage of contributing towards the sponsor's share of the sum of money that was attracting grant aid.

It was reported to the Brightwell Recreation Association meeting of April 5th 1989 that: all grants had been received together with the £5,000 interest free loan from the Sports Council; the final amount of £66,077.20 had been paid to the contractor D. W. Clark Drainage Ltd; there were no amounts outstanding, apart from the repayment of the £5,000 loan from the Sports Council.

From the first covenant, pledged on November 16th 1986, to the final payment to the contractor was a period of two years and four months.

A chronological listing of further works after the main scheme was completed
(Notes by Russ Mallace, Chairman
of Brightwell from 1991)

1989: A sub committee of the Brightwell Recreation Ground Association was formed to discuss the provision of a new pavilion. It was in favour of one large multi-sport building adjacent to the bowling green.

1990: A referendum was held regarding a new pavilion in the central location. Of 490 forms sent out, 30 were returned – 20 for, 10 against.

1991: R. Mallace was appointed Chairman of Brightwell by Byfield Parish Council. A working party was set up to discuss the pavilion with a three month deadline to report.

Football and Cricket Pavilion

1991/1992: Plans were drawn up by Rod Healey for an agreed Cricket/ Football pavilion.

An estimate from Cherry's builders of Cropredy was received for £70,000

Grants were sought and obtained from:

March 1992	Daventry District Council	£15,000
October 1992	Foundation for Sport and the Arts	£25,000
January 1993	Sports Council	£15,000
January 1993	Loan from D.D.C	£6,000
	BRGA money	£9,000
	Total	£70,000

The building is owned by BRGA. The Football and Cricket clubs paid annual sums as their contribution to the running costs. Other organisations wishing to use the facility would pay a user fee. People were to be asked to covenant to pay off the loan.

At the Village Festival in 1993, the new cricket and football pavilion was officially opened by The Right Hon. Tim Boswell MP. £5,000 raised at the festival was shared between the BGRA and the Byfield Council of Churches.

September 1993: Byfield Athletic Football Club moved on to the site from their Woodford Road ground.

Summer 1995: Byfield Cricket Club moved on to the site from their ground behind the Old Rectory.

Agreements regarding maintenance of the grassed areas were: the Byfield Cricket Club to cut all of the cricket and football playing areas; BRGA to receive a grant from the Byfield Parish Council for cutting all of the playing areas, as the whole of the Brightwell complex is a public recreational area; contractors to be employed directly by Byfield Parish Council to cut fringe areas.

1995: Discussions took place regarding the provision of a bowls and tennis pavilion. There were two basic options: either extend the Village Hall, or provide a new purpose-built building. The decision was to build a purpose-built building.

The Bowls and Tennis Pavilion.

The new building was designed and the necessary plans drawn up again by Rod Healey. The first single-storey design was rejected by the Bowls Club due to inadequate floor area. A second two-storey building was designed with a brief "not to look like a barn".

Estimates received for the construction, varied from £99,000 to £150,000.

Local builder Will Montgomery's tender of £99,000 was accepted with certain deletions, as funding available was only £91,000. (No plastering in the changing rooms etc., these tasks to be completed later by the user clubs Byfield Bowls and Tennis Clubs).

Further grants were obtained as set out in the following table.

January 1997	Daventry District Council	£15,000
February 1997	Lottery Sports Fund Award	£59,000
	Byfield Bowls Club	£14,000
	Byfield Tennis Club	£3,000
	Total	£91,000

August 25th 1997: There was an official opening of the Pavilion by Russ Mallace Chairman of BRGA.

The new building is owned by BRGA. Byfield Bowls and Tennis Clubs were given delegated authority to manage the buildings on behalf of the BRGA and to pay all the running and upkeep costs.

March 1998: Floodlighting provision on two of the three tennis courts, cost £14,617. Grants obtained were

National Lottery	£9,700
Byfield Tennis Club	£4,917
Total	£14,617

The Adventure Playground

This was originally an "offshoot" of the school Parent Teacher organisation.

1989: After a referendum it was agreed to relocate the adventure play area, from what is now in 2004 the lower car park area to a position below the slope, closely adjacent to the footpath to the Church.

1990: The climbing tower and slide purchased by the Playground Committee was handed over to the Byfield Parish Council.

The Byfield Parish Council intended to use the existing play equipment from the old play area on the new site, with an ever-resourceful Mr Frank Beasor heading the team. The equipment, much of it installed in the 1940s, was in a worse and more dilapidated state than originally envisaged.

1996: The new play equipment was installed by Byfield Parish Council from plans drawn up by Alan Hamblett and Bill Gibbon, and £700 was contributed by BRGA; Mrs Irene Vokes ran a coffee morning to raise money for equipment; Daventry District Council contributed £500. The balance was paid by Byfield Parish Council on a total cost of £5,000.

The Youth Building.

1991: A meeting was organised for January 15th chaired by Nick Leonard, who was the Outreach Youth Worker employed by Northamptonshire County Council. The meeting agreed to investigate the possibility of obtaining a Portakabin-type mobile classroom for use as a youth building on Brightwell land. In February and March Byfield Parish Council and BRGA agreed to accept the building and also agreed its location.

In September the local " Right Angle Project" agreed to forward £250 as surety should the occasion arise that the building had to be removed.

Note: The Right Angle Project was the title given to a Government-funded organisation, set up by Northamptonshire County Council, which was to examine ways to improve the quality of life in deprived areas. The area around Woodford Halse was deemed to be one such area, and this included the village of Byfield. This youth project was part of that initiative.

Protracted negotiations continued between BRGA, Byfield Parish Council, Thames Water and the Charity Commissioners regarding the suggested siting of the building.

September 14th 1993: The youth building was officially opened.

February 3rd 1998: Brightwell Recreation Ground Association, became Brightwell Recreation Ground Committee.

1998: The Youth Club folded and the building, from which so much had been expected to enable the youth of Byfield to form their own individual identity, became unused and subsequently quickly deteriorated. The building was dismantled using the funding that had been put aside for that very purpose.

The non- turf all weather cricket wicket.

May 13 1999	Daventry District Council grant	£1,500
July 5 1999	National Lottery grant	£2,648
	Byfield Cricket Club funds	£2,050
	Total	£6,198

Continuing improvements by Byfield Cricket Club.
(Notes by J.R., President of the club)

Clock tower
2000: Byfield Cricket and Football Club erected a clock tower on the top of the Cricket and Football Pavilion, in the memory of that stalwart player, officer and staunch supporter of Byfield sport and Byfield village activities, Keith Anderson. Keith's name is inscribed on the clock face, a visual reminder to all of the efforts of another of Byfield's characters.

Electronic scoreboard.
2002: Byfield Cricket Club installed a new electronic score board in memory of Mick Moyce, who served the cricket club as player, untiring worker, groundsman, coach to junior members and as an elected officer. He was held in such high regard that the memorial was funded by public donation.

External pavilion enhancement.
2003/2004: Byfield Cricket Club, under the guidance of Geoff Broad, built a veranda and extended barbeque area to the Cricket and Football Pavilion. This was funded from the closing balances of Byfield Sports and Social 400 Club, which had been discontinued due to lack of support after raising considerable revenue continuously over many years.

CHAPTER NINETEEN

BYFIELD VILLAGE HALL

The builders of the hall were Wootton Bros. from Sulgrave, who made an offer to the Village Hall Committee that, if the final settlement of £300 was made on time, they would discount £75. This money was raised by interest-free loans from villagers and the promised discount was obtained.

On Saturday November 12th 1960 the hall was officially opened by Doctor Waine, who had been the medical practitioner in Byfield from 1939 to 1946. He was one of the parishioners who were instrumental in the building of the hall.

At an initial meeting following the opening, the committee members were asked for ideas for money raising. One that was suggested was bingo, this idea was taken up and the first bingo session took place on Friday February 14th 1961, and in fact the sessions ran for 31 years.

The amount of money raised in comparison with what had been raised before was considerable, and the Hall Committee were able to provide both furniture and fittings for the new building.

One important provision that was made was actually outside the responsibility of the Committee. This was to put a hardcore foundation and tarmac surface to the car park, it previously having been only surfaced with ashes, which were not compatible with a new hall having a mahogany block floor.

In 1966, sadly, Doctor Parkinson the village general practitioner died. Because the doctor's family did not wish to move from the traditional doctor's house, the surgery facilities, which had served the village and surrounding area for many years, suddenly became unavailable.

The Village Hall Management Committee had a request from Doctor John Holland then living in Essex, but who had been born in Priors Marston. John expressed a wish to take over the Byfield medical practice and enquired as to the possibility of using the Village Hall as a doctor's surgery. It was agreed to grant this request if the surgery could be accommodated in the under-stage rooms. The under-stage rooms were converted for the Doctor's use. One problem was security, due to the fact that the practice dispensed drugs to patients. This was overcome by improving the quality of the locks, fitting bars to the windows etc. Another problem was access to toilet facilities, both for convenience and the taking of samples. This was solved by the patients climbing the stairs from the under-stage rooms onto the stage, and then down and through the main hall to the toilets.

One thing not generally known was that the sink fitted for surgery use had its waste outlet directed into the roof down-pipe gully. It was assumed at the time that this gully discharged into the foul drain system; in fact it ran into a "soak away" which discharged into the original ex-British Rail ash and clinker base of the village bowling green! Obviously this was not ideal, but sufficed until the situation was regularised with a connection to the main drainage system through the good offices of the Brightwell Committee, who provided an extra manhole to serve the lower area of the Village Hall, at the time when the new bowls and tennis pavilion was built.

Another problem with the accommodation was lack of soundproofing. Other hall users had to be asked to bear in mind the fact that it was difficult for doctors to consult with patients if excessive noise was coming from the main hall. It was difficult to separate the beat of the heart from the beat of the hall. With an increasing use of the hall, the furniture and other equipment had to be stored at the rear of the stage, to enable sufficient floor space to be available. This was a tedious and heavy job. Other difficulties were a lack of space to accommodate the caretaker's equipment, also there was no "milling space" in the main hall area for large functions, and no space to accommodate a licensed bar. The problems were also not helped with the loss of the under-stage rooms for general use, the doctors now having exclusive use of this area.

With the money available from bingo it was decided by the committee to extend the hall on the west side. Some of the older committee members were initially shocked, apparently because the hall had only recently been built. This was understandable considering the tremendous effort put into money raising, much of it raised from functions in the old hall in Church Street to get the original building in the first place. But all members were totally supportive.

Plans were drawn up, and a 50% grant obtained from the Department of Education and Science. The hall extension was built in 1968 by the building firm of Parratts of Badby at a cost of £2,000. The new accommodation was greatly appreciated, comprising an extension measuring an area of 33 feet by 14 feet, which with the aid of folding doors could be separated from the main hall. A storeroom for furniture and other equipment was accessed from the main hall. An area with a wide hatchway was accessible from the new extension suitable for use as a bar. A store behind the bar area was available to accommodate the caretaker's equipment. This had drains in the floor for possible use as a shower room accessed from the gents toilets, if showers were ever required. All windows and doors etc. that were reusable due to their relatively short lifespan to date, were reused.

It was possible to build in extra improvements within the kitchen area, including new worktops and sink units. The stage was improved with the fitting of two rolled steel joists running from front to back of the stage; one on each side to act as a guide for a movable backdrop. Wings were fitted to the sides of the stage mounted under the RSJs. The new furniture storeroom was fitted with bi-fold doors to enable the room to be used as a dressing room for live shows.

One of the early problems in the building, due to the fact that the water pipes were too close to the eaves of the roof, was these freezing. This was cured by the fitting of frost protection using various strategically located horticultural electrical tube heaters of varying sizes and electrical pipe lagging operated by a frost stat, which was fitted in the apex of the loft area. This solved the problem and the £50 outlay was to prove very good value for money.

On setting up the hall for an annual Cricket Club dinner, it became apparent that, for such popular functions as this, the main hall was not big enough. The Village Hall Chairman stated "This hall wants extending again!" "What do you want to do now?" was the question. "Build the same width as the other extension but a bit longer," was the reply. The suggested extension was drawn on a blackboard. Some discussion took place and with some modifications it was agreed in principle by the Committee.

Plans were again drawn up. These were purposely drawn up to give an opportunity to build the extension in three phases, if total funding for the whole scheme was not readily available.

The first phase was an extension of the entrance hall and toilets.

The second phase was an extension and enlargement of the main hall floor area.

The third phase was to extend the doctors' under-stage surgery facility, and to include an extension to the stage area at stage level.

The scheme was put out to tender to three builders. Quotations came in; one at £6,000 one at £8,000 and one for £12,000. One of the reasons for the considerable variation was that in 1974 inflation was running at 26%, making it very difficult for contractors to tender realistically.

A grant application was submitted on the quotation of £8,000. Grants were obtained from Daventry District Council and Northamptonshire County Council of 60% of the cost.

It became apparent to the Village Hall Chairman that the Management Committee might have difficulty in finding the sponsor's share of the cost. He discussed the problem with Doctor John Holland, pointing out that if the project was phased the third phase might not be done. The Doctor immediately agreed to write out a cheque for £1,000 in lieu of rent to assist the funding of the scheme, which was gratefully accepted.

The Village Hall Management Committee decided it was possible to build the whole of the planned extension in one go, and to award the contract to the building firm of Parratts of Badby. The firm had built the west side extension and had also submitted the lowest tender.

To save professional fees for the general construction work the Village Hall Chairman agreed to supervise the work.

The construction of the extension was not straightforward due to a number of factors. The main one arose because the original hall was constructed as a Portal Frame Structure. This meant that two of the vertical stanchions of two of the portal frames needed to be removed to allow a larger unobstructed floor area. Then, because of the bending moments at the ridge and at the eaves of the roof, it would be necessary to construct a frame running across the ceiling and down the outside walls of the new extension to arrest the force of these bending moments.

The removal of the stanchions also meant that a rolled steel joist, 40 feet long and of 22.5 inch by 8.5 inch section and weighing one ton, was needed to support the roof structure in the place of the two removed vertical stanchions. This RSJ was to be supported by two stanchions, one at each end. The stanchion at the stage end had to have a foundation at the foundation level of the under-stage rooms, the other was built into the dividing wall between the main hall and the newly-constructed main hall entrance/exit. The underground concrete reinforced footings, that were formed to support the steelwork, were such that they were outside the outer walls and at right angles to the building, because of the forces of the bending moments of the new roof structure.

The specification for the design of the steelwork was determined by a structural engineer, to the satisfaction of the Building Control Department of Daventry District Council.

When the steelwork was being erected, major errors were made, inasmuch as when the Portal Frame sections of the existing steelwork were being cut, no allowance was made for the Portal Frames to fit into the new main beam section and so the new main beam with both its supporting stanchions were located 4 inches out of alignment.

The error was clear to see because the steelwork, which should have been fitted in the outside wall, was 4 inches inside the building and the main supporting stanchion at the stage end of the main beam was fitted in a position that would not allow the stage access doors to open.

The village hall Chairman rang the Director of the steel erectors who had been on site and politely informed him of the error! At first the error was denied. The outcome was that, after consultation with the Structural Engineer and the Daventry District Council, the main beam was left in position, but the supporting stanchion at the stage end was moved to its correct position. A bracket was welded at the top end of the stanchion to support half the width of the main beam, the other half being supported by the stanchion. Two 4 inch spacing brackets were fitted, one to each end of the cross beams, this resulting in the vertical sections aligning with the outside wall as originally intended.

Various practical additions were made during construction. One was the provision of a large capacity store cupboard accessed from the doctors' consulting rooms, built under the floor of the main hall. This was designed to accommodate securely prescription drugs which were dispensed by the doctors. A separately metered electricity supply to the under-stage area was provided.

A void was left in the suspended concrete ceiling of the new consulting rooms to allow a staircase to be fitted between the floor level of the main hall and the lower floor level, should this facility be required at a later date. This void was filled by a suspended wooden panel.

All fittings, including doors and windows, were re-used where possible and prudent to save expenditure.

The building was completed by Parratts of Badby in 1975.

It was then possible to enhance the whole building further. The new stage extension had a set of stairs made from part of the original flight of stairs, which had been removed. This enabled the stage extension to be readily accessed from the main hall. A set of wrought iron safety railings was fitted, together with a set of folding doors located behind the safety railings, which enabled the new stage extension to be separated from the main hall.

One problem with completely separating the under-stage area from the rest of the building was the inconvenient access to the toilets. The doctors had to have a key to the outside door of the new toilet that was installed in what had previously been the main doors of the original hall. This was obviously far from ideal with patients who were very unwell, especially in inclement weather. This access to the toilet was also used by the Byfield Tennis Club.

The Village Hall Management Committee contacted the District Valuer to ascertain a fair and reasonable rent for the doctors' accommodation. An amount was agreed between the Medical Practice and the Village Hall Management Committee. The previously advanced sum of £1,000 was converted into a time factor and the Practice used the premises rent free for an agreed period.

The biggest problem was the cost of the finished project. Due to high inflation the final cost of the building was £13,000 as against the sum of £8,000 originally budgeted. At a special meeting of the Village Hall Management Committee the Chairman announced this disturbing news, which meant that there was a £3,000 shortfall in the finances.

It was agreed that we should submit an application to "The Nene Foundation", a charity formed by the American Timken family to assist communities in which there were a number of British Timken workers living. This fund was set up to give financial assistance for the provision of recreational, educational and/or social facilities within those communities.

The case was put with the specific point that the primary cause of the shortfall was the very high inflation situation running at 26%. The Committee was very pleased and greatly relieved that the charity was able to assist, and a cheque was received from the American-based headquarters of the company for the amount of the shortfall, £3,000.

Following the Byfield Medical Practice's construction of a purpose-built Medical Centre in Church Street in the late 1980s, the under-stage area of the Village Hall became vacant.

The disadvantage of this was that the hall suffered a loss of income; the advantage was that the complete under-stage area of the hall was available for other uses.

The Village Hall Management Committee decided that the under-stage area containing various small rooms did not lend itself to maximum usage, so it was decided to knock out all the interior walls in the original under-stage area to make a room 25 feet by 18 feet, and to support the span of the stage with a beam across the centre supported by two piers.

Byfield Parish Council had always used the hall for its meetings, with the disadvantage of needing to "set up" and "take down" the chairs and tables etc. required for its meetings. It was considered it would be ideal if the Parish Council furnished the rooms, retaining ownership of any furniture or fittings, to make the rooms suitable for meetings for any organisations to use. The Parish Council were also having problems with the storage of documents.

They enquired of the Village Hall Committee whether the council could pay a retainer for the storage of the Council's documents in what had been the doctors' old consulting rooms, perhaps utilising the secure cupboard under the Village Hall floor, in addition locating a number of filing cabinets securely bolted to the wall.

In addition they sought agreement for the Council to hire the under-stage rooms for its meetings, to display "The Byfield Time Line" which depicted the events that had occurred in Byfield in each year of the first one hundred years of Byfield Parish Council, 1894 to 1984. Also to display various maps of the village, for use of the council, as well as being of general local interest.

Notes by Jean West, Byfield Village Hall Treasurer
By 1997 the flat roofed extensions had reached the end of their life span. The interior ceilings and in some areas the walls had become extremely damp, with fungal growth in parts. The ceiling in the stage annex collapsed in March with signs of the ladies powder room ceiling joining it. There were also problems with water coming in under the emergency exit doors, wetting the carpets, and loss of heat due to draughts and single glazed windows.

The Management Committee decided to consult with the residents of Byfield to find out their views on the premises.

A questionnaire was produced which asked:

1 Whether the existing building should be refurbished, or the provision of a new hall should be attempted.

2 What help would each household offer in financial donations, attendance at fund raising events and donations of time and talents.

To ensure as many replies as possible were returned, the committee members collected them by hand. This resulted in a 40% return.

The overwhelming opinion was that the existing building should be brought up to modern standards. Armed with this result, plus offers of financial help and promised support for fund-raising activities, the Trustees then prioritised the work on an achievable basis with a long-term plan.

To help the improvements a fund-raising event would be held every month; each covering a wide area of activities and designed to appeal to a wide range of tastes. This plan worked well and events were supported by the community.

In addition to this, research was carried out to source grant-making trusts giving mainly to rural communities, as well as investigating those available from statutory authorities.

The flat-roofed areas and the damp internal ceilings were the biggest problem and also the most expensive to correct, taking the greatest time to plan the work and access the money. It was decided that as all the ceilings were to be replaced, it would be sensible to incorporate new heating and lighting systems into this part of the project. Considerable thought was given to the heating, and it was decided that electrical heating would be the best. This was to be by two different methods Using:

1 Night storage heaters to maintain the fabric of the building and to ensure that it was more comfortable for users.
2 Electrical heaters (some infra-red and some ceramic) to be used through the meter system.

The proposal took a considerable time to put together. However, in the summer of 1999 an application to the National Lottery Charities Board was submitted with a request for £43,735.

Whilst waiting for the outcome of this application, the refurbishment was started with other parts of the project which could be completed in the meantime. The installation of a disabled toilet for the main hall area was carried out in 1998 at a cost of £1,900, towards which a grant of £1,000 was received from the Maud Elkington Trust.

In 1999, the windows and doors were replaced with double glazed units, including the emergency exits. This was carried out by Styleglaze at a cost of £6,650, and a grant of £3,000 was received from Daventry District Council. New curtains were purchased for the main hall from the ongoing fund-raising at a cost of £1,200, and a new carpet was fitted in the entrance area.

By 1999 the Bowls Club, who had been renting the lower annex (after the doctors' surgery moved out), had moved into a new purpose-built bowls and tennis pavilion. It was decided that this part of the building would be used by a greater number of groups if it had its own toilet facilities. A manhole adjacent to the hall had been provided through the good offices of the Brightwell Committee when they put main drainage to the new pavilion.

Consequently, a toilet suitable for disabled use and improved access was installed. The total cost of this was £4,910, with a grant received from Awards for All of £4,755.

In January 2000 the Management Committee were told that the application to the National Lotteries Charity Board had been successful and that the full amount requested had been awarded.

The contract for re-roofing the flat roof areas, and re-felting the pitched roof area, was awarded to Cross and Blackham from Everdon. When building flat roofed areas now, much greater ventilation is built into the structure than had been the previous practice, thus reducing the

potential damp risks, and this company was chosen because of their expertise and the quality of their work. They began work in April 2000 and the job was completed in May at a cost of £28,000.

The internal work had to wait until the summer, when the bookings had been suspended for several weeks to give sufficient time for the work to be carried out. The ceilings were removed, the electrical work carried out, then new ceilings installed and plastered. The ceilings and plastering work was done by A. J. Head; the electrical work by Tobias Electrical Services. This work was completed in five weeks. The interior was then painted by the Management Committee and volunteers. The total cost of both the internal and external work was £49,201, with £43,735 coming from the National Lottery Charities Board grant (now called the Community Fund).

Sufficient funds were available, following this work, to buy new curtains for the stage, and replace the wooden shutters on the stage annex with matching curtains with a sound-reduction lining. This was at a cost of £860.

With the building refurbished and new curtains fitted, attention turned to furniture and fittings. In 2001, 150 new chairs were purchased at a cost of £813 with money from fund raising. It was not expected that all the required new chairs could be bought at the same time because of the cost, however there had been a cancelled order for 130 that could be bought at half price, which meant that the full 150 could be purchased immediately as long as we had green ones.

Twenty small Gopak tables were bought from the Village Hall's share of the proceeds of Cabaret 2001 (£933), and the Parish Council bought ten large Gopak tables for use of parishioners both in and out of the hall.

Also in 2001, the Committee upgraded the ladies' powder room and the gent's toilet, and installed a children's toilet with financial assistance from Swindon and Oxford Co-op. Total costs were £1,035.

It was then necessary to look at the implications for the village hall of the new Disability Discrimination Act, which had to be fully implemented by October 2004. Also the noise pollution problem which had arisen due to the increased use of sections of the premises.

In 2002 the Management Committee decided that the next step must be to improve facilities in the lower annex, which was now being used to a greater extent. In addition to the use by the Parish Council there were two art classes a week, plus other regular meetings.

This plan was to replace ceilings and cover bare brick walls with sound-check plaster board, install insulation, fit emergency lighting and add an induction loop system, which is a requirement under the Disability Discrimination Act.

The plaster work was carried out by A. J. Head, the electrical work by Tobias Electrical Services and the induction loop system by Hilltop Audio of Nottingham.

The total cost was £4,100, which included new floor coverings. Grants were received from the Maud Elkington Trust £1,000: Leeds and Holbeck Charitable Trust £500: the Benham Trust £300 and the Daventry District Council £413.

In 2002 there was a sound induction loop system installed in the main hall. This was at a cost of £2,000. This loop system was also installed by Hilltop Audio of Nottingham.

In 2003 the access conditions to meet the Disability Discrimination Act were tackled. Planning permission was obtained and funds were sought to finance the necessary work. For access to the main hall area to comply with the Act, three interior doors had to be widened, and the fire exit in the entrance hall was changed into the main entrance, with a new ramp leading to the new doors. It was also necessary to alter the taps in the kitchen. This work was carried out by J. P. Charles of Middleton Cheney.

The access to the lower annex will also have to be altered to comply; it is intended that this work will be done in 2004. Planning permission has been obtained and an application for a 50% grant from Northamptonshire County Council is being submitted.

To date the Management Committee has received grants from the following bodies to assist with the Disability Discrimination Act compliance work: Northamptonshire County Council £5,000 for the main Hall: Byfield Parish Council £2,000: Lloyds TSB Charitable Trust £2,600: Yorkshire Bank Charitable Trust £350: £1,000 from a Trust which gives anonymously: £301 from Byfield Village Fete.

INDEX

"Sitting down and indexing a book is – in our experience – the most painful,
horrible, mind-numbing activity you could ever wish on your worst enemy."
Real World Adobe InDesign CS by Olav Martin Kvern and David Blatner

136

Cornell, signalman 47
Corner House 149
Correction, House of 84
Cosy Corner 78, 79, 80, 128
Cotswolds 7
Cottingham, Joseph 84
Coventry 13, 71, 110
Coventry blitz 13
Cox, Davis Fox 50
Cox, Joseph 35, 49, 75, 128, 130
Cox, Samuel 97, 122, 156
Cox, Thomas 34, 35, 36, 40, 57, 59, 88, 121, 166
Cox, William 48, 49
Coy, Mrs 163
Cramp, Edward Cornelius Dodd 29
Crampton, T. R. 19
Cravens of Sheffield 47
Cricket Club 34, 56, 125, 171, 176, 177, 179
Crook Alley 85
Cross, Ancient Bartering 32
Cross, Mrs Chris 156, 173
Crossings Farm 73
Cross and Blackham 181
Cross family 166
Cross Street 85, 109
Cross Tree Cottages 85, 121, 127
Cross Tree Elm 33, 163
Cross Tree Public House 24, 32, 119, 161, 166
Crown Land 103
Crustaceous Millipede 70
Cugini, Donald 89
Curgenven, Reverend Francis Henry 28, 52, 53, 87, 152

D

Dalton, Les 72
Daniels family 36
Darbishire, Dorothy 127
Darbishire, Gratton 29, 31, 98, 127
Darbishire Farms Ltd 48, 61, 87, 90, 127
Darby, Mrs 72
Dashwood Road School 55
Dassett Beacon 13
Daventry District Council 47, 58, 127, 173, 176, 177, 179, 181
Daventry New Street Car Park 172
Daventry Rural District Council 40, 54, 57, 75, 88, 126, 127
Daventry Weekly Express 36
Davidson-Houston family 49
Davies, Mrs Frances 149, 166
Davies, Richard 19, 120
Davies, Mr and Mrs Tom 89
Davies family 34, 89, 124
Day, William Allen, Police Sergeant 84
Days, William 45, 47
De- Witts 159
Deacon, Brian 95
Deacon, Patricia 2, 95

Deene Cottage 57, 87
Denis Price Ltd 22
Department of Education and Science 178
Dester, George 108
Devonshire, Abraham 139
Devonshire, Elizabeth 139
Devonshire, Robert 139
Devonshire-Lawrence, Mrs 140
Devonshire family 122
Dexter, Mrs Sheila 112
Dexter, P.C. 88
Dickens, Charles 93
Dickens: Bleak House 93
Disability Discrimination Act 181, 182
Displaced Persons 72
District Valuer 180
Doctors Close 19
Doctor Barnardo's 118, 149
Dodd, Charles 122
Dodd, Richard 64, 111
Dodd, Sarah 122
Dodd, Sarah Bloxham 122
Dodd, William 97, 141
Dodds Well 141
Dodford, Northants 49
Dolls Hill 40, 85, 89, 90, 145
Doomsday Book 1, 9
Douglas, Annie 113
Douglas, Daniel 152
Douglas, Rob 94
Douglas, Stuart 19
Douglas family 121
Dove House Close 134, 169
Dowler, George 154
Drake-Brockman, Gervase Alan 142
Drilling Rig 16, 17
Dring family 155
Driver, John 76
Driver's children 76
Drott Bulldozer 172, 173
Dugan family 120
Dumbleton, John 112
Dumbleton, Samuel 76
Dunkley, William 76
Dunlop, Janet 128
Dunlop, John 128
Durham 66, 93
Durran, Benoni Pearson 29
Dutch Elm Disease 32
Dutton, Victor H. 156

E

Eales 36
Eastern seaports 7
East and West Junction Railway 19, 43, 46, 65, 145
Eatock family 57
Ecumenical Bees 55
Eden, Charles 156
Edgecote, Battle of 9

H